PREVENTING
SCHOOL
DROPOUTS

PREVENTING SCHOOL DROPOUTS

Tactics for At-Risk, Remedial, and
Mildly Handicapped Adolescents

Thomas C. Lovitt

8700 Shoal Creek Boulevard
Austin, Texas 78757

Printed in the United States of America

Library of Congress Cataloging-in-Publication Data

Lovitt, Thomas C.
    Preventing school dropouts : tactics for at risk, remedial, and mildly handicapped adolescents / by Thomas C. Lovitt.
      p.   cm.
    Includes bibliographical references (p.   ) and index.
    ISBN 0-89079-454-5
    1. Dropouts—United States. 2. Handicapped youth—Education—United States. 3. Special education—United States.   I. Title.
LC146.6.L68   1991
373. 12'913—dc20   90-27493
                                             CIP

pro·ed

**8700 Shoal Creek Boulevard
Austin, Texas 78757**

3   4   5   6   7   8   9   10   95

CONTENTS

11 PARTICIPATION

PREFACE

Dropouts, youth who have failed to graduate from high school, have always been a problem for educators. Recently, however, educators have been particularly concerned about the numbers of youth who exit the system. According to some reports, about 25% of the pupils drop out of school each year ("Technology," 1988). This number is even higher for individuals with mild handicaps. Zigmond and Thornton (1985) found that over 50% of LD students did not complete their secondary education. A study by Blackorby, Kortering, Edgar, and Emerson (1987) corroborated those data in Seattle.

This dropout situation has serious implications, and they depend to some extent on which authority is quoted. According to Rumberger (1987):

> Individual dropouts suffer because many have difficulty finding steady, well-paying jobs not just when they first leave school but over their entire lifetimes. Society suffers as well because unemployment and lost earnings lower tax revenues and increase demands on social services. But the consequences of dropping out go beyond simple economic losses, no matter how large they may be. They cover a wide range of individual and social outcomes that need to be better understood. (p. 112)

Students drop out of school for a number of reasons. An article in *The Seattle Times* ("Many tacks," 1986) cited the following motives for dropping out of high school as expressed by the students: expelled or suspended, made poor grades, decided that school was not for me, believed that the school ground was too dangerous, didn't get into desired program, couldn't get along with teachers, married or planned to be, became pregnant, had to support family, followed my friends who had dropped out, couldn't get along with students, became ill or disabled, offered a job and chose to work, entered the military, moved too far from school, and wanted to travel. Those reasons are much in accord with the ones noted by Rumberger (1987).

Most of those reasons for dropping out of school are rather general. Following are a few specific problems that prompt students to drop out of school: difficulty reading and with other basic skills, inability to organize their lives in general, failure to see relevancy in school subjects, poor study habits, difficulty knowing who or when to ask for help. And teachers sometimes nudge students out of school by failing to provide one of the following: current and valid rationales for learning certain tasks, proper and ample motivation for students, regular and adequate time for students to study in their classes, direct and frequent feedback on their efforts, and clear and regular communication with the youths' parents.

Youth who are likely to drop out of school are referred to in various ways . A current and popular label for potential dropouts is "at risk." Other youth who are likely to drop out of school are "mildly handicapped," those more specifically referred to as "remedial" or "learning disabled."

The numbers of youth who drop out vary from one state to another. According to data in *USA Today* ("States," 1989), the highest dropout rates were in the District of Columbia, Florida, and Louisiana; whereas the lowest rates were in Minnesota, Wyoming, and North Dakota. The dropout rate is to a large extent dependent on the location of the school, either in suburbs, rural areas, small cities, or large cities. In Washington State, for example, whose rank order was 35th in the *USA Today* poll, the highest dropout rates were in the cities— that is, Seattle and Tacoma—whereas the lowest were in affluent suburbs such as Mercer Island and Bellevue ("Eastside Dropouts," 1989). Some interesting exceptions to this were noted, however.

Potential dropouts are in regular and special education classes. They are in science, social studies, language arts, music, physical education, home living, and industrial arts classes taught by regular teachers. They are in special education classes and resource rooms taught by special education teachers. There, some of those students are given assistance with their regular science, social studies, or other classes. In other situations, students are provided instruction in content areas by special education teachers. In yet other instances, these youth are in content classes that are co-taught by regular and special education teachers. But whoever might teach these students in whichever situation, teachers must be cognizant of the dropout problem and knowledgeable of tactics for addressing the issue. This book is a collection of tactics that should be useful for those teachers, particularly since they relate to specific reasons for dropping out of school.

When it comes to presenting these tactics, a number of arrangements are possible. For one, teachers could go directly to the tactics, identify those that are suitable for their classes, and arrange them for their youth. The tactics could also be explained to teachers by instructors of preservice or inservice situations. This collection of tactics would be a useful text for (a) instructors who prepare teachers to work with diverse types of youth in middle schools, junior highs, and high schools; (b) instructors who train consulting or resource teachers at the secondary level; and (c) staff development and inservice instructors in public and private schools who assist teachers at the secondary level.

Throughout, the activities in this book are referred to as *tactics.* That term was chosen because the suggested activities could be arranged by teachers without greatly changing major features of their instructional approaches. Moreover, most of these tactics *support* the content that teachers have chosen to deliver. Teachers are not asked to alter the material they present, just the way in which it is delivered.

I believe that thousands of youths can be assisted to stay in school when these tactics are properly arranged. Obviously, more drastic approaches—that is,

strategies—must be developed to assist others to remain in school. A number of such strategies that require teachers and schools to significantly modify their curricula or approaches are available (e.g., Guthrie, Long, & Guthrie, 1989).

This book has 120 tactics arranged in 11 categories: study skills, social behaviors, attendance, motivation, health, basic skills, compliance, self-concept, attitude, goals, and participation. Those categories were determined from a survey of more than 400 regular secondary level teachers from Florida, Montana, Washington, and Utah. Those teachers—who were in high schools, junior highs, or middle schools, in large cities, suburban areas, small towns, and rural villages— were asked to list the characteristics of at-risk and remedial youth, those who were likely to drop out of school. On analyzing those data, I came up with the 11 categories.

To locate the tactics, hundreds of articles in leading educational and psychological journals, chapters, monographs, unpublished papers, and books were surveyed. Once potential tactics were selected, they were condensed and paraphrased. They were written so that the procedures were understandable and appealing to teachers, while maintaining the intent of the authors.

Each tactic is written in a format that includes five sections: background, who can benefit, procedures, modifications and considerations, and monitor. In the first section, comments as to the origin of the tactic and its theoretical background are provided. In section two, the type and age of the individuals in the referenced article are identified, and comments are offered on the type of youth for whom the tactic would be most suitable. A step-by-step plan is provided for carrying out the tactic in the procedures section. In the next part, suggestions are included on how to modify the technique so it would be suitable in situations other than the one described in the write-up. Also included in that part are comments on matters that should be taken into account before or while the tactic is implemented. Suggestions for evaluating the tactic are available in the monitor section. At the end of each tactic, the references that stimulated the write-up are provided.

When the collection of tactics was initially written, it was sent to a number of secondary teachers for their review. All the tactics were evaluated by at least two teachers, several by three, and a number by four or five. For their evaluations, teachers were given a form like that sent out by journals. Referring to it, the teachers could accept the tactic as is, accept it with modifications, or reject it. In addition to offering those overall recommendations, the teachers were encouraged to write comments and suggestions about the tactics. Based on those recommendations and suggestions, a few tactics were eliminated and several others were substantially revised.

The tactics in this book are written in a format that has

proven successful in another book, *Tactics for Teaching* (Lovitt, 1984). Numerous teachers and instructors throughout the country have consulted that book, designed for elementary level teachers, and have been quite pleased with it. Other tactics, in this same format, were also written for a successful pre-referral project, RIDE (Weast et al., 1986).

In addition to this collection of 120 tactics, the book contains three related parts. One is a "Monitor" section (Appendix A), which is included to give teachers a number of ideas for evaluating tactics beyond the suggestions in the monitor section of each tactic. In Appendix A, 19 ways to measure pupil performances are briefly described (e.g., frequency, duration, percentage, rating scales, interviews, video recordings). When reading a tactic, the teacher is referred, in the monitor section of the tactic, to one or more of the 19 ways to evaluate data in Appendix A. Between the two descriptions, the teacher should have considerable information on how to evaluate each technique.

In the second section that accompanies this book, "How to Present the Tactics" (Appendix B), rationales are offered for learning about these techniques. This part would be particularly helpful for instructors of courses or inservices who offer these ideas to teachers.

The third added feature is a Supplementary List of Program Contents (Appendix C). For that section, five additional topics were identified around which teachers or instructors might categorize the tactics. They are different from the 11 original themes and are the following: self-management, involving peers, metacognitive approaches, involving parents, and instructional modifications.

In summary, considerable data and testimony support the format and content of this book: (a) The categories for the tactics were derived from a survey of teachers; (b) the majority of the tactics were based on published research; (c) the tactics were reviewed by teachers, and their suggestions were taken into account; (d) other tactics in a similar format have been successfully scheduled by hundreds of teachers and instructors; (e) based on experience with teachers and instructors who have arranged the tactics, a separate appendix is included that expands on the information in the monitor section of each tactic; and (f) based on experience with describing the tactics to teachers, a section on how to present the tactics is included.

References

Blackorby, J., Kortering, L., Edgar, E., & Emerson, J. (1987). Dropouts from special education. Unpublished manuscript. Experimental Education Unit, University of Washington, Seattle.

Eastside dropouts are few overall. (January 11, 1989). *The Seattle Times*, p. H1.

Guthrie, L.F., Long, C., & Guthrie, G.P. (1989). *Strategies for drop-out prevention*. San Francisco: Far West Laboratory for Educational Research and Development.

Lovitt, T.C. (1984). *Tactics for teaching*. Columbus, OH: Merrill.

Many tacks tried to keep students from dropping out. (September 2, 1986). *The Seattle Times*, p. A3.

Rumberger, R.W. (1987). High school dropouts: A review of issues and evidence. *Review of Educational Research, 57*, 101-121.

States are at a standstill in educational progress. (May 4, 1989). *USA Today*, p. 6D.

Technology and the at-risk student. (1988, November/December). *Electronic Learning*, pp. 35-49.

Weast, J., Beck, R., Gabriel, S., Bornstein, P., Lovitt, T., & Conrad, D. (1984). *Project RIDE (responding to individual differences in education)* [Computer program]. Longmont, CO: Sopris West.

Zigmond, N., & Thornton, H. (1985). Follow-up of postsecondary age learning disabled graduates and dropouts. *Learning Disabilities Research, 1*(1), 50-55.

STUDY
SKILLS

READING: MULTIPASS TO INCREASE COMPREHENSION

Background

This strategy was developed to assist secondary age students to deal with increased amounts of content material. The Multipass approach requires students to make three "passes" through the assigned reading material, with a different purpose in mind each time. Because students must perform a number of behaviors in each pass, each pass is taught as a unit and in succession.

Who Can Benefit

The research in the cited study was conducted with eight LD adolescents. Remedial and at-risk students, including those with learning disabilities, can use Multipass to handle the reading assignments in their science, history, and social studies classes. Many other students who are neither remedial nor at risk should also profit from the Multipass reading strategy.

Procedures

Steps. As mentioned, Multipass is made up of three steps or passes. In the first, students skim through a passage in the text to identify main ideas and note its general organization. This should take only a few minutes. The purpose of the second pass is to gain information and facts from the passage without reading it thoroughly. During the third pass, the pupils sort out the information gained from the first two passes. Following is a detailed description of the three passes (see Multipass Worksheet in Figure 1.1):

1. *Survey Pass:* Focus on these items:

    TISOPT
    T: Titles/Subtitles
    I: Introduction
    S: Summary
    O: Organization/Outline of chapter

P: Pictures (read captions)

T: Table of Contents (note how the passage fits in with other passages)

(No more than 30 seconds should be spent on each page for this pass.)

2.   *Size-Up Pass:* Students should read the captions for all illustrations and raise questions about them. They should then scan the pages for more information about which to ask more questions. As students go through the passage they should paraphrase the information and take notes. The following letters can serve as memory cues:

IQWH:RASPN

I: Illustrations

Q: Form Questions about illustrations

W: Words in bold type (ask what they mean)

H: Headings (form questions about them)

R: Read

A: Ask

S: Scan

P: Paraphrase

N: Note

3.   *Sort-Out Pass:* For this final pass, students should answer the questions that are generally at the end of a section or chapter. Students should read the questions and follow these instructions:

If You Know the Answer
a.   Say it and write it.
b.   Write a check mark beside that question.
c.   Say and write next question.

If You Don't Know the Answer
a.   Mark it with a square.
b.   Look at the subheadings.
c.   Decide on the likely one(s) to use.
d.   Look there for answer.
e.   Say it and write it.

Instructions

1.   Analyze students' current reading habits: Have them read a section in a textbook; ask them what procedures they used to read and learn the material.

2.   Describe the new strategy as an alternative to methods they may have been using (e.g., "Here's

a way that's been proven to work." "Students can go through material faster and understand more.").

3. Give students reasons for learning the new technique (e.g., they will be more efficient and get better grades).

4. Model the new strategy (e.g., "Here's how we do the Survey Pass.").

5. Conduct verbal rehearsal exercises for each sort (e.g., TISOPT and IQWH:RASPN).

6. Assign easy passages for the students to read as they learn the strategy.

7. Provide positive and corrective feedback to students, according to their performances.

8. Practice on content materials at grade level after students have used the strategy with easier materials.

9. Provide more feedback and reinforcement to them.

Modifications/ Considerations

See the MultipassWorksheet in Figure 1.1 for a simplified checklist of the three passes. These can be used individually or with groups of students. The teacher may instruct the pupils to use letters such as TISOPT to serve as reminders for certain passes. If they are confusing or otherwise not helpful, other letters or symbols could be selected, or that feature of the program could be dropped.

Students will be given a number of suggestions and a fair amount of feedback during the various stages of learning the Multipass strategy. It is important that they learn to accept and deal with that information, particularly those comments that may be critical of their current methods of reading and studying from textbooks.

Monitor

Teachers may want to monitor the extent that students remembered the steps for the various phases (e.g., TISOPT). To obtain these data, teachers could develop a checklist (see MONITOR 6 in Appendix A) and occasionally assess students' ability. Beyond knowing the steps, teachers might want to know whether the tactic helped students retain more information from their textbook passages. To do so, teachers might develop a set of questions from passages

FIGURE 1.1   Worksheet for Use in the Multipass Strategy

MULTIPASS WORKSHEET

Survey Pass

1.   Write title. _____

2.   What is the main idea in the introduction? (one sentence)

_____

3.   What is the main idea in the summary? (one sentence)

_____

4.   Write main headings.

5.   Which pictures, titles, maps, time lines are most important?

6.   How does this chapter fit in with the whole book?

Size-Up Pass

1.   Write questions.

2.   Write subheadings.

3.   Write vocabulary words, italicized words, key words.

Sort-Out Pass

Write answers to questions:

Can't answer question number _____ .

Scanned for answer on pages _____.

Write answer

Still can't answer? Mark it and move on.

Return to marked question(s).

_____

for which the reading tactic was scheduled and some for passages for which Multipass was not used (see MONITOR 12). Data from passages studied with and without Multipass could be compared to determine, for each student, whether the technique was helpful.

Schumaker, J.B., Deshler, D.D., Alley, G.R., Warner, M.M., & Denton, P.H. (1982). Multipass: A learning strategy for improving reading comprehension. *Learning Disability Quarterly, 5,* 295–304.

Reference

READING: COMPREHENSION MONITORING

Background

A number of strategies are available that help students derive specific information from a text, but they do not necessarily help them monitor their comprehension *while* they read. When students make the shift from teacher-directed discussions to independent reading, it is important for them to have a way to monitor their comprehension of the material. Self-monitoring, the approach explained here, will help students raise their awareness of what they comprehend as they read, and will stimulate them to take corrective action.

Who Can Benefit

In a study by Smith and Dauer (1984), this tactic was taught to middle and high school level students by home economics, social studies, biology, English, and industrial arts teachers. This approach would be suitable for many remedial or at-risk students, or others who have difficulties comprehending what they read.

Procedures

1. Analyze the material to determine which judgments you want the students to make as they

read. This would depend on a number of factors, the characteristics of the material and the curriculum objectives among them. A code for reading from a U.S. history book could be the following: A = agree, B = bored, C = confused, D = disagree, M = main idea.

2. Explain the code to the pupils, and offer a rationale for its use.
3. Model the process by showing an excerpt of text on an overhead projector and marking in the letters.
4. Request the students to study the code before they begin reading.
5. Write the code on the board.
6. Require the students to record the designated letters on strips of paper affixed to the margins of the pages as they read.
7. Discuss with the students, after they read the passage, what they cited as main ideas, the points they agreed and disagreed with, and the sections they found boring or confusing.

Modifications/ Considerations

Teachers should explain to the students why the strategy is helpful and why the specific codes are used. Teachers should also develop codes that are applicable to a variety of materials. Furthermore, students should be encouraged to develop their own codes, once they can use the strategy independently. One such category might pertain to interest.

Monitor

In addition to having pupils develop their own codes, once they are familiar with the process as directed by the teacher, they should be encouraged to keep data on the extent to which they enter the various marks (see MONITOR 1 in Appendix A). Those data could be revealing. If, for example, a pupil consistently indicates that he or she agrees or disagrees with most of the statements, or believes that the majority of the phrases are confusing or boring, he or she should probably make some adjustments or seek help to come up with a set of more balanced judgments. One might hope that if students did have a category that indicated their interest, they would read more in that area and, perhaps because of the depth of reading on the topic, generate interests in other, related topics.

Smith, R.J., & Dauer, V.L. (1984). A comprehension-monitoring strategy for reading content area materials. *Journal of Reading, 28*, 144–147.

Schewel, R.H., & Waddell, J.G. (1986). Metacognitive skills: Practical strategies. *Academic Therapy, 22*, 19–25.

References

READING: VISUAL IMAGERY AND SELF-QUESTIONING TO IMPROVE COMPREHENSION

Remedial and at-risk students in middle and high school must learn to acquire information from content materials. The learning strategies model, with its emphasis on learning *how* to learn, has proven to be particularly valuable for adolescents of this type.

Two learning strategies that have been advocated to improve reading comprehension are *visual imagery* and *self-questioning*. In a study by Clark, Deshler, Schumaker, Alley, and Warner (1984), these two approaches were taught to LD adolescents to increase their interaction with the content and enhance their reading comprehension.

Background

The referenced study was conducted with six LD adolescents from 13 to 17 years old. These strategies can be adapted to the content and needs of students in intermediate grades and taught to students of average intelligence who may be low achievers or non-motivated learners. The authors of the research recommend, however, that to benefit most fully from this approach, students should be able to read at the fourth-grade level.

Who Can Benefit

Instructional Steps

1. Administer a pretest.
2. Test each student's ability to use the Visual Imagery Strategy with grade-level material.

Procedures

3. Test each student's ability to use the Self-Questioning Strategy with grade-level material.
   a. Present a passage and instruct students to tell about the content when they finish reading.
   b. Test comprehension further by asking students some questions about the passage.
4. Describe the steps of the strategy to the students and explain how it will help them (see next section for the steps).
5. Model the strategy: Demonstrate all the steps.
6. Instruct students to verbally rehearse the steps of the strategy. Require 100% accuracy.
7. Require students to practice using the strategy with materials that have been written at their ability levels.
8. Expand the practice when students are comfortable with easier material, to include grade-level materials.
9. Provide positive and corrective feedback to the students.
10. Administer a posttest (a readministration of the pretest).

Visual Imagery Strategy (RIDER)

1. READ (Read the first sentence.)
2. IMAGE (Make an image or a picture in your mind.)
3. DESCRIBE (Describe your image.)
   a. If you cannot make an image, explain why you cannot and go on to the next sentence.
   b. If you can make an image, decide whether it is an old one (an image in memory from the most recent sentence), an old image that has been modified, or an entirely new image.
   c. Once you have an image, describe it.
4. EVALUATE (Evaluate your image for its completeness.)
   a. Make certain that the image includes as much of the sentence's content as possible. If some content is missing, adjust your image and continue.
   b. If your image is comprehensive, continue.
5. REPEAT (Read the next sentence and repeat steps 1 through 4.)

Self-Questioning Strategy (RAM)

1. <u>R</u>EAD a paragraph. Ask "WH" questions as you read to help keep yourself engaged in reading.
2. <u>A</u>NSWER your questions as you read.
3. <u>M</u>ARK your answers with the appropriate symbol for the type of "WH" question. (Establish symbols for each type of question: a clock face for "when" questions, a circle face for "who" questions, a square for "what" questions, an arrow for "where" questions, a capital Y for "why" questions, and a capital H for "how" questions.)

Modifications/ Considerations

For the visual imagery strategy, pupils are encouraged to form an image after each sentence. Depending on the density of material in a passage, that may be difficult. It may be more appropriate to conceive of images following each paragraph. The opposite instruction may be appropriate for the self-questioning strategies. Whereas it was recommended that pupils develop questions following each paragraph, it may be helpful, depending on the richness of material, to form questions following each sentence.

Although the two strategies are independent of each another, they could be used together. That, of course, would depend on the type of material and on the ability of the pupil.

Whether one strategy or another or a combination of the two is scheduled, pupils, to gain the most from the approaches, should be taught when to rely on one or the other. Generally, it might seem that the imagery approach would be an appropriate selection if, in the material, several objects or scenes were described. The questioning strategy might be a wise choice if a number of facts or statements were included in the passage.

Monitor

There are a number of ways to measure the effects of these approaches. One would be to ask students to say or write facts or summaries of stories they had read prior to being instructed to use one of the approaches (see MONITOR 10 in Appendix A). Those data might then be charted as number of words, facts, judgments, or whatever per unit of time (see MONITOR 1). Following this baseline—when neither technique was involved—those same data could be gathered while one or both tactics were being instructed. Data from the two phases could then be compared to determine whether the comprehension techniques improved students' performance.

Reference
Clark, F.L., Deshler, D.D., Schumaker, J.B., Alley, G.R., & Warner, M.M. (1984). Visual imagery and self-questioning: Strategies to improve comprehension of written material. *Journal of Learning Disabilities, 17,* 145–149.

WRITING: AN ERROR MONITORING STRATEGY (COPS)

Background
One of the important goals of education is to instruct students to express their thoughts in writing in a concise, cogent manner. Another goal is to develop independent behaviors. The COPS strategy explained here was designed to focus on both those goals: to assist youngsters to improve their writing and to be independent in the process.

Who Can Benefit
Junior high students of normal intelligence have learned to use this strategy. It has also been effective with learning disabled students and students who generally have poor study habits. In all of these cases, COPS has proven to be a beneficial tactic when students are required to write sentences.

Procedures
Introduction

1. Explain to the students that it is important for them to check their own writing for errors.

Encourage them to offer suggestions on how to do this.

2. Introduce the COPS tactic as a simple way to remember specific features when self-checking their written work. Explain the meaning of the acronym COPS. Check for:

   C: Capitalization (first words, proper nouns, dates, etc.)
   O: Overall editing and appearance
   P: Punctuation
   S: Spelling (handwriting, neatness, margins, complete sentences, etc.)

Implementation. Encourage students to follow these steps as they self-check their writing assignments.

1. Write on every other line (this makes it easier to make corrections).
2. Re-read each sentence, asking the COPS questions.
3. Write the appropriate letter (C, O, P, or S) at the beginning of each sentence in which an error or correction is found.
4. Indicate the location of the error or correction with a check mark.
5. Go back over the assignment and make the necessary corrections.
6. Rewrite the paper, and read it over carefully. Then hand it in.

Modifications/ Considerations

One way of modifying the COPS tactic is to write the COPS acronym on a note card and tape it to the desks of students who particularly need to employ the steps (see Figure 1.2). Review the COPS method and remind students to use it when writing papers. COPS can also be modified for the appropriate level of instruction (elementary, junior, or senior high). The teacher can go into as much detail as necessary for individual students.

To help students check their spelling, which is often a difficult chore, provide them with a "Bad Spellers Dictionary." Students could also exchange their papers with one another to check on not only the spelling but other features of writing as well.

FIGURE 1.2 Reminder for Students Learning the COPS Strategy

COPS

C Have I capitalized the first word and proper names?

O How is the overall appearance?

P Have I put in commas where needed and punctuation at the end of sentences?

S Have I spelled all the words correctly?

For this tactic to be truly effective, students must apply the steps consistently. Check students' papers to see that they are relying on the COPS components. Reinforce their efforts to do so and point out instances when they should have used certain features.

If teachers are to assist youngsters to be good, or at least adequate writers, they must schedule times for them to write. Too often, too little time is set aside for writing, and what is scheduled is generally devoted to rules and principles, not to actual writing.

Another important point for instructors to keep in mind is to schedule instances for their students to write that are functional, meaningful, and motivating. Too often, assignments for adolescents are patronizing, boring, and meaningless.

Monitor To monitor the extent to which students relied on the COPS technique while checking their papers, a checklist could be developed (see MONITOR 6 in Appendix A). On it, the four letters could be written vertically, and across the top a succession of days could be printed. With that chart, the teacher, a peer, or pupils themselves could mark the features that were incorporated in their corrections for each session. As a measure of ability, the teacher could use ideas explained in MONITOR 10; someone could count the number of words written each session and plot those frequencies on a graph.

Reference Deshler, D. (1984). COPS tactic presented in a study skills workshop sponsored by Lake Washington School District #414, Kirkland, WA.

NOTETAKING: SEVERAL SUGGESTIONS

Background

Good notetaking skills make important information more accessible to students. Taking notes requires them to consider and evaluate the content of their lessons in ways that merely listening cannot. Furthermore, students who take and review their notes over lectures learn more than those who just listen. It's not enough to simply tell them to take notes.

Students must be convinced, first, that there are good reasons to improve their notetaking skills, and next, that they can learn to do so and profit from their notes. This tactic offers suggestions for helping students recognize the need for notetaking, and presents a variety of ways for instructing them to take notes.

Who Can Benefit

Secondary students will profit from learning to take notes, since the majority of lesson content in junior high and high school is delivered through lectures and texts. Teachers who take the time to instruct students in sound notetaking practices will provide their students with valuable, generalizable skills that can help them learn more in nearly every learning situation they will encounter.

Procedure

1. Present a brief (10–15 minutes) lecture:
    a. Ask students to take notes.
    b. Test them on the information in the lecture the next day.
    c. Ask them to evaluate their ability to take notes.
2. Teach students two formats for notetaking (see Figure 1.3).
3. Provide students with a list of hints for taking notes (see Figure 1.4).
4. Use video- or audiotapes to provide practice in listening and notetaking by:

FIGURE 1.3 Two Formats for Notetaking

Sample Two-Column System

Topic: _____

Date: _____

Triggers or Key Concepts   Class Notes

Sample Three-Column System

Topic: _____

Date: _____

Triggers or Key Concepts   Class Notes   Text Notes

---

    a. Allowing students to replay a tape to watch or listen for main ideas.

    b. Playing a short segment of a taped lecture, having students list the cues and explain their importance.

    c. Replaying the segment to let students verify their list of cues.

5. Teach students to review notes for tests by:

    a. Using key concepts to formulate questions.

    b. Finding or developing answers from notes.

6. Elicit discussion about other classes in which notetaking skills would be helpful.

FIGURE 1.4 Hints for Taking Notes

1. Take notes using either a two- or three-column system.
2. Take notes on only one side of the paper.
3. Date and label the topic of the notes.
4. Use a modified outline format, indenting subordinate ideas and numbering ideas when possible.
5. Skip lines to note changes in ideas.
6. Write ideas or key phrases, not complete sentences.
7. Use pictures and diagrams to relate ideas.
8. Use consistent abbreviations (e.g., w/ = with, & = and).
9. Underline or asterisk information the lecturer stresses as important.
10. Write down information the lecturer writes on the board or transparency.
11. Draw a line if you miss an idea you want to include so you can fill it in later.
12. Spell a word the way it sounds or the way you think it looks if you cannot remember how to spell a word.
13. Review the previous sessions' notes immediately before the lecture.
14. Read the information before listening to the lecture, if the lecture is about an assigned reading topic.
15. Go over your notes as soon as possible after a lecture. Fill in the key concept column, and list any questions you still have.
16. Summarize the major points presented during the lecture after going over your notes.
17. Listen actively! Think about what you already know about the topic being presented and how it relates.
18. Review your notes before a test!

Note. From Bos, C.S., & Vaughn, S. (1988). *Strategies for teaching students with learning and behavior problems* (p. 209). Boston: Allyn & Bacon. Reprinted by permission.

7. Help students develop a simple monitoring procedure to examine the effectiveness of their notetaking in other classes, including:
   a. Length of notes
   b. Format
   c. How well they think they have taken notes
   d. Test scores

Match the complexity of your lectures to current levels of notetaking and listening instruction by:

Modifications/ Considerations

1. Beginning with short, well-organized lectures
2. Using several visual aids

3. Basing lectures on simple, familiar material
4. Gradually increasing lecture length, difficulty, and novelty of material; reducing number of visual aids

Table 1.1 provides an overview of the events of instruction involved in teaching good notetaking, and how they help students learn more.

To assist students to discriminate between good and poor sets of notes, develop some models of each type. These sets could be evaluated by individuals, small groups, or as a class.

Monitor   As is the case with other tactics in the Study Skills category, it is important to measure the extent to which students learn the skill and how, by learning that skill, they are better able to acquire knowledge or information. For this technique, teachers could assess students' ability to take notes by judging the extent to which they wrote main ideas, organized the information, or incorporated other features of proper notetaking. A rating scale (see MONITOR 5 in Appendix A) or checklist (see MONITOR 6) could be developed for this purpose. To determine whether students acquired more information from textbooks or lectures because of improved notetaking skills, arrange a test or two; several options are available. For one, consider the ideas in MONITOR 11 or MONITOR 12. Write questions for students to answer from the content to be given before and after the notetaking instruction. Pupils' scores on those tests could be charted as frequency or percent (see MONITOR 2).

Reference   Bos, C.S., & Vaughn, S. (1988). *Strategies for teaching students with learning and behavior problems.* Boston: Allyn & Bacon.

NOTETAKING: A SIMPLE FORMAT

Background   Notetaking is a skill that becomes increasingly important as the emphasis shifts from skill building

TABLE 1.1 Notetaking and the Events of Instruction

Instructional Event	Lecturer Might Operationalize This Event in the Following Ways	Which Encourages Notetakers to Do the Following
1. Gaining attention	Physical movement (e.g., move to podium). Arrange lecture notes. Switch on overhead projector. Verbal interaction. "Good morning. Let's begin." Overview the lecture content.	Prepare to listen. Locate place to take notes.
2. Informing learner of objective	Suggest how the information will be useful.	State why the material should be noted. Retrieve critical information.
3. Stimulating recall of prerequisite learning	Review terminology. Summarize main points from previous lecture. Ask questions to determine if students recall key terminology, concepts, principles. Provide a few minutes for students to review notes from an earlier session.	Search for past associations. Review earlier notes.
4. Presenting the stimulus material	Speak at a comfortable pace. Organize the points of the lecture. Pause to allow for questions, clarification.	Alternate between your own words and lecturer's words.
5. Providing "learning guidance"	Use verbal cues such as "Note the following," "This is important to remember," "Record this in your notes." Use chalkboard, overhead transparencies to highlight major points. Raise questions to test comprehension of an idea. Provide an outline.	Discriminate between essential and nonessential information. Use mnemonics.
6. Eliciting performance	During lecture, provide sample questions/problems similar to those that will be presented on an examination.	Practice performance by overtly or covertly responding to questions/problems. Highlight notes, material relevant to responses.
7. Providing feedback about performance correctness	Request students to respond to other students' answers. Model responses to questions/responses.	Correct inaccuracies. Attend to essential information.
8. Assessing the performance	Encourage distributed and massed review of lecture content.	Rehearse notes in preparation for examination.
9. Enhancing retention and transfer	Present divergent examples, nonexamples, and problem situations during lectures. Explicitly link information from previous lecturer with current lecture.	Integrate new information into existing notes.

Note. From Carrier, C.A. (1983). Notetaking research: Implications for the classroom. Reprinted from the *Journal of Instructional Development, 6*, p. 25, by permission of the Association for Educational Communications and Technology. Copyright 1983 by AECT.

FIGURE 1.5 Form for Use in Notetaking Format

NOTETAKING FORMAT

TOPIC _____

Basic Ideas	Background Information	Questions
5″	2″	1″
(Include information necessary for tests, reports, etc.)	(Related or interesting information)	(Comments on points about which there should be more information or clarification)

at the elementary school level to the acquisition of content information at the secondary level. The tactic explained here takes a unique approach to notetaking in that a structure is provided for writing notes and comments about them.

Who Can Benefit The article that stimulated this tactic is a review of notetaking procedures for secondary age learning disabled students. This tactic should be considered, however, for at-risk, remedial, or average students who have difficulty taking notes in content area classes where lecture and textbook notes are required.

Procedures 1. Instruct students to divide a sheet of paper into three columns, or give them paper that has already been divided. The first and largest column (about 5 inches) should be labeled BASIC IDEAS. Label the middle column (about 2 inches) BACKGROUND INFORMATION. QUESTIONS is the label for the last column (about 1 inch). Provide a line at the top of the page for the topic (see Notetaking Format in Figure 1.5).
2. Instruct students to use the form as they take notes, and tell them what each space is for:

a. *Topic*—Identify the main idea (e.g., what started WW I; how seeds germinate; steps for administering CPR).
b. *Basic Ideas*—Write in the facts, figures, dates, names of people, and places. Include here the material that will be needed to pass tests and write reports.
c. *Background Information*—Include information that is related to the basic ideas or is of interest to the student.
d. *Questions*—Include comments about information that is unclear and questions that should be asked.

3. Teach students to use the form by guiding them through several lectures. Tell them what to write in the various columns. You may need to write the notes for some students. This could be done on an overhead projector.
4. Require them to identify relevant and irrelevant information from lectures or textbook activities.
5. Give students a topic sentence and have them complete notes from the textbook or lecture.
6. Move about the room and check on the students' ability to write notes. Assist those who have problems.

Modifications/ Considerations

Following the steps noted here will not of itself ensure independent notetaking. It is necessary to teach students several related skills—subordinating, listening, abbreviating, studying, and test-taking strategies—that they can rely on before and during the time they take notes. Learning to subordinate helps students organize notes. Learning to listen orients students to verbal clues from lectures (e.g., "The first reason . . ." or "The most important point . . ."). Learning to abbreviate helps students write more information. Learning appropriate study and test-taking strategies helps them prepare for tests and to do as well as possible when they take them.

Students could assist one another with notetaking. One way to promote their willingness to help others would be to have them compare notes and make suggestions for improving each other's notes. Most students should realize that by helping others take notes, they may themselves benefit. Knowing this could provide an opportunity for discussing why good citizenship involves working not only for oneself, but for others as well.

To increase their motivation to take notes, you may wish to announce occasionally that students will be allowed to refer to them during tests.

Monitor To monitor the effects of this technique, the suggestions in the previous tactic could be followed. In addition, the ideas in MONITOR 10 in Appendix A could be considered. Pupils could write about what they had read for a few days before receiving instruction on notetaking, and for a few days after they had been offered instruction. Data, in terms of number of words written, concepts detailed, or other features from the two phases, could be graphed and compared.

Reference Saski, J., Swicegood, P., & Carter, J. (1988). Notetaking formats for learning disabled adolescents. *Learning Disability Quarterly, 6*(3), 265-271.

COMPLETING HOMEWORK: SELF-MONITORING

Background To move through a curriculum at an acceptable pace, teachers must rely on students to complete their homework regularly. Doing homework, however, is more than simply setting aside the time to do it. Most students require some assistance in successfully completing their assignments.

Teachers can provide students with a checklist to follow as they tackle their assignments. By referring to the checklist, parents can help their youngsters work through the trouble spots.

Who Can Benefit The cited study was written for LD students at the middle and high school levels. Students of about any type or age, however, could benefit from learning approaches for completing homework assignments.

1. Distribute the checklist to students and review the steps with them (see Checklist for Monitoring Study in Figure 1.6).
2. Answer any questions students might have about the checklist.
3. Encourage pupils to review the checklist with their parents at home. This will give them another chance to familiarize themselves with the checklist while involving their parents. The checklist provides parents with a guide for assisting their youngsters with homework assignments.
4. Request students to rely on their checklists consistently, and address any additional questions that arise after the lists have been used for a few days.
5. Ask students to discuss how the checklists helped them with other students.

Procedures

The checklist provided in Figure 1.6 may be used for many types of homework, but teachers should modify it depending on the type of students, the subjects, and other considerations. The pupils' opinions should certainly be considered with respect to modifying the lists.

Modifications/ Considerations

If time permits, students may practice using the checklist in class for assignments that are to be completed at home. This way, they will be able to ask questions as they come up.

Since the checklist is to be used primarily at home, students will soon discover how important it is to get all the information they need to complete an assignment before they leave school. Knowing this should increase their attention to directions in class and encourage them to ask questions about what they don't understand. Some teachers, to ensure that students know how to do the homework before they take it home, require them to do a bit of it at school, then check on their abilities to do it and provide assistance to those who need it.

To monitor the extent which homework is completed, turned in, and satisfactorily carried out is a rather simple process. Beyond those matters, the teacher should reflect on *why* the homework is assigned in the first place, then design a fitting means to evaluate it. If, for example, the point of homework assign-

Monitor

FIGURE 1.6 Checklist for Use in Self-Monitoring

CHECKLIST FOR MONITORING STUDY

Before Study

☐ 1. Have I organized the necessary time, space, and materials for study?

☐ 2. Do I know exactly what the assignment involves? If I am unsure about anything, have I asked the teacher?

☐ 3. Have I previewed the assignment?

☐ 4. Do I need to ask the teacher to give me more background on the subject?

☐ 5. Have I checked the words for which I do not know the meanings?

(List with page numbers.) _____

_____

☐ 6. Have I thought of questions that could be answered from what I read?

☐ 7. Have I checked with the teacher on the kind of organization that is expected? (Check the appropriate types.)

  ☐ underline

  ☐ list

  ☐ take notes

  ☐ outline

  ☐ retell

  ☐ write a summary

  ☐ write practice exam questions (comparison/contrast, draw conclusions, explain procedures)

☐ 8. Have I attempted the following when I don't understand? (Choose one or more.)

  ☐ re-read

  ☐ jump ahead

  ☐ use an outside reference (glossary, dictionary, map)

  ☐ ask someone

  ☐ write down questions to ask the teacher

After Study

☐ 1. Have I reviewed the question?

☐ 2. Have I listed questions to ask the teacher?

☐ 3. Is my material organized properly? (See number 7 on previous list.)

☐ 4. Have I rehearsed the information in an appropriate way? (Check those that apply.)

    ☐ reading the next assignment

    ☐ solving problems

    ☐ doing laboratory assignments

    ☐ writing a paper

    ☐ taking a test

Note. Adapted from "Help for the Homework Hassle" by L.M. Clary, 1986, *Academic Therapy, 22,* pp. 58, 59. Copyright 1986 by PRO-ED, Inc. Reprinted by permission.

ments is to offer pupils more opportunities to practice on vocabulary, problems, or identifications, then tests should be scheduled periodically to see if there are effects on those abilities. For this, the teacher might consider 10, 11, or 12 in the MONITOR section (Appendix A). There could be, of course, other reasons for scheduling homework assignments, but whatever they are, the teacher should design a suitable approach for evaluating their impact.

Reference

Clary, L.M. (1986). Help for the homework hassle. *Academic Therapy, 22,* 57–60.

TAKING TESTS: RESPONDING TO VARIOUS QUESTION TYPES

Background

Most schools and many businesses rely heavily on testing to evaluate the potential and current performance levels of students and employees. Difficulty with the test-taking process itself can be a major stumbling block for some individuals. Specific hints for responding successfully to several types of objective tests are included in this tactic.

Who Can Benefit   Learning more effective ways to respond to various kinds of test questions would benefit anyone faced with a testing situation. At-risk and remedial students could experience marked improvement in test scores, which might in turn result in improved self-concept and school success.

Procedures   **Introduction.** List and explain the major characteristics of the following types of test questions:

1. *Questions of Fact*—Generally short, requiring answers consisting of a few words.
   EXAMPLES: Who discovered Australia?
                     Where did Marie Curie work?

2. *Sentence Completion*—A common form of question, usually written out with blanks where important words have been omitted. Students are to provide the missing word or words that best complete the statement.
   EXAMPLES: Lewis and _____ explored the Northwest.
                     Molecules are made up of _____.

3. *True/False*—Written in statement form, these questions are often found on teacher-made, textbook, and achievement tests. The student determines whether the statement is completely correct.
   EXAMPLES: All soda pop is free of sugar.
                     Some oceans contain salt water.

4. *Analogies*—Probably the most difficult, in which students are given three bits of information and expected to establish a relationship between two of them, and then identify a mate for the remaining item. The outcome should be that both sets resemble one another.
   EXAMPLES: Day is to night as light is to _____.

                     Lead is to pencil as ink is to _____.

5. *Matching*—A popular form found on many tests. Pupils are to select items from one list that match items on a second list.
    EXAMPLES: 1. dog   a. VCR
                      2. ice   b. canine
                      3. TV   c. frozen water
    Another common format is to write blanks to the left of the numbers in the first column, on which the letters of the correct answers from the second column are to be written.
6. *Multiple Choice*—Probably the most common type of test question. A statement is presented along with a number of words, phrases, or symbols from which to choose. The correct choice completes the statement or answers the question.
    EXAMPLE: A noun is the name of a person, place, thing, or _____.
                        ape   rock   idea   verb
7. *Essay*—Generally the most difficult to respond to (or grade). Pupils must come up with answers on their own, ordinarily without cues.
    EXAMPLE: Explain photosynthesis.

Helpful Hints. Once an understanding of the differences in the most common types of tests has been demonstrated, teachers should provide pupils with strategies to employ in each case.

Questions of Fact

1. Inform students that they must be able to perform these operations:
    a. Identify the key word: *who, what, when, where, why,* or *how.*
    b. Consider the type of word or phrase prompted by each of these terms.
        WHO =   a name
        WHAT =   something or an act
        WHEN =   a date or period of time
        WHERE = a location
        WHY =   defend some act or decision
        HOW =   explain something
2. Provide several questions that include all the asking words. Instruct students to mark their answers as follows:
    a. Circle or check the key words.
    b. Write answers to the questions.

Sentence Completion: Teach students to recognize and respond to the following cues:

1. Number of blanks = number of words in answer.
2. Look for a missing part of speech in the incomplete statement. (If there is no action word in the statement, then the missing word must be a verb.)
3. A conjunction before the blank indicates type of word to follow. (It should be the same type of word as the one before the conjunction.)

True/False

1. Remind students that they should read directions carefully and study sample items to find out how to mark the answers.
2. Explain that the words *all, every, none, more, exactly, always,* and *never* set absolute conditions. Since things are rarely absolute, statements with these words are often false.
3. Discuss the fact that qualifiers such as *some, sometime, usually, occasionally, rarely,* or *frequently* are not as bold as those in the first set, so questions containing these words are more likely to be true.
4. Suggest that the longer the statement, the greater the chance that it will be false, since it would be rare for every part to be accurate.

Analogies. Prepare several sets of analogies to use as examples. Point out that a relationship exists between two words in each analogy. Assist students as they:

1. Identify these relationships.
2. Study the third (unattached) word and determine how it corresponds with its match.
3. Identify a term to link with the third word.

Matching

1. Remind students to read directions carefully to discover if they are to identify the correct answer by placing a letter in a blank, drawing a line between the two related items, or doing something else.
2. Point out that sometimes there are more items in the second column than in the first; therefore, some items will have no match.

3. Suggest that it is best to match the easier parts first, then attempt to join the harder ones. Checking off items in the second column as they are used will help students avoid using an item more than once.

Students should practice on several tests of this type, mastering first the easy statements that are readily matched, and have the same number of items in each column, then moving on to more complex test questions with more items in the second column than in the first.

Multiple Choice

1. Instruct students to determine from the directions which approach to answering multiple choice questions they should take:
    a. Circle the appropriate choice.
    b. Write the number of the correct choice alongside the number of the corresponding statement.
2. Instruct pupils to watch for the following types of incorrect answers:
    a. Words that sound or look a little like the correct word
    b. Choices that may be reasonable, but not the best answer
    c. Obviously absurd possibilities
    Reading the statement and *all* choices before making a decision should help eliminate the obviously incorrect answers first, thus leaving less information to deal with.
3. Teach students to look carefully to see if the words *a* or *an* precede the choice word. These words provide clues as to choosing an answer that begins with a vowel or a consonant.

Essay

1. Stress again the importance of reading directions. On an essay question this is especially important, as there will be no other cues.
2. Instruct students to identify "determiners" (words that tell what to write, how to write it, what style to employ, and how much they should write).
    DESCRIBE   Write about some setting, circumstance, or event they are

	familiar with so that others "get a feel" for the situation.
OUTLINE	Write about familiar events in outline form (e.g., their three daily meals).
TRACE	Write about, for example, the first 10 events of the day (begin with dressing, eating breakfast).
PARAPHRASE	Listen to or read something, then write about it in your own words, retaining the accuracy and order of the original.
INTERPRET	Read a statement and explain it in terms of message, moral, metaphor, or allegory.

3. Progress from simple messages and very short stories with obvious morals to more sophisticated passages.
4. Teach these general techniques for writing responses to essay questions:
   a. Write an outline.
   b. Restate the questions.
   c. Respond to all queries.
   d. Proofread.

Modifications/ Considerations

In each of the training phases, example questions should proceed from extremely simple to gradually more complicated.

Allow students to make initial responses orally, followed later by written answers. This will provide more opportunities for immediate feedback. Teachers could assist pupils to improve on essay tests if they gave a few as "open book" and "open note" tests. This approach would reinforce students' efforts to read more thoroughly and take better notes.

A good follow-up to determine how well students actually understand the differences between the various types of questions they have studied would be to ask them to compose their own questions.

Monitor

The expected outcome from this tactic is that, having been taught a number of test-taking strategies, pupils will do better on actual tests. Thus, it is important for them to have this information and to be able to readily access it. One way to determine this ability would be to quiz the pupils on the important points for taking certain types of tests prior to testing. To obtain those data, a checklist could be developed (see MONITOR 6 in Appendix A).

Reference

Menard, C., Mickelson, G., Orumchian, J., Cassidy, R., Koehl, E., & McCaffrey, A. (1984). *Study strategies for secondary students: Goal setting, time management, test taking* (pp. 42–64). Lake Washington School District No. 414, Kirkland, WA.

TAKING TESTS: DEBRIEFING

Background

Tests are such a regularly occurring event in most educational settings that students are bound to take a lot of them. For at-risk students, who seldom do well on tests, this can become a major stumbling block in their educational paths. They may find the test-taking process so unrewarding that the last thing they would want to do is go back through the test, analyzing their mistakes and approaches for taking the test. Whereas some successful students commonly review their performances on tests, thus learning from their mistakes or poor test-taking strategies, at-risk students seldom profit from their errors, or "learning opportunities." If remedial and at-risk youngsters can be convinced that it is in their best interest to do well on tests, that it is up to them to improve their abilities, and that techniques are available for increasing their scores on tests (apart from knowing more about the content), they will begin to experience more success on tests, and perhaps more success in school.

Who Can Benefit

The approach explained here was designed for mildly handicapped youngsters of secondary age. These steps for debriefing students following a test should, however, be suitable for secondary age youngsters of many types, including those identified as at risk or remedial.

Procedures

1. Develop a checklist of skills and behaviors students need in order to succeed in testing situations. Following are a number of items to consider:

   a. Determine if students put their names and date on the test.

   b. Point out students' scores on the test; tell them how many answers were correct and incorrect, and how many were left out.

   c. Analyze students' performance by type of question (e.g., essay, true/false, multiple choice, matching).

   d. Evaluate students' handwriting; was it legible?

   e. Determine whether students carefully read all the directions.

   f. Ask them if they read the entire test, including directions, before responding to any of the items.

   g. Discover if by reading all the items before responding, they found answers for a few items.

   h. Ask if students paced themselves while working, in order to respond to all the items.

   i. Find out if they responded to the easy questions first.

   j. Ask if they checked their work when finished.

   k. Ask if they requested help during the test for items or directions they didn't understand.

   l. Ask them if they know where the items on the test came from (i.e., lecture, text, video).

   m. Ask them to describe how they studied for the test and how much time they devoted to this.

2. Determine *what* students should concentrate on for the next test by reviewing with them the points in the list they failed to observe.

3. Give students a copy of the checklist to use as they prepare for the next test.

4. Emphasize to students that if they pay attention in class, listen to lectures, read the textbook assignments, study their notes, and consider the steps proposed here for taking tests, that they will most certainly do better on tests and make better grades.

5. Provide time during class for students to prepare for tests and to evaluate tests that are returned.

6. Conduct private interviews with students who require individual assistance on test taking, at which time general problems and concerns may also be brought up. Encourage students to comment on the points of this approach that are, for them, particularly difficult or helpful.

Modifications/ Considerations

Solicit suggestions from students on ways to prepare for tests and for taking tests. Some novel and useful approaches will result.

A more general test-taking strategy, SCORER, has been proposed by Carman and Adams (1972). Following are the six points of that approach:

S = Schedule your time for responding to all the test items.

C = Clue words, be certain to identify and react to them.

O = Omit difficult questions and do the easy ones first.

R = Read test items and directions carefully.

E = Estimate your answers to see if they are "in the ballpark."

R = Review your work after responding to as many items as possible.

Monitor

Keep track of the students' scores on tests during the period you work with them on the debriefing approach. After all, the point of this procedure is to raise test scores. As they go up, point out the reasons for the increases to the students. Inform them that it is not related to chance. If, however, their scores do not improve, determine why not, and make suitable adjustments. If the test scores are reported as percentages, a chart of that type could be developed on which the scores were entered (see MONITOR 2 in Appendix A).

References

Carman, R.A., & Adams, W.R., Jr. (1972). *Study skills: A student's guide for survival.* New York: Wiley.

Lovitt, T.C. (1983). *Debriefing performance on tests.* Unpublished manuscript. University of Washington, Seattle.

LEARNING FROM TEXTBOOKS: STUDY GUIDES

Background   Study guides take a variety of forms, many of which can be useful when adapting textbook passages for remedial and at-risk students. Researchers have pointed out that some textbook passages are so poorly organized that comprehension becomes quite difficult for many students. Providing organized supplementary material as described in this tactic can to some extent alleviate that problem.

Who Can Benefit   Study guides designed in a framed outline format have proved effective in research with both LD and non-LD adolescents. In this approach, ideas are arranged so that there is a train of narration and a sequence of thought, both of which help students grasp the main ideas of a passage.

Procedures   **Constructing Study Guides**

1. Scan the entire book and mark the chapters that will and will not be covered.
2. Note the sequence in which the chapters will be assigned.
3. Read every part of the first chapter including the introduction, summary, figure captions, study questions, graphics (i.e., tables, figures, charts), and other material carefully.
4. Pay particular attention to the featured words and phrases (i.e., headings, words that are italicized, boxed text, or words that are highlighted in other ways) and to information in summary or review sections.
5. Read the passage again, and underline all important ideas and concepts. Err on the side of underlining too much, since some of the important ideas may appear in several places. Cross out material you do not intend to cover.

6. Divide the chapter into logical sections of about 1,000 to 1,500 words each, depending on how detailed the material is and how much is important.
7. Write down the main ideas.
8. Sequence the main ideas (this may vary from the order the ideas appear in the text). Type this sequence on a sheet and review it. Check to see that the ideas and their arrangement are coherent.
9. Write brief sentences containing the main ideas. Arrange them so that a story unfolds. Develop a narration that brings it all together so that one idea leads to another. Write as simply as possible while maintaining the style of the text.
10. Leave out a few words in each sentence: nouns in some, verbs in others, and other parts of speech in still others. Vary the number of words omitted depending on the ability of the students. If writing is a slow process for a student, leave out only a word or two. On the other hand, if writing speed or skill is not a concern, several words may be omitted.
11. Prepare two copies of the sequenced study guides for the teacher. On one, all the words are provided; on the other, a few words are missing. Prepare one study guide for the students, on which some words are not included.
12. Allow 2- to 3-inch margins on either side.

See Figure 1.7 for an example study guide.

Presenting Study Guides

1. Require pupils to read the text passage before using the study guides.
2. Designate a pupil to pass out the study guides after students have read the material. There are a number of ways to select this person:
   a. Ask the same student to hand study guides out each day, or give this task to a different pupil each day.
   b. Ask for a volunteer to pass them out.
   c. Require students to earn the privilege of passing them out by achieving a certain standard of performance.
   d. Have students take turns handling this task as they generally do other classroom chores.

FIGURE 1.7 Example of a Study Guide

STUDY GUIDE

STUDENT _____   TEACHER _____

DATE _____   PERIOD _____

TOPICS *Compounds (pages 139, 144–146)*

Mixtures (page 147)

1. A compound is made up of 2 or more different elements. The *molecules* in a compound have 2 or more different kinds of *atoms*.
2. For example: Water is a *compound*. Its molecules have 2 hydrogen *atoms* and 1 *oxygen* atom.
3. Although compounds are different from each other, they have some similar *properties* and can be classified according to these *properties*.
4. Two major kinds of compounds are *acids* and *bases*. Another kind of compound is *salt*.
5. All *acids* have hydrogen atoms joined to 1 or more other kinds of atoms. Acids taste *sour*.
6. All *bases* contain atoms of some kind of metal. Each *base* contains 1 atom of oxygen joined to 1 atom of hydrogen; this is called a *hydroxyl* group. Bases taste *bitter*.
7. *Indicators* such as litmus paper change *color* in the presence of an acid or *base*. They tell us whether something is an *acid* or base.
8. When an acid and a base react, they *change* chemically and form 2 new *compounds*, a salt and water.
9. Salt is formed when an *acid* reacts with a metal oxide. It does not taste bitter or sour—it tastes *salty*!
10. A metal oxide is a *compound* formed when oxygen and a metal combine. *Rust* is a metal oxide, formed of oxygen and iron atoms.
11. Mixtures are different from *compounds*. In mixtures, different kinds of matter are joined together in one place. They do not form a new *compound*.
12. *Solutions* are one kind of mixture. Solutions are mixtures that appear to be the *same* throughout.
13. Solutions can be liquid, gas, solid, or a combination of these. One kind of solid solution is an *alloy*. Alloys are usually made up of one or more *metals*.

3. Begin the lecture. Place the transparency that has missing words on the overhead projector. Show only the first sentence, and ask students to take out their copies of the outline and a pencil.

4. Explain to the students that they should listen to the lecture and, as the topics on the outline are discussed and the missing words are filled in on the transparency, fill in the blanks on their copies in pencil.

5. Keep the lesson active and moving. Vary the style of presentation and sustain student involvement by doing the following:
   a. Stop from time to time and ask questions, rather than merely reading the sentences and filling in the missing words.
   b. Illustrate concepts with examples.
   c. Review phrases when necessary, and reiterate certain facts or phrases.
   d. Supply linking ideas when the transition from one thought to another is not clear.
   e. Ask pupils, occasionally, to say what should be filled in before writing in the missing words.
   f. Elicit both individual and unison responses.

6. Roam about the room during the lecture to be sure that all the youngsters are filling in the blanks.

7. Ask students to turn over their outlines when all the points have been covered and they have filled in all the blanks.

8. Pass through all the sentences quickly, several times.

9. Write notes on the outlines, and encourage pupils to do the same on their sheets.

10. Remind students to store their outlines in a folder or some type of notebook where they can be quickly retrieved.

11. Administer a quiz on the material.

Modifications/ Considerations

There are many additional ways to incorporate framed outlines into the teaching routine:

1. *Pair (or Peer) Teaching*—One student (as the teacher) uses the filled-in version of the outline while the other student (as the pupil) fills in the blanks. The student acting as teacher may read the material while the "pupil" fills in the blanks.

Or, the two students simply take turns asking each other for answers.

2. *Homework*—Students may take the sheets home and ask a parent or other family member to drill them, or students can simply practice with the materials themselves.

3. *Review*—If students keep their sheets in an organized and sequenced manner they can review them for 6-week, semester, and end-of-year quizzes and tests.

4. *Odd Moments*—When there isn't enough time to begin a new activity, but order must be maintained and time used productively, ask questions from the study guides. This could be developed into an ongoing game by dividing the class into teams. A running score could be kept, and a winner announced at the end of a period of time.

Keep in mind when developing the "story" from main ideas in the chapter that the primary concern is for students to understand the subject. Ask yourself, if you had read only the sequenced main ideas and not the entire chapter, whether you would have enough information about the passage.

To move from a teacher-directed to a student-directed activity, print page numbers alongside the sentences in the study guide to show students where to look in the text to find the missing words. Then, require students to fill in the blanks on their own.

Print the vocabulary words on the bottom of the sheets as cues to increase response rates during the initial phase of instruction and to reinforce correct spelling.

Monitor A number of possibilities are available for monitoring the influence of study guides on pupils' performance. In a study by Lovitt, Rudsit, Jenkins, Pious, and Benedetti (1986), the researchers scheduled chapter tests developed by publishers (see MONITOR 12 in Appendix A). In that study, the publishers' tests were administered following chapters for which study guides were available and following others without study guides. The sequence of the chapters alternated from those "with study guides" to those "without study guides." With those data, the researchers learned about the comparative effects of the guides on groups of youth and for each individual.

References

Lovitt, T.C., & Horton, S. (1987). How to develop study guides. *Journal of Reading, Writing and Learning Disabilities, 3,* 213–221.

Lovitt, T., Rudsit, J., Jenkins, J., Pious, C., & Benedetti, D. (1986). Adapting science materials for regular and learning disabled seventh graders. *Remedial and Special Education, 1,* 31–39.

LEARNING FROM TEXTBOOKS: GRAPHIC ORGANIZERS

Background

Most regular content area classes contain heterogeneous groupings of nonhandicapped, remedial, at-risk, learning disabled, and behaviorally disordered students. Considering the range of abilities inherent in such settings, classroom teachers may have justifiable concerns about providing for individual needs.

With this tactic, teachers will learn to construct and implement graphic organizers (GOs) to teach content to all of these students in the same setting at the same time. Two types of GOs, hierarchical and compare/contrast, are presented, and three techniques for implementing GOs are suggested.

Who Can Benefit

Middle and high school age learning disabled, remedial, and regular education students were included in the studies on which this tactic is based. Students in each group demonstrated gains in the acquisition of information when GOs were employed to teach science, social studies, and health. A major benefit to students and teachers alike is that GOs can be implemented without changing classroom location, textbooks, grouping arrangements, or existing sequences of instruction.

Procedures

Constructing Graphic Organizers

1. Determine which textbook chapters will be taught and arrange them in sequence.
2. Divide chapters into 1,500- to 2,000-word instructional units.
3. Outline the main ideas in the passage.
4. Choose a format:
   a. *Hierarchical*—Most text information converts easily to this format (arranged by major and minor categories). Can be approached either top-down (deductive) or bottom-up (inductive). (See Figure 1.8 showing the classification system. This is a modification of the hierarchical format.)
   b. *Compare/Contrast*—Best for materials arranged by similarities or differences. (See Figure 1.9 for information on two types of colonies.)
5. Develop teacher and student versions of the GO:
   a. Prepare the teacher version first.
   b. Keep it to a single page.
   c. Select and number specific items to be completed by students.
   d. Remove some information from the student's copy.

Implementing Graphic Organizers

1. Decide when to use the GOs:
   a. Before reading a passage (advance organizer)
   b. During instruction (intermediate organizer)
   c. After reading (post organizer)
2. Choose the type of activity for the lesson:
   a. In-class
   b. Large or small group
   c. Homework
3. Determine which method of implementation to use:
   a. Teacher directed
   b. Student directed with text references
   c. Student directed with clues

Teacher Directed

1. Have students mark the pages in their textbook that are involved in the GO.
2. Instruct students to read and re-read the passage for 15 minutes.

FIGURE 1.8 Example of a Graphic Organizer Using a Hierarchical
Format

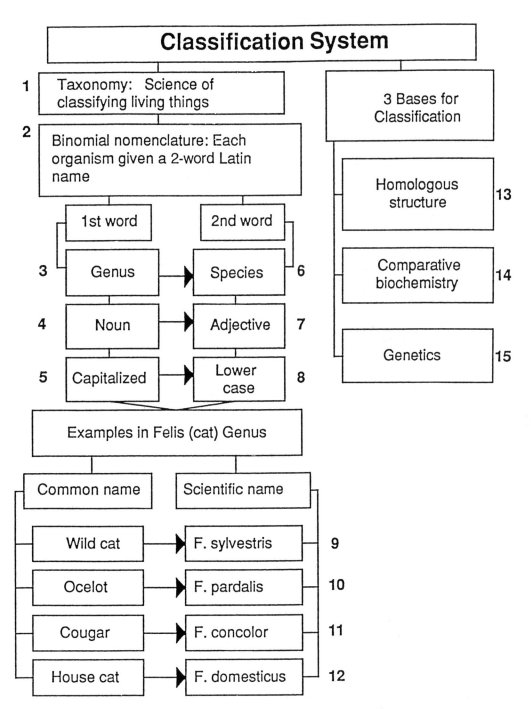

Note. From Lovitt, T.C., & Horton, S.V. (1985-1988). Material developed from grant from
U.S. Government. Department of Education.

FIGURE 1.9 Example of a Graphic Organizer Using a Compare/Contrast Format

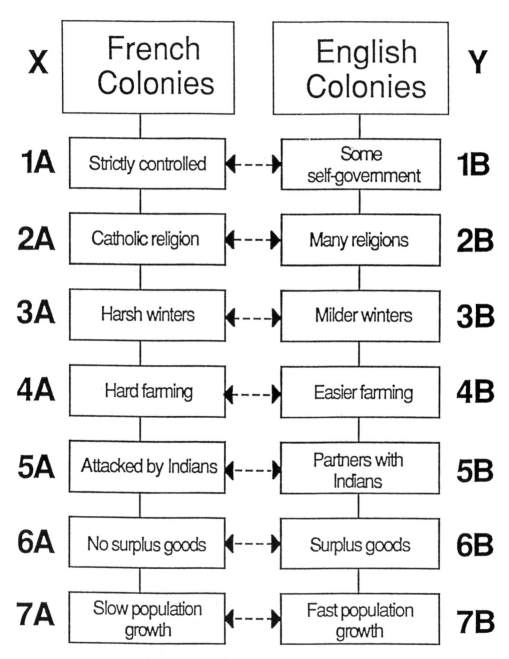

COMPARE AND CONTRAST

	French Colonies	English Colonies	
X			Y
1A	Strictly controlled	Some self-government	1B
2A	Catholic religion	Many religions	2B
3A	Harsh winters	Milder winters	3B
4A	Hard farming	Easier farming	4B
5A	Attacked by Indians	Partners with Indians	5B
6A	No surplus goods	Surplus goods	6B
7A	Slow population growth	Fast population growth	7B

Note. From Lovitt, T.C., & Horton, S.V. (1985–1988). Material developed from grant from U.S. Government. Department of Education.

3. Tell students to close their books. Give each pupil a copy of the student version of the GO.
4. Place a transparency of the teacher's version on the overhead projector, and point out the relationships between items shown on the diagram.
5. Help students fill in the answers on their copies:
   a. Cover an answer on the transparency.
   b. Call on a student to provide the answer orally.
   c. Uncover the answer.
   d. Request students to write the answer on their copies.
   e. Repeat until all answers have been filled in.
6. Allow 3 minutes for students to study their completed GOs.
7. Pick up student copies and give a test.

Student Directed with Text References

1. Repeat steps 1 through 4 of teacher-directed GOs.
2. Attach a cover sheet that shows the page and paragraph number for locating each answer.
3. Direct pupils to use that information to complete their diagrams.
4. Circulate among the pupils to keep them on task and to provide assistance as necessary.
5. Review the filled-in GOs by placing a transparency of the teacher's version on an overhead. Ask students to correct their copies.
6. Allow 3 minutes for students to study their completed GOs.
7. Collect the completed GOs and give a test.

Student Directed with Clues

1. Arrange the answers to the numbered boxes on the GO in random order on a cover sheet. Include directions for completing the GO.
2. Attach the cover sheet to the student's version.
3. Follow steps described in the "Student Directed with Text References" section above, except for number 5. Instead, have students complete the diagram by studying the relationships between categories, referring to a list of clues, and checking the reading passage in the textbook.

Modifications/ Considerations   Research with mildly handicapped youngsters indicates that information acquired through GOs transfers more readily to both testing formats (graphic-to-graphic and graphic-to-prose) than that presented in a prose style.

When selecting chapters to present with graphic organizers, you may wish to pick those that are poorly organized, or have caused problems for students in the past. Dividing those chapters into shorter reading passages lessens the chance that students will be overwhelmed by too much information, and makes it easier for teachers to analyze the material.

Generally, GOs are most effective under the following conditions: when used as post organizers; when based on specific reading passages rather than overall content; and when presented to students of secondary and college age.

According to many content area teachers who have continued employing GOs after studies were completed, their reason for doing so is that GOs are effective with large heterogeneous groups.

Monitor   An effective way to determine the effects of this technique is to follow the suggestions in MONITOR 14 in Appendix A: Rely on a fill-in-the-blanks or a cloze procedure. One way to set this up would be to require students to fill in some of the information on graphic organizers when they are provided only the geometric shapes and a few clue words. Students could be required to fill in this information on forms that *were not* presented to them as graphic organizers and on forms that *were* scheduled as organizers. As for data, a point could be given for each blank that is filled in properly. There were 14 opportunities, for example, to supply information for the boxes underneath French and English in Figure 1.9. Data from both conditions—with and without graphic organizer instruction—could be compared.

References   Bergerud, D., Lovitt, T.C., & Horton, S.V. (1988). The effectiveness of textbook adaptations in life science for high school students with learning disabilities. *Journal of Learning Disabilities, 21,* 70–76.

Horton, S.V., & Lovitt, T.C. (1989). Construction and implementation of graphic organizers for academically handicapped and regular secondary students. *Academic Therapy, 24,* 625–640.

LEARNING FROM TEXTBOOKS: VISUAL-SPATIAL APPROACH

Background

In the visual-spatial (V-S) approach, an association is made between key words and certain shapes, which are then linked together to form a visual representation of the relationship among main ideas in a written passage. This format works best with materials that fit two classic styles of organization: (a) Present a main idea supported by subordinate ideas, or (b) show interrelationships among main ideas. As explained here, the Direct Instruction method of teaching is used to instruct the concepts and relationships in V-S.

Who Can Benefit

In a study by Lovitt, Stein, and Rudsit (1985), the V-S technique was employed with mildly handicapped seventh graders in a resource room. Although the subject matter in these studies was science, V-S formats can be applied to most content areas. Using visual cues to aid retention of facts should be especially beneficial to students who have difficulty processing written information.

Procedures

Creating a Visual-Spatial Display

1. Read the chapter carefully, looking for arrangements such as those mentioned in the Background section above. Also note pictures and ideas that could serve to enhance the V-S approach.
2. Highlight the main points in the chapter. Indicate related and subordinate features as well.
3. Arrange and group these key facts and related items on a page arranged like an organizational chart (see Figures 1.10 and 1.11).
    a. Start with main ideas, branching out and adding others that pertain to primary and subordinate ideas.
    b. Use different shapes to indicate degrees of importance and relationships and to trigger students' memory.

FIGURE 1.10 Sample Framework for a Visual-Spatial Display

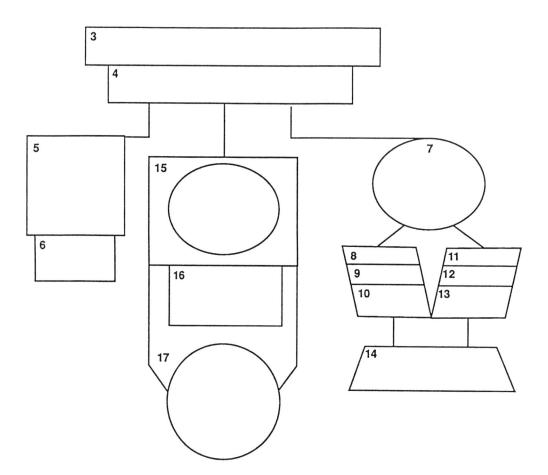

MONITOR'S QUESTIONS:

on dice	question	on dice	question
3	What words go in space 3?	11	What words go in space 11?
4	What words go in space 4?	12	What words go in space 12?
5	What words go in space 5?	13	What words go in space 13?
6	What words go in space 6?	14	What words go in space 14?
7	What words go in space 7?	15	What words go in space 15?
8	What words go in space 8?	16	What words go in space 16?
9	What words go in space 9?	17	What words go in space 17?
10	What words go in space 10?		

Note. From Dixon, R. (1983–1984). Material developed from contract from U.S. Government. Department of Education.

FIGURE 1.11   Example of a Completed Visual-Spatial Display

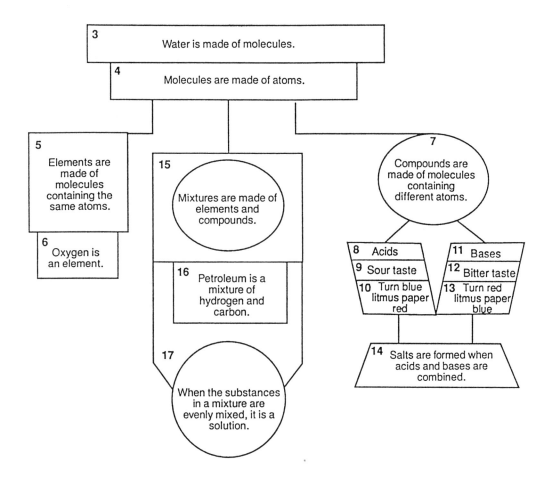

DIRECTIONS

1. Form groups of three players and one monitor.
2. Players memorize the facts in each space of the filled-in chart.
3. When the game starts, each player is given a blank chart. The purpose of the game is to remember the facts that belong in each space.
4. Players take turns rolling the three dice. The number on the die corresponds with a fact on one of the spaces. The monitor asks the player to recall the words from that space.
5. Players have 30 seconds to answer. Correct answers earn one point. Incorrect answers earn no points.

Note. From Dixon, R. (1983–1984). Material developed from contract from U.S. Government. Department of Education.

Initial Teaching Presentation

1. Provide each student with a copy of the completed visual-spatial chart, and display an identical copy on the overhead projector.
2. Direct students to look at the first piece of information, for example, 3 in Figure 1.11.
3. Read aloud the words in that space, "Water is made of molecules."
4. Instruct students to repeat the fact or phrase you just read. (CUE: "SAY IT.")
5. Provide related information and further explanations as appropriate.
6. Follow up by telling students to remember the phrase, its position on the chart, and the shape that encloses it.
7. Drill students over the other phrases and words using this same approach.

Expanded Teaching Presentation

1. Place a transparency of the incomplete visual-spatial chart on an overhead projector.
2. Give each student a copy of the blank chart.
3. Tell students to look at the first blank shape.
4. Instruct them to listen to the words that go in the blank.
5. Read the words to them.
6. Require students to repeat what you have just said.
7. Repeat the process with all facts needed to fill in the chart.
8. Ask students to look at the first blank space again.
9. Request them to say the words that should go in the blank.
10. Repeat this procedure for all the facts.

V-S Game

1. Begin playing the V-S Game when students demonstrate familiarity with all items.
2. Form teams. Either the teacher or the students may choose the team members.
3. Appoint the highest performing student in each group as the monitor for that team.
4. Explain that the teams are to take turns throwing the dice, one team member at a time.

5. Give each team monitor a script of the questions and a list of all the pupils on their team.
6. Instruct monitors to ask a student the question that corresponds to his or her roll of the dice (e.g., if a student rolls a *3*, ask him or her to supply information to number 3).
7. Direct the monitor to mark a *1* next to the name of each pupil who gives a correct answer. For incorrect answers, the monitor will read the correct answer and ask the student who erred to repeat it.
8. Alternate this question-and-answer procedure between the teams until all the questions have been answered.
9. Award prizes of some sort to teams, individuals, or both.

Modifications/ Considerations

Once pupils have learned to play the V-S Game, the teacher should allow them to manage the game themselves, stepping in only if necessary to ensure that it runs smoothly. It would be a good idea to establish a few basic management rules before turning things over to the students.

The V-S procedure could be expanded by having students develop their own V-S for later chapters, and including other subjects in the process. Examples of other sets of facts or features that could be represented visually would be (a) a diagram of the atom, showing electrons, protons, and neutrons; (b) a chart explaining the metric system; (c) maps, including rivers, cities, mountain ranges; (d) derivations of words; (e) a schematic of the automobile's electric system; or (f) the families of instruments in the orchestra.

Monitor

To ascertain the effects of this technique, the procedures explained in MONITOR 14 in Appendix A could be followed. The V-S approach could also be evaluated in a more traditional way. The teacher could give students a test he or she had developed or one prepared by the textbook publishers, some of which are accompanied by the V-S Game and others that are not.

References Lovitt, T.C., Stein, M., & Rudsit, J. (1985). *The use of visual spatial displays to teach science facts to learning disabled middle school students.* Unpublished manuscript, Experimental Education Unit, University of Washington, Seattle.

Engleman, S., Davis, K., & Davis, G. (1986). *Your world of facts I: A memory development program.* Tigard, OR: CC Publications.

LEARNING VOCABULARY: PRECISION TEACHING VOCABULARY SHEETS

Background It is extremely important to learn the important words of a subject to fully understand it. Following are a few of the physical science words that seventh graders are expected to know: *observation, experiment, probing, investigate, environment, chemistry, solution, amplify, voltage, molecule, compound, nuclear,* and *dissolve.* The approach for teaching vocabulary described here is based on features of Precision Teaching (PT): setting performance aims, charting performances, making instructional decisions from those data, and practicing on those materials until aims are reached.

Who Can Benefit Mastery of the specialized vocabulary of some content area classes can be especially difficult for students whose reading ability is below average. In a study by Lovitt, Rudsit, Jenkins, Pious, and Benedetti (1985), pupils from several seventh-grade science classes were instructed in the PT sheets. Those students were instructed in groups of six: two high-performing, two average-performing, and two low-performing students.

Constructing Vocabulary Sheets   **Procedures**

1. Identify the key words in a chapter or passage in one of the following ways:
    a. Select the italicized words or those the publisher has otherwise highlighted.
    b. Copy the words the publisher identified in a vocabulary section (often located at the end of the chapter).
    c. Pull out the essential words from the introduction or summary section of the chapter.
    d. Select those words identified in the book's glossary.
    e. Choose key words from the index.
    f. Require a few pupils to read the chapter, and note words they cannot pronounce or those for which they don't know the meaning.
2. Write simple definitions for the words that were identified, following these guidelines:
    a. Include words familiar to the students.
    b. Keep definitions short (4–10 words) with no unnecessary words.
3. Print the words and definitions at the top of the vocabulary sheet. Below these words, print the vocabulary words over and over on the grid so that each term appears three or four times (see Figure 1.12, Answer Side of PT sheet).
4. Print only the vocabulary words (no definitions) at the top of the other side of the sheet (see Figure 1.13, Question Side of PT sheet). Below these, write only the definitions over and over on the grid so that they correspond with the words on the other side of the sheet.

Completing the Precision Teaching Package

1. Give each student a manila folder. Attach an acetate sheet to one of the inside flaps; on the inside of the other flap, tape a chart (see illustration of Precision Teaching folder in Figure 1.14).
2. Personalize the folders. Ask students to write their names on the folders. Students could decorate their folders according to a theme of their choice.

FIGURE 1.12 Sample of Answer Side of Precision Teaching Vocabulary Sheet

ANSWER SIDE

buoyancy	= upward push on an object placed in a liquid	**hypothesis** = proposed answer to a question or tentative solution to a problem
displacement	= way to determine the volume of an odd-shaped piece of matter	**observing** = taking notice and gathering data; using senses to find out things
SI	= international system of units (Metric System)	**inference** = conclusion based on observation
standard	= fixed quantity used in measuring	**scientific method** = orderly way to solve problems: observing, measuring, explaining, and testing

SI (SI)	observing (ob)	standard (stan)	displacement (dis)	SI (SI)
hypothesis (hyp)	buoyancy (buo)	inference (in)	hypothesis (hyp)	scientific method (s.m.)
displacement (dis)	observing (ob)	scientific method (s.m.)	inference (in)	displacement (dis)
inference (in)	scientific method (s.m.)	SI (SI)	observing (ob)	hypothesis (hyp)
standard (stan)	buoyancy (buo)	standard (stan)	observing (ob)	buoyancy (buo)

FIGURE 1.13 Sample of Question Side of Precision Teaching Vocabulary Sheet

QUESTION SIDE

buoyancy (buo)
displacement (dis)
SI (SI)
standard (stan)

a hypothesis (hyp)
observing (ob)
an inference (in)
scientific method (s.m.)

Student _____

Date _____

Teacher _____

Period _____

_____ is an international system of units (Metric System).

_____ is a proposed answer to a question or tentative solution to a problem.

_____ is a way to determine the volume of an odd-shaped piece of matter.

A conclusion based on observation is called _____.

A fixed quantity used in measuring is _____.

_____ is taking notice and gathering data; using senses to find out things.

The upward push on an object placed in a liquid is called _____.

A fixed quantity used in measuring is _____.

_____ is a way to solve problems: observing, measuring, explaining, and testing.

_____ is an international system of units (Metric System).

A fixed quantity used in measuring is _____.

The upward push on an object placed in a liquid is called _____.

_____ is a way to determine the volume of an odd-shaped piece of matter.

_____ is a proposed answer to a question or tentative solution to a problem.

A conclusion based on observation is called _____.

_____ is taking notice and gathering data; using senses to find out things.

_____ is an international system of units (Metric System).

_____ is taking notice and gathering data; using senses to find out things.

The upward push on an object placed in a liquid is called _____.

_____ is a way to solve problems: observing, measuring, explaining, and testing.

A fixed quantity used in measuring is _____.

FIGURE 1.14 Illustration of Precision Teaching Folder

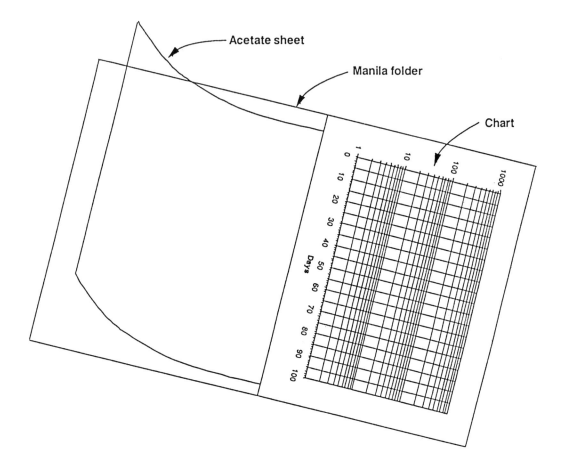

3. Establish a management system for storing and handing out folders. Choose methods that are smooth and fit in with your management style.
4. Purchase erasable marking pens for the students.

Teaching with This Package

1. Pass out folders and pens.
2. Give the following directions:
   a. Turn the folder lengthwise so that the hinge of the acetate sheet is in the middle and opens nearest to you.
   b. Place the practice sheets under the acetate with the "blanked" definitions facing you.

    c. With the special pen, fill in the blanks on your sheets with the proper vocabulary words as fast as you can.

    d. Start with the item farthest to the left on the top row, move one at a time across that row, then to the item on the left on the next row. Don't skip around.

    e. Write as neatly and as rapidly as you can.

    f. Refer to the list of words at the top of the page if you need to check your spelling.*

    g. Flip the sheet over and look at the filled in definitions if you can't remember the meaning of a word.*

*Tell students to rely on (f) or (g) only if absolutely necessary.

3. Begin the timings. Allow students to work for 1 minute.

4. Instruct students to check and count their answers, when finished, in the following manner:

    a. Flip the practice sheets over and compare your responses with the answers on the sheet.

    b. Circle incorrect answers and write in the correct word.

    c. Count the number of correct and incorrect answers.

5. Explain the components of a graph to students and how to chart their data:

    a. Vertical lines = *Day Lines* (Sunday is represented by heavy lines, with each succeeding line representing successive days of the week.)

    b. Horizontal lines = *Rate Lines* (Explain what the 1s, 10s, 100s, and the lines in between them indicate.)

    c. Place data from the first timing on the first day's line of the first week, and so on.

Note: Four timings, one after another, 3 times a week, is recommended.

6. Ask students to evaluate their scores by comparing their best score with a classroom goal.

7. Collect folders and pens. This should be done quietly and quickly. File folders so they can be accounted for and distributed easily the next session. Count pens to see that they've all been returned.

Modifications/ Considerations   PT vocabulary sheets can be altered in several ways. For instance, the number of words could vary, or abbreviations might be used in place of whole words for definitions. The advantage to using the shortened form is that students can cover more ground during the 1-minute timings. A word of caution, however: Test students periodically to make sure they still know what words the abbreviations stand for.

As with other study skills approaches, these vocabulary sheets can be used for peer tutoring, pair teaching, homework, or review sheets.

The classroom goal mentioned in number 6, "Teaching with This Package," may be based on the performance of one of the best students in the class. The suggested rate is about 20 correct answers per minute.

Monitor   Suggestions for monitoring appear in numbers 4 and 5, "Teaching with This Package." Pretests and Post-tests would provide an additional evaluation. See MONITOR 1 in Appendix A for other suggestions for evaluating this approach.

References   Lovitt, T.C., Rudsit, J., & Bergerud, D. (1984). *Physical science vocabulary program.* Lehi, UT: Precision Teaching Materials.

Lovitt, T., Rudsit, J., Jenkins, J., Pious, C., & Benedetti, D. (1985). Two methods of adapting science materials for learning disabled and regular seventh graders. *Learning Disability Quarterly, 8,* 275–285.

MEMORIZING INFORMATION: MNEMONICS

Background   The ability to learn multiple attributes is an important factor in the mastery of concepts. Research on the use of keywords and pegwords to teach associations between facts—such as vocabulary words and definitions, or mineral names and hardness levels—has shown mnemonic strategy instruction to be effective. The techniques described here would be helpful in remembering related facts in a variety of areas (e.g., geography—multiple features of states and countries; biology—multiple functions of organs and systems).

The referenced study examined four methods for teaching multiple attributes of a concept: direct instruction, mnemonic instruction, reduced-list direct instruction, and free study.

Who Can Benefit

Fifty-six junior high school LD students participated in this study. The improvements in learning and retention they achieved indicated that mnemonic procedures can be more effective for students than any of the other three instructional approaches mentioned above.

Procedures

Basic Concepts

1. Develop an understanding of the basic terms and concepts of mnemonic instruction:

   Keywords: Incorporate the "3 Rs" of associative mnemonic techniques: recoding, relating, and retrieving.

   Recoding—An unfamiliar term is transformed into a concrete, familiar word that sounds like a part of the new word to be learned and can be easily pictured.
   EXAMPLE: new term—*viaduct*
   keyword—*duck*

   Relating—A keyword is linked to desired response via an interactive picture.
   EXAMPLE: *viaduct* = *bridge*; interactive picture: *duck* crossing *bridge*.

   Retrieving—Learner is led systematically from the stimulus to the response.
   EXAMPLE: *viaduct* (stimulus)—duck (keyword)—duck crossing bridge (interactive picture)—*bridge* (correct response).

Pegword: Numbers 1 through 10 are recoded as familiar rhyming words (e.g., 1 = *bun,* 2 = *shoe,* 3 = *tree,* etc.).

The combination of keywords and pegwords results in a mnemonically interactive picture to be used by students to learn the attributes of a concept.
EXAMPLE: Concept: The mineral *wolframite* has a hardness level of *4* (see Figure 1.15).
Keyword: *wolf*
Pegword: *floor*
Interactive picture: A *wolf* sitting on a *floor* in front of lights.
Additional attributes can be represented by expanding the pictorial representations, adding color (if a relationship can be drawn), and establishing more acoustical links. Of the three, pictorial representations are usually the most effective.

2. Determine which concepts contain multiple attributes that students will need to learn. Identify those attributes and decide how to represent them mnemonically.
3. Prepare the following materials prior to instruction: A set of interactive illustrations drawn on $8\frac{1}{2} \times 11$-inch paper. Each illustration should include some or all of the following, depending on the number and nature of the attributes to be mastered:
   a. The name of the fact to be learned and its keyword
   b. Numerical information and its pegword
   c. A color that would enhance association
   d. A representation of the use or importance of the fact

Instruction

1. Inform students that they are to learn information about minerals, and there will be a quiz over this information at the end of the period.
2. Explain to them that they will be using a new technique that will help them remember what they were taught.
3. Teach students the rhyming pegwords for numbers 1 through 10 (if numbers are among the attributes to be learned).

FIGURE 1.15   Example of Mnemonic Instruction

WOLFRAMITE

Note. From Scruggs, T.E., Mastropieri, M.A., Levin, J.R., & Gaffney, J.S. (1985). Facilitating the acquisition of science facts in learning disabled students. *American Educational Research Journal, 22*(4), p. 580. Copyright 1985 by the American Educational Research Association. Reprinted by permission.

4. Teach the keywords as follows:
   a. Show students a picture of the keyword and the new word to be learned.
   b. Say, "The keyword for (*word to be learned*) is (*word the picture represents*)."
      EXAMPLE: "The keyword for *bauxite* is *box*."
5. Present the interactive illustrations for each concept to be learned and explain the relationships between the cues and facts as succinctly as possible. Be consistent in wording.
   EXAMPLE: (Refer to Figure 1.15 illustration for the mineral *wolframite*.)
   a. Say, "*Wolframite* is *4* on the hardness scale, *black* in color, and is used for making *light bulbs*."
   b. Explain that the word cue for *wolframite* is *wolf*, and *4* is *floor*.
   c. Point out that the wolf in the picture is *black*, because that is the color of the mineral *wolframite*, and that the *light bulbs* are a reminder of the mineral's use.
6. Discuss the retrieval process. Give examples of how students should use the mnemonic cues to respond to specific questions.
   EXAMPLE: If asked, "What is the hardness level of wolframite?" students should:
   a. Think first of the keyword (*wolf*).
   b. Go back (mentally) to what is happening to the wolf in the picture.
   c. Find the pegword (*floor*) and answer "*4*."
   d. Use the same process to answer questions about color and use (or whatever attributes students are learning for a particular topic).
7. Teach the remaining concepts in a like manner, but omit the pegword instruction.

Modifications/ Considerations

Direct instruction is often recommended for remedial and at-risk students, but results of the cited study indicated that it was considerably less effective than the mnemonic strategy. Of all the methods attempted, free study was least effective, probably due to the poor organizational skills of most students of this type.

It may be necessary to involve students in the development of materials, since this can become a time-consuming and expensive aspect of this type of instruction. In most cases commercially produced illustrations tend to be more recognizable than student-drawn pictures, so it might be advisable to make photocopies of pictures from magazines and newspapers or to trace over illustrations in books. This could become a class project, or could be offered to individuals as an extra credit option. If there are artistically talented students in the class, they could submit designs for the mnemonic picture clues.

One approach for evaluating the effects of mnemonics, as explained in this technique, would be to follow suggestions in MONITOR 12 in Appendix A. A way to involve that approach would be to select several sets of words for which youth were to learn definitions, then alternate the technique. Do not arrange mnemonic training for the first set, arrange it for the next, not the next, and so forth. Administer a test following practice or training on each set of words. Check each student's paper for the various sessions, chart those data, and compare scores across conditions.

Monitor

Scruggs, T.E., Mastropieri, M.A., Levin, J.R., & Gaffney, J.S. (1985). Facilitating the acquisition of science facts in learning disabled students. *American Educational Research Journal, 22*(4), 575-586.

Reference

MANAGING TIME: STAYING ON TASK

With this tactic, students monitor their own behavior. The benefits of having students assume this responsibility include an increase in the time they spend working and improved self-confidence. This translates into more time devoted to instruction and

Background

greater success for students. Self-monitoring is a technique that is easy to implement, cost-free, and useful in a wide variety of settings.

Who Can Benefit   The cited research was conducted with emotionally disturbed and mentally retarded children between the ages of 10 and 16 who were not able to complete daily work without constant supervision to keep them on task. They were described by their teachers as being impulsive, having short attention spans, and having difficulty concentrating during independent seatwork assignments. The tactic could benefit students who need to be actively involved in order to stay on task.

Procedures   **Prerequisite.**   Record a series of tones on a tape recorder. These tones should occur at random intervals between 10 and 90 seconds. The mean interval length should equal 45 seconds. Be sure to record enough tones to last for the duration of the period.

Steps

1. Define clearly the behaviors to be monitored. In the referenced research, the behaviors were paying attention and not paying attention. Paying attention can be defined as doing the assigned work. Not paying attention would be defined as doing anything that was not the assigned work, such as talking, looking about the room, drawing, or cleaning out one's desk.
2. Introduce students to self-monitoring by explaining that you want to help them pay more attention to their work and by describing the expected behaviors as defined above.
3. Distribute the Self-Recording Sheets (see Figure 1.16). Tell the students that they are for keeping track of paying attention and not paying attention.
4. Model examples of paying attention and not paying attention and ask the students to mark yes or no on their recording sheet based on your examples.

FIGURE 1.16   Self-Recording Sheet for Use in Managing Time

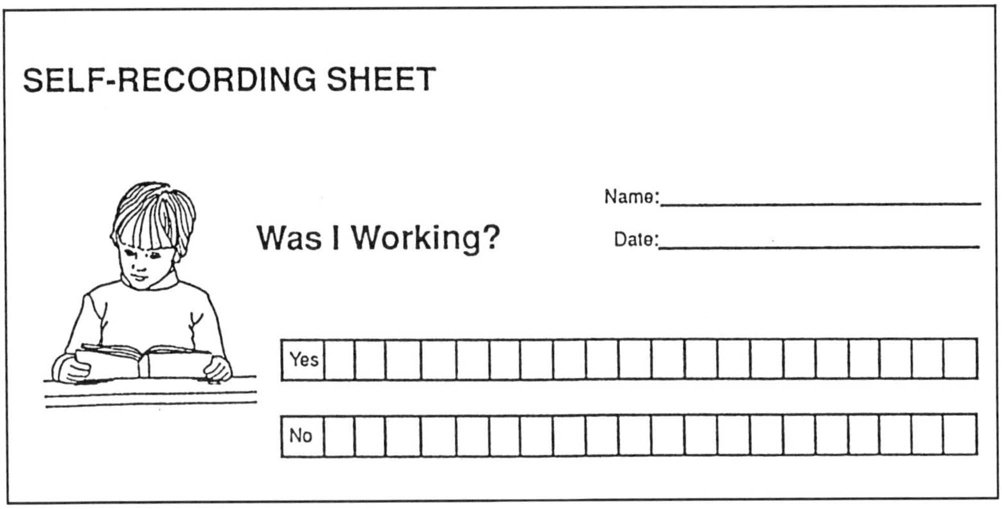

Note. From Osborne, S.S., Kosiewicz, M.M., Crumley, E.B., & Lee, C. (1987). Distractible students use self-monitoring. *Teaching Exceptional Children*, *19*(2), p. 66. Copyright 1987 by The Council for Exceptional Children. Reprinted by permission.

5. Explain to the students that they will hear a tone from a recorder at random intervals and it will be a signal to mark on their sheets either a yes for paying attention or a no for not paying attention, according to the following instructions:
    a. "When I hear a tone, I ask myself if I was paying attention to my work."
    b. "If I was, I mark yes and keep working."
    c. "If I was not paying attention to my work I mark no and tell myself to get back to my work."
6. Begin the tape recorder and model as if you were the student. Then let the students practice listening to the tone to cue self-recording while they work.
7. Perform a final check by asking the students to repeat the definitions of both paying attention and not paying attention and the self-monitoring questions given above. (This training should take only a few minutes on intermittent occasions.)

Modifications/ Considerations

Although the approach of using tones on the tape is an effective means for cueing students, it is possible to do without it. The teacher could, instead, signal times to record by raising his or her hand or making marks on the board. In either case, the teacher should be sure that the cues are random, so that students cannot predict their occurrence.

Students showing the most improvement could earn the privilege of setting up the tape and/or passing out the recording sheets.

This procedure may be used whenever a reminder is needed, such as following a school break. It shouldn't be used any more than is necessary, however. The best indicator of when to put this technique into operation is when the production of the students begins to fall off.

Impress on the students that they must try to be as honest as possible when they mark their Self-Recording Sheets. Point out that their reward will be more work completed, which could translate to better grades. Always stress the fact that the more dependable they are in self-monitoring, the more independence they will gain.

Monitor

Follow the suggestions in MONITOR 4 in Appendix A. If a pupil checked that he or she was on task seven intervals on the example recording sheet, that would indicate 70% of the time. That score might then be entered on a percentage chart. A teacher could evaluate this technique by setting up a before-during-after study. In the before phase, the teacher could monitor the student's ability to stay on task for a few days. For the during phase, the pupil would self-record as explained in this technique. Throughout the third phase, the teacher would again record the pupil's intervals of attention. Data from the three phases could be compared to determine whether the technique was effective.

Reference

Osborne, S.S., Kosiewicz, M.M., Crumley, E.B., & Lee, C. (1987). Distractible students use self-monitoring. *Teaching Exceptional Children, 19*(2), 66–69.

MANAGING TIME: STUDY SKILLS INVENTORY

One of the most pronounced distinctions between good students and those who do poorly is their understanding of and ability to apply study skills. All too often students respond to low grades on tests and quizzes with the plaintive cry, "But I *did* study!" when, in reality, they merely read or skimmed the material. Although they may have the intent to remember, on which dependable learning is based, they may not have developed the study habits needed to be efficient learners.

This tactic is based on the premise that students who say they are bored by learning are actually frustrated by their own inability to learn, and that finding a good place to study, learning to organize their study time, and becoming aware of the study skills they need to improve can help them overcome some of that frustration and dispel many of their negative feelings about learning.

Background

Content teachers interested in improving their students' ability to learn can help them develop ways to manage their study time more effectively. Students who are aware of their weaknesses in this area, and are willing to learn and apply good study habits, should begin to experience more success in mastering content in the classroom.

Who Can Benefit

1. Take a careful look at the subjects you teach and the way you teach them, and determine what study skills would most likely benefit students in your classes. Consider the importance of the following: managing time, reading textbooks, underlining passages, taking notes, outlining, using maps, taking essay tests, taking objective tests.
2. List the skills you identified and develop a rating scale (see Study Skills Inventory in Figure 1.17).

Procedures

FIGURE 1.17 Suggestion for a Study Skills Inventory Form

STUDY SKILLS INVENTORY

_____

Student

_____

course/period

_____

Date

Directions: Study skills will be important to your success in this course, and this inventory is designed to find out what your strengths and weaknesses may be in these areas. Think carefully about each of the following statements and then answer as honestly as you can. This is NOT a test!!

Circle 1, 2, 3, or 4 next to each statement to indicate whether the statement would be true for you usually, sometimes, seldom, or never.

	Usually	Some-times	Seldom	Never
Managing Time				
1. I spend about 45 minutes each day studying for each of my courses.	1	2	3	4
2. When I study, I can stick with it until I am finished.	1	2	3	4
3. I study where I will not be interrupted.	1	2	3	4
Using a Textbook				
4. I use the table of contents to help me understand how topics are related.	1	2	3	4
5. I use the index in my studying.	1	2	3	4
6. I use the glossary to find meanings of unfamiliar words.	1	2	3	4
Underlining				
7. I underline all important ideas as I read.	1	2	3	4
8. I underline only key words or phrases, not whole sentences.	1	2	3	4
9. I underline details and examples.	1	2	3	4
10. I underline almost everything.	1	2	3	4
Notetaking				
11. When I study, I take notes from my reading.	1	2	3	4
12. When I take notes from my reading, they are clear enough to make sense several weeks later.	1	2	3	4
13. When I take notes from my reading, I put down the page numbers where I got the information.	1	2	3	4

	Usually	Some-times	Seldom	Never
14. When a teacher is lecturing in class, I take clear notes of what is said.	1	2	3	4
15. In my lecture notes, I make sure to write down the main ideas.	1	2	3	4
16. In my lecture notes, I include details and examples that help me clarify ideas.	1	2	3	4
Outlining				
17. I outline the major things I learn when I study.	1	2	3	4
18. In my outlines, I include main ideas in the primary headings.	1	2	3	4
19. In my outlines, I include details as subheadings that clarify the main ideas.	1	2	3	4
Using Maps				
20. I can use the keys and legends when reading maps.	1	2	3	4
21. I can interpret what the maps suggest about historical trends.	1	2	3	4
Taking Essay Tests				
22. When taking essay tests, I read the directions and all the questions before beginning to answer any of the questions.	1	2	3	4
23. When taking essay tests, I think about what I want to write before beginning.	1	2	3	4
24. When taking essay tests, I organize my answer so my ideas will be clear to the instructor.	1	2	3	4
25. I proofread my answers when I am finished and before I turn in my paper.	1	2	3	4
Taking Objective Tests				
26. When answering a multiple choice question, I try to eliminate first the obviously incorrect choices.	1	2	3	4
27. I trust my first guess when unsure of an answer.	1	2	3	4
28. I proofread to make sure no question is left unanswered, even if the answer is a wild guess.	1	2	3	4
29. I read through all of the choices before marking an answer, even if the first or second one seems correct.	1	2	3	4
30. I look for clues in other questions that can help in answering questions of which I am unsure.	1	2	3	4

Note. From Estes, T.H., & Vaughn, J.L., Jr. (1985). *Reading and learning in the content classroom: Diagnostic and instructional strategies*, pp. 124–125. Boston: Allyn & Bacon. Reprinted by permission.

3. Go over every item on the list with the students, providing examples. Make certain that they understand the items and how to rate the extent to which they use them.
4. Ask the students to rate themselves on the items.
5. Fill out a survey form for each of your students.
6. Compare your ratings with theirs.
7. Identify the areas of strengths and weaknesses and the items for which their judgments and yours were alike and different.
8. Discuss those findings with your students.
9. Design a program to teach study skills based on your data and discussions with students.

Implementing Training. Following are suggested activities for instructing one of the more important study skills, managing time.

1. Discuss the main components of good work-study habits:
   a. Organizing study time and daily scheduling
   b. Establishing a comfortable and familiar place for study
2. Ask students to think of words and phrases they associate with time (e.g., "time is money," "killing time").
3. Generate a discussion on setting priorities with reference to school, work at home, outside work, and leisure activities.
4. Extend the discussion by asking students to identify benefits that might come from a plan for managing their study time.
5. Instruct students to keep daily records of how they spend their time.
6. Assist them to construct a pie chart that illustrates how they distribute their time.
7. Ask them to comment on the proportion of time they spend studying.
8. Discuss with them how they might reallocate their time so as to spend more time studying.
9. Instruct students to keep records of their study time.
10. Assist students, later, to keep records of their production and its quality; that is, the number of assignments or papers completed and the grades they receive.

11. Point out the relationships between amount of time studying, amount submitted, and grades.
12. Reassess the quality of students' study time if positive relationships are not noted.

Corresponding activities should be scheduled for other study skills components that may be lacking (e.g., reading from textbooks, underlining).

Students could be required to fill out the complete inventory every now and then to determine whether or not they are (or think they are) improving. Apart from evaluating their improvement, with respect to incorporating study skills, these periodic reviews should serve to remind students of specific skills they should attend to. Learning about study skills should therefore become a set of specific and clearly defined activities.

Students' needs for specific study skills will change as they master those initially targeted for improvement, and as lesson content changes throughout the year. Ask students to help revise the original list from time to time.

Modifications/ Considerations

Suggestions for monitoring this activity were included in the Procedures and Modifications/Considerations sections. See MONITOR 6 in Appendix A for more information on using checklists to evaluate activities.

Monitor

Estes, T.H., & Vaughan, J.L. Jr. (1985). *Reading and learning in the content classroom: Diagnostic and instructional strategies.* Boston: Allyn & Bacon.

Reference

MANAGING TIME: BEING PREPARED

Many of us employ a variety of behavioral techniques to manage our own behaviors. We reward ourselves

Background

with special items for our accomplishments, make arrangements with ourselves so that we take on necessary but undesirable tasks, withhold things we normally enjoy if we don't behave in certain ways, and assess and revise our methods, depending on how well they work.

When we teach students to self-monitor their behaviors, we are encouraging them to use the same techniques. Initially, we can supplement their self-monitoring programs by providing frequent feedback and rewards. Later, random checks and intermittent rewards should be sufficient to ensure maintenance of the students' programs.

Who Can Benefit

This study was conducted with eight behaviorally disabled boys, ages 10 through 12, who had a variety of behavior problems. Like many students, they had been exposed to a number of behavior management systems, all of which were controlled by teachers. The technique described here is an ideal tactic for students of that type, for it gives them an opportunity to manage their own actions.

Procedures

1. Identify the behavior or collection of behaviors that will be evaluated (e.g., being prepared for school).
2. Develop a checklist for self-rating components of that topic (see Figure 1.18):
   a. Has all necessary supplies
   b. Assignments completed
   c. Assignments turned in on time
   d. Papers organized in notebook
   e. Arrives on time
   f. If absent, obtains missed assignments
3. Establish a criterion for the behaviors and for accurate self-rating. A criterion for the preparation behaviors might be that if all six items are checked, the student will earn a few minutes of free time. To increase the probability that students will rate themselves accurately, they could earn a reward (e.g., time to read a magazine, talk to a friend, or go to the library) if their ratings matched those of the teacher.

FIGURE 1.18   Checklist for Use in Managing Time

CHECKLIST ITEMS

Name _____

Date _____

	M	T	W	T	F
Has all necessary supplies	☐	☐	☐	☐	☐
Assignments completed	☐	☐	☐	☐	☐
Assignments turned in on time	☐	☐	☐	☐	☐
Papers organized in notebook	☐	☐	☐	☐	☐
Arrives on time	☐	☐	☐	☐	☐
If absent, obtains missed assignments	☐	☐	☐	☐	☐
TOTAL COMPLETE	___	___	___	___	___

X = student rating (mark for each completed task)
+ = teacher verification (mark for each completed task)

Modifications/ Considerations

There are a variety of applications for this technique at home or school. The referenced study focused on clean-up activities at a summer camp. It is important to note that, initially, students will probably need some type of reward to encourage them to carry out the desirable behaviors, and to assure that they accurately record them.

As students progress with this type of management and their needs change, so can the items on their checklists. Eventually, students could even establish their own performance goals.

Monitor

Suggestions for monitoring the effects of this technique were provided in the Procedures section. For more details on the makeup and evaluation of checklists, see MONITOR 6 in Appendix A.

Reference

Layne, C.C., Rickard, H.C., Jones, M.T., & Lyman, R.D. (1976). Accuracy of self-monitoring on a variable ratio schedule of observer verification. *Behavior Therapy, 7,* 481–488.

THINKING: MAKING INFERENCES

Background   Certain assumptions lie at the heart of this tactic: that thinking can be taught; that certain thinking skills are involved in learning how to study; and that there are strategies for teaching thinking skills. The author of the cited research contends that thinking skills such as making inferences, predicting, drawing conclusions, identifying main points, following sequences, organizing, comparing, contrasting, and relating can be taught in the classroom, and that the acquisition of those skills is not totally dependent on intelligence. Of those thinking skills, making inferences is the key to the others, and the topic of this tactic.

Who Can Benefit   Since many at-risk and remedial students are not noted for their thinking skills, among them the ability to make inferences, the set of techniques outlined here would aid them in acquiring a skill believed to be fundamental to other thinking skills. If these youngsters learn about making inferences, then acquire other related thinking skills, they will learn more content, which may enable them to experience more success in school.

Procedures   1. Introduce the concept of inferences by encouraging students to make guesses about characters and actions in stories, TV shows, and skits.
   a. "What do you think the young people on the corner are planning to do?"
   b. Help students direct their thinking by asking questions such as, Why do you say that? Are there clues in the story? Are you comparing them to yourself and your friends? Have you read about or seen other characters in other stories who are like the young people in this one?
2. Point out that these guesses are called *inferences*, and that people tend to make better inferences

about things they know a lot about (e.g., if they know quite a bit about art, they should be able to make good inferences about artists, schools, movements, and other related matters).

3. Give examples of incorrect inferences made by people who know little or nothing about a subject.

4. Inform students of the basic distinction between inferences and facts: that factual statements can be verified.

5. Set up situations where students make inferences. Lead them through the process first, then provide practice opportunities—for example: (a) Mrs. Sands's class has already gone to lunch. (b) We are supposed to go to lunch before they do. (c) Either our class is late to lunch or hers went earlier than usual.

6. Ask students to make 10 or more inferences ("things the writer didn't say, but we know are probably so") from printed text (e.g., newspaper articles, textbook passages, stories in magazines).

7. Explain to students that writers don't tell their readers everything because readers are able to make some inferences based on what they already know.

    a. Talk about "slot-filling" (i.e., if certain things are true, then other things must also be true).

    b. Discuss "scheme-making" (i.e., a person develops a concept, or scheme, from existing knowledge made up of common elements distinguishing it from other possible objects, actions, and events, and this scheme helps him or her make sense of new information).

8. Assist pupils to make predictions from story titles.

    a. Guess what the story is about.

    b. Predict the setting.

    c. Guess what the characters may be like.

9. Ask students to verify their predictions from the content of the story.

Provide examples of backward inferencing. Present information from familiar scenes (e.g., changing a tire, going to a movie) and ask questions such as the following:

Modifications/ Considerations

CAUSALITY: "If this happened first, and then this, was one the cause of the other?"

DRAWING CONCLUSIONS: "Based on what we have seen or heard, can we conclude that thus and so will or has occurred?"

Monitor   One way to evaluate this technique, before and after training, would be to show videotapes to students of daytime "soaps." Throughout the 20 or so minutes of the shows, students could jot down as many inferences as they could think of. Later, a teacher or another could replay the episodes and evaluate the inferences to determine whether they were or were not plausible. That number could be charted as frequency of "correct" and "incorrect" inferences (see MONITOR 1 in Appendix A). Because of training on inferences, one would hope that pupils would generate reasonably high rates of correct responses.

Reference   Devine, T.G. (1987). *Teaching study skills.* Boston: Allyn & Bacon.

ORGANIZING LECTURES: ADVANCE ORGANIZERS

Background   Students in the intermediate grades and at the secondary level are faced with a different set of problems than those encountered by lower elementary children. These secondary age students are required to use information-processing skills, which they often lack or fail to activate, to deal with content areas. One way to assist at-risk and remedial students in meeting the demands of content teachers is to instruct them to listen for and use advance organizers.

Seven regular and seven learning disabled adolescents were the pupils in the original research. Junior and senior high school students in content area classrooms could also benefit from the ability to apply advance organizers.

1. Plan lessons in which advance organizers are presented either verbally, in writing, or with a visual aid, or are elicited through questions throughout the lesson.

2. Introduce the following 12 advance organizer components to students, beginning with this introductory statement:
   "Advance organizers are a set of behaviors that precede the learning act and generally incorporate one or more of the following components."
   a. Inform the learner of the purpose of the advance organizer.
   b. Clarify the task's physical parameters in terms of actions to be taken by the teacher.
   c. Clarify the task's physical parameters in terms of actions to be taken by the student.
   d. Identify the topic of the learning task.
   e. Identify subtopics related to the task.
   f. Provide background information.
   g. State the concepts to be learned.
   h. Clarify the concepts to be learned.
   i. Motivate students through rationales.
   j. Introduce or repeat new words.
   k. Provide an organizational framework for the learning task.
   l. State the outcomes desired as a result of engaging in the learning activity.
3. Provide students with a worksheet on which the components of advance organizers are listed.
4. Demonstrate the types of information that might be written alongside the components (e.g., identify topic).
5. Instruct students to listen for and take notes on advance organizers presented in class.
6. Tell students that once they are able to consistently identify components of advance organizers, they should attend to those features as they listen to lectures, but they needn't rely on the worksheets.

Modifications/ Considerations

Critical to the effectiveness of this tactic is the teacher's own use of advance organizers and his or her ability to activate students to attend to them. It was shown in the cited study that teacher behaviors alone were not enough; students must specifically be educated to attend to advance organizers and make use of them, if there are to be positive gains in their performance.

The purpose of this tactic is to teach students one of the all-important attributes for success in school and on the job: how to get information before starting a task. Armed with the ability to listen for and identify key information, students will be better prepared to complete assigned work in a variety of situations. Although it is important for students to be able to recognize and put into use the 12 steps that make up this advance organizer, the true measure is whether or not they acquire more information from lectures and are able to assimilate that knowledge because of learning about the organizers.

Monitor

As with some of the other study skills, teachers may want to evaluate the extent to which students learn the study skill and determine the effects that learning may have on their ability to acquire information from lectures or textbooks. For the former, a teacher could develop a checklist on which some features of advance organizers were listed (see MONITOR 6 in Appendix A). With that list the teacher, or another, could periodically monitor the extent to which pupils relied on advance organizers. To determine whether students learned more from lectures or textbooks as a function of advance organizers, suggestions from MONITORS 11 and 12 could be incorporated.

Reference

Lenz, B.K., Alley, G.R., & Schumaker, J.B. (1987). Activating the inactive learner: Advance organizers in the secondary content classroom. *Learning Disability Quarterly, 10,* 53–67.

SOCIAL
BEHAVIORS

GETTING ALONG WITH OTHERS: STRUCTURED LEARNING WITH SELF-MONITORING

Background

With an increased emphasis on vocational training and community placement of at-risk and mildly handicapped youth, knowledge and practice of appropriate social skills are becoming more and more important for this population. One of the main reasons for failure in job placements is a lack of interpersonal and social skills. Often, the effects of social skills training in schools are limited to only that setting. The following study sought to ensure that skills taught in a structured situation would transfer to circumstances outside of that setting and last after training had ended. The authors implemented a four-phase intervention consisting of modeling, role-playing, performance feedback, and self-monitoring with and without reinforcement. The purpose of the first three phases of the intervention was to teach the social skills, and the purpose of the self-monitoring phase was to promote generalization and maintenance of the learned behaviors.

Who Can Benefit

An 18-year-old mildly retarded and behaviorally disordered male resident of a mental health and developmental center was the focus of training for the cited study. The following intervention would be successful in an environment in which there was both a structured and nonstructured setting to observe behaviors. This technique would be best suited for youth who had rather severe, chronic behavior problems.

Procedures

1. Set aside 30 minutes per day for training, which should consist of four components: modeling, role-playing, performance feedback, and self-monitoring (with and without reinforcement).

2. Select the behaviors to be taught by having several teachers report which behaviors they believed the student(s) needed to improve most (e.g., initiating conversation, greetings, saying thank you and please).
3. Simulate a situation for the students in which one of the targeted skills can be performed, and ask the students to perform the skill.
4. Require students to describe the steps taken to perform the behavior. From the description and observation of the behavior, the teacher can determine a criterion for the functioning level of the skill that is based on the students' ability and need for improvement.
5. Decide what additional steps should be added to the target behavior to make it socially acceptable.
6. Continue training until the students master 100% of the steps of the target behaviors.

Modeling

1. Form a small group of students and include the targeted individual(s).
2. Break the skill down into component parts and model each part for the students.
3. Model the target behavior with several examples of its application in several settings for the students.

Role-Playing

1. Start a group discussion on what the students saw and heard and how the behaviors relate to their lives.
2. Ask the students to role-play or practice the skills taught in the modeling situations. Ask them to role-play true-to-life situations.
3. Encourage students to coach and support those who are role-playing the parts.

Performance Feedback

1. Elicit performance feedback (i.e., praise, compliments, approval, constructive criticism) from the group members following the role-playing.
2. Give support as well as constructive suggestions to students so as to improve their performance of the target behaviors.

Self-Monitoring

1. Model self-monitoring for the students. Explain to them that self-monitoring is the systematic monitoring and recording of one's performance of a target behavior.
2. Allow students to role-play the self-monitoring behavior and provide feedback on their performance.
3. Give students a self-monitoring form, and ask them to take it with them at the beginning of each day and record, by circling a number each time the targeted skill was performed correctly (see Figure 2.1).
4. Ask the students to use the form outside of the classroom (i.e., in the cafeteria, study hall, gym, outside school grounds).
5. Instruct students to return the form on the following day, and give them praise or reinforcement for returning the form promptly.

Self-Monitoring with Reinforcement

1. Continue the self-monitoring, but give points to students for the number of times they performed the target behavior correctly.
2. Allow students to exchange the points for privileges or other rewards.

Modifications/ Considerations

In the referenced study, generalization and maintenance of the learned social skills were the most pronounced under the self-monitoring plus reinforcement phase. The authors reported, however, that the target behavior did improve after only the training.

Before initiating training, teachers might rehearse the modeling and instruction of the target behaviors. Performance criteria should be set up beforehand, based on the students' ability and time limits. An example of a criterion for initiating a conversation is the student saying, "It's a nice day," or "What did you do over the weekend?" 10 seconds after an opportunity. In that example, opportunity is defined as being within 3 feet of the other person with no other persons between the student and the other person. The other person must not be engaged in conversation. The student must make eye contact, use a

FIGURE 2.1   Self-Monitoring Form

Name: _____

Date: _____

Date Due: Next day

SELF-MONITORING FORM FOR BEHAVIOR X

Circle the number that answers the question.

1. Number of times I encountered a situation where I could use
    behavior X?

    1   2   3   4   5   6   7   8   9   10

2. Number of times I actually performed behavior X appropriately?

    1   2   3   4   5   6   7   8   9   10

moderate tone of voice, make content-appropriate statements, and make the initiation statement only once.

Types of reinforcement for the self-monitoring phase could be free time, points toward a field trip, or a night without homework.

Monitor   The effects of this rather extensive approach could be evaluated qualitatively; that is, a number of individuals, familiar with the youth being assisted, could be interviewed before and during the treatment period (see MONITOR 9 in Appendix A). The youth's parents, friends, or siblings, for example, could be asked to comment on specific and more general social behaviors of the individual and to judge whether or not they had noted improvement.

Data regarding this set of techniques could also be obtained in a role-playing situation (see MONITOR 19). A teacher or other observer could, by using a checklist, mark the times that designated incidents occurred, and write out descriptions of other happenings as well.

Kiburz, C.S., Miller, S.R., & Morrow, L.W. (1984). Structured learning using self-monitoring to promote maintenance and generalization of social skills across settings for a behaviorally disordered adolescent. *Behavioral Disorders, 10*(1), 47–55.

Reference

GETTING ALONG WITH OTHERS: ARRANGING PSYCHOSOCIAL ACTIVITIES

Background

The addition of psychosocial activities to the curriculum of underachieving adolescents can help improve scholastic learning by providing a more interesting class environment, creating more opportunities for personal development, and allowing the acquisition of new interpersonal skills. The inability to get along with others manifests itself in disruptive classroom behavior making it nearly impossible for others to learn or get any work done.

The most common problem of misbehaving youth is a lack of autonomous and responsible behaviors. In an effort to enhance student social relations and, in turn, make a more favorable classroom learning environment, the following group activities were implemented. The goals of the activities were to teach students to listen to one another, respect others and their opinions, and become aware of the emotions of their peers.

Who Can Benefit

Nine seventh-grade learning disabled and behaviorally disordered students participated in the study. Their ages ranged from 12 to 14 years. This tactic would be most suitable for adolescents who had difficulty relating to others. It is important for teenagers to develop these skills, because it can make a significant difference in their future employability and general well-being.

Procedures   Implement each of the following group activities for 90 minutes a day for 3 weeks.

Relaxation Sessions.   These sessions are created to reduce fidgety and tense behaviors in students.

1. Center discussions around personal development such as functions of the body during sleep (i.e., rapid eye movement, sleep cycles, muscle relaxation, and respiration).
2. Instruct students to lie on the floor with their eyes closed and lights out after the daily discussion.
3. Ask students to begin by tightening the muscles in their feet and then releasing the tension.
4. Work up through the entire body as students progressively tighten and relax their muscles.
5. Continue until all muscles are relaxed and students feel the release of tension and anxiety from their bodies.

Magic Circle Activities.   These activities are implemented to decrease the incidence of teasing, criticizing, and laughing at one another among students. This is achieved through the nonjudgmental, accepting atmosphere of the Magic Circle.

1. Form a circle, and engage the class in a group discussion.
2. Select the topics for discussion either ahead of time or by having the group members choose a topic pertinent to them.
3. Encourage input into the group discussion and the selection of topics for discussion. This helps to develop motivation and autonomy among the students.
4. Stop the activity if the behaviors become disruptive.
5. Point out disruptive behaviors to the offenders and remind them of the rules of the Magic Circle: to be accepting and nonjudgmental of others.
6. Require the person who ridicules or annoys another to explain how that person must feel.
7. Give students who interrupt the opportunity to speak when they are not interrupting. Often, students interrupt just to receive attention and don't really have anything to contribute.

Art Sessions. The goal of the art sessions is to assist students to gain a better understanding of themselves through self-expression and to work cooperatively with others.

1. Ask students to draw a picture of themselves and to share the picture with the group. This promotes self-awareness and expression.
2. Discuss with students how the picture might reflect their classroom conduct and how that conduct affects others.
3. Allow students to doodle while they state their feelings; this is another technique aimed at increasing self-awareness and expression.
4. Encourage students to work together on a large mural to instill cooperation, planning, and organizational skills.

Future-Planning Groups. These sessions are aimed at getting students to think more realistically about their future in consideration of their limited educational abilities and performances.

1. Center discussions around the plans and aspirations students have for their future.
2. Help students to understand the limits of their options, at their current educational level.
3. Illustrate how important education is to the attainment of loftier goals and jobs.
4. Discuss other topics with respect to the future: marriage, family, type of home, travel, city in which to live.

Decision-Making Groups. The goal of these groups is to aid students to make proper decisions in order to create more responsible and autonomous behaviors.

1. Pick an issue on which a decision must be made, for example, a class song, field trip, or project.
2. Discuss the pros and cons in making a choice.
3. Determine the feasibility of each option, in terms of availability of materials and the interest of the other students.

Miscellaneous Activities. These suggestions allow teachers to devise activities that allow consequences to be given for good and bad behaviors. The following are examples:

1. Develop a point system whereby students who gained the most points for good conduct at the end of the week were able to skip one class period.
2. Write all the students' names on the board in columns, and place a check next to those who spoke out of turn or misbehaved. This will enable students to become more aware of the frequency of their disruptions.

Modifications/ Considerations

The use of psychosocial activities in the classroom effectively reduced disruptive behaviors in the referenced study. Students were also able to disclose more of their feelings. Girls spoke and participated in the activities more than before, and felt more comfortable in their interactions with boys. There was also an increase in school attendance during the class activities, and students developed a more positive attitude toward school.

Students in the cited study reported enjoying the relaxation technique the best. The Magic Circle gave them the most difficulty at first, but they believed that it had the greatest impact on their understanding of others' feelings and how similar their problems were to their peers.

Teachers should take care in setting up any of these practices to see that students don't become overdependent on them and rely on them too much. Although these techniques should be arranged as required, teachers should be reinforced by the generalized results of the training, not so much by the process of carrying out the techniques. Moreover, trainers should make every effort to transfer as much control for carrying out the procedures to the students as possible.

Monitor

The effects of these activities could be evaluated specifically and globally. For the former, a teacher could pinpoint one or more critical behaviors that might be influenced by training (e.g., being disruptive, interacting with others, contributing to discussions). Over time, frequencies of those behaviors (for individuals or groups) could be acquired and graphed (see MONITOR 1 in Appendix A).

To ascertain the effects of one of these techniques on more global social skills (e.g., "How does he get along with others?"), one might set up a structured interview with a few of the youth's relatives and acquaintances (see MONITOR 9). Those individuals could be asked a series of questions from time to time as the training was being conducted. Their responses to those queries could then be summarized and studied to determine whether progress was being noted in real-life settings.

Mills, M.C. (1987). An intervention program for adolescents with behavior problems. *Adolescence, 22*(85), 91–96.

Reference

GETTING ALONG WITH OTHERS: SOLVING INTERPERSONAL PROBLEMS

The Teaching, Learning, and Caring (TLC) curriculum is an interpersonal problem-solving skills training program. It was developed to teach specific social problem-solving strategies to exceptional adolescents. Following are some of the problems the TLC curriculum addresses: being impulsive, identifying and responding to the affective state of another, generating a range of responses to problem situations, evaluating consequences of behaviors before acting, communicating wants and needs, and responding to the desires of others.

Background

Eight components make up the TLC curriculum: communication mode, empathy, goal identification, cue sensitivity, alternative thinking, skills implementation, consequential thinking, and integration. This tactic outlines procedures for teaching five of those components.

Who Can Benefit

The curriculum described in this tactic was designed for severely emotionally handicapped (SEH) and learning disabled adolescents. It was developed and field-tested for a 2-year period in a program where some students were in a self-contained SEH classroom and others were mainstreamed. The 18 students who participated in the cited study were between the ages of 14 and 18. The tactic, as paraphrased here, was geared toward at-risk, remedial, and learning disabled secondary students. Because the ability to listen and respond appropriately in typical day-to-day conversations is a prerequisite to adequate social competence, students who have not developed these skills are most likely to benefit from this tactic.

Procedures

Goal Identification

Purpose: Teach students to identify problems; discern what they and others want when a problem situation arises; establish both long- and short-range goals and differentiate goals from needs.

1. Ask students to list academic subjects in which they would like to improve.
2. Help them select one thing that they could do immediately to improve their performance in the subjects they have listed.
3. Request students to offer their proposals to the class for constructive feedback.
4. Instruct pupils to keep personal written records (journals) of their progress to help them share information in weekly class discussions.
5. Repeat this process, but extend the goal-setting period from weekly to monthly periods, and then to longer periods in the future.
   EXAMPLE: *Monthly*—Read four books in October
   Long Range—Pass all classes with at least a C average for a semester
6. Encourage students to incorporate personal goals into their plans after they have had some success with academic goal planning.

Cue Sensitivity

Purpose: Help students understand both verbal and nonverbal messages consistently.

1. Provide students with the following examples of nonverbal communication:
   Smile = Approval
   Furrowed eyebrows = Confusion
   Touch = Intimacy
   Stepping backwards = Person must leave
2. Cut out pictures from magazines and ask students to identify possible nonverbal messages that people in them could be giving. Direct students to consider dress and body language as well as facial expression.
3. Ask students to summarize some real-life situations in terms of verbal and nonverbal cues.
   EXAMPLE: "I knew Bill didn't understand what I was saying to him when he furrowed his eyebrows, so I tried to explain it a different way. The smile on his face when I finished told me that this time he understood."
4. Present several role-play situations for students to observe and note verbal cues.
5. Arrange for students to observe each other to identify and evaluate the cues they are sending to others.

Empathy

Purpose: Teach students to recognize their own feelings and the feelings of others.

1. Teach students the meanings and applications of words that indicate feelings, such as *frustrated, disgusted, jealous, perturbed, disappointed, delighted, concerned, furious, outraged,* and *embarrassed.*
2. Ask students to take turns describing emotional situations and how they would feel if placed in those situations.
3. Discuss the possible consequences of various responses to the situations described above. For example, students could discuss the consequences of Mike's possible responses in the following situation. (*Note:* The goal is for him to select a response that is beneficial to both him and Charlie.)
   > Charlie is instantly upset when he sees his girlfriend talking to Mike. Mike knows that Charlie is upset. How could Mike respond to Charlie?

(One answer could be to explain to Charlie that he was only answering her question about a missed assignment. Another might be to greet Mike enthusiastically, saying something like, "Oh, there you are, Charlie! I was just telling *(girl-friend)* that I've been looking all over for you.")

Alternative Thinking

Purpose: Provide a strategy for generating solutions to a problem, rather than acting impulsively.

1. Make a "problem box" and place it somewhere accessible to students.
2. Ask students to write a note about a problem they have or have had with others (peers, neighbors, parents, or teachers) and place the note, without their name on it, in the box.
3. Take one or two notes from the box every day for several days, and have students discuss possible solutions to the problems mentioned in the notes.

Consequential Thinking

Purpose: Help students develop the ability to anticipate the possible consequences of a behavior before engaging in it.

1. Write the following questions on the board:
   "What might happen next if I do . . . (the intended behavior)?"
   "What will happen in the long run if I do . . . ?"
2. Compile a list of examples from the lesson on alternative thinking to be discussed in the context of the questions in number 1 above.
3. Ask students to provide examples from personal experiences of times when they "thought ahead."
4. Conduct a class discussion about the consequences of thinking ahead and not thinking ahead in a variety of situations (see Table 2.1 for TLC Skill Checklist).

Modifications/ Considerations

Teachers may wish to use all or only parts of this tactic depending on their students' skills. For example, it may be that all of the students in a particular group seem to understand verbal and nonverbal cues and are able to recognize feelings, yet have difficulty set-

TABLE 2.1 TLC Skill Checklist

COMMUNICATION MODE

1. Repeating the content of another's message
2. Identifying the main idea of the content of another's message
3. Identifying the stated feelings in another's message
4. Identifying the underlying feelings in another's message
5. Identifying the main idea of the content of one's message
6. Identifying the underlying feeling in one's message
7. Using self-disclosure appropriately
8. Using open and closed questions appropriately
9. Listening to the problems of another with discounting
10. Listening to the problems of another and to hypothetical situations that influence behavior

EMPATHY

1. Identifying words that convey emotions (e.g., jealous, hurt, angry, hostile, shy, afraid, furious)
2. Matching past situations and the feelings associated with the situations
3. Discussing the importance of identifying emotional states as the first step in responding appropriately to them
4. Identifying how you would feel in hypothetical situations
5. Identifying the feelings of others in pictures, films, and hypothetical situations

GOAL IDENTIFICATION

1. Defining own goal(s) when in a problem situation
2. Defining the goal(s) of another when in a problem situation
3. Identifying immediate and long-term goals
4. Sharing identified goals with the student group and accepting feedback
5. Listing the steps to reaching identified goals

6. Charting progress toward reaching goals
7. Identifying and describing the needs and goals of others

CUE SENSITIVITY

1. Identifying environmental cues in pictures and responding by asking questions and summarizing content and feelings
2. Identifying environmental cues in real situations that influence behavior
3. Identifying the personal cues people use and what they mean in role-plays and films
4. Identifying the personal cues used by others in real situations
5. Identifying own cues when interacting with others and what they mean
6. Identifying several cues you want to include in your repertoire
7. Identifying cues of others, your typical response to them, and possible alternative responses

ALTERNATIVE THINKING

1. Identifying likely alternatives to solving hypothetical problems
2. Identifying likely alternatives to solving real problems
3. Identifying nonaggressive alternatives to solving hypothetical problems
4. Identifying nonaggressive alternatives to solving real problems

SKILLS IMPLEMENTATION

1. Identifying the best procedure for implementing the selected alternative
2. Identifying a person who implements the alternative well and describing what they do
3. Describing the step-by-step process for implementing the selected alternative
4. Role-playing, practicing, and rehearsing the selected alternative
5. Using feedback from self and others to make changes in the procedures

(Continued)

TABLE 2.1 (Continued)

6. Implementing selected alternative	7. Identifying the consequences of selected behaviors in interpersonal situations involving self
7. Evaluating the outcome and the procedure	8. Implementing a "stop and think" approach to solving interpersonal difficulties
CONSEQUENTIAL THINKING	
1. Predicting the likely consequences of a series of events that do not involve them	**INTEGRATION**
2. Predicting the likely consequences of hypothetical stories and role-play situations	1. Observing models (counselors, teachers, and peers) integrate the problem-solving process in solving hypothetical problems
3. Predicting the likely consequences of interpersonal interactions of others	2. Observing models (counselors, teachers, and peers) integrate the problem-solving process in solving real problems
4. Identifying short-run and long-run solutions to solving hypothetical problems	3. Integrating the problem-solving process in solving group problems
5. Identifying problems in the long run when implementing short-run solutions to hypothetical situations	4. Integrating the problem-solving process in solving hypothetical problems
6. Identifying the consequences of selected behaviors in interpersonal situations involving others	5. Integrating the problem-solving process in solving real problems

Note. From Vaughn, S. (1987). TLC—Teaching, learning, and caring: Teaching interpersonal problem-solving skills to behaviorally disordered adolescents. *The Pointer, 31*(2), p. 28. Reprinted with permission of the Helen Dwight Reid Educational Foundation. Published by Heldref Publications, 4000 Albemarle St., N.W., Washington, D.C. 20016. Copyright 1987.

ting goals. The teacher could choose to skip Cue Sensitivity and Empathy to spend more time on Goal Identification.

This tactic could be expanded by analyzing interpersonal social situations in terms of more than one component. Students might also analyze the behaviors of their "most admired person" in terms of the various components.

Monitor This project, like others intended to assist students to get along with their peers, could be evaluated by arranging a sociometric instrument (see MONITOR 8 in Appendix A). Youth could be asked, before and after the training program, to identify a best friend or a person with whom they would like to work, or in other ways rate their peers.

Students might keep a detailed notebook that includes subheadings for each category and notes from the class discussions. As personal situations arise, they could refer to their notebooks for help in deciding how to handle various social situations. Recording their approaches to problem situations and the outcomes would provide ongoing documentation of their growth in this area. For example, they could keep track of the number of times a day they acted with empathy, thought of alternative solutions, or thought about the consequences of an action.

Vaughn, S. (1987). TLC—Teaching, learning, and caring: Teaching interpersonal problem-solving skills to behaviorally disordered adolescents. *The Pointer, 31*(2), 25-30. **Reference**

GETTING ALONG WITH OTHERS: A FOUR-STEP PROCESS

Background

Individuals who lack opportunities to learn social behaviors in their natural environments may end up with social skill deficits that negatively affect their interactions. Teaching social skills incidentally within either natural environments or deliberately created social situations has proven to be an effective process. In the tactic explained here, practice in getting along with others is gained through role-playing. In this tactic students are taught a few simple steps for analyzing a problem, planning ways to solve it, and evaluating the outcome.

Who Can Benefit

This tactic was developed from a comprehensive social skills training package that was originally written for elementary age children. It has been modified, however, and used successfully with a variety of populations. The examples explained here are suitable for students at the secondary level who have not developed adequate skills for getting along with others in difficult situations. Students with limited experience in interpersonal relations should benefit most from learning to interact successfully with others.

Procedures
1. Tell students that the subject for the day is "solving problems related to getting along with others."
2. Write the following target behaviors on the board:
   Listening carefully
   Treating others respectfully
   Joining in with others
   Maintaining a good attitude
   Taking responsibility for self
   Staying calm and relaxed
   Solving problems
3. List the following situations where problems can occur:
   Neighborhood
   Home (parents, siblings, other relatives)
   School (peers, teachers, administrators)
4. Ask students to provide examples of people getting along and not getting along in each of the above situations to be sure they understand these concepts. (Sources such as Ann Landers's column or other advice columns in newspapers or magazines could provide several ideas.)
5. Explain the following four-step process for solving problems to students:
   a. Take a deep breath in an attempt to create a calm body and a good attitude.
   b. Identify the problem.
   c. Think of at least three possible solutions to the problem.
   d. Select the best one and try it.
6. Model an example of this four-step process (see role-plays sheet in Table 2.2). For example, to show students how to stay calm and relaxed when there is a problem involving parents, model the following steps:
   Take a deep breath—Remind students that this is to develop a *calm body* and a *good attitude*.

TABLE 2.2   Role-Plays

Situations/ Target Behaviors	School Problems (Teacher/Peers)	Neighborhood Problems	Sibling Problems	Parent Problems
Listen carefully	During reading the teacher calls on you to read out loud, but you don't know where to start.	You're taking care of the neighbors' cat, and you can't remember where they said the key would be.	Your sister asks you to do her a favor and says she'll bring you a treat for doing it. You forgot what she asked you to do.	You are at a friend's, and you aren't sure what time your mom said to be home.
Treat others nicely	A kid that everyone calls "nerd" asks you to help her with her math during free time.	A neighbor kid you don't like trips and falls down. One of the lenses in his glasses breaks out and rolls away.	Your sister comes in your room when you are outside and plays with your toys.	You're eating dinner with your family, and you don't like what was cooked.
Join in with others	At lunch a group of kids are talking about skiing: You'd like to talk to them, but you don't know anything about skiing.	You feel really bored and are riding your bike. You see a group of kids playing basketball. You've never met these kids.	Your mom is taking you and your sister to the movies. They are talking about seeing a movie that is not what you'd choose.	Your aunt is visiting, and she and your family are deciding where to go sightseeing.
Keep a good attitude	You get a C on your report card, but you think you deserved a better grade.	You are playing ball with a friend, and another kid comes up and takes the ball away from you.	Your little brother hits you, and just as you hit him back, your dad walks in and gets mad at you.	Your dad is watching TV, and it's almost time for your favorite show.
Take responsibility for self	A group of kids are fighting at recess. The teacher is standing close, but you're not sure she will see them.	You and your neighbor are at a movie, and you want some popcorn, but you don't have any money. You still owe this kid money.	Your brother and you are at the store getting some things for your mom. You also want some candy, but there isn't enough money.	You run the vacuum cleaner over a hairpin because you don't think it will matter. Then it makes a loud, awful noise.
Stay calm and relaxed	You are on the playground; three kids gang up on you and start calling you a nickname you hate and threatening to hit you.	You are playing softball in front of your house. You hit the ball, and it goes through a neighbor's window. She is very mad.	You have been waiting all day to get home and have a special snack that you bought yesterday. Your sister ate it.	Your mom promised to take you roller-skating, but then tells you she forgot and made plans to get your haircut.
Solve problems	You spent your whole allowance over the weekend. On Monday you need some money to buy something at a bake sale at school.	A friend invites you to a movie. You agree, but you forgot you already promised to go over to another friend's house.	You're playing a game with your brother, and he keeps moving your "man," taking your turn, etc.	Mom tells you to clean your room before school, and then she leaves. You remember that you have to be at school early today.

Note. From Jackson, N.F., Jackson, D.A., & Monroe, C. (1983). *Getting along with others: Teaching social effectiveness to children* (Skill Lessons and Activities; p. 11). Champaign, IL: Research Press. Copyright 1983 by the authors. Reprinted by permission.

Identify the problem—Your mom promised to give you a ride to the roller-skating rink, but then tells you that she forgot, and made plans to have your hair cut.

Think of three solutions—These could be to: (a) Yell at your mom, run to your room, and refuse to come out; (b) keep the appointment to have your hair cut without objecting, but then give your mom the silent treatment for the rest of the night; (c) remind your mom of her promise, and ask her if your haircut could be rescheduled.

Select the best solution and try it—Tell students that the best choice for this situation is the last one.

7. Read several other examples from the role-plays sheet in Table 2.2 and guide a student discussion of possible solutions following the four-step solution process. Point out that the target behaviors offer clues to solutions.

8. Provide students with a few more examples from the same sheet to role-play with their partners. Encourage pupils to come up with their own solutions for the sample problems.

9. Organize a class discussion of ideas and outcomes.

Modifications/ Considerations

The subject of getting along with others is broad enough to allow teachers to modify procedures by choosing examples that are appropriate to the specific needs of their students. Teachers may also wish to expand on specific behaviors that might fall under each category of the role-play sheet to better prepare students for the exercises in this tactic.

To add variety to the approach, the problem-solving activities could be handled as a written exercise. Students could choose examples from the list, write out three solutions for each one, then rank them in order of appropriateness to the situation. The ranking could also be done by means of a group discussion and vote. The voting could focus on either picking the "best" one, or on counting how many offered similar solutions.

For this approach, data on its effects could be obtained in the role-playing situations (see MONITOR 19 in Appendix A for more detail). In those settings, any of the themes suggested in the role-plays sheet in Table 2.2 or others could be acted out. Then, with a checklist to indicate which behaviors were being emphasized, an observer could tally the extent any of the individuals engaged in them.

Monitor

Jackson, N.F., Jackson, D.A., & Monroe, C. (1983). *Getting along with others: Teaching social effectiveness to children*. Champaign, IL: Research Press.

Reference

LEARNING TO COMPROMISE: THE ART OF NEGOTIATION

The tactic outlined here is a program for teaching teenagers the art of negotiation as an alternative to inappropriate, harmful, or disruptive behaviors. ASSET (Hazel, Schumaker, Sherman, & Sheldon-Wildgen, 1981), the program from which this tactic is derived, provides professionals with a comprehensive array of social skills training techniques. Whereas a variety of media make up the ASSET program, with special consideration given to coordination of a videotape and training manual, the tactic explained here relies mainly on direct instruction and role-playing to help students learn and practice the basic steps for successful negotiation.

Background

Although all students can benefit from opportunities to improve their negotiation skills, this type of training has special significance for secondary students who have failed to learn these skills either at home, at school, in the neighborhood, or anyplace else.

Who Can Benefit

FIGURE 2.2 Negotiation Checklist for Use in Learning to Compromise

NEGOTIATION CHECKLIST

Student's Name _____ Date _____

Criterion Tests

1	2	3	4	Did the student:
—	—	—	—	1. Face the person during the conversation?
—	—	—	—	2. Maintain eye contact with the person?
—	—	—	—	3. Keep a neutral facial expression?
—	—	—	—	4. Use a normal tone of voice—positive and nonaccusing?
—	—	—	—	5. Maintain an erect posture?
—	—	—	—	6. Ask to talk to the other person?
—	—	—	—	7. State what he or she wanted?
—	—	—	—	8. Give a reason for the request?
—	—	—	—	9. Wait for a response?
—	—	—	—	10. If the response was positive, thank the person? If the response was negative, ask the person if he or she could think of anything the student could do to get what was wanted?
—	—	—	—	11. Listen to the other person's response?
—	—	—	—	12. If satisfied with the solution, agree and thank the person? If not satisfied, propose a compromise?
—	—	—	—	13. If the other person agreed with the compromise, thank him or her? If the other person did not agree, ask for another solution and continue negotiating?
—	—	—	—	14. Pay attention to the other person while he or she was talking by giving head nods and saying "mm-hmm" and "yeah"?

Note. From Hazel, J.S., Schumaker, J.B., Sherman, J.A., & Sheldon-Wildgen, J. (1981). *ASSET: A social skills program for adolescents* (p. 112). Champaign, IL: Research Press. Copyright 1981 by the authors. Reprinted by permission.

1. Explain to the students that they will be learning to come to an agreement with another person. Tell them that this is the skill of negotiation.

2. Discuss the importance of negotiating and give examples of amicable negotiations throughout the world, in the community, and in the school.

3. Hand out a Negotiation Checklist (Figure 2.2) to the students and go over the 14 points that are listed.

4. Role-play the situation of a parent and a teen-ager who is asking for a larger allowance. Below is a suggested sequence to follow.

   S: (Initiates conversation.) Asks for a raise in allowance from $7.50 to $10.00/week.
   P: Responds with, "I don't think so."
   S: Asks for another solution. ("Can you think of anything else I can do?")
   P: Gives an alternative that the teenager finds unreasonable, such as a 50-cent increase.
   S: Suggests an alternative, such as performing a specific household duty.
   P: Still refuses, but offers to raise the allowance to $9.00/week if the student helps with one extra chore.
   S: Agrees or continues the negotiation.

5. Discuss what happened during the scene, identifying negotiating skills that were and were not used (see number 3).

6. Explain the rationales of negotiation. Ask why it would have been important to use good negotiation skills in the allowance scene. Make clear the following points:
   a. If you negotiate you will probably get what you want more often, but you will probably have to give up something, or do more of something else.
   b. Proper negotiation often leads to compromise and makes both parties reasonably happy.
   c. Being able to compromise and negotiate often leads to immediate, and long-term, benefits.
   d. Negotiation can get you through difficult situations without loss of respect or friendship.

7. Give examples of situations that could require negotiation, such as:
    - You want to stay out later than the curfew your parents have set.
    - You want to drive the family car, but your parents say that you are not responsible enough to drive.
    - You and a friend want to see a movie, but can't agree on which one to see.
    - You want some extra time to complete an assignment at school.
    - Your boss has given you more work than you can do in the allotted time.

8. Ask students to think of additional examples.

9. Instruct them to choose partners and have the pairs role-play various negotiations, following the steps in the checklist. Teachers might make suggestions depending on how well the negotiations proceed.

10. Evaluate the situations with the Negotiation Checklist. Fill in one for each participant.

11. Lead a class discussion about the dramatizations, emphasizing alternative solutions that could have been offered.

Modifications/ Considerations

Figure 2.3 is a Home Note form that could be helpful in efforts to involve family members who might encourage the development of these negotiating skills at home. Students could be asked to return the notes with comments from adult caregivers regarding evidence that training has generalized into the home setting.

Videotaped depictions of adolescents involved in situations requiring negotiation skills could be used to help students see the need for these skills. Moreover, those tapes could focus on particular behaviors that are or are not effective in various situations, and could stimulate discussion and further exploration of solutions.

Throughout training, there should be emphasis on the fact that being able to negotiate results in compromise, not one-sided victory. Students should be made to understand that a negotiable position is required when establishing objectives for the intended negotiations.

FIGURE 2.3   Home Note Form to Involve Family Members

HOME NOTE

Dear _____:

The group discussed and practiced negotiation this week.

_____ has agreed to practice this skill with you three times this week. We would appreciate it if you would record what the practice situation was and how well the skill was performed. Figure 2.2 is a Negotiation Checklist which shows the steps for correctly carrying out this skill. Please check your teenager's performance against these steps. For each of the three practice situations give a check mark for a correct performance only if the teenager made no more than two mistakes during the practice. Please sign the form after the practices, and encourage your teenager to return it. Thanks for your help.

Situation	Performed Correctly?	Steps Omitted
1. _____		
_____		
_____		
_____		
2. _____		
_____		
_____		
_____		
3. _____		
_____		
_____		
_____		

Signed: _____   Date: _____

Note. Adapted from Hazel, J.S., Schumaker, J.B., Sherman, J.A., & Sheldon-Wildgen, J. (1981). *ASSET: A social skills program for adolescents.* Champaign, IL: Research Press. Copyright 1981 by the authors. Reprinted by permission.

Monitor   As noted, one way to monitor this approach would be with film. In fact, a series of videocassettes could be made of various groups of students engaged in role-playing situations. Those cassettes could be used for training individuals or to evaluate the effects of a program. For the latter, a group could be filmed interacting on some topic prior to and following training. Those films could then be shown to judges, unfamiliar with either the students or the training, who could comment on the differences noted, if any (see MONITOR 15 in Appendix A for more detail).

Reference   Hazel, J.S., Schumaker, J.B., Sherman, J.S., & Sheldon-Wildgen, J. (1981). *ASSET: A social skills program for adolescents*. Champaign, IL: Research Press.

MAINTAINING YOUR POSITION: DENYING INAPPROPRIATE REQUESTS

Background   This tactic is based on a program that provides social skills instruction in four general areas: basic social interaction skills, conversing with others, being positive and making friends, and being assertive. The tactic explained here is concerned with only a specific skill within that program, denying requests.

Who Can Benefit   Often, adolescents give in to inappropriate requests from peers, requests they would rather refuse. But, because they are uncomfortable with the situation, or simply cannot say no, they give in. Adolescents, particularly those who are at risk, can benefit from learning to deny unreasonable requests in a manner that is convincing yet polite.

1. Inform students that they will learn a technique for denying requests that they believe are inappropriate.

2. List the following social interaction skills on the board. Review them with students, and ask if there are any questions.
    a. Getting the person's attention and maintaining eye contact
    b. Speaking with appropriate voice and volume control
    c. Maintaining a proper distance
    d. Waiting until the other person pauses before speaking

3. Teach students to decide when it is appropriate to deny requests—giving thought *first* to their relationship with the person making the request, and *second*, to the consequences of denying the request. Teachers and students might come up with a variety of examples to discuss. Some suggestions are listed in number 6 below.

4. Teach a variety of denial and rejection statements appropriate to the situation under consideration. The following are some possibilities:
    a. "I'd like to, but I'm busy at that time."
    b. "No, thank you."
    c. "I'm sorry, but I am unable to . . ."
    d. "Let me think about it."
    e. "I would prefer not to . . ."
    f. "I'm not allowed to . . ."
    g. "No, please excuse me."

5. Teach the art of "polite" rejection by modeling examples of some of the above responses to unreasonable requests.

6. Ask students to form pairs to practice role-playing the denying of requests in the following hypothetical situations:
    a. You have gone to a party and someone offers you something to eat that you really don't want.
    b. Your mom asks you to go to the store for her, but you're expecting a phone call.
    c. A friend wants to borrow five dollars from you, but you don't like to loan money.
    d. A classmate asks to copy your homework assignment. You have worked on it for quite a while, and you don't want to give it to him or her.

Procedures

e. An acquaintance asks if you would like to try a new drug.
f. Your teacher has just asked you to take part in the school play. You have a part-time job and don't have time.
g. Some friends ask you to skip school with them.
7. Summarize with the class what they learned in the role-play exercises through class discussions. Respond to questions that come up.
8. Give each student several forms for Denying Inappropriate Requests (Figure 2.4). Ask them to fill these in on the occasions they deny requests. Later, some of this information could form the basis for class discussion.

Modifications/ Considerations

Students should be encouraged to supply situations of their own for the role-playing exercises. The teacher should note these, and over a period of time will have quite a collection.

With the prevalence of threats to the well-being of adolescents, including the use of drugs, alcohol, and sexual abuse, students should be taught to err on the side of being "old-fashioned" and conservative. Parents and teachers should make it clear to youth that the consequences for those errors will be understanding and reassurance. Training of this type is an ongoing process; it is not like mastering a few addition facts. Role-playing is only one way to get the message across. Training of this type should be the responsibility of every teacher and should be engaged in within the contexts of all situations at the secondary level.

Monitor

Suggestions for monitoring this technique were sprinkled throughout the write-up; teachers could rely on role-playing situations (see MONITOR 19 in Appendix A) and checklists (see MONITOR 6). Teachers could, in fact, set up two phases to evaluate the impact of their training. Throughout a phase before instruction they could gather data from the checklist as students role-played a few situations. Similar data could be acquired on a few occasions after the treatment had been scheduled. The teacher and participants should then study those data to see if there were changes.

FIGURE 2.4   Form for Use in Maintaining Your Position

DENYING INAPPROPRIATE REQUESTS

Monitoring Form

Trial # _____   Date _____

Briefly describe the situation: _____

_____

_____

Preskills

Did the person who was practicing Denying Inappropriate Requests (Check items that apply):

☐ 1.   Get the other person's attention and maintain eye contact?

☐ 2.   Speak with appropriate voice and volume controls?

☐ 3.   Maintain an appropriate distance?

☐ 4.   Wait until the other person paused before speaking?

Denial and Rejection Statements

Which statements were used? Were they effective? (Check items that apply and comment in the space provided.)

Comments

☐ 1.   "I'd like to, but I'm busy at that time."

☐ 2.   "No, thank you."

☐ 3.   "I'm sorry, but I am unable to . . ."

☐ 4.   "Let me think about it."

☐ 5.   "I would prefer not to . . ."

☐ 6.   "I'm not allowed to . . ."

☐ 7.   "No, please excuse me."

☐ 8.   Other (Please write in.)

Note. Adapted from Cheney, D., Morgan, D.P., & Young, K.R. (1984). *Assertiveness skills for adolescents.* Logan: Department of Special Education, Utah State University. Reprinted by permission.

Reference Cheney, D., Morgan, D.P., & Young, K.R. (1984). *Assertiveness skills for adolescents*. Logan: Department of Special Education, Utah State University.

ACCEPTING CRITICISM: LISTENING AND RESPONDING

Background The steps outlined in this tactic are a combined and expanded version of methods advocated by Black and Downs (1984) and Hazel, Schumaker, Sherman, and Sheldon-Wildgen (1981) in their programs for assisting disruptive students. Accepting criticism is identified by those authors as a skill of great importance, because it is so much a part of life in both the structured academic settings of school and in the more independent areas of home and work.

Who Can Benefit Because individuals with demonstrated social skills deficits are likely to receive more than the average amount of negative feedback, it is crucial that they learn to accept and act positively on criticism, rather than react negatively, thus increasing the levels of criticism they will receive.

Procedures Following are some suggestions for reacting to criticism. These points are not listed in an order to be followed, and some are more important than others.

1. Face the person who is delivering the criticism, and make eye contact with him or her.
2. Maintain a neutral expression, and speak with a normal tone of voice.
3. Stand up straight and near the critic.
4. Listen attentively to the critic so you will know exactly what he or she is saying. Don't interrupt.

5. Nod occasionally or in other ways let the critic know that you are listening.
6. Ask the person to clarify anything you do not understand. Say something like, "I don't quite understand what you mean or what you think I did wrong," or "I'm not sure why you're so upset; please fill me in."
7. Apologize, if you agree, or say that you understand why he or she is upset. If it is not obvious what you should do or not do on future, similar occasions, ask for suggestions.
8. It may be that you understand why the person is upset, but you believe he or she has somehow misinterpreted what happened. In such a case, ask the person to listen to your version of what took place.
9. As you try to defend your position, keep in mind the status of the person who gave you the criticism. If it is an authority figure, you may want to back off after you calmly and succinctly presented your case. That, of course, would depend on the nature of the criticism, the intensity of the criticism, how justified it may have been, how frequently this person had criticized you in the past day or so, and on a number of other factors.
10. After the first wave of criticism has been delivered, and depending on how you feel and the critic's acceptance of your reaction, you may want to excuse yourself and say that you will think about the person's comments and get back to him or her in a day or so.

Modifications/ Considerations

It might be effective to approach this topic by asking students to role-play a number of different, but typical situations in which they may need to deal with criticism. Begin with situations that might occur at school, and later ask students to suggest other scenarios. Discussions about why certain approaches worked (or did not) might generate additional options that could help students.

Monitor

The teacher might want to gather data on the extent that pupils dealt with criticism in role-playing situations (see MONITOR 19 in Appendix A) and in actual encounters. For the former, some type of checklist could be designed to acquire data as students acted out a variety of scenarios as critics and recipients of the criticism.

To determine whether those role-playing episodes had any impact on real life, students could keep records of the times they were criticized, noting the critic, the criticism, and their reaction.

References   Black, D.D., & Downs, J.C. (1984). *Administrative intervention workshop manual: Procedures for assisting disruptive students.* Boys' Town, NE: Division of Education, Father Flanagan's Boys' Home.

Hazel, J.S., Schumaker, J.B., Sherman, J.S., & Sheldon-Wildgen, J. (1981). *ASSET: A social skills program for adolescents.* Champaign, IL.: Research Press

MAKING REQUESTS: APPROPRIATE AND EFFECTIVE QUESTIONING TECHNIQUES

Background   Knowing how to make requests appropriately can be critical to successful interactions in classroom situations, at work, at home, or elsewhere. The method described here was adapted from the Teaching-Family Model, a group home and residential treatment program for behaviorally disruptive youth. This is a tactic derived from the *Administrative Intervention Workshop Manual* (Black & Downs, 1984) developed at Father Flanagan's Boys' Town.

Who Can Benefit   Requests make up a large part of our daily conversations. In school, teachers and students spend a good part of their time making requests of one another (e.g., "Please hand in your papers now," "May I be excused?"). We usually begin our phone calls with a request to speak to a certain person, often followed by a request for information. Many jobs require the ability to make appropriate requests, such as "How may I help you?" Because requests are such an integral part of our everyday lives, and at-risk and remedial youth are generally weak with respect to communication skills, such youth should profit from this technique.

Procedures

Following are a few steps to consider when assisting students to make requests properly:

1. Offer a rationale to students for learning to make requests. Include in the rationale:
   a. A benefit to students that will result from employing the skill
   b. A negative consequence that will occur if they do not
   c. A concern for the effect their actions have on others
2. Explain to students that they will now be expected to use this social skill:
   a. Before they use something that belongs to someone else
   b. When they approach someone to ask for help
3. Explain and model the following steps for making a request:
   a. Wait until the person is not busy to make your request.
   b. Maintain eye contact with that individual.
   c. Stand close to that person and remain still.
   d. Keep a pleasant facial expression.
   e. Say "please" when making your request.
   f. Say "thank you" after the individual reacted to your request.
4. Point out that not all requests will be granted, and outline ways to deal with denials through negotiations and compromises such as the following:
   a. Maintain eye contact and close proximity; don't fidget and move around.
   b. Verbally acknowledge denial, maintaining a quiet voice and pleasant facial expression.
   c. Ask, if you do not understand, why your request was denied.

d. Wait to discuss it at a later time with the individual if you disagree or still don't understand the reason for the denial.

e. Ask to talk privately to the individual again about the matter, and at a time convenient to him or her.

f. Make a statement of empathy or concern to the person about his or her decision.

g. State your disagreement or misunderstanding.

h. Offer your rationale for disagreeing with the person.

i. Thank the individual for listening.

Modifications/ Considerations

This is only one of a number of social skills included in the Boys' Town program. Others include accepting criticism and consequences, greeting others, getting the teacher's attention, disagreeing appropriately, and following directions. Suggestions for teaching students to compromise are included in this tactic as a way to deal with the denial of requests. Another tactic in this series pertains specifically to teaching individuals to compromise.

Monitor

One approach to consider for evaluating the impact of this treatment would be for students involved in the training to self-record the times they made requests. They could begin taking these notes a week or so before training begins and continue for some time during and after the program. In addition to obtaining data on the number of requests, information could be acquired as to the results of the requests and about the episodes generally. Those frequency data could be charted and evaluated (see MONITOR 1 in Appendix A).

Data regarding the training itself could be obtained by setting up role-playing situations. Those interactions could be videotaped and evaluated later with the assistance of checklists.

Reference

Black, D.D., & Downs, J.C. (1984). *Administrative intervention workshop manual: Procedures for assisting disruptive students*. Boys' Town, NE: Division of Education, Father Flanagan's Boys' Home.

COMMUNICATING EFFECTIVELY: TALKING TO TEACHERS ABOUT PROBLEMS

Students who get the best grades at school are generally not afraid to approach teachers. Other students, those who aren't as successful, don't seek out their teachers when they have problems because they are afraid that teachers will embarrass them, yell at them, or they will not know what to say and teachers will think they are stupid. This scenario is replayed by students from grade school through college. Students can benefit from learning to interact with those in authority by applying the technique introduced here at home, school, and work.

Background

Most students will benefit from explicit instructions on communicating with authority figures. Students who are at risk especially need this skill. If they can communicate their willingness to deal with problems, they may be able to work out plans with their teachers to overcome them.

Who Can Benefit

1. Ask students to think of a problem they have in one of their classes. It might be one of the following: They do not understand the work, they want to change their seat, they believe they deserve a higher grade, they are missing assignments or classes.
2. Discuss ways in which students can deal with the problem. They could let it slide, give excuses, or offer a possible solution.
3. Model for students how to set up a discussion with a teacher: "Mr. Jones, I'd like to talk with you about _____. When would be a good time for me to come by?" Explain to the students that they must agree on a time that is acceptable to

Procedures

both parties, and they must keep track of it and show up at the right place at the right time.

4. Show students the difference between owning a problem and blaming it on others. The first is positive, the second negative. Compare "I statements" to "Blaming statements": "I don't understand . . . the assignment is too hard for me." "Your assignments and grades are unfair." Inform students that the former statements are more apt to get positive results than the latter.

5. Inform students that they must act as though they are willing to work with the teacher on the problem. To indicate this attitude, they might ask, "What do you think I could do about this?"

6. Discuss with the students how they could offer their ideas in an acceptable manner. "I've thought about it. Maybe I could . . . or maybe it would help if I . . ."

7. Explain to students that they need to listen as the teacher offers suggestions.

8. Tell the students that they must be responsible to end the discussion by agreeing to an acceptable solution. They should write it down and put it into practice.

9. Assign students to partners, particularly to boys or girls they don't know, and have them take turns role-playing these aforementioned steps.

10. Ask students, following the role-playing, to write a paragraph about their experiences, explaining what it was like for them to play the teacher, how closely they followed the proper steps, where they got stuck, and what they learned.

11. Instruct students to fill in the following form at the end of an instructional period:

When will you approach a teacher with a problem using what you learned today?

SET IT UP: "Write below what problem you have thought of and a date when you'll talk to the teacher."

_____

_____

_____

Turn this page in to your teacher today. The teacher will check back with you on _____.

After students have communicated a concern to one of their teachers, they could discuss the interaction: What did they say? What did the teacher say? How did the conversation come out?

When students have become reasonably successful with this interaction approach at school, they should be encouraged to apply it to situations at work and at home.

Modifications/ Considerations

Role-playing was the suggested approach for training youth to make requests in this project. Data from those situations could be acquired with the help of a checklist (see MONITOR 6 in Appendix A). Interaction data could also be acquired in these situations. For that, an observer would mark each statement of the person who initiated the request and those of the other individual. Furthermore, those data would be coded to indicate the "tone" or type of remark, either positive/negative, acceptable/unacceptable, or some other way. By analyzing those data, the teacher may learn that when the frequency of these interactions increases (between two people), the chances for a favorable result are increased (see MONITOR 18).

Monitor

Stoker, J. (1980). *Grab H.O.L.D.: Help overcome learner dropouts. Classroom guidance manual.* San Jose, CA: Resource Publications.

Reference

PEER TUTORING: GUIDELINES FOR SETTING UP PROGRAMS

Peer and cross-age tutoring has a long history as an effective method for educating students. The benefits for the tutee include individualized instruction and extra practice. Tutors may benefit academically,

Background

socially, and personally. Research has indicated that peer tutoring programs are the most cost effective, and they produce the greatest gains in learning, when compared with other interventions such as decreasing class size or lengthening the school day.

Who Can Benefit

This tactic is based on a review of research that supported tutoring at both the elementary and secondary levels. Tutoring is designed to assist students with a variety of academic skill levels, and can be effective in most content areas. The increased amounts of time on task inherent in this approach are particularly valuable for low achieving students. Students who serve as tutors not only acquire a better understanding of subject matter, they also develop useful management skills in the process.

Procedures

1. Secure support for establishing a peer tutoring program from school administrators, staff, and parents.
2. Select tutors. Teachers suggest to higher achieving students that they become tutors. An application form should be completed by students who express an interest. Signed permission letters should be obtained from parents of tutors who have been selected. (See Peer Tutor Application in Figure 2.5 and example permission letter in Figure 2.6.)
3. Select tutees. Teachers identify the students who could benefit from tutoring. Students could also request assistance for themselves.
4. Recruit a good note-taker from the target class to take notes on lectures and reading assignments. Provide tutors with a copy of these notes. Training may be provided for note-takers.
5. Train tutors. This training should be extensive, covering communication skills, analysis, instructional methods and strategies, and study skills.
6. Match tutors and tutees. The more experienced tutors could be placed with those students having the greatest difficulty. Depending on the specific requirements of the tutees, tutors may be able to assist groups of two or three.
7. Specify goals and steps of tutoring for individual students.

FIGURE 2.5 Form for Use in Setting Up Peer Tutoring Program

PEER TUTOR APPLICATION

Applicant _____ Present Grade Level _____

Mailing Address _____

_____

_____

What subject areas do you consider to be your strongest? Would you be comfortable tutoring someone in these areas? (Please rank order the subjects below with number 1 being the highest priority for you.)

_____ Art   _____ Language Arts

_____ Business Education   _____ Math

_____ Home Economics   _____ Reading

_____ Industrial Education   _____ Science

                                         _____ Social Studies

In 100 words or less, please tell us:

1. Why you would like to be a peer tutor.

2. The qualities you feel you have that would make you a good peer tutor.

---

   8. Supervise tutors and tutees. Circulate about the classroom to be sure that tutoring sessions are proceeding appropriately. Assist students as questions arise.
   9. Maintain tutors' involvement and interest. Options for doing this are discussed in the Modifications/Considerations section below.
  10. Tutees might keep records of their assignments and test scores while they are being tutored.

FIGURE 2.6 Suggestion for Permission Letter for Peer Tutors

PERMISSION LETTER

Dear Parents:

Your son or daughter is applying for a position as a Peer Tutor.
Peer Tutors are a select group of students who will be trained to provide
specific kinds of assistance to students with special learning needs.

I hope you will support your son's or daughter's application.

Sincerely,

_____   _____
(Parent Signature)   (Date)

Tutors could monitor these records to see how their assistance helped the tutees' progress. Teachers, in turn, could supervise all record-keeping and set up a bulletin board on which students may post their scores.

Modifications/ Considerations

Tutors can be honored in a number of ways. Reinforcers might take the form of a school display with tutors' photos, an awards assembly, a page of the yearbook, or a reception. Positive feedback from tutees and teachers can also help maintain tutors' interest.

One of the most important attitudes students will need to develop in the tutor-tutee relationship is flexibility. No matter how specific the task, or how well structured the procedures, situations will arise that have not been covered in training or instruction. Students must be able to adjust their approaches as necessary, and be willing to ask for and accept assistance if they cannot.

Monitor

Because this is an organizational tactic, one designed to establish a program, it would be appropriate to measure the extent to which the program got under way and how the participants initially felt about it. As for the former, records should be kept of the numbers involved: tutors, tutees, and teachers. Information should also be obtained on the time required for start up, for daily involvement, and for administrative matters.

To acquire data on the impressions of affected individuals, a series of interviews could be scheduled (see MONITOR 9 in Appendix A). Teachers, tutors, tutees, and perhaps parents of tutors and tutees could be interviewed to determine how they felt about the program, what changes they would suggest, and whether they believed the program should be continued.

To properly evaluate a tutoring program, data should also be acquired on the primary goal of the program—the improvement of tutees in various subjects. Data should also be kept on the tutors, to determine whether they, as a result of teaching, are also acquiring important skills. Data of these types are discussed in the peer tutoring projects that follow in this chapter.

Reference

Jenkins, J.J., & Jenkins, L.M. (1985). Peer tutoring in elementary and secondary programs. *Focus on Exceptional Children, 17*(6), 1–12.

PEER TUTORING: DEVELOPING BETTER WRITING SKILLS

Background

In recent years researchers have emphasized the need for a return to the concept that writing is a process, and that it should be taught as such. As a result, several teachers have modified their lessons to systematically teach students to write. Specifically, the instruction provided has been in the areas of idea development, sentence generation, and paragraph organization. The tactic described here involves peer tutoring of effective strategies to facilitate the writing process.

Who Can Benefit

The procedures in a study by Whitt, Paul, and Reynolds (1988) were used with middle school students classified as learning disabled. Because writing abilities vary greatly, this tactic would be suitable for remedial and at-risk high school students as well.

Procedures

1. Assign each student to a partner. Students should be matched so that the better writers (tutors) are with those who need the most assistance (tutees).
2. Stimulate the selection of a writing topic by providing a variety of experiences such as role-play, drama, speakers, interviews, demonstrations, or field trips.
3. Assist students to develop an outline for their paper. Tutors can help the tutees they are working with. Teachers can respond to the questions of tutors.
4. Check outlines of all the students.
5. Ask the students to write a lead sentence and two or three supporting sentences.
6. Instruct the peer tutors to help tutees combine their lead and supporting sentences into a topic sentence.
7. Ask students to begin working on their draft, using their outline as a guide.
8. Circulate about the room checking progress and providing assistance as required.
9. Conduct conferences in which the pairs of students (i.e., tutors and tutees) share their rough drafts with each other orally and provide each other with feedback. Provide dictionaries and the following list of questions about revisions to students:
   a. Did you describe events by giving concrete details?
   b. Are your paragraphs in a proper sequence?
   c. Can you use more precise verbs?
10. Model revisions by helping students to rewrite or combine sentences, to choose more appropriate or imaginative vocabulary, and to add interesting examples or details.

11. Encourage students to make revisions with the help of their peer tutors. Point out to students that the concerns of these writing assignments are content, organization, and style.
12. Provide a few standard editing symbols to student pairs and help them proofread their drafts.
13. Conduct teacher conferences when pairs of students are ready to turn in their final drafts. Students should read and discuss their compositions with the teacher at this time. Teachers can point out ways to make improvements and encourage the students to make additional revisions.
14. Approve final drafts and have students write a neat final copy.
15. Students could keep a folder containing a checklist to monitor their progress through the writing process. It could serve as a guideline to help them remember to go through each step in a sequential manner, and as a visual record of just where they are in the process. The following points should be on the checklist:

Brainstorm	Revision
Outline	Editing
Lead sentences	Teacher conference
Rough draft	Final copy
Peer conference	

Modifications/ Considerations

Selecting a topic on which to write and establishing a purpose for writing are important matters. Teachers may initially stimulate writing by one of the following prompts: Write to a friend or relative, describe a favorite scene or possession, explain how to do something, write directions on how to get someplace, describe your feelings when you are happy or sad, detail the events of a typical or favorite day, write about your future plans.

Teachers should also lead discussions and stimulate students to identify reasons for writing. They should write to organize their thoughts, to inform and make requests of others, to supply information, to chronicle events and keep records. From those reasons and others, students should be encouraged to come up with their own justifications for writing.

Tutors should, of course, write their own compositions as well as help their partners. This allows them to use their work as examples, and provides them with additional practice.

Tutees should be encouraged to provide input to tutors about writing and tutoring, thus making the relationships ones of mutual exchange. By doing so, tutees are provided needed experience in expressing their ideas, and tutors are given opportunities to hear other viewpoints and to deal with them.

Teachers might make arrangements to publish selected students' compositions in the school newspaper. A weekly or monthly newsletter could be started for this purpose as well.

Not only will tutees acquire information about specific subjects in these tutoring situations, they can acquire other, highly negotiable skills as well: getting information before beginning assignments, following directions, and paying attention.

Monitor   One way to evaluate tutees' progress in these programs would be for them to keep notebooks of their selections. To evaluate their progress, a few of their writings, over a period of time, could be shown to a judge. That person could be the youth's parent, another teacher, or someone else. It would be the judge's task to put the passages in order according to specified criteria such as the following: fluency or number of words, mechanics (such as grammar, punctuation, and spelling), sequence (logical progression of events), or other features. If the passages the judge believed to be the better ones were written last, it would appear that the student was making progress (see MONITOR 13 in Appendix A).

Reference   Whitt, J., Paul, P., & Reynolds, C.J. (1988). Motivate reluctant learning disabled writers. *Teaching Exceptional Children, 20*(3), 37–39.

PEER TUTORING: MOVING TOWARD BETTER RELATIONSHIPS

Tutors must demonstrate mastery of the subject matter they intend to instruct and be able to communicate and interact personally with their tutees. This tactic provides a model whereby tutors can identify and possibly adjust to a number of interpersonal situations that might arise as they work with tutees. In the cited research, this approach was initially involved to teach social skills to students. Later, it was arranged for students in academic situations.

Background

The purpose of this tactic is to alert tutors to the fact that they will probably experience interactions of several types with their tutees, not all of which will be positive for either party. There will be times when they, the tutors, are reinforced by the event, and times when they are not. Moreover, there will be occasions when their tutee is reinforced and at other times not.

In the cited study, students trained with this model served as tutors in a college learning center. This tactic could benefit most secondary students.

Who Can Benefit

1. Distribute the sheet listing examples of interactions (see Figure 2.7, Interaction Place Map).
2. Introduce students to the sheet by stating the following:
    a. Tutors are identified by mortarboard caps.
    b. Interactions are one-on-one.
    c. A plus sign indicates a positive effect from the interaction, a minus sign indicates a negative effect, and a zero indicates no effect.
    d. Reading across the top, the tutor in each case is enhanced by the tutor-tutee relationship.
    e. Reading across the bottom, the tutor is detrimentally affected by the relationship.

Procedures

FIGURE 2.7 Interaction Place Map

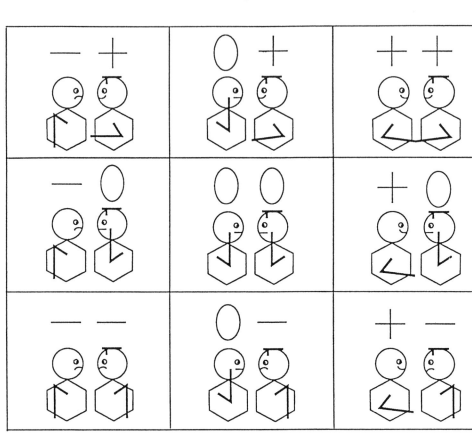

Note. From Leary, B.B. (1987). Interaction place maps: A tool for tutor training. *Journal of Developmental Education, 10*(3), p. 9. Reprinted by permission of author.

f. On the right side of the figure the tutee is enhanced, but on the left the tutee is adversely affected.

3. Present examples of the student–peer tutor scenarios.

a. (+,+) A student comes to the learning center for help with a research paper. The tutor recognizes that the tutee has put a great deal of time and effort into the paper. The tutee has specific questions about spelling and references, and the tutor is helpful. When the session is over, both individuals are pleased, and the goal of improving academic achievement has been met.

b. (+,0) In this situation the tutor experiences no change, even though the tutee benefits. This could happen if a tutee recited a number of facts while the tutor merely listened and gave occasional feedback.

c. (+,-) An example of the student benefiting and the tutor being adversely affected would be if a student came late to the tutoring session or came unprepared. Although the tutee could profit from the session, the tutor lost valuable time waiting for the student or helping him or her organize materials.

d. (0,-) The tutee in this situation comes to the learning center for help but doesn't pay attention to the tutor during the session. The tutee doesn't gain from the experience, and the tutor is frustrated by the interaction.

e. (-,0) The tutor in this case is burned out from tutoring unmotivated or unprepared students. Meanwhile, a well-prepared tutee comes to the learning center only to receive a half-hearted session. In this case the tutee is detrimentally affected, and the tutor is unaffected.

4. Request students to offer examples from their experiences that fall into each of the nine categories on the Interaction Place Map in Figure 2.7 and discuss each one.

5. Discuss additional examples as they come up.

6. Ask students to role-play some of the interactions and have other students identify which type of interaction is occurring.

Modifications/ Considerations

Beyond learning to identify the various types of interactions that might occur in tutoring situations, tutors should be prepared to deal with some of them. After all, the goal for these tutoring encounters would be that every session would be positive for both parties. Therefore, if a tutee came to the session unprepared, unmotivated, or in other ways not receptive to proper instruction, the tutor should have a few ideas in mind to deal with that. Furthermore, by being aware of the interactions that take place in tutoring sessions, tutors should realize more fully their responsibilities. For not only are they expected to coach the tutees on some subject, they are expected to deal with related social and motivational matters.

Monitor Tutors should keep track of the types of tutoring sessions by developing a checklist (see MONITOR 6 in Appendix A). Across the top the nine types of interactions would be printed, and down the left the names of individuals being tutored would be printed. On each day for each tutee the tutor would write the date alongside that student's name in the box that corresponded to the type of interaction. Those data, when studied over time, should reveal where certain interventions were required. If, for example, the data showed that with one student the tutor was never rewarded but the tutee was, the tutor should consider some change so that he got more out of the situation.

Reference Leary, B.B. (1987). Interaction place maps: A tool for tutor training. *Journal of Developmental Education, 10*(3), 8–12.

PEER TUTORING: A CLASSWIDE PROGRAM IN SOCIAL STUDIES

Background One idea behind this tactic is that many students, particularly those characterized as mildly handicapped, need opportunities to practice the facts, ideas, and concepts that are dealt with in secondary content classes such as social studies. To increase those opportunities, peer tutoring has been recommended. Another point that supports this particular peer tutoring program is that students who are mildly handicapped work with peers who have not been labeled as handicapped; this is certainly in keeping with the current Regular Education Initiative. A related point, one that is emphasized in several tactics in this set, is that students are often motivated to learn if they are allowed to work with other students, and there is a "payoff" for group as well as individual production.

Who Can Benefit

The referenced study was carried out by a regular classroom teacher with three classes of 10th graders. There were a number of mildly handicapped students mainstreamed into these classes. The tutoring program arranged in those social studies classes was an extension of a tutoring system developed by researchers at the University of Kansas (e.g., Delquadri, Greenwood, Whorton, Carta, & Hall, 1986).

Procedures

Following are procedures for implementing the program:

1.   Divide the class into two teams. Have students draw a red or a blue colored square from a box, then form a Red Team and a Blue Team.
2.   Randomly pair students within each team to form tutoring dyads.
3.   Set up a few sessions to train all the students on how to tutor. Those steps are detailed in number 6 below.
4.   Arrange 30-minute tutoring sessions in which one member of the pair serves as the tutor and the other as the tutee for the first 15 minutes. Schedule two sessions per week.
5.   Dictate the items on a 30-item study guide to the tutee.
6.   Require the tutee to write and say the answers to the questions. If the answer was correct, say "That's right" or "Correct" and provide three points for the response. If the answer was incorrect, say "That's wrong" and tell him or her the correct answer. Then require the tutee to write the correct response three times. Award 2 points for correcting the answer.
7.   Reverse roles at the end of the 15-minute period or when all 30 items on the study guide have been answered. Follow the same procedures noted above.

8. Award up to 10 bonus points for "good tutoring": clear and accurate dictation of questions, appropriate use of the error correction procedure, contingent and accurate delivery of points, and use of praise and support statements. (To deliver these, the teacher moved about the classroom during the sessions.)

9. Ask students to total up the number of points they earned during the session and record that number at the top of their paper.

10. Schedule a "surprise day" when the teacher checks the students' papers and awards 10 bonus points for each team member who correctly totals the points.

11. Post the students' scores on a laminated chart in front of the class.

12. Calculate the daily team totals.

13. Administer a weekly quiz on the study guide items and award students 5 points for each correct answer.

14. Calculate all the points for both teams following the weekly quiz and announce the winner.

15. Form a new set of teams following each 2-week period.

Modifications/ Considerations

Data from this research indicated that most students, including mildly handicapped ones, improved their scores on tests and corresponding grades as a result of the peer tutoring sessions. The authors noted that this program was carried out without disrupting other classroom features. They did point out, however, that it required considerable time to prepare adequate study guides. (Refer to Learning from Textbooks: Study Guides in Chapter 1 for a detailed outline on how to prepare study guides.)

This final tactic in the peer tutoring set has features similar to the tactics in the next group, those on cooperative learning. Sharan (1980) has detailed the differences between peer tutoring and cooperative learning situations in Table 2.3.

Monitor

In the Maheady, Sacca, and Harper (1989) article, the students' weekly scores on the quizzes were charted in terms of percentages (see MONITOR 2 in Appendix A). These scores were charted for a few weeks

TABLE 2.3 Differences Between Peer Tutoring and Cooperative Learning

Peer Tutoring	Cooperative Learning
Source and Variety of Information and the Nature of the Learning Task	
1. Information is transmitted by the teacher or a text.	Information is gathered by the pupils.
2. Learning sources are limited to cards, a worksheet, or lecture.	Learning sources are varied in number and kind.
3. Tasks emphasize information and/or skill acquisition.	Tasks stress problem-solving, interpretation, synthesis, and application of information.
Interpersonal Relations and Communication	
4. Peer communication in teams is primarily unilateral or bilateral (dyadic).	Communication in teams is primarily bilateral and multilateral (discussion).
5. Peer communication is for rehearsal of teacher-taught materials.	Peer communication is for interpretation and exchange of ideas.
6. Peer interactions frequently imply status distinctions ("I teach, you listen").	Interactions are primarily based on mutual exchange.
7. Pupils interact sporadically or in dyads.	Group members coordinate activities on a groupwide basis.
Academic Product, Evaluation, and Rewards	
8. Academic product is independent (i.e., there is cooperation in means but not in goals).	Academic product is interdependent (i.e., there is cooperation in means and in goals).
9. Evaluation is primarily individual (individual tests and scores).	Rewards are primarily intrinsic (self-directed interest in topic).
10. Rewards are extrinsic (reinforcement in the form of personal praise).	Evaluation is both individual and group (group report or project as collective project).
Classroom Organization	
11. The class functions as an aggregate of teams that are uncoordinated or engaged in a uniform task.	The class functions as a "group-of-groups" with between-group coordination and division of labor and tasks.

Note. Adapted from Sharan, S. (1980). Cooperative learning in small groups: Recent methods and effects on achievement, attitudes, and ethnic relations. *Review of Educational Research, 50*(2), p. 264. Copyright 1980 by the American Educational Research Association. Reprinted by permission of the publisher.

during a baseline, when the peer tutoring intervention was not in effect, and for a few weeks while the tutoring was scheduled. In fact, the researchers set up a multiple baseline design across classrooms: The intervention was scheduled in one class, then in another, and finally in the third.

References Delquadri, J., Greenwood, C.R., Whorton, D., Carta, J.J., & Hall, R.V. (1986). Classwide peer tutoring. *Exceptional Children, 52,* 535–542.

Maheady, L., Sacca, M.K., & Harper, G.F. (1989). Classwide peer tutoring with mildly handicapped high school students. *Exceptional Children, 55,* 52–59.

Sharan, S. (1980). Cooperative learning in small groups: Recent methods and effects on achievement, attitudes, and ethnic relations. *Review of Educational Research, 50*(2), 241–271.

COOPERATIVE LEARNING: CIRCLES OF LEARNING

Background According to Johnson, Johnson, Holubec, and Roy (1984), the essence of cooperative learning is positive *interdependence*—students recognize that they are in this together; they sink or swim as one. These situations are also characterized by *individual accountability*: Every student is accountable for both learning the assigned material and helping other group members learn.

Who Can Benefit The Johnsons (Johnson et al., 1984) maintain that at their best, cooperative learning experiences lead to the following: positive interactions, feelings of psychological acceptance, psychological success, self-acceptance and high self-esteem, and understandings of other students. The Johnsons recommend that teachers resist the advice they may have been given as beginning teachers to isolate students who pester others; teachers should, instead, integrate those students into cooperative groups.

Specify Objectives.   Teachers should specify objectives of two types: those that pertain to academic expectations and those that detail which collaborative skills will be emphasized.

Procedures

Make Decisions.   Teachers must decide on the size of the groups (i.e., from two to six; Johnson et al., 1984, recommend groups of two or three). Decide on how to assign students to groups and how long the groups will remain together (Johnson et al. recommend that the groups be as heterogeneous as possible, and stay together until some unit of work is finished). Decide how to arrange the room to facilitate the cooperative groups. Decide how the materials or information will be provided to the groups, and whether the members of the groups will be assigned roles (e.g., summarizer, checker, recorder).

Explain the Academic Task.   Explain the objectives of the lesson and relate the concepts and information to be studied to students' past experiences. Furthermore, explain the criteria for success on the academic task and inform students what is expected of them collaboratively.

Structure Positive Goal Interdependence.   Inform students that they have a group goal and must work collaboratively. Ask the groups to produce a single product, report, or paper. When completed, each member should sign the paper to indicate that he or she agrees with the report and can summarize its content. Provide group rewards.

Structure Individual Accountability.   Assess frequently the level of performance of each group member (e.g., give intermittent tests to each member, select at random one paper from the group to grade, ask members to explain answers, require members to edit each other's work).

Monitoring and Intervening. Teachers should roam about the room while the cooperative groups are functioning, and provide feedback and assistance as they do so.

Modifications/ Considerations

The authors (Johnson et al., 1984) noted that cooperative relationships are just as effective with teachers as they are with students; teachers are more effective when they have positive support from colleagues and can solve problems together. The enhanced product of collaborative groups has been supported in the context of teacher assistance teams by R. Beck (personal communication, 1990). When a group of teachers is asked to come up with a variety of interventions to arrange with academic and social concerns, the group will identify about three times as many as will a single teacher.

Monitor

Johnson et al. (1984) recommend that teachers use a formal observation sheet to count the number of times teachers observed appropriate behaviors of students. At first teachers may simply record who talked in each group to get a notion of the participation patterns. Later, they could gather data on the following: contributing ideas, asking questions, expressing feelings, actively listening, expressing support and acceptance, expressing warmth and liking, encouraging all members to participate, summarizing, checking for understanding, relieving tension by joking, and giving direction to the group work. It is important also to acquire data on the product of the groups' efforts on the academic task, and to evaluate the extent to which the various groups worked together.

Reference

Johnson, D.W., Johnson, R.T., Holubec, E.J., & Roy, P. (1984). *Circles of learning*. Alexandria, VA: Association for Supervision and Curriculum Development.

COOPERATIVE LEARNING: STUDENT TEAMS– ACHIEVEMENT DIVISIONS (STAD)

According to Slavin (1986), Student Teams–Achievement Divisions (STAD) is one of the simplest of all cooperative learning methods, and is a good model to begin with for teachers who want to get started with these arrangements. STAD is one of the oldest and most extensively researched forms of cooperative learning.

Background

This would be an excellent choice if a teacher's intent were to increase cross-racial friendships, because evidence to support the effectiveness of this approach in this area is strong. Researchers have also reported that youngsters' self-esteem was positively influenced when STAD procedures were arranged.

Who Can Benefit

Preparation

Prepare materials. Make a worksheet, answer sheet, and a quiz for each unit. This could be in the form of a study guide or a graphic organizer.

Assign students to teams. Organize teams in groups of four or five students who, to the extent possible, represent a cross-section of the class in terms of academic performance, sex, and race or ethnicity.

Determine initial base scores. Calculate each student's average score on a number of past quizzes.

Schedule of Activities

Teach. Tell students what they are about to learn and why it is important. Review any prerequisite skills or information. Stick close to the objectives

Procedures

that will be tested. Assess students' comprehension by asking questions. Require students to solve problems or in other ways become involved with the lesson. This might take one or two class periods, depending on the amount of information to cover and other factors.

Team study. Students study the worksheets in their teams. They have two copies of the worksheets and one answer sheet. Teams study the sheets until everyone knows the items. Have students explain answers to one another instead of merely checking one another's answers. If someone has a question, he or she should ask all members for help. While the teams are working, the teacher should circulate among them to keep them on track, to praise those who are doing well, and to help out those who have problems. This could take one or two class periods.

Test. Distribute quiz and inform students to work on it individually. When finished, ask students to exchange papers with members of other teams, or give them to the teacher for scoring. This might take up only a part of a period.

Figure Individual and Team Scores

Individual improvement scores. Students earn points for their teams based on the degree to which their quiz scores exceed their base scores. For example: score of 10 points above = 10; score of 20 points above = 20.

Team scores. Record each team member's points on a team summary sheet; add them up and divide by the number of members on the team.

Recognize team accomplishments. Give awards that indicate three levels: good team, great team, or super team. Those awards should be based on team averages.

Return quizzes. When the first set of quizzes (with base scores, quiz scores, and improvement points) are returned, the scoring system should be explained.

Every so often, recalculate the base scores. This should serve to gradually raise pupils' scores. After 6 weeks or so, change teams. This will give the students opportunities to know more of their classmates, and give them experiences in working with a wide range of individuals. Although the greatest proportion of a student's grade should be based on his or her actual quiz scores, or perhaps improvement scores, a student's team scores could make up a percentage of the grade.

Modifications/ Considerations

To evaluate the effects of this cooperative approach on academic performance, two phases could be arranged. During the first, or baseline, phase, pupils would work independently on their lessons, and in the next phase, they would be in cooperative groups. Data could be studied to determine which youth did better during which condition. Furthermore, the latter data would indicate which groups were generally productive and which ones were not. If the teacher wished to evaluate the students' self-esteem, a measure such as the *Coopersmith Self-Esteem Inventory* (Coopersmith, 1967) could be administered.

Monitor

Coopersmith, S. (1967). *The antecedents of self-esteem.* San Francisco: W.H. Freeman.

Slavin, R.E. (1986). *Using student team learning* (3rd ed.). Baltimore: Johns Hopkins University, Center for Research on Elementary and Middle Schools.

References

COOPERATIVE LEARNING: TEAMS–GAMES– TOURNAMENT (TGT)

Teams–Games–Tournament (TGT) is the same as STAD in every respect but one: Instead of the quizzes and the individual improvement score system, TGT

Background

uses academic tournaments in which students compete as representatives of their teams with members of other teams who are at the same academic level.

Who Can Benefit   A few studies have indicated that students in TGT groups gained significantly more friends outside their own racial group than did control students. Other studies have reported that more students in TGT groups believed it was important to do well in class than did control students, and that students in these groups named more friends than did youth in control situations.

Procedures   **Preparation.** Make a worksheet, a worksheet answer sheet, and a quiz for each unit you intend to teach. The worksheet could be a study guide or a graphic organizer. In addition, prepare a set of cards numbered from 1 to 30 for every three students. A question is written on each card.

Class Presentations. Material is initially introduced in a class presentation, in the form of direct instruction or a lecture-discussion conducted by the teacher.

Teams.   Teams are made up of four or five students who represent a cross-section of the class in every respect.

Games.   The basis of the games is content-relevant questions designed to test students' knowledge from the class presentation and team practice. Games are carried out with numbered questions on a sheet. They are played at tables of three students, each of whom is from a different team. A student picks a numbered card and attempts to answer the corresponding question. Players are allowed to challenge one another's answers.

Tournaments.   The tournament is the structure in which the games take place. For the first one the teacher assigns students to tables on the basis of their past performance: the top three students to table 1, the next three to table 2, and so on. This equal competition enables students of all levels to contribute to their team scores. On following weeks, students change tables depending on their performance in the most recent tournament. The winner at each table is promoted to the next higher table; the second scorer stays at the same table; and the lowest scorer is moved to a lower table.

Team Recognition. Determine individual improvement scores and team scores. For individuals, give points on an arrangement such as the following: more than 10 points below base score = 0 points; 10 points below to 1 point below base score = 10 points; base score to 10 points above base score = 20 points. To figure team scores, record each member's improvement points on a summary sheet, total the points, and divide the total by the number of members.

Schedule of Activities. Follow this cycle: Teach for one or two class periods, team study for one or two periods, and schedule tournaments for one class period.

Modifications/Considerations

After 5 or 6 weeks, assign students to new teams. For additional variety, use TGT for one part of your instruction and other cooperative methods for other parts. For example, use TGT in combination with STAD, either by having quizzes one week and tournaments the next, or by having a quiz the day after each tournament and counting both the quiz score and the tournament score toward the team score.

Monitor

The primary concern with this type of cooperative learning might be to determine the best possible combinations of students in which to place handicapped or at-risk youth. If so, it would be necessary to systematically place those boys and girls in a variety of groups and compare their data across groups.

Reference

Devries, D.L., & Slavin, R.E. (1978). Teams–games–tournament (TGT): Review of ten classroom experiments. *Journal of Research and Development in Education, 12,* 28–38.

COOPERATIVE LEARNING: COOPERATIVE INTEGRATED READING AND COMPOSITION (CIRC)

Background

According to its developers, a major objective of CIRC is to use cooperative teams to help students learn broadly applicable reading comprehension skills. Various aspects of reading—for example, story structures and reciprocal teaching—are incorporated in the approach and directed toward that objective.

Who Can Benefit

Although CIRC was designed as a comprehensive program for teaching reading, writing, and language arts in the intermediate grades, it would be an appropriate procedure to set up for at-risk or remedial youth in middle school or high school.

Procedures

Major Components of CIRC

Reading groups. Assign students to reading groups according to their reading level.

Teams. Assign students to pairs within their reading groups, then assign the pairs to teams composed of partners from two reading groups. Team members receive points based on their individual performances on quizzes, compositions, and book reports, and these points form a team score.

Basal-related activities. Assign a reading passage to the youth. This could be a story from a book of literature or a passage from a science or social studies text. Teachers set the purpose for reading by introducing new vocabulary, reviewing old vocabulary, and discussing the story after students read it.

Reading Activities

Partner reading. Students read the entire passage silently, then take turns reading it aloud with a partner, alternating paragraphs. Teacher circulates about the room as this is going on.

Vocabulary study. Students are given a list of new, difficult, or important words from the passage. They are asked to look up the definitions, write out the definitions in their words, and write sentences using each word.

Retell. After reading the story and discussing it in reading groups, students summarize the main points to their partner.

Subsequent Activities

Partner checking. After students complete each of the above activities, their partners initial a form indicating that they completed the task.

Tests. Students are given a comprehension test over the passage at the end of three class periods. Students work on their own.

Direct instruction in reading comprehension. Students receive direct instruction in specific reading comprehension skills (e.g., identifying main ideas) once a week.

Writing. Students write paragraphs or letters on topics of their choice or on specific, teacher-directed lessons. Students submit drafts of their writing to their teammates and the teacher.

Independent reading and book reports. Students are asked to read a trade book for at least 20 minutes every evening. Parents initial forms indicating that students read for the required time.

Other related activities could be involved in the CIRC program; for example, spelling, laboratory exercises, and special projects. Whereas classroom teachers could make use of the CIRC approach in a number of subjects, it would be quite appropriate for special teachers to arrange CIRC for students in resource rooms or in basic skills classes.

**Modifications/
Considerations**

Monitor There are some natural features to measure in a program such as this, but since the main emphasis is on reading, it would be a good idea to keep track of the time spent reading, number of books read, and rate at which the youth read orally and silently. Furthermore, data could be kept on the rate at which students write or say facts (or other features) about the passage.

Reference Stevens, R.J., Madden, N.A., Slavin, R.E., & Farnish, A.M. (1987). Cooperative integrated reading and composition: Two field experiments. *Reading Research Quarterly*, *22*, 433-454.

COOPERATIVE LEARNING: JIGSAW II

Background The original Jigsaw approach was developed by Aronson and colleagues (Aronson, Blaney, Stephan, Sikes, & Snapp, 1978). A few words about it are included in the Modifications/Considerations section below. A more practical and easily adopted form, Jigsaw II, developed by Slavin (1986) is described here.

Who Can Benefit Jigsaw can be used whenever the material to be studied is in written form. It is appropriate for students in subjects such as social studies, literature, and science in which it is important to learn facts and concepts and to relate them to one another.

Procedures **Preparation.** Select several chapters, stories, or other units, each covering material for two or three days. Identify four topics within the unit and make an *expert sheet* for each topic. A summary of important facts and concepts is included on the expert sheet, along with the definitions of necessary key words. To the extent possible, material on each topic should appear throughout the unit. Develop a quiz for each unit made up of at least eight questions (two for each topic).

Assign Students to Teams. There should be four or five students to a team; teams should be as heterogeneous as possible.

Assign Students to Expert Groups. Members of each team are assigned to expert groups. Each group is assigned a different topic within each unit. There should be no more than six students in each expert group.

Reading. Students receive expert topics and read assigned material to locate information on their topics (one class period).

Expert-Group Discussions. Students with the same topic meet in groups. Appoint a discussion leader for each group who keeps the discussion going and sees to it that everyone participates. While the expert groups are working, the teacher roams around the room and spends time with each group (one-half class period).

Team Report. Experts return to their teams and, in turn, teach their topics to the team members. Experts may question their mates after their report to see if they learned the material (one-half class period).

Test. Distribute quizzes. Students work alone on tests. When finished, they exchange quizzes with members of other teams for scoring (one-half class period).

Scoring. Give points for individual improvement and for team averages.

In the original jigsaw, each student within a team read material from different sources. This has the benefit of making the experts on each topic (who had read the same material) possessors of unique information. The drawback to this method, however, is

Modifications/ Considerations

that the teacher would have to find four (or as many as there are students in each group) related but different passages for students to read. Another way to vary the Jigsaw approach would pertain to evaluation. After the experts gave their reports, the students could write essays or give oral reports instead of taking written quizzes.

Monitor   If the major concern is to raise the performance level of students, then measures of some academic activity should be acquired for a few sessions before introducing the jigsaw procedure and a few sessions while it is in operation. Likewise, if the teacher believes that this cooperative learning technique might influence peer acceptance, locus of control, or something else, then measures that pertain to those attributes should be gathered before and during the process.

References   Aronson, E., Blaney, N., Stephan, C., Sikes, J., & Snapp, M. (1978). *The jigsaw classroom.* Beverly Hills, CA: Sage.
Slavin, R.E. (1986). *Using student team learning* (3rd ed.). Baltimore: Johns Hopkins University, Center for Research on Elementary and Middle Schools.

COOPERATIVE LEARNING: GROUP INVESTIGATION

Background   Group Investigation has its origins in philosophical, ethical, and psychological writings from the early years of this century. John Dewey would have promoted this approach to learning, because he viewed the classroom as a place to develop social skills for dealing with the complex problems of life.

According to Slavin (1990), Group Investigation is appropriate for integrated study projects that deal with the acquisition, analysis, and synthesis of information to solve multifaceted problems. The task should allow for diverse contributions from group members, and not be designed simply to obtain answers to factual questions. It would be ideal for teaching about the history and culture of a country, or major assignments of that sort. **Who Can Benefit**

In this approach, students progress through six stages. **Procedures**

Stage 1: Identifying the Topic and Organizing Pupils into Groups. The teacher presents a broad problem or issue. Students meet in small groups and write down all the things they would like to learn about the topic. Those ideas are shared in a class discussion. The idea is to come up with one list. Those ideas are written on the board and then classified. Students are grouped on the basis of their interest in any of the categories. The teacher may want to limit the size of groups or subdivide some popular categories in an effort to have equal numbers of students per group.

Stage 2: Planning the Investigation in Groups. After joining their respective groups, students select subtopics for themselves. They determine, as a group, which resources will be required to carry out their investigation. Each group comes up with a plan that details who is going to do what and how they will do it. The plans are posted.

Stage 3: Carrying Out the Investigation. Each group carries out their plan. While they are doing so, the teacher serves as a facilitator. When individuals complete their tasks they convene the group and present their findings. Other members discuss their work in progress. Summaries of the reports could be written and collected by one of the group members.

Stage 4: Preparing a Final Report. During this stage the essential ideas of the various reports are abstracted and combined. Each group appoints a

member to serve on a steering committee. Those individuals listen to the preliminary reports of all the groups and offer suggestions on drafting their final reports.

Stage 5: Presenting the Final Report. At this stage, the class as a whole is convened and the groups present their reports.

Stage 6: Evaluating Achievement. Teachers should evaluate students' higher level thinking about the subject they studied. They might do this by having the students tell or write about how they investigated certain aspects of the subject, how they applied their knowledge to the solution of new problems, how they used inferences from what they learned in discussing questions requiring analysis and judgment, and how they reached conclusions from sets of data.

Modifications/ Considerations

Following are some broad topics that would lend themselves to the Group Investigation approach: the Reconstruction era, the thirties and the Depression, chemistry and cosmetics, biology of the rain forests, natural disasters, the judicial system, U.S. Congress, civil rights.

Monitor

If evaluative information beyond that detailed earlier is desired, teachers could monitor pupils' affective experiences during the study, including their level of motivation and involvement. It might also be informative to interview the pupils, asking their opinions about the approach. The teacher could reconvene the steering committee as a focus group to evaluate the process.

References

Sharan, S., & Sharan, Y. (1976). *Small-group teaching*. Englewood Cliffs, NJ: Educational Technology Publications.

Slavin, R.E. (1990). *Cooperative learning: Theory, research, and practice*. Englewood Cliffs, NJ: Prentice-Hall.

COOPERATIVE LEARNING: CO-OP CO-OP

Co-op Co-op is similar to Group Investigation. It places teams in cooperation with one another to study a class topic. With this approach, students work together in small groups first to advance their understanding of themselves and the world, then to provide themselves with opportunities to express their new knowledge to their peers.

Background

This cooperative learning approach would be most suitable for students who had participated in other, more basic cooperative learning situations, such as STAD or Jigsaw II. Students should have acquired skills for working together and should trust one another.

Who Can Benefit

Following are the steps for carrying out Co-op Co-op.

Procedures

Step 1: Student-Centered Class Discussion. Encourage students to express their interests in the subject to be covered. That general topic might be the timber industry in the Northwest. The teacher could lead a discussion on this topic and attempt to discern what the students know about the topic, and should encourage students to express themselves freely on the subject. The success of this procedure is greatly dependent on the collective interest of the students that are involved.

Step 2: Selection of Student Learning Teams and Team Building. Assign students to four- or five-member heterogeneous teams.

Step 3: Team Topic Selection. Allow students in teams to select specific topics they intend to work on. Guide them to select topics that relate to the major theme—in this case, the timber industry. Inform all the groups of all the topics; point out how the topics are all connected. Roam about the room while the students work on their specific tasks and provide assistance.

Step 4: Minitopic Selection. Each member of a team should select a topic within the major topic; it should cover one aspect of their collective subject. Although some students may be able to take on more complex assignments than others, every student should make a contribution. Peers should support one another as they work on their assignments.

Step 5: Minitopic Preparation. Students should work individually on their assignments. Their preparation might involve library research, data gathering through interviews, or an expressive activity such as writing.

Step 6: Minitopic Presentation. When students have completed their assignments they present their results to their team. These presentations should be rather formal. Following the individual presentations, the team members discuss the total topic. They blend information from all the individual reports. During these presentations one team member might take notes and another could serve as a critic. Other students should be assigned specific roles. After this first meeting, students might go back to work on their individual assignments. They could clarify points that were raised during the meeting or expand on some of their commentary. Following that, they could reconvene.

Step 7: Preparation of Team Presentations. At this time, the team combines their individual reports into a common presentation. The form of the presentation would be determined by the content of the material. Nonlecture formats such as the following are recommended: displays, demonstrations, skits, and team-led class discussions.

Step 8: Team Presentations. For these, the teams control the classroom. They are responsible for using the time, space, and resources of the class. A timekeeper from another team should keep track of time. The team may wish to include time for comments and feedback from the class members.

Step 9: Evaluation. Consider evaluation of three types: (a) team presentations, to be evaluated by the class; (b) individual contributions to the team, to be evaluated by the teammates; (c) write-up or presentation of the minitopic by each student, to be evaluated by the teacher.

Particularly successful teams could be held up as models. During postpresentation interviews, the teacher might detect strategies that could help other teams in future Co-op Co-op units.

Modifications/ Considerations

In addition to the evaluations just suggested, the teacher could acquire data regarding pupils' impressions and opinions about the approach. Those suggestions could be considered when setting up future cooperative learning situations.

Monitor

Kagan, S. (1989). *Cooperative learning resources for teachers.* San Juan Capistrano, CA: Resources for Teachers.

Reference

ATTENDANCE

3

PUNCTUALITY: CLOSE THE DOOR ON LATECOMERS

Background

The following technique was designed as a measure to curtail tardiness to class, a chronic problem with students at the secondary level, particularly at-risk and remedial students. The approach explained here is quite natural: When it is time to begin the period, the door is shut and latecomers are not admitted.

Who Can Benefit

The technique explained here was one of several identified from a survey of 713 secondary schools throughout the country for dealing with late students. This procedure could be arranged by most secondary schools, particularly those that have "in-school suspension rooms" or other monitored locations for youngsters to attend when they are not in class.

Procedures

1. Stand at the classroom door to greet students as they pass in the hallway or enter into the classroom.
2. Close the door of the classroom immediately after the tardy bell and begin class activities without delay. Do not admit latecomers.
3. Notify students ahead of time that if they are late, for whatever reason, they are to report to the in-school suspension room and remain there for the remainder of the period. At the end of the period, or at some time during the day, check with the monitor of that room to see that they attended.
4. Assign a student to check attendance from a seating chart.
5. Schedule an activity to begin after the tardy bell.
6. Ask students to raise their hands if they have a current event to offer.
7. Give students points for sharing their reports. Make them brief so that several youth can present their information and earn points.

8. Enlist the help of a recorder to keep track of who offered the events.

9. Explain to the students what the points are worth. The points could be calculated into the youths' grades, or exchanged for secondhand books or school supplies.

Modifications/ Considerations

For this tactic to be successful, the following guidelines must be followed: (a) The consequence of coming in late must be precise and consistent (the door must always be shut when the bell rings, and no one should be admitted); (b) an important or interesting activity must be scheduled; and (c) a plan must be made to properly acknowledge those who *do* show up on time.

This tactic, designed to increase punctuality, was quite natural: If you don't show up on time, you don't get in. A number of other natural arrangements can be made with respect to time: If you don't show up on time, you miss the bus, train, or plane (unless they too are late); if you arrive late for some appointments, your meeting is canceled; if you are late for some shows or concerts, you don't get in; if some applications, letters, or payments aren't sent in on time, you are ignored, reprimanded, or fined. In all, it's a good idea to learn early on that it generally pays off to be prompt.

Monitor

The most obvious way to monitor this technique would be to keep track of the number of pupils who were tardy each day. To determine whether this tactic was effective for one teacher, a multiple baseline design across classes could be arranged. Baseline data in all of that teacher's classes would be obtained on the number of tardy pupils per day. Those data could be charted as frequency per day (see MONITOR 1 in Appendix A). After a few days, the intervention could be scheduled in one class, then in a few days in another, and so forth until the intervention was in place for every class. To evaluate the effects of the intervention, the teacher would compare the frequency of latecomers before the intervention with the number after, for each class.

Purvis, J., & Leonard, R. (1985). Strategies for preventing behavioral incidents in the nation's secondary schools. *The Clearing House, 58,* 349–353. **Reference**

PUNCTUALITY: THREE TECHNIQUES

As young adults, secondary level students must learn to take responsibility for their own successes and failures. Furthermore, career readiness is a vital part of secondary school instruction. The dependable, prompt individual will obtain and keep the job. Youth must learn to accept the responsibility for showing up for school on time just as they must later show up for work at the appointed hour.

Background

This tactic is especially suitable for remedial and at-risk students, because one of the prime characteristics of those youth is that they are often late for school. Regrettably, these are the students who can least afford to miss hours or even minutes of instruction. They need all the help they can get to stay in school, make acceptable grades, graduate, and move on to the world after high school.

Who Can Benefit

Three techniques are explained here to reduce tardiness. The following steps should be taken before any of them are introduced:

Procedures

1. Explain your desire to eliminate tardiness. Inform students that you want to assist them to develop positive job skills. Remind them that all jobs have rules and responsibilities.
2. Inform the students that you are disappointed in their behavior when they are tardy. There is no need to lecture or threaten them, however. Explain to them that when they arrive at class on time they will be given something they want, and

when they are tardy they will not receive the reward. Let them know that they are now in control of the situation, and that your job as the teacher is simply to record the attendance pattern accurately.

3. Be consistent. Explain clearly what you expect, what you will do, and the consequences for successful behavior. Keep an accurate record that is open and accessible to the students.

Daily Report Card

1. Develop a card such as that shown in Figure 3.1 or Figure 3.2. Negotiate with the student the reward he or she will be given for acceptable behavior. Rewards might include stereo time, free reading time, 5 extra minutes of break time.
2. Involve the parents. Require the student to take the card home each day. Parents can record the number of successful days and perhaps arrange a reward for acceptable behavior.
3. Drop this procedure when the student has been on time for an extended period.

Contract Card

1. Develop a contract similar to that shown on Figure 3.3. The contract specifies the behavior to be improved, how the pupil intends to improve it, how success will be measured, the time requirements, and the reward.
2. Post the contract where students can see it and record their progress.
3. Select this technique for more difficult cases and for maintaining attendance over extended periods of time.

Grade-Point Credit

1. Award points for completed assignments. Give additional points each day the student comes in on time.
2. Post the number of points required to earn each grade on the board, and explain this arrangement to the student.
3. Select this technique for students who need to be nudged not only to attend school but to get to work once they get there.

FIGURE 3.1 The Daily Report Card

Daily Report Card—Attendance
Name _____ Date _____ Class _____
Attendance: ☐ on-time ☐ tardy
Teacher's initial _____

Note. From Potthoff, J.O. (1979). Late again? Three techniques to reduce tardiness in secondary learning handicapped students. *Teaching Exceptional Children,* pp. 146 and 147. Copyright 1979 by The Council for Exceptional Children. Reprinted by permission.

FIGURE 3.2 The Daily Report Card Can Be Expanded to Include Other Behavioral Areas

Daily Report Card
Name _____ Date _____ Class _____
Attendance: ☐ on-time ☐ tardy
Classroom Behavior: ☐ good ☐ OK ☐ poor
Work/Participation: ☐ good ☐ OK ☐ poor
Comment _____
Teacher's initial _____

Note. From Potthoff, J.O. (1979). Late again? Three techniques to reduce tardiness in secondary learning handicapped students. *Teaching Exceptional Children,* pp. 146 and 147. Copyright 1979 by The Council for Exceptional Children. Reprinted by permission.

These techniques could be more or less complex. Certainly, more situations and different consequences could be written into any of the three.

The matter of showing up on time could be tied into a group activity in which some reward is granted to all individuals in a group if all of them attended school on time for a few days or so (or turned in acceptable assignments).

Modifications/ Considerations

FIGURE 3.3 The Contract Card

Daily Individual Contract				

Name _____ Date _____ Class _____

I would like to improve: _____

To improve I will: _____

This will be measured by: _____

Time limit: _____

Mon.	Tues.	Wed.	Thurs.	Fri.

Reward _____

Student signature _____

Teacher's signature _____

Note. From Potthoff, J.O. (1979). Late again? Three techniques to reduce tardiness in secondary learning handicapped students. *Teaching Exceptional Children,* pp. 146 and 147. Copyright 1979 by The Council for Exceptional Children. Reprinted by permission.

Monitor   In this project, as in many others, students could be encouraged to take on the responsibility of record-keeping, or it could be the joint responsibility of the youth and the teacher. An ongoing graph or record of prompt attendance (see MONITOR 1 in Appendix A) and performance could be displayed either privately or publicly.

Reference   Potthoff, J.O. (1979). Late again? Three techniques to reduce tardiness in secondary learning handicapped students. *Teaching Exceptional Children, 11,* 146–148.

ATTENDING: PEER GROUP SUPPORT PLUS REWARDS

Background

This tactic is based on the notion that if students are involved with their peers, they may be encouraged to attend class regularly. Certainly, at the secondary level youth are more reinforced by peers than by adults.

When students miss a day of school now and then, teachers must spend time with them, telling them what they missed and explaining how to do it, if they want them to stay on track. When students are chronically absent, dedicated teachers must take even more time explaining, providing examples, and generally helping them stay afloat. All of this special, individualized attention takes time that teachers could devote to other students, many of whom attend school regularly. To cut down on the expenses of extra, after-hours teaching is a goal of every teacher.

Who Can Benefit

In a study by Morgan (1985), marked improvement in daily attendance was noted for the pupils. The students in that research were 92 elementary students from lower socioeconomic backgrounds, many of whom had records of excessive unexcused absences. Since the procedures explained here are neither linked to a particular subject, nor dependent on the length of class periods, there would be no problem with applying them to the needs of remedial or at-risk secondary students. This technique might be administered by a teacher or counselor.

Procedures

1. Identify the pupils with records of poor attendance.
2. Place each of these target pupils with two other students who attend school regularly. If possible, identify triads of pupils who are good friends.

3. Explain to each trio that they will have the opportunity to earn rewards by working together as a group. Present these rules to them:
   a. If all three members attend school on a particular day, each member will earn one token.
   b. If the target member is absent that day, no one receives a token.
   c. If only the target pupil comes to school, he or she will get the reward, and if he or she and one other mate show up, they will be rewarded. Earning tokens is strictly dependent on the behavior of the absent-prone pupil.
4. Set the requirements for exchanging the tokens: For a certain number of tokens, students could earn privileges such as an extended lunch hour, a midday break, homework time in class, or the granting of a reasonable request. When tokens are exchanged for one of those privileges, that should be indicated on the Attendance Rewards Chart (Figure 3.4). Pupils who attend school for a certain number of days could earn larger rewards (e.g., points toward a class party in celebration of their effort).
5. Give immediate reinforcement in the form of tokens every morning or at the beginning of the class period.

Modifications/ Considerations

This tactic can be adopted for individual or total class attendance. In either case, a daily chart should be maintained. This will serve as an immediate source of feedback for the individual or class.

One method of determining which rewards might be effective would be to question the students. Some of them will have ideas for rewards that either they or other students would enjoy.

This tactic, as originally set up, provides two motivating factors: (a) the prospect of immediate rewards and (b) peer persuasion. Since the participation of individuals who are important to the target pupils is involved, the target student stands to learn the values of responsibility and working with others.

When setting up the triads—the target student and two pupils with better attendance records—the teacher may want to involve peers of the target youngster who are not necessarily their friends, par-

FIGURE 3.4   Form for Use with Attending: Peer Group Support Plus Rewards

ATTENDANCE REWARDS CHART

Week of _____

Rewards	1	2	3	4	Groups 5	6	7	8
Extended lunch period								
Midday break								
Class time for homework								
Personal request								
Class party								

Record date on which award was earned in correct space under group number. (Must be initialed by teacher.)

Constance Ballew, 1988.

ticularly for at-risk students. One of the characteristics often noted of those youth is that they associate too much with other at-risk students. This tactic might provide an opportunity for them to acquire friends, at least acquaintances, of a different type.

Monitor

This technique can, to some extent, be evaluated by the data from the Attendance Rewards Chart (Figure 3.4). By calculating the number of times the group (a triad) earned rewards, the teacher would learn about the effects of this tactic. If some groups never received a reward, then obviously a different technique should be arranged or a different combination of the students should be formed. By studying the groups' choices of "rewarding" events, the teacher would learn about their relative strengths. In addition to those data, the teacher should, of course, take data on the number of absences over a period of time (see MONITOR 1 in Appendix A).

Reference   Morgan, R. (1985). An exploratory study of three procedures to encourage school attendance. *Psychology in the Schools, 12,* 209–215.

ATTENDING: CONTRACTS AND LOTTERIES

Background   For this tactic, students open up "bank accounts" for which they receive "funds" each day they attend class. In addition, students can deposit a small amount once a week and have a chance to win a large amount in a lottery. In the referenced study, each method proved to be effective in increasing both attendance and participation in an aerobic exercise program.

Who Can Benefit   A study was conducted with 41 female college students over two academic quarters (Epstein, Wing, Thompson, & Griffin, 1980). The interventions explained here could be arranged for a variety of situations at the secondary school level, and would be particularly beneficial for remedial and at-risk youth.

Procedures   Contracting

1. Determine which students might benefit from the intervention.
2. Develop an "account" form for each student, with places to indicate a beginning balance, deposits, withdrawals, and daily balance.
3. Translate the value of "money" into school supplies that students can earn.

4. Tell students that they will start out with a balance of one dollar, to which they can add 25 cents every day they come to class.
5. Inform students that they will lose 25 cents for each day they miss class.
6. Require students to balance their accounts at the end of each week. Allow them to either cash in their funds for school supplies or bring their balance forward to the next week.

Lottery

1. Inform students that at the end of each week, those who were present all 5 days are eligible to take part in the lottery.
2. Require eligible students to donate 25 cents on the day of the lottery.
3. Conduct the lottery by placing slips of paper with the students' names on them in a container. Ask a volunteer to draw a name.
4. Give the winning student the total amount that was in the lottery.

Modifications/ Considerations

Epstein et al. (1980) have suggested that contracting works better than the lottery for initial attendance, but the lottery was more effective for maintaining attendance.

One way to increase the motivation for the bank account aspect of this tactic would be to pay interest on money held in student accounts; of course, the amounts given each day or for the beginning of the contracting program could be different from those suggested here. Furthermore, the amounts the students were allowed to place in the lottery could vary.

A way to enhance the effects of a lottery would be to hold it on random days of the week, so that students would be less likely to skip class for fear of missing their chance of winning the lottery.

Monitor

As with other attendance programs, the most straightforward way to measure the success of the ideas presented here would be to acquire data, over time, on the number of absences and who was absent. The teacher or counselor should, of course, gather these data prior to scheduling these techniques and during their involvement. Furthermore, the evaluator could determine the comparative effects of the techniques by relating the frequency of absences when "contracting" was in place to the frequency when "lottery" was scheduled (see MONITOR 1 in Appendix A).

Reference   Epstein, L.H., Wing, R.R., Thompson, J.K., & Griffin, W. (1980). Attendance and fitness in aerobic exercise: The effects of contract and lottery procedures. *Behavior Modification, 4*, 465–479.

ATTENDING: PRAISE AND REWARDS

Background   The idea behind this tactic is that a combination of praise and rewards can improve attendance. Although it should go without saying, teachers or administrators don't ordinarily praise youngsters for showing up at school. They expect them to do so and when they don't, they are disappointed and fuss at them for their nonattendance. As for rewards, the following are a few suggestions: Post the names of students with good attendance, send congratulatory letters to the students or parents, and award certificates to the students. In a study by VanSciver (1986), when rewards and praise were given to pupils, their attendance records were better than those of students who attended other schools that employed the usual policies of lowering grades and suspending students for poor attendance.

Who Can Benefit   The study was conducted with a sophomore class of approximately 100 students in a rural high school (VanSciver, 1986). This tactic could be arranged, however, for urban schools and for middle schools as well as high schools.

1. Explain the attendance improvement program to students. Inform them that copies of letters or awards received for good attendance will be included in their permanent files, and that future recommendations to employers or colleges will include mention of those outstanding attendance records.
2. Send a letter containing the same information to the youths' parents.
3. Deliver a statement about the importance of good attendance on several occasions during the first period of the day. Vary the message from week to week, but always emphasize the fact that teachers and administrators appreciate the responsible and positive behaviors that students show by coming to school each day.
4. Post the names of students who had perfect attendance on the school bulletin board at the end of each month.
5. Call parents midway through the marking period to congratulate them if their son or daughter had a perfect attendance record.
6. Send congratulatory letters at the end of the marking period to students with perfect attendance.
7. Publish the names of these "perfect attenders" in the local newspaper.
8. Send similar congratulatory letters to students who maintained their perfect attendance throughout the next marking period.
9. Award attendance certificates to students who had perfect attendance through two marking periods at a special school ceremony.

Modifications/ Considerations

The length of time that students must maintain perfect attendance to receive recognition may be modified, depending on their previous attendance records. Students who have especially poor attendance records may benefit from more frequent congratulatory letters and phone calls to their parents. For students who have fairly good attendance records, the procedure described here should be adequate. But whatever the "reinforcement schedule," it shouldn't be too lean. As indicated earlier, we generally and mistakenly take good attendance for granted.

In addition to the procedures that were explained, an attendance contest was held between homerooms in the study (VanSciver, 1986). For the contest, T-shirts donated by a local car dealer were awarded to students in the homeroom that maintained the best overall attendance for each marking period. The T-shirts were printed in the school colors, and on the front they read, "My homeroom maintained the highest daily attendance in the 1st (or 2nd) marking period of the 1984–85 school year." This proved to be an extremely popular part of the attendance program.

The general tone of this tactic is positive; therefore, it should create an environment for many opportunities to model positive attitudes. One could hope that the positive approach used to increase attendance could also promote more attention to assignments, better grades, and better attitudes toward self, school, and community.

Monitor The primary way to monitor the effects of this program would be to gather data on absences before and after the program was in effect. It would be informative also to interview or provide questionnaires to a number of students, teachers, and parents following the involvement of these techniques to learn which of the program's features were the most effective. Certain aspects may have been more influential for some youth than for others and some of the practices more difficult or expensive to carry out than others. That information would be helpful in making future plans for increasing attendance (see MONITOR 9 in Appendix A).

Reference VanSciver, J. (1986). Use rewards to boost student attendance (and public goodwill). *The Executive Educator, 6,* 22–23.

ATTENDING: SOCIAL REWARDS

Background This tactic is designed to help students improve their attendance at school by involving individuals who are

important to them in the process. Teacher cooperation is required for this tactic, because secondary students generally have multiple classes. Teachers who
wish to initiate this tactic may begin by helping students design contracts that exchange attention (in
the form of phone calls or special outings) from individuals who are important to them for attendance.
Contracting is cost-free, takes little time to implement, and has been shown to be effective.

A study (Bizzis & Bradley-Johnson, 1981) was **Who Can**
conducted with a 17-year-old, 11th-grade girl who **Benefit**
was classified as delinquent due to a history of truancy and other problems. This tactic should be considered for chronically absent high school students,
because it is based on naturally occurring consequences (attention from others). Those consequences
increase the likelihood that the positive results of an
intervention will generalize to other situations.

Design a chart on which students can record their **Procedures**
hourly attendance (see Attendance Chart in Figure
3.5).

1. Define attendance as being present when the
    morning bell rings and remaining in school for all
    class periods.
2. Help each student create a contract between him-
    self or herself and an individual of his or her
    choice who has agreed to participate in the
    project.
3. Incorporate telephone calls into the contracts by
    allowing students to call their designated friends
    at a specified time on those days they arrived on
    time and attended every class.
4. Provide bonuses in the contract such as outings
    with the student's partner for being in atten-
    dance a specified number of days in a row.
5. Instruct students to keep their attendance charts
    in their lockers and record a yes or no for whether
    they attended each class.
6. Inform target students to ask a neighbor at
    school to keep a chart in his or her locker on
    which the neighbor records whether the target
    students were present at the beginning and end
    of each day.

FIGURE 3.5 Form for Use with Attending: Social Rewards

ATTENDANCE CHART

Student _____

Class   Dates

Class														
English														
Social Studies														
Algebra I														
Study Hall														
Shop														
Computers														
Biology														
Checked by														
Call Made?														

Comments:

ATTENDANCE CHECK FOR _____

Class   Dates

Class														
Morning														
Afternoon														

Checked by _____
Locker # _____

Constance Ballew, 1988.

7. Compare target students' attendance records with teachers' records and reports from their school neighbors. Resolve any disagreements in these sets of data.
8. Renegotiate the contracts as attendance patterns change.

Modifications/ Considerations

Something to consider when scheduling this technique is that target students might try to contact their partners even though they were absent. Steps should be taken so that the partner is not available for calls on days when the student is absent. A daily message for the partner could be left at his or her office or home, stating whether the target student was in attendance for that day.

This tactic could be modified in a number of ways: The friends who are called could change from time to time, a number of friends could be identified as contacts, the friends could initiate the calls to the attending pupils rather than the other way around, target pupils might be allowed to call someone long distance if they showed up for school several days in a row.

An important benefit from this approach could be the increased interaction of students with those with whom they contact. Their partners could be prompted to reinforce the pupils for good attendance, and converse with them about matters that are generally reinforcing. Yet another source of reinforcement and communication to be derived from this technique could be the attention of those who might answer the phone for the designated individual being called. Those individuals, like the partners, could be cued to reinforce the absent-prone students and spend a few moments talking with them before they call the designated persons.

Monitor

Data regarding the effects of this technique are available from the attendance chart. In fact, those data indicate the specific classes the student attended. It might be revealed that a student "cut" only one or a few of his or her classes from time to time but showed up regularly for others. That would be informative to the student's teachers and counselor. The person who was called could also keep data. He or she could note when the calls came, how long they chatted, and what they talked about. That information might also be useful for future planning. If those conversations are recorded, they could be evaluated later (see MONITOR 16 in Appendix A).

Reference
Bizzis, J., & Bradley-Johnson, S. (1981). Increasing the school attendance of a truant adolescent. *Education and Treatment of Children, 4*, 149-155.

ATTENDING: THE QUARTER CREDIT PLAN

Background
Many students who are frequently absent from school never return. They have fallen so far behind it is no longer profitable to show up. This tactic attempts to remedy the problem by providing students with credit for attending class for brief periods. Because of this arrangement, students may be inclined to come to school more often.

To implement the Quarter Credit tactic, each subject is divided into two grading periods per semester. Students receive credit for those quarters they attend regularly.

Who Can Benefit
When this tactic was implemented in two high schools, as reported by Garcia (1979), the following improvements over the previous year were reported: 19% for attendance, 31% for tardiness, and 50% for missed classes. Related to increased attendance of the pupils, there were 25% fewer failing marks.

This method of improving attendance would be possible in those secondary schools where students could retake one-half of a semester to receive one quarter credit. The idea is that youth have more opportunities to acquire credits and are not "penalized" on an "all or nothing" basis as is often the case. When some students know that they can earn credits for a shorter period of time, they might muster enough energy and consistency to stick it out that long.

1. Explain the Quarter Credit concept to the classes and each pupil individually. Emphasize the fact that absences result in lower grades and fewer credits, whereas regular attendance is associated with better grades and credits earned toward graduation.
2. Set attendance standards for each quarter. In the cited article (Garcia, 1979), pupils were permitted no more than two unexcused absences per quarter. A third absence resulted in a failing grade due to attendance for that quarter.
3. Inform pupils that failure to maintain attendance standards for any one quarter will result in a lowering of the final grade for that class and will prompt a meeting between the teacher and the student's family.
4. Require pupils to sign an absentee form for each unexcused absence. This makes them aware of their "illegal" absences and keeps them informed of their progress.
5. Hold a meeting with the pupil's parents if their youth has not maintained the agreed on attendance requirements for any one grading quarter. Inform parents that students will have to take the class (or a portion of it) over again in summer school, or the next year, if they fail the attendance requirements for any grading period.
6. Explain to the students that if they fail to maintain attendance standards in classes that are required for graduation, they will have to take that quarter of the class over again, either in the summer or the next semester. Tell them that the grades earned during the two quarters they receive credit will be averaged together for their final semester's grade.
7. Point out to students each quarter how they stand with respect to grade-point average and credits earned toward graduation. Keep a detailed accounting for each student. Make certain that they know how many credits are required to graduate, how many they have, and how many they will have to earn each quarter to graduate at a predetermined time.

Procedures

8. Emphasize to students, in addition to the information just noted, the importance of credits and grades. Point out to them, vividly and accurately, what kinds of jobs or opportunities are available to them if they have certain grade-point averages and credits earned.

**Modifications/
Considerations**

It was found that the abilities and skills of the pupils in the study (Garcia, 1979) increased as a result of their improved attendance. They were relieved to have guidelines that mandated attendance that superseded peer pressure to skip class. An added benefit of this tactic is the involvement of parents in the student's education and school procedures. Furthermore, the incidence of crime and vandalism within the school in the cited study was remarkably reduced.

The well-defined consequences in this tactic should serve as a vivid illustration of the importance of dependability. Students will experience basically the same treatment they could expect in a work situation: that too many absences or late arrivals can result in dismissal.

Monitor

This project can be monitored by using the two forms in Figures 3.6 and 3.7. In the first, data are acquired on absences, tardies, and grades across the four academic quarters. Data pertaining to parent contacts throughout the year are summarized in the second form (see MONITOR 1 in Appendix A).

Reference

Garcia, E. (1979). Instant quarter credit concept: An answer to class cutting? *NASSP Bulletin, 63*, 39–43.

ATTENDING: SELF-RECORDING AND PUBLIC POSTING

Background

The idea behind this technique is that if young people keep their own records of attendance and perfor-

FIGURE 3.6   Form for Use with Attending: The Quarter Credit Plan

QUARTER CREDIT PLAN

Record of Student Attendance

Attendance
Standard:_____

_____

_____

	Quarter 1	Quarter 2	Quarter 3	Quarter 4
Tardies				
Absences				
Total T/A				
Attendance Grade				

Constance Ballew, 1988.

mance, and if those records are publicly posted, they will be motivated to increase their attendance and improve their performance. A number of investigations have indicated that both these practices are motivating.

The youngsters in the research (McKenzie & Rushall, 1974) were 16 boys and 16 girls who were from 9

Who Can Benefit

FIGURE 3.7   Form for Use with Attending: The Quarter Credit Plan

QUARTER CREDIT PLAN

Record of Parent Contacts

Parent Contacts	Date	Comments
Quarter 1		
Quarter 2		
Quarter 3		
Quarter 4		

Summary of Concerns/Action Taken/Results/Future Recommendations

Constance Ballew, 1988.

to 16 years of age. They were members of a swim team. The concern of this study was that those members had a poor attendance record, and when they did come to practice, many of them left early, didn't complete their workout, and in some instances, never entered the pool. Not surprisingly, the team had a poor performance record. They came in near the bottom in most of their competitions. The coaches, in an effort to turn that situation around and to develop a more competitive team, became harsh disciplinarians for behavior problems rather than trainers for swimming. This lack of positive attention and instruction created animosity between coaches and swimmers, and soon the attendance became even worse.

When self-management procedures and the public posting of records were introduced, the swimmers were able to monitor their own attendance and performance and see, over time, their improvements and those of others. As a result, the coaches were able to resume their roles as instructors, and team morale and performance improved.

This tactic would be suitable for teams of all sports: volleyball, football, basketball. It would also be an appropriate technique to arrange for classes where youth were engaged in cooperative activities, where everyone's performance influenced the reward or grade of everyone else.

Procedures

1. Record attendance and daily performance (i.e., laps per pupil) of each student before initiating the self-management and public posting procedures. (These data serve as a baseline.)
2. Design a team chart on which every member's name is written. Assign a different color to each member, and instruct them to chart the number of laps they swam each day (see Team Chart in Figure 3.8).
3. Provide each pupil with a colored marker that matches his or her color.
4. Determine individual goals for each student. They should be decided on by a trainer and each pupil.
5. Post the chart in plain view so that all team members can see the performances of all participants.

FIGURE 3.8 Team Chart for Use in Attending

TEAM CHART

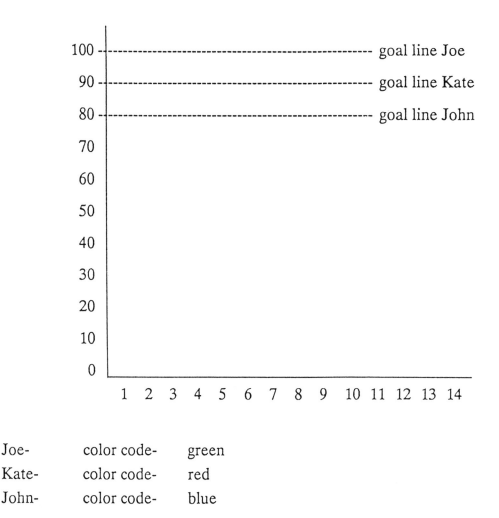

Joe-	color code-	green
Kate-	color code-	red
John-	color code-	blue

Kathleen Opie, 1988.

6. Raise the goals of students periodically as they become more proficient and more motivated to succeed.
7. Tie in these attendance and performance gains with the results that will hopefully occur in the various competitions.

8. Encourage the swimmers to similarly record data on other features of their swimming program: weight training, running laps, other exercises, and measures of diet.

Self-recording and public posting alone were successful in the cited study (McKenzie & Rushall, 1974), but in some instances it is necessary to arrange a consequence for the improved behavior in addition to self-monitoring. In those situations it would be a good idea to monitor the accuracy with which students self-record, and perhaps give them bonus points for counting reliably.

 For some students, a public display of performance may be aversive. This could further deter them from coming to practice and participating in the exercises. It might be a good idea to have them keep their records privately at first, then if they become more comfortable with their progress, they could join in with the group.

Modifications/ Considerations

In this project, data on the number of laps swum each day for each student are kept on the Team Chart (Figure 3.8). For additional information on recording frequency, see MONITOR 1 in Appendix A. As indicated in number 7 of the Procedures section, data should also be kept on the performances of team members at the various competitions. It is anticipated that a team would win more awards as they become more disciplined.

Monitor

McKenzie, T.L., & Rushall, B.S. (1974). Effects of self-recording on attendance and performance in a competitive swimming training environment. *Journal of Applied Behavior Analysis*, *7*, 199–206.

Reference

ATTENDING: INVOLVING PARENTS AND THE COMMUNITY

Recent studies have suggested that absenteeism is most common among students who have lower class

Background

standings, receive poor personality ratings from teachers, and don't participate in extracurricular activities. Those students usually have average or above average intelligence, but below average achievement levels. Because of a lack of interest or poor achievement, they often feel alienated from the school environment.

To get students back into the classroom these problems must be identified and alleviated. Toward that end, this tactic involves the cooperation of parents, schools, and the community.

Who Can Benefit   The study (White, 1979) was concerned with truant students in the upper grades. Since truancy typically leads to dropping out, which in turn means that students lose opportunities for education and schools lose portions of their state and federal funding tied to attendance, successful implementation of this tactic would be beneficial to students, schools, and society in general.

Procedures   1.   Inform students and parents, in writing, of the school's attendance policy, and clearly explain the consequences of absences.
2.   Remind students and parents of the attendance policies.
3.   Enforce these policies consistently.
4.   Write letters to notify parents of students' absences. Include the name of someone they can reach to answer their questions, such as a teacher, an administrator, or a counselor.
5.   Involve parents by asking them to call the school to excuse students when they are legitimately absent.
6.   Reward good attendance to show students that their school system is interested in their being at school.

Following are additional suggestions from the study (White, 1979):

1.   Schedule special activities on Mondays and Fridays, the worst days for absenteeism. For example, social events could be planned, or class scheduling could be varied by beginning school

later with shortened lunch or homeroom periods. School yearbooks, rings, or activity tickets could be distributed on those days as well.

2. Invite someone from a local business to visit the class to discuss the importance of a good attendance record for seeking employment.

3. Sponsor attendance contests, giving specific, tangible rewards (e.g., special seating at assemblies or class parties).

4. Establish a "buddy" system in which each student is responsible for someone else's attendance and for seeing that students who are absent receive makeup assignments.

5. Review attendance records at the beginning of the year with each student to establish the importance of regular attendance.

Modifications/ Considerations

Students must be given a feeling of being an important part of the school system. They must believe that their presence matters to everyone involved. Teachers might help convince students of this by offering incentives and rewards for good attendance. Some rewards might be extra free time, music in class, or bonus points toward a final grade. Donations from the community could be solicited and offered as prizes. Class contests could be arranged for special parties, awards, or seating in assemblies.

Students are usually good at offering their ideas for rewards. Class members could vote on suggestions made by students that were acceptable to teachers. Special consideration should be given to those rewards most likely to work for the students who are frequently absent.

Monitor

Beyond keeping data on attendance, and reviewing those data carefully with regard to who was absent, when, and for what reasons, data could be kept on several of the suggested interventions in this program. Students involved in the buddy system, for example, could keep track of who they called, when, and what the results were. And students could be interviewed, using either a structured set of questions or an open-ended format, following the talks given by civic leaders on the importance of education, school, attendance, and other matters. They could be asked about their impressions of what was said and, importantly, whether the individual's message caused them to value schools and education more highly (see MONITOR 9 in Appendix A).

Reference   White, E. (1979). How to reduce absenteeism, save money, help kids. *The Executive Educator, 1,* 24–26.

ATTENDING: PARENTAL INVOLVEMENT AND IMPROVED INSTRUCTION

Background   This tactic is based on the idea that students will be influenced to attend classes if their parents encourage them to do so. Students in the referenced study indicated that they would welcome family interest in their lives. Teachers reported that parents were receptive to comments about their children that were timely and indicated their concern or interest.

Since it was also learned in the study (Suprina, 1979) that the best deterrent to absences was a stimulating class, an effort was made to improve instruction. In addition to parental involvement and improved instruction, activities were outlined in case substitute teachers were called on. The latter activity was carried out because a survey of students indicated that a significant opportunity for skipping classes was when substitute teachers took over.

Who Can Benefit   The referenced study (Suprina, 1979) was conducted with students in a New York high school. This tactic would be appropriate for at-risk and remedial students in most locations.

1. Identify students with frequent absences.

2. Ask students what they think about the class routine as it is, and what they would do to make it more interesting. By asking about this, teachers will obtain insights as to the students' perceptions, and thus be able to make changes to encourage their attendance. Particular attention should be paid to the comments or expressions of agreement of students who are frequently absent.
3. Identify activities with the students that are interesting to them, to be used later, when the class is managed by a substitute. A current and relevant video or film, or a visiting speaker such as a local athlete or person from industry, may be interesting enough to prompt students to attend class.
4. Meet with parents and students together to address any special concerns and to explain the following guidelines that were established in the referenced study:
   a. Upon determining that an illegal absence has occurred, the teacher will discuss it with the pupil and mail an illegal absence report to his or her home.
   b. If a second illegal absence occurs, the teacher requests a parent conference through the guidance office. At this conference the criteria necessary to maintain enrollment in the class are discussed and an agreement is signed by all concerned.
   c. If continuous attendance is not maintained, the student is permanently withdrawn from the class. It must be clearly understood that such action may delay the student's graduation from high school.
   d. Students withdrawn from class are assigned to a restricted study hall during that class period. Cutting this study hall, or behaviors resulting in disciplinary problems, are grounds for suspension.

An important part of this tactic is the parent conference that takes place when there is a second unexcused absence. At this conference, there should be discussion about the pupil's performance in class, his or her attitudes, and efforts to get along in school. In the cited study (Suprina, 1979), these meetings improved the relationships among the students, educators, and parents. The initial meeting could cover some of the same topics to establish a rapport between those involved, without waiting for unexcused absences to stimulate a conference.

This tactic relies heavily on parental involvement. Parents might incorporate a reward system to further encourage regular attendance. Rewards could be privileges, relief from household duties, or additions to savings accounts for special purchases.

Monitor   Attendance may be checked against a seating chart and recorded on a master list. This allows a substitute to take attendance quickly without having to call out names. Students can also keep track of their own attendance by checking off days on a calendar or on another form.

In addition to keeping those data, valuable information could be gathered from parents. Periodically, parents of "absent-prone youth" should be interviewed to determine what they were doing to keep their youth in school (particularly if they were successful). A compilation of those techniques could be of great help to other parents and teachers, and counselors as well (see MONITOR 9 in Appendix A).

Reference   Suprina, R.N. (1979). Cutting down on student cutting. *NASSP, 63*, 27–31.

DEALING WITH ESTHETICS: RENOVATING URBAN SCHOOLS

Background   The dismal picture of America's urban schools, particularly the high schools, is now widely known:

shattered windows and leaky roofs, malfunctioning plumbing and inadequate heating, crowded classrooms and noisy hallways, limited supplies and antiquated textbooks, spattered walls and dirty floors. Should anyone be expected to work, creatively and productively, under such wretched and dismal conditions? Educators, psychologists, anthropologists, and architects have for some time recognized the effects of physical settings on production and learning. If we are to expect individuals to teach and learn, we must provide them with better settings than many of them now have.

Who Can Benefit

If schools were more esthetically pleasing, everyone would benefit. Certainly the youth who are expected to show up, learn, and socialize would profit from more pleasant surroundings. Likewise, teachers would be more motivated to attend regularly and teach, because not only are the circumstances appalling for youth, they are just as bad for teachers. Many of them do not have adequate offices or places to prepare for teaching, and their "teacher lounges" are unappealing and uncomfortable. Professionals in other occupations would not be expected to function in such drab settings.

Most parents would be delighted if schools were more appealing. It cannot be too reinforcing for them when they visit schools to see the old and unkempt structures that house the future leaders of America.

Many at-risk youth would be particularly motivated by school buildings, classrooms, and related facilities if they were more appealing, because many of them come from dreary and dingy circumstances. Not a few of them live in homes that are in states of disorganization and disrepair; the homes of their friends are similarly wretched; the shops and stores at which they interact are shabby and cluttered. Many of these youngsters rarely see buildings that are functional and beautiful. We contrast this state of affairs to the environments of many suburban youth who live in beautiful and organized homes, shop in functional and pleasing centers, and generally live in a world that is visually pleasing. If schools were more appealing, they would be sanctuaries for many at-risk youth.

Procedures   What can be done about it?

1. At the very least we could attend to the interiors of schools. As it is, many of the walls are barren (except for graffiti), and there are no flowers, paintings, or sculptures. Certainly, the members of the home living, industrial arts, and art departments could do something about this.

2. Most schools are terribly noisy. Some of this could be overcome by carpeting a few rooms or hallways, staggering schedules so that everyone does not move from one location to another at the same time, placing a few hangings along hallways or in classrooms to absorb some of the noise (and at the same time provide beauty). Several departments could help out with these matters.

3. Much of what comes over the public address systems in high schools is boring, threatening, or disruptive. Very little entertainment or beauty comes out of the speakers. Certainly the music, drama, and communication departments could see to it that more pleasing sounds came over the airwaves.

4. Businesses could be encouraged to provide money to repair or remodel. Many of them could donate money for specific projects, ones that would bear their names.

5. Architectural firms and landscape designers could be contacted to provide ideas and plans for renovating and restructuring the buildings and grounds.

6. Contractors, developers, and builders could be persuaded to donate services for remodeling and repairing the exterior and interior of buildings.

Modifications/   It is particularly important to renovate urban
Considerations   schools, because these crumbling, poorly maintained, uninviting inner-city schools distract teachers and students from the business of education. Toward this end, according to Piccigallo (1989), we need to ask two questions: To what degree can city youths be expected to believe that education is the principal route out of urban squalor and despair when society is either unable or unwilling to rescue their schools from similar conditions? And what message of self-worth and societal expectation does the

abysmal physical state of inner-city schools convey to students who have no choice but to attend them or drop out?

Data of several types could be kept on the effects of improving school environments: numbers of drop-outs; numbers of drop-backs; teacher attendance; parent involvement with schools; parent, administrator, teacher, and student impressions of the physical plant; involvement of business, industry, and community in the school (see MONITOR 1 in Appendix A).

Monitor

Piccigallo, P.R. (1989). Renovating urban schools is fundamental to improving them. *Phi Delta Kappan, 70,* 402–406.

Reference

TRANSITION FROM MIDDLE SCHOOL TO HIGH SCHOOL: BRIDGE

The transition from middle school to high school is a rough one for most students, but it can be especially difficult for disadvantaged and at-risk youth. A curriculum guide developed by the Northwest Regional Educational Laboratory (1989) is designed to bridge that gap and to keep discouraged learners and at-risk students in school while enhancing their employability.

Background

As indicated, the referenced curriculum is designed particularly for disadvantaged and at-risk students. Many other youngsters could profit from this program, because more students drop out of school at

Who Can Benefit

around the ninth grade than at any other time. The BRIDGE curriculum provides a structured sequence of activities designed for high school freshmen and sophomores.

Procedures

The activities in this curriculum revolve around skills that are seldom addressed in the standard high school curriculum. According to the program's author, Andrea Baker, "If students don't experience success right away, they may opt to leave. They often don't have the social skills and self-esteem to battle what can be a tough environment."

Recent studies on student retention have identified elements of school programs that make a difference for at-risk students, the most critical of which are (a) integration of academic skills, personal growth, and work; (b) individualized and personalized instruction; (c) cooperative and team learning; (d) use of real-life problems and situations as learning context; (e) experiential learning strategies; (f) consistent rewards for success; and (g) making connections between learning and earning. BRIDGE is designed to address those elements.

The curriculum guide contains 18 units, each of which is to be covered in about 2 weeks: (a) self-esteem; (b) self-responsibility; (c) decision making; (d) time management; (e) conflict resolution; (f) communication; (g) peer relationships; (h) career awareness; (i) leadership; (j) career goals and expectations; (k) multicultural/multiethnic awareness; (l) me, myself, and I; (m) traditional and nontraditional roles; (n) substance abuse; (o) self-preservation; (p) community resources; (q) planning for summer; and (r) using leisure time.

Each unit begins with an overview of the topic and responds to the question, "Why should I care about this topic?" The second component of each unit features relevant and provocative quotations on the topic for the students to think about and discuss. In each unit there is also a presentation of terms that are particularly relevant to that topic. Some words in the self-esteem section are *goal*, *cooperate*, and *success*. There is a series of about eight activities for each unit that range from role-plays to word jumbles, discussions, and reading assignments.

BRIDGE was conceived by Public/Private Ventures (P/PV), a Philadelphia-based educational agency. Cost of the BRIDGE Curriculum Guide is $115.95. To order the guide, contact The Private Industry Council, 520 S.W. Sixth Avenue, Suite 400, Portland, OR 97204, (503) 241-4600. For information or technical assistance, contact Andrea Baker at 1-800-547-6339.

Modifications/ Considerations

At the end of each unit, the students have an opportunity to synthesize and reflect on what they learned and to think about ways to apply the new information to their lives. The true evaluation of this program would come from interviews of selected youth who participated in the BRIDGE program a few weeks after they began high school. They should be asked about the difficulties they are experiencing in their adjustment, how the program prepared them to cope with high school, and what more could be done in middle school to make the transition even smoother. Parents of these youth and a few of their high school teachers should also be interviewed to learn about their impressions of the BRIDGE program and the general process of transition (see MONITOR 9 in Appendix A).

Monitor

Curriculum guide provides "BRIDGE" to high school. (May, 1989). In *Northwest Report, The Newsletter of the Northwest Regional Educational Laboratory,* 101 S.W. Main Street, Suite 500, Portland, OR 97204.

Reference

DROPOUT PREVENTION: WHAT SCHOOLS CAN DO

In 1985–86 more than 600,000 young people dropped out of public schools at an estimated cost to society of

Background

$120 billion in lost productivity throughout their life-times. Beyond that startling figure there are incalculable losses in terms of wasted or unfulfilled lives because of not graduating from high school. According to the author of the cited research, there are a number of areas—attending among them—that educators must consider to cut down on the number of dropouts.

Who Can Benefit

To curtail the number of dropouts, educators must make early and continuous contacts with students who often miss school, and devise ways to keep them coming to school. Attendance is a particular area of concern for at-risk youth.

Procedures

Following are a few activities that schools might consider to reduce the number of dropouts:

1. Develop a comprehensive attendance policy and communicate it to students, parents, and civic leaders. This policy should state clearly that every student should be in school and that the school values attendance.
2. Devise a systematic accounting system for early identification and continuous monitoring of student absences with special attention to students with chronic absenteeism.
3. Inform parents immediately when their child is absent by writing letters, using volunteers or automatic calling machines to notify them, or asking a local radio station to announce daily the names of student absentees.
4. Develop a makeup program for excessive absences that is flexible enough to accommodate a wide range of situations, but rigid enough to discourage abuses.
5. Identify incentives for good attendance for individuals, classes, and schools. Reward individuals and groups for perfect and near perfect attendance for a period of time by recognizing them in local newspapers or on radio and television stations, or by issuing tickets with which students can select items from a menu of prizes. Schools can also acknowledge attendance with ribbons, buttons, trophies, plaques, certificates, savings bonds, and coupons from restaurants.

6. Encourage teachers to communicate the importance of being in school by using statements such as the following each day: "I'll see you in the morning," "Tomorrow we will talk about . . . ," "Next Tuesday is the day our special . . ."
7. Organize peer groups whose members call one another each morning to encourage others to show up for school, particularly those who are inclined to find other things to do.

Modifications/ Considerations

When students must be removed from a class for disciplinary reasons, an in-school suspension program is better than out-of-school suspension for at least four reasons: It keeps students under supervision; it ensures that they keep up with their academic work; it pays economic dividends when funds are allocated on the basis of attendance; it does not allow them the opportunity to find things to do away from school, many of which are not socially acceptable. We should point out to students a saying of Woody Allen's: that 80% of success is simply showing up.

Monitor

It is rather simple to monitor attendance. Attendance secretaries could keep a running record of how many students come to school each day (see MONITOR 1 in Appendix A). They could be encouraged to alert teachers to students who have a certain number of absences in a row or who miss school intermittently but more than they should. These attendance data, if plotted daily, could serve as baseline measures from which systematic efforts to cut down on the rate of absences, hence dropouts, could be evaluated.

Reference

Hamby, J.V. (1989). How to get an "A" on your dropout prevention report card. *Educational Leadership*, February, 21–28.

DROPOUT PREVENTION: A THREE-WEEK PLAN

Background

Chronic attendance problems create difficulties for teachers and students. Although teachers take roll, they don't ordinarily get further involved in their students' attendance problems. A practical procedure for chronic absenteeism is the attendance contract and a 3-week monitoring period. Using a support group—parents, counselors, other teachers—a designated teacher can take charge of a particular student's attendance. This involvement requires teachers to address the students' attitudes about attendance, and to counter them actively with motivational support.

Who Can Benefit

Students who miss classes fall behind in credit and as a result have a poor image of themselves. They need support to break the cycle and should benefit from this tactic.

Procedures

1. Plan time for being an active attendance monitor. Approximately 5 hours are required to set up the program. Familiarize yourself with the details of the program and your school's attendance procedures. Interest other teachers and students in helping students with attendance problems. Identify other school resources: counselors, psychologists, administrators.

2. Identify a student with poor attendance (e.g., absent 3 days out of 10) in one of your classes. Check the school attendance records to see if the student was absent 20 or more full school days the previous school year. Obtain the student's address, parent's name, phone number, and current class schedule.

3. Confer briefly with the student's counselor; establish contact with the home. Maintain contact with the counselor on a weekly basis, as he or she can determine whether the student has followed through on his or her commitments.

4. Schedule a special meeting with the student. Plan at least one day in advance if you need to remove him or her from class for the meeting, so you can leave a hall pass in the teacher's box the day before.

5. Inform the student as to the purpose of the meeting.
   a. Explain that you want to become more active in encouraging the student's attendance. Discuss the student's past perfor-

mance. Ask permission to take notes on the conversation.

b. Explain the 3-week attendance monitoring program, including the daily check-in procedures.

c. Gain a commitment from the student to attend classes. Discuss his or her class schedule and requirements, credits earned, and strategies for being a successful student. Outline the help available if the student agrees to become a better student. Discuss career and educational goals with the student and the relationships among long-range goals, school attendance, and success.

d. Write a behavioral contract for attendance; explain that you will contact the student's parents and other teachers, and will share the results of those discussions at the next meeting. Stress both positive and negative consequences of attending school. Positive consequences include successful feelings in school, friendly conversations, points, and counseling. Negative consequences are pre-arranged with the teacher the first time, a call to parents the second time, a vice principal/case conference the third time, and the loss of credit for the fourth infraction.

e. Sign the contract.

f. Arrange a meeting for the next day.

6. Schedule daily meetings with the student. Require the student to carry an attendance slip to each class for 3 weeks. Each teacher signs the slip and indicates whether the student arrived on time, completed his or her work, brought proper materials, or if a conference was needed. The student brings the completed slip to the teacher each day and makes plans for the following day. If pupils cut a class during the program, they must begin again until they achieve 15 days of perfect attendance.

7. Arrange meetings with the student's other teachers. Send them notes stating that you will contact them at a specified time unless they contact you at their convenience.

8. Call the student's parent(s) or guardian(s). Introduce yourself, your role, and establish your interest in their student:

      a. Discuss student's past performance; ask permission to take notes.

      b. Explain the attendance monitoring program, including the sequential consequences of a phone call home and a case conference.

      c. Encourage parents to provide positive reinforcement at home for their youth's success.

9. Chat with the student's other teachers by phone or in person. Explain your role in the student's attendance program. Discuss the student's previous and current attendance pattern; ask about the teachers' concerns regarding the student; explain the daily attendance check and set up a weekly communication appointment. Other teachers play an important role by reinforcing the student daily and providing feedback on class performance.

10. Go over parent and teacher contacts at the second student interview. Check attendance of the previous day(s), and go over problems and successes of the previous day(s). Give out the daily attendance sheet for the following day. Arrange for positive and negative consequences. If the student does not show up, call his or her parents. If the student arrives, the positive consequence may be points, a coke with a peer or counselor, or some other article or event. If you are unavailable for one of the daily checks, arrange for someone else to take over.

11. Call parent(s) and contact teachers with information about the process after one week.

12. Continue daily student contacts and weekly parent and teacher contacts, *unless:*

      a. The student has perfect attendance for 3 weeks, in which case drop to weekly teacher, parent, student contacts.

      b. The student arrives without a slip, in which case contact a parent. If the student does not arrive with a slip after parent is contacted, contact the counselor who will talk to student and/or parent(s). A further infraction leads to a referral to the vice principal for case conferences, or a parent visit to school is scheduled.

13. Send a congratulatory letter to the parents on completion of the 3-week daily program, and give an award to the student. The student carries

attendance slips for 6 weeks more, but only one day per week. If a student backslides on attendance during the weekly checks, reschedule the daily monitoring.

Following completion of the six weekly checks, the student should take charge of his or her attendance. Send a congratulatory letter to the parents, and invite the student for counseling as needed. Thereafter, make occasional attendance checks, especially during the first weeks of each quarter.

Modifications/ Considerations

Students with chronic attendance problems often have better attendance in some classes than in others. Discuss their personal preferences with them, and take their comments into account with regard to other classes.

This program was field-tested with chronic absentees, and with an attendance counselor rather than the teacher as the initiator. Although teachers would be in the best position to carry out the program, as explained here, it may be too time-consuming for them to do so, particularly if they have two or three students in their classes who are absent a great deal. It may be necessary, therefore, in some schools to hire personnel whose primary responsibilities are to work on attendance and dropout prevention programs. Perhaps those individuals' salaries could be paid by industries or businesses in the district.

Monitor

Like the other projects in this set, the primary data to be kept are in regard to attendance. Those data should be kept before and during the involvement of a program. In this particular program, data might be gathered on various features of the intervention: parent contacts, interviews with the pupil, conversations with other teachers (see MONITOR 9 in Appendix A).

Reference

Stoker, J. (1980). *Grab H.O.L.D.: Help Overcome Learner Dropouts. Classroom guidance manual.* San Jose, CA: Resource Publications.

DROPOUT PREVENTION: A CHECKLIST

Background Early identification of potential dropouts can be the key to prevention and intervention. An inexpensive and reliable instrument for teachers to use to identify these students is Fox's Potential Early Leaver Profile (Fox & Elder, 1980).

Who Can Benefit The obvious students to profit from this approach are those who evidenced characteristics of a dropout but were identified and encouraged to stay in school.

Procedures Periodically, fill out the Fox Profile (Fox & Elder, 1980) on students, particularly those who are at risk of dropping out of school.

Potential Early Leaver Profile

Variable	Indicator
1. Age	Two or more years older than classmates
2. Physical size	Small or large for class group
3. Health	Frequently ill, fatigues easily
4. Academics	One or more years behind in basic skill areas
5. Father's job	Unskilled or semi-skilled
6. Parents' education	Grade 7 or below
7. Family size	Five or more
8. Transfers	Pattern of jumping from school to school
9. Learning rate	Below 90 IQ or 30th percentile
10. Adjustment	Fair or poor

Variable	Indicator
11. Graduation	Negative parental attitude toward diploma
12. Broken home	Absence of father or mother or both from family
13. Activities	Little or no participation in school activities
14. Other activities	Little or no participation in acceptable community activities
15. Attendance	Chronic absenteeism (20 or more days per year)
16. School grades	High proportion of Ds and Fs
17. Authority	Resents school control
18. Peer relations	Not liked or accepted by fellow students
19. Interest	Little or no interest in schoolwork
20. Reading	Two or more years below grade level

Two other important considerations not mentioned by Fox:

21. Minority group membership, especially Hispanic or black
22. Works more hours per week than attends school

Modifications/ Considerations

It is important to keep in mind that these 22 points are only red flags, and that the identification of five of them (as suggested by the author) is not totally correlated with dropping out of school. Certainly, there are youngsters who drop out of school who had fewer factors noted, and students who stayed in school who had more than five identified items. Furthermore, some factors on the list are more important for certain youngsters than are other items. We must also be aware that there are factors other than those listed that have prompted students to exit schools. Nonetheless, teachers, counselors, and administrators should be on the lookout for youngsters for whom a number of the noted factors are true. Correspondingly, something should be done about that in an effort to counter those forces and help the youth to stay in school.

Monitor Certainly, schools should keep data on dropouts (see MONITOR 1 in Appendix A). To do so, they must adopt a suitable and agreed-on definition of dropouts. For example, high school dropouts are those students whose school status meets the following criteria: (a) no longer enrolled in school, (b) not formally transferred to another institution, and (c) not awarded a high school diploma or its equivalent. It could also be important to note why some students had been told not to come to school: habitual disruptive behavior, delinquent behavior, suspension from building, age over mandatory limit, poor attendance/nonattendance.

References Fox, W.M., & Elder, N. (1980, February). *A study of practices and policies for discipline and dropouts in ten selected schools.* North County, NY: North County High Schools. (ERIC Document Reproduction Service No. ED 191 974)

Ohio State Department of Education. (1983). *Reducing dropouts in Ohio schools: Guidelines and promising practices: A guide to dropout prevention, intervention, and remediation.* Columbus, OH: Author. (ERIC Document Reproduction Service No. ED 262 316)

MOTIVATION

4

MODIFYING THE CLASSROOM: EFFECTS ON ATTITUDES AND ACHIEVEMENT

Background

The physical environment of the classroom can affect students' motivation to learn just as the environment of a factory can affect workers' production. In most classrooms, the teacher stands at the front of the room and students sit at desks arranged in rows and columns. Seating arrangements can have a great impact on students' motivation and their interactions in a class. There are a number of other factors that can affect student behaviors, hence comfort and motivation, such as room lighting, color of the room, type of furniture, number of people in the room, and room temperature. Although it is easier to control some of those variables than others, teachers should survey their situations from time to time to see that they are conducive to learning.

Who Can Benefit

Most of us work better in environments that are comfortable, esthetically pleasing, and nondistracting. It is hard to be productive, much less creative or enthusiastic, if our surroundings are dingy, crowded, and noisy. It is particularly important to arrange attractive environments at school for at-risk and remedial students, because many of them come from homes that are drab, cluttered, and disorganized. There is the chance that some students would be motivated, hence more productive, if their classrooms were more attractive and pleasant.

Procedures

1. To make your classroom a more motivating place, examine the following features or conditions:
   - *Lighting*—Ask students if they would like any changes in lighting. Your pupils may prefer open window shades to those that are shut.

Use natural lighting to balance fluorescent lights, as fluorescent lighting can put students to sleep more easily than regular lighting.

● *Color*—Coordinate the colors in your classroom to increase school achievement, production, and morale and to lower absenteeism. Keep walls at the front and back a nondistracting, neutral tone. Place materials that are light and reflect sunlight opposite the windows. If your classroom is exposed to the north, use light-colored material on the walls to compensate for the sun's rays.

● *Overcrowding*—Brief periods of overcrowding have negative effects on individuals' moods and their satisfaction with tasks and the environment. If you have an overcrowded classroom, remove some furniture to create more open space. You may seem distant to students toward the rear of classes that are arranged by traditional rows and columns if you constantly teach from the front. Large classes often benefit from arranging seats in ways other than the ordinary row and column configuration.

● *Furniture*—Classroom seats are designed to last for many years and to make it easy for janitors to sweep around them. They are not designed for comfortable use 6 hours a day. Consider adding out-of-seat activities to your curriculum, especially in winter months or rainy periods.

● *Temperature*—Excessive heat has negative effects on pupils' moods, their impressions of the environment, and the assigned tasks. Use windows, fans, and/or air conditioning to maintain a moderate temperature during extreme hot and cold weather.

● *Noise*—It may be possible to reduce the noise in your environment through simple changes: using a fan instead of an open window, appointing door monitors to shut the door when appropriate, or putting rubber pads on metal chair legs.

● *Attractiveness of surroundings*—Cover up parts of the room that are ugly with screens or fabrics. Tidy up those areas of the room that are messy. Transform "institutional" rooms to more attractive settings by adding travel posters, plants, and student artwork. Unattractive surroundings have a negative effect on pupils' moods and efforts.

2. Include in your examination of the classroom observations of the student-teacher interactions. If the desks in your classroom are arranged in rows and columns, you might expect students in the center front to interact the most often. Furthermore, observe students to determine whether those who sit outside the action zone participate. Do you tend to walk in the center front, the middle of the room, or around the perimeter? Use your observations and objectives to adjust the seating assignments and your movements until you get the type and frequency of student involvement you desire.

3. Match the seating pattern to the classroom activity.

    ● *Situation 1*—You may wish to minimize interactions between students in situations such as test taking or independent seatwork. Structure your environment in rows and columns to achieve this goal.

    ● *Situation 2*—You may want students to work in small groups. Plan for the least amount of distractions by pushing desks together so that students in each group are face to face with each other and away from other groups.

    ● *Situation 3*—If small groups of students are presenting a report to the class, you may want them to stand or sit at a table at the front of the room. Arrange seats for the pupils in a large horseshoe or semicircle.

    ● *Situation 4*—For large group discussions, rearrange seats to maximize student involvement and minimize your role as controller of the discussion. Use a hollow rectangle or circular arrangement, and sit where you can assume leadership as the situation demands.

    ● *Situation 5*—If you use a film, slide, or overhead projector to show images on a screen at the front of the room and want students to interact with you, divide chairs into two lines along the sides of the room, leaving a wide aisle in the center, so that students can alternate between looking at the screen and at you as the activity dictates.

4. Allow students a few days to become adjusted to the changes before making your decisions about their continued use. Determine whether students participate to the extent you want, and evaluate their academic performances. Survey the pupils to see if they noticed or liked the changes.

Modifications/ Considerations

Other changes could be made in classrooms to make them more conducive to learning, some of which are more easily accomplished than others. A number of good ideas for arranging comfortable and attractive situations could be gathered by observing other classrooms or businesses, or by looking through magazines that focus on living and working environments.

Monitor

Data of two types should be gathered to evaluate the effects of any (particularly major) environmental change. One type has to do with pupils' production or achievement: Do the students, in general, learn more as a function of the change? The other type of data, which is probably related to the first, has to do with pupils' impressions of the changes. Students should be interviewed to determine these thoughts: Are they more comfortable? Do they interact more? Is it easier to attend? Do they learn more? Are they more inclined to come to school, at least to this class? (See MONITOR 9 in Appendix A regarding interviews.)

Reference

Bassett, R.E., & Smythe, M. (1979). *Communication and instruction.* New York: Harper & Row.

MODIFYING THE CLASSROOM: ARRANGING PEER FORUMS

Background

In this tactic, forums were established that involved students as panelists, who discussed a number of matters of great importance to them. The idea behind this technique is that youth will listen to their peers when they discuss social and academic matters more than they will adults, and will be particularly impressed by youth who have turned their lives around.

Who Can Benefit

This tactic is appropriate for remedial and at-risk students, and those who are turned off by school or generally not motivated. Lewandowski (1989) noted that the major lesson to be learned from this project is that success is the accomplishment of personal goals. According to the author, the most noted effects from this technique were on the panel members themselves. They gave advice about attitudes, accomplishments, self-concepts, and the need for education. Because of their responsibilities, the panelists believed that they must live up to their own advice.

Procedures

Preparation

1. Choose six students to serve on the panel. They should have a variety of abilities and experiences. Some of them may have experienced serious behavior problems in and out of school, others may have dealt successfully with a drug or alcohol problem, and so forth. Panelists should be perceived as real people who have overcome problems familiar to other youth. In addition, they should meet as many of the following criteria as possible:
   - Be successful and interested in academics
   - Be involved and successful in extracurricular or out-of-school activities
   - Be well known and respected by other students
   - Be known to have overcome significant school problems
   - Be able to communicate their "story"
2. Obtain permission to proceed with the plan from administrators and parents.
3. Issue formal, written invitations to prospective panelists. State the purpose of the forum and why they were asked to participate.

4. Introduce the plan to all students. Point out that one goal is to become aware that real people with real problems can set reasonable goals and achieve them.
5. Prepare students by having them think about problems they have at school or at home.
6. Prepare the panel members by asking them to think about problems they had, how they handled them, how they dealt with them, what their goals are, and when they began setting them. Have them consider what kinds of positive advice they would offer about courses to take, attitudes to develop, and study strategies to learn.

Implementation

1. Seat the panel at a table in front of the classroom. Place a name card in front of each panel member, and provide a pitcher of water and glasses.
2. Moderate the panel and formally introduce each member.
3. Ask each member to comment briefly on a selected topic.
4. Open the floor to questions. You may have to ask the first one or two to get things going.

Follow-up

1. Send written thank-you notes to all participants.
2. Allow time for discussion the next day.
3. Refer back to the discussions that arose from the panel throughout the year, as appropriate occasions come up.

Modifications/ Considerations

Teachers might invite graduates to come back and serve as panel members. They could talk about how their academic problems affected them on the job, in college, or at technical school. Most high school students are eager for information about what it is like "out in the world."

In setting up these situations the teacher should avoid putting the audience on the spot so that they feel they are being admonished. Point out that many of them will have a turn later as a panelist. The class members would probably feel more comfortable about this technique and more motivated to participate if they had a part in its structure.

One way to monitor this procedure would be to keep track of the interactions that develop between the panelists and between them and the audience (see MONITOR 18 in Appendix A). Another idea for evaluating the effects of the panel discussions would be to ask students (particularly those in the audience) to respond to a few items on a questionnaire or to write (without a structure) their comments about the event, and note their suggestions for future meetings.

Monitor

Lewandowski, J.A. (1989). Using peer forums to motivate students. *Teaching Exceptional Children*, Spring, 14–15.

Reference

INCREASING INTEREST IN SCHOOLS: PROMOTING READING

It is extremely important to read, because reading meets the intellectual and emotional needs of individuals. But motivating some adolescents to read can be difficult. Offered here is a list of activities to increase the pleasure in classroom reading while giving students more responsibility for learning.

Background

Students who read very little on their own should benefit the most from these activities. At-risk, remedial, and mildly handicapped students can profit from the stimulation of these ideas.

Who Can Benefit

1. Plan sustained silent reading periods. For lower ability students the emphasis should be more on "covering material" than on accuracy. Students should read materials at their own level and pace.

Procedures

2. Read aloud and stop occasionally at highly interesting spots. In science classes, expose students to the thrill of discovery and the accuracy required to obtain reliable results.

3. Provide newspapers and encourage students to read them. Vary the sections required to maintain interest. Younger secondary students prefer news and comics sections, whereas older pupils prefer editorials. Organize files on several topics in which students can put articles they have read that are of particular interest to them.

4. Create a library corner and use it for free-time activities. Give students material on topics about which they have expressed interest. Adolescents are confronted with developmental concerns such as establishing peer and sex roles and independence from parents. Provide materials on those topics. Teens enjoy reading young adult books, those that deal with problems they must cope with now or in the near future. Look for books in your subject area that touch on their interests: biographies, science fiction, romance, and sports. Ask students for recommendations.

5. Provide enrichment activities that involve microcomputers. Encourage pupils to read text passages that have been prepared with Hypercard formats, those that allow readers to obtain information related to specific passages: definitions, illustrations, examples.

6. Encourage students to read sources of general information such as encyclopedias, directories, almanacs, and yellow pages. Point out to students that different types of reading require different styles of reading and attention.

7. Short drama activities can often enliven textbook narrations. Consider this approach, and on occasion schedule sessions for reading poetry.

8. Pair students for writing research reports so they can generate creative ideas together. See to it that ample resource materials are on hand, and give pupils suggestions for finding the necessary resources quickly.

9. Plan book swaps. Ask students to bring in books and magazines from home (preferably good ones or those they can recommend), and encourage them to make trades.

10. Plan activities for home that relate to reading in class such as investigations or surveys. A unit on oral histories or scientific patents in your community may appeal to some students.

11. Bring the class (or part of it) together as a literate community by asking them to read, review, and discuss books, magazines, or newspaper articles.

12. Integrate reading and writing. When a task features one skill, involve the other. For example, pupils could be asked, on occasion, to write reviews of books that were read.

13. Provide students instruction on specific reading skills such as paraphrasing, skimming, or scanning.

14. Encourage students to write reviews of events they attended, and read the newspaper reviews about them.

15. Make a portion of the grade dependent on an oral book report.

16. Schedule expressive writing events—perhaps a personal journal—that you neither read nor grade.

17. Invite guest speakers to discuss or amplify materials that have been featured in the class. Instruct students to write out questions for the speaker.

18. Locate and bring nontraditional books to the classroom:
    ● Histories of your community
    ● Student-authored materials
    ● Science and model-building books
    ● Creative mathematics activities

19. Encourage class members to come up with other reading activities.

Rank order by importance the activities you intend to schedule. Write out goals for individual pupils, and indicate when the goals should be reached.

Modifications/ Considerations

Keep track of how many new activities you introduce each week. If 2 weeks go by without adding variety to your reading programs, identify a different activity and schedule it.

Monitor

Ask students to keep a log of what they read and the amount of time they read. Data, over a period of time, regarding the minutes that students spend reading each day should be charted and studied to determine whether pupils are reading enough to become more fluent (see MONITOR 3 in Appendix A).

References

Davey, B. (1987). Team for success: Guided practice in study skills through cooperative research reports. *Journal of Reading, 30*, 701–705.

Ammann, R., & Mittelsteadt, S. (1987). Turning on turned off students: Using newspapers with senior high remedial readers. *Journal of Reading, 30*, 708–716.

INCREASING INTEREST IN SCHOOLS: ALLOWING STUDENTS TO PARTICIPATE IN GRADING

Background

This procedure can ensure uniformity of grading when implemented throughout the elementary, middle, and high school levels. When these ideas are practiced, more time is available for teachers to work individually with students. Students become more independent and involved in their learning with this technique, because they have access to lesson plans they helped to develop. Furthermore, the immediate feedback and clearly stated goals, which are a part of this procedure, can also help students achieve their goals.

Who Can Benefit

This tactic would be suitable for many at-risk and remedial students and others who appear to be overwhelmed or disfranchised by the grading process.

This approach is particularly appropriate for students who require more precise feedback more often with respect to their assignments and grades.

Part A. Structuring for Planning and Grading

1. Design a weekly lesson plan based on the academic status for each student involved in the program (see Weekly Lesson Plan in Figure 4.1).
    a. Separate by subject matter.
    b. Place the title of the textbook or workbook, pages to be completed, and related objectives in the appropriate spaces (by subjects).
2. Check assignments immediately after they are completed.
3. Provide corrective feedback, in the form of written comments on the work and individual conferences for students.
4. Record the number correct over the number possible below the specific assignment on the lesson plan.
5. Calculate and record daily percentages in the space below that.
6. Figure weekly averages by adding the percentages obtained on each assignment and dividing by the number of total grades for the week. Record the weekly average in the appropriate box.

Part B. Involving Students. Involve students in the grading process by having them check their own work and calculate their daily and weekly percentages.

1. Explain to students that by taking on additional responsibilities for their work they will learn to become more independent.
2. Hand out copies of individual lesson plans (see Weekly Lesson Plan in Figure 4.1).
3. Discuss the format of the weekly lesson plan. Probe for their understanding of the plan by asking questions such as the following:
    a. "In what order will you complete each day's assignments? How is this shown on the weekly lesson plan?"

Procedures

FIGURE 4.1 Weekly Lesson Plan for Allowing Student Participation in
Grading Process

WEEKLY LESSON PLAN

_____ Middle School
Resource Room

Name _____ Date _____

Subject	Monday	Tuesday	Wednesday	Thursday	Friday
Reading Oral/Silent Comprehension					
Weekly Average					
English					
Weekly Average					
Language Arts					
Weekly Average					
Vocabulary					
Weekly Average					
Spelling					
Weekly Average					

Subject	Monday	Tuesday	Wednesday	Thursday	Friday
Phonics					
Weekly Average					
Skill Series					
Weekly Average					
Math					
Weekly Average					
Homework Science History English Math/Other					
Weekly Average					
Independent Work					
Weekly Average					

Note. From Zoboroski, J. (1981). Planning and grading LD students. *Academic Therapy,* *16*, pp. 466 and 467. Copyright 1981 by PRO-ED, Inc. Reprinted by permission.

    b. "How will you know which book to use and what pages to complete for each subject?"

    c. "What have you done so far in any of the subjects?"

4. Ask students to raise their hands when they have completed an assignment so you can check it and provide immediate feedback.

5. Explain to pupils that you will write their scores on each assignment showing the number correct over the number possible (e.g., 9/10), and review how to figure percentages.

6. Show students where to enter these scores on the weekly lesson plan, explain how to figure a weekly average, and indicate where to enter this figure.

7. Set aside a time at the end of each week or at the beginning of the following week during which students average their weekly grades and hand in their completed lesson plan sheets.

Monitor   Copies of all lesson plans and scores should be kept on file to document student performances. The information on these forms will be helpful in parent conferences, staffings, and other situations that require discussions of and decisions about educational progress and future planning for students.

As an incentive for students to improve in a specific area, chart (or have them chart) information that would illustrate their performance—for example, daily scores, percentage of assignments completed (see MONITOR 2 in Appendix A), number of lesson plans turned in. This could be done on an individual basis, or could become a class project if competition is effective with your students.

Reference   Zoboroski, J. (1981). Planning for and grading LD students. *Academic Therapy*, *16*, 463–471.

INCREASING INTEREST IN SCHOOLS: IMMEDIATE APPLICATIONS

Background

The idea supporting this tactic is that most youth, particularly those referred to as at risk and remedial, are unimpressed with much of the school's curriculum. They have a number of common complaints about schools and the subjects that are offered, but one that is heard often goes something like this: "What's the point in learning about _____? I don't see any need to know that." Teachers, in their efforts to convince students to attend to those subjects, tell students that in time they will need to know about _____. But most of the students are unimpressed with that line, and pay little attention to either the teacher or the subject.

Who Can Benefit

The students who should benefit most from this tactic—an attempt to explain the immediate gains from subjects that are taught—are those referred to as remedial or at risk. Many of those youth are motivated only by the immediate. They are totally unmoved by pleas to learn something for tomorrow, much less next month or next year. For them, the future is now. This activity should benefit teachers as well, because many of them need to carry out sessions of self-inquiry to assess the gains, immediate or otherwise, that can come from their teachings. Some teachers may learn that they are presenting content to students that is questionable, in terms of its relevancy, either now or later.

Procedures

Teachers should survey the content of their subjects and list carefully the arguments or rationales that can be offered students to defend the relevancy of their material. They should also discuss this matter with other teachers in their department. When fortified, teachers should present these justifications to students in an effort to motivate them to take the courses more seriously. Following are some reasons that could be communicated to youth for needing certain skills taught at school:

1. To find a job
2. To perform on a job
3. To survive as an adult
4. To assist in learning a more desirable skill
5. To be mainstreamed into a regular class
6. To stay in a regular class and not be sent to a special class
7. To enter some type of postsecondary training: vocational school, community college, 4-year college
8. To be accepted into the armed services
9. To complete the courses and earn the credits required for high school graduation
10. To pass the GED examination
11. To enjoy or participate in a desired leisure activity
12. To function like their more adept peers
13. To participate in extracurricular activities
14. To deal with parents and other adults
15. To help cope with stress
16. To be better able to live with others, particularly with one's own family

Modifications/ Considerations

The above list of reasons is certainly not exhaustive; parents, teachers, and citizens at large can think of many others. The justifications are greatly dependent on the subject that is taught. It is easier to make the case for immediate relevancy for home living and driver's education courses than it is for U.S. history and physical science.

Many of the suggestions for immediate application of content could come from students themselves. After the teacher had made an effort to bring his or her subject "back to the present," some of the responsibility for coming up with rationales could be delegated to students.

It would be a good idea to encourage some pupils —those who became more understanding and accepting of the course content because they saw how it fit into their immediate lives—to extend the period of gratification. Perhaps some of them could see how certain content would benefit them in one week, one month, even one year.

Counselors and administrators, as well as teachers, should be brought into this process. They too should be required to justify various subjects and their content.

Monitor

One way to monitor this activity has been mentioned. After students are informed as to how certain content is immediately relevant, they could be given other content and asked to write out or discuss how they believe it fits into their lives (see MONITOR 10 in Appendix A).

Reference

Zigmond, N., Sansone, J., Miller, S.E., Donahoe, K.A., & Kohnke, R. (1986). *Teaching learning disabled students at the secondary school level: What research and experience say to the teacher of exceptional children* (CEC monograph). Reston, VA: The Council for Exceptional Children.

SELF-MANAGEMENT: INCREASING PERFORMANCE

Background

The notion that supports this tactic is that we are motivated when allowed to take on aspects of our instruction. Ordinarily, teachers "call all the shots." They identify what is to be taught, when it will be scheduled, how it will be presented, how the pupil will respond, when the pupil will do it, what the pupil will receive for his or her efforts, and how much of it will be granted. Although it is probably important for teachers to assume most of these responsibilities, many students are motivated when allowed to manage one or more of those features. In the project explained here, a young man was allowed to determine the number of points he would receive for correct academic responses.

Who Can Benefit This type of project would be most effective for students who have been exposed to token economies. If students have been in situations where teachers have given them points for a specified number of academic responses, and they were allowed to exchange those points for tangible objects or minutes of time, there is a great chance that they would be motivated by the activity explained here. Their motivation would show up in increased rates of performance. The pupil in the research (Lovitt & Curtiss, 1969) was a 12-year-old boy.

Procedures
1. Set point-per-correct-response ratios for the pupil in a number of subjects. Following are a few of the ratios for the student in the cited study:
   math: 10 problems = 1 minute of free time
   reading: 1 page = 2 minutes
   spelling: 18 words = 1 minute
   writing: 20 letters = 1 minute
2. Establish a plan for correcting the work and keeping track of the points earned.
3. Arrange a situation whereby pupils can spend the minutes they have earned. In the referenced study (Lovitt & Curtiss, 1969), the teacher set up a leisure-time area. There were a number of games, puzzles, and other activities in that location.
4. Establish a way to monitor the exchanges of points for time, and the pupil's behavior in the free-time area. Make certain that the pupil is in that area for only the amount of time he or she earned. Set up rules for behavior in the area. If, for example, a pupil bothers someone else, or is otherwise disruptive, the pupil should be asked to return to his or her desk and to start working.
5. Assist the pupil to understand the various ratios. In math, for example, the pupil's ratio in the cited study was 10 to 1. Ask the pupils now and then how many points they would earn if they correctly answered 20 or 30 problems. Carry out similar exercises to help them understand other response-to-point relationships.

6. Allow pupils to set their own ratios when you are convinced that they understand the process. (You may want to specify a limit on the ratios.)

One consideration was mentioned earlier: The chances that this tactic will be successful are increased if the student has experienced token economies, ratios, and exchanges.

As indicated in number 6 of the Procedures section above, it may be necessary to set a limit on the ratios. Some pupils might be too liberal in their specifications. Those limits could be set with or without the pupil being aware of them.

In the referenced project (Lovitt & Curtiss, 1969), the pupil was allowed to self-select his ratios in every subject. A teacher may want to go about this gradually, by encouraging the student to set ratios in only one or a few subjects at a time.

As indicated earlier, there are a number of other instructional features from which students could be allowed to choose. They could determine when they would work on certain activities, how they would respond, and could even select their own rewards.

Modifications/ Considerations

In the cited research (Lovitt & Curtiss, 1969), data were obtained during conditions when the teacher set the ratios and when the ratios were arranged by the boy. Those data were kept in terms of frequency of correct responses per day (see MONITOR 1 in Appendix A).

Monitor

Lovitt, T.C., & Curtiss, K.A. (1969). Academic response rate as a function of teacher- and self-imposed contingencies. *Journal of Applied Behavior Analysis*, *2*, 49–53.

Reference

SELF-MANAGEMENT: IDENTIFYING ANTECEDENTS AND CONSEQUENCES OF BEHAVIOR

Background

The desire to change or improve one's own behavior and a willingness to be responsible for this are essential to the success of any attempt to self-manage. A positive introduction to the basic principles of self-management is the first, and possibly most important, step in the process. Students need to understand that if they can manage their own behaviors, others will have less reason to control behaviors for them, which translates to greater independence.

This tactic provides guidelines for teaching students what self-management is, and how to apply it to their own lives. The main idea is to help students identify events that cause or trigger behaviors and anticipate the consequences or results of those behaviors.

Who Can Benefit

The increased freedom of choices available to individuals who manage their own behaviors can benefit adolescents in a number of ways. As they are given more opportunities to select activities and set goals they can achieve, they may develop stronger self-concepts, all of which may combine to help them lead more successful and happier lives.

Apart from those personal gains, students who control their own behaviors responsibly will contribute to a more productive, focused classroom atmosphere, thus benefiting other students and their teachers as well as themselves.

In a society where adults are able to complete jobs satisfactorily with minimal supervision, more time and money can be spent on improvement and innovation rather than on training and repairing.

| Introduction | **Procedures** |

Introduction

1. Set the tone for a positive learning experience.
   a. Treat students as responsible persons.
   b. Present the self-management program as a privilege, an opportunity to control one's own life.
   c. Maintain a positive, interested attitude.
2. Define *self-management* and give examples of how it can be applied to the students' lives.
3. Briefly trace the progression of control in all our lives.
   a. Young children—virtually all behaviors managed by adults
   b. Adolescents—a transition from management by adults to gradually assuming responsibility for themselves
   c. Adults—expected to manage their own behaviors in a responsible manner that does not infringe on the rights of others
   d. All ages—must learn to function within the range of rules and expectations of society

The ABCs of Behavior

1. Write on the board (or display on a poster) an explanation of the ABCs of Behavior:
   A = Antecedent: What happens to *trigger* your behavior
   B = Your Behavior: What you do or say
   C = Consequence: What happens as a *result* of your behavior
2. Present examples (see Examples of Antecedents, Behaviors, and Consequences in Figure 4.2).
3. Ask students for personal examples of events that trigger certain behaviors, what the behaviors are, and what might result. Record their responses in the corresponding columns.

Discriminate and Predict

1. Present a lesson on how to discriminate between triggers (antecedent events) that cause students to act appropriately and triggers that cause them to act inappropriately (see Table 4.1).
   a. Set up six columns, three under POSITIVE (Triggers, Behaviors, Results) and three under NEGATIVE (Triggers, Behaviors, Results).

FIGURE 4.2 Examples of Antecedents, Behaviors, and Consequences

("You," "Your," and "You're" refer to the student.)

Antecedents (Triggers)

1. Your friend keeps throwing paper wads at you during seatwork.
2. You're supposed to be at work by 3:30, but your friends always want you to hang out after school.
3. Your teacher gives you a book report assignment that's due in one week.
4. Your dad tells you that you have to baby-sit Friday night.
5. The girl that you want to go to the dance with asks you for help with homework after school.
6. You go out to the parking lot after school and find that you have a flat tire.
7. Your teacher gives an assignment that you don't understand.
8. One of your teachers announces that there will be a chapter test on Friday.
9. Your mom asks you to come home right after school to help her out.
10. You're walking down the hall and someone you don't get along with comes up behind you and shoves you.

Behaviors (Numbers in parentheses indicate "matching" antecedents.)

(9) 1. Even though your friends are going out for cokes, you go right home and help out.
(6) 2. You kick in your front fender and punch the side window, cracking it.
(2) 3. You get to work an hour late for five days in a row.
(5) 4. You go shopping with your friend because you'd rather do that than help her with schoolwork.
(4) 5. You really want to go out, but you stay home as you've been asked to do.
(10) 6. You're really mad, but you just walk away from him or her.
(1) 7. You punch your friend and yell swear words at him.
(3) 8. You schedule your study time so that you work on your report a little each night and have enough time to rewrite it neatly the night before it is due.
(8) 9. You'd rather be out partying, but you decide to study each night between now and Friday.
(7) 10. You go to the teacher during seatwork time and ask for clarification on the assignment.

Consequences

- (9) 1. Your mom really appreciates your help and offers to treat you and your girlfriend/boyfriend to a movie on Friday.
- (4) 2. Your dad lets you borrow the car Saturday night and gives you $5.00.
- (1) 3. Your teacher sends you to the principal's office.
- (10) 4. The hall monitor sends the "other guy" to detention, but you're doing fine.
- (6) 5. Instead of just having to change a flat tire, you have to come up with $100 for body work.
- (3) 6. You get a B+ on your paper.
- (8) 7. Even though you missed a couple of nights out, you ace the test.
- (2) 8. Your boss fires you and you lose the income you were saving for a new car.
- (7) 9. You are able to complete the assignment accurately and get a good grade.
- (5) 10. When you ask her to go to the dance with you, she says, "Forget it!"

Note. From Young, K.R., West, R.P., Smith, D., & Morgan, D.P. (1987). *Teaching self-management strategies to adolescents: Instruction manual* (pp. 39 and 40). Logan: Department of Special Education, Utah State University. Reprinted by permission.

  - b. List three to five events (triggers) that would elicit positive results in the first column. (These steps correspond to those on the chart in Table 4.1.)
  - c. Record student responses to "What would you do if (*trigger*) happened?" in the second column.
  - d. List three to five triggers that would cause negative results to occur in the fourth column.
  - e. Record student responses next to each one in the fifth column.
2. Go back to the first two columns and discuss the probable results of each trigger/behavior. List student responses in the POSITIVE RESULTS column.
3. Repeat this procedure with the second set of triggers/behaviors. Record student responses in the NEGATIVE RESULTS column.
4. Transfer the trigger in the fourth column to the first column immediately after students acknowledge the negative results of each inappropriate behavior, and elicit suggestions for more appropriate responses.

TABLE 4.1 Predicting Consequences

POSITIVE				NEGATIVE		
Triggers	**Behaviors**	**Results**		**Triggers**	**Behaviors**	**Results**
(Step 1b) Teacher asks class to work individually and quietly.	(Step 1c) You work on your own without talking.	(Step 2) You finish your work and are allowed to talk to friends for the last 5 minutes of class. You also have less homework.		(Step 1d) Your friend keeps throwing paper wads at you during seatwork.	(Step 1e) You think it's funny and start throwing paper wads back at him.	(Step 3) You both get sent to the principal's office. Because you missed the rest of class, you have more homework.

(TO CHANGE *NEGATIVE* TO *POSITIVE* SEE *STEP 4*, BELOW.)

(Step 4) Your friend keeps throwing paper wads at you during seatwork.	) (Step 5) You ignore your friend and finish your work.	Your friend gets tired of bothering you and gets his work done, too, so you both have more time to have fun after school.

Note. These steps correspond to those in the Procedures section. Developed by Constance Ballew, 1988.

5. Discuss and list the positive results that might follow each amended behavior.

EXAMPLE

Trigger: Your English teacher hands back a paragraph you wrote with several punctuation and capitalization errors underlined, and asks you to make corrections and recopy it in ink for tomorrow. She tells you to look it over now so you can ask questions about anything you don't understand.

Behavior: You glance at the paper and stick it in your notebook, thinking you will get to it later. When you get home, you discover that there are several errors you don't know how to correct.

Consequence: You get a "zero" on the paper, and have to do it over again.

Ask the student to *change the behavior*: You look over the paper in class, and ask for help on the errors you don't know how to correct. Once all the corrections have been made, you recopy it in ink, and turn it in on time the next day.

So that the *consequence changes*: The teacher congratulates you for getting your work finished on time, and changes your F to a B.

6. Encourage students to employ self-talk statements to help make better choices (e.g., counting to 10, saying things like, "If I don't control myself, someone else will," "If I manage my own behavior, I will have more freedom to do what I want").

7. Repeat steps 1–5 with new examples to provide additional practice in discriminating between events that are likely to trigger appropriate and inappropriate behaviors, and in predicting the consequences of those behaviors.

Role-Play and Discussion

1. Arrange for students to role-play a few ABC sequences. (You may wish to refer to examples from previous lessons or present new ones such as those listed in Figure 4.2.)

2. Discuss the concept of self-management as it relates to what students learned:
   a. What the ABCs stand for
   b. How that arrangement can be applied to students' lives and those of others

c. The advantages to controlling one's own behavior

d. Ways to manage themselves so that others will not have to

Modifications/ Considerations

Since the desire to change or improve one's own behavior is an important prerequisite to learning self-management, the teacher should consider how each student in the class may react to the concept before introducing it to the group. If you anticipate that someone will respond negatively, it may be best to ask privately if he or she would like to participate, after explaining the basic notions of self-management to the student. If the response is negative, do not include the student in the instructional group.

Throughout this tactic there are opportunities to reinforce positive attitudes and to help students accept criticism. From the introduction on, the emphasis is on the positive aspects of self-management. During the "discriminate and predict" phase, students will have to deal with feedback from their negative responses. Since the next step is to rethink those negative responses and come up with positive alternatives, students will again be exposed to the concept of a positive attitude in practice.

In the lists shown in Figure 4.2, ask students to match up the 10 antecedents with the 10 behaviors and consequences. (The "matches" are indicated in parentheses.) They could also start with one set and predict events in the other two sets.

Monitor

A determination of the degree to which students are able to apply these concepts would be to ask them to record examples of situations that occurred throughout their day that showed their awareness of events that triggered behaviors, how they reacted, and what the results of those actions were (see MONITOR 7 in Appendix A).

Reference

Young, K.R., West, R.P., Smith, D., & Morgan, D.P. (1987). *Teaching self-management strategies to adolescents: Instructional manual.* Logan: Department of Special Education, Utah State University.

SELF-MANAGEMENT: SAVING A LIFE

The life you save could be your own. That is the message of this tactic. More precisely, the idea is that if individuals are taught to self-record important behaviors, that skill could save their life. A number of self-recording tactics have been described in other sections of this program, but the context in which self-recording is explained here should be the most motivating.

Background

The tactics explained here should be appealing to most youth, particularly at-risk and remedial students, because they are generally most anxious to be convinced that teachings in school are relevant. What could be more relevant than saving one's own life?

Who Can Benefit

Because procedures for carrying out self-recording are rather simple, they are only reviewed here: Pinpoint as precisely as possible the behaviors of concern, count the frequency with which those behaviors occur, chart those frequencies, and, if possible, establish aims or goals for those frequencies.

Procedures

The remainder of this section is devoted to summaries of three instances in which individuals monitored extremely important behaviors of their own and, by so doing, helped themselves deal with a serious accident or disease.

Norman Cousins. Several years ago this famous author and editor contracted a serious blood disorder. His doctors were unable to come up with a treatment for the problem, so Cousins took charge of his own care. He began taking measures and charting them on a number of vital functions: sedimentation rate, amount of blood sampled for diagnoses, and others. In addition, Cousins prescribed large doses of ascorbic acid and laughter. The latter was stimulated by watching old "Candid Camera" highlights. Careful records were maintained throughout a lengthy but successful period of rehabilitation.

Israel Goldiamond. About 30 years ago this famous psychologist was in an automobile accident and suffered a spinal injury. Following surgery he was unable to move any of his limbs and realized that, if he was to improve, he would have to take charge of his treatment. He began recording all the efforts of the doctors to aid him, but more importantly, he set up his own exercise program and kept careful records of his movements. Although he has yet to recover fully, he is more mobile than he would have been without the involvement of his own program.

Ken Campbell. Several years ago this Florida teacher wrote about being in a hospital following surgery to remove cartilage and its effect on his quadricep muscles. He began exercising and imagining that he was charting the frequency of the movements. "I had no charts—was too doped up to draw a dot anyway—but thought chart. Within a day or so the movement hovered around 1 P.M. During the second day I increased to about 3 P.M. After a week I was up to around 80/90—any faster would not be exercise, nor control." After months of therapy and self-recording his behaviors, Ken was back to normal.

Modifications/ Considerations

Within a medical setting, it is also important to monitor important behaviors of friends or loved ones. This is particularly true when they are unable to do it for themselves. A friend told me that he once went with his wife to the hospital. She had undergone minor surgery. Although he took along some reading materials, he also went with pencil, stopwatch, and chart paper in hand. When she returned to her hospital room following surgery, the data gatherer began recording her blood pressure readings, the rates her IVs were flowing, the frequencies of visits from doctors and nurses, and many other happenings. Over a period of 60 minutes, he had noted three "irregularities," and when he reported them to the head nurse, they were dealt with. My friend wasn't terribly upset by those events, because he was certain that she would have survived the mistakes; however, he was glad he had kept data, because when a person is down and out that is no time to take chances.

Perhaps the best way to monitor circumstances such as those described here would be to keep a rather detailed log, because there are so many things that occur, many of which are unforeseen. The data gatherer should, however, make a point to acquire data on the events that are predictable and somewhat consistent over time: vital signs, body movement, diet, toileting, sleep patterns. Many of those data could be plotted across time as frequency (see MONITOR 1 in Appendix A) or duration (see MONITOR 2).

It would be helpful in the instances described here if there had been standards—normal and personal rates on sedimentation flow, blood pressure, leg and arm movements, and other important vital signs—prior to gathering the data during unusual circumstances. With that information, the recorder would know the extent to which the client's rates were off the mark.

Monitor

Cousins, N. (1977). Anatomy of an illness (as perceived by the patient). *Saturday Review, 5*(28) 4-6, 48-51.
Goldiamond, I. (1973). A diary of self-modification. *Psychology Today*, November, 95-101.

References

STAYING IN SCHOOL: A SCHOOLWIDE PROGRAM

The content of this tactic can be applied in one of two ways: (a) as a checklist for a school's staff to consider as they evaluate their program (or lack of) for handling students at risk of failing or dropping out of school or (b) as an outline to follow in developing such a program.

The author of this material (Conrath, 1988), an educational consultant specializing in dropout prevention, recommends that prior to evaluating an existing program, or budgeting funds to set up a new one, three questions must be addressed: What makes

Background

a dropout prevention program effective? What makes teachers in dropout programs effective? What are the needs of probable dropouts from adults and a dropout prevention program? Recommendations will address these basic concerns.

Who Can Benefit

Students from grades K through 12 should be served by the type of program outlined here. These students are not "dumb"; often, they are simply discouraged. A program that acknowledges this and deals with the factors that cause them to fail (i.e., too few credits or too many absences) in a serious way will help more than will programs that label youth as "reluctant learners" or "slow learners" and provide watered-down curricula and "fun" activities to the exclusion of work that must be done to remain in school. Furthermore, the avoidance and hostility demonstrated by many students who are likely to become dropouts is exacerbated by anonymity. This approach seeks to avoid that by treating students personally.

Procedures

Program Effectiveness. Address the question, "What makes a dropout prevention program effective?" in the following ways:

1. Make the program part of a system-wide, K–12 strategy.
   a. Talk about dropout prevention in faculty meetings.
   b. Involve all staff members.
   c. Consider the program to be essential (not something that may be cut from the budget in the future).
2. Identify which students will be best served by the program.
   a. Place only those students in the program.
   b. Do not overload it with all students who have special needs.
3. Clarify roles within the program.
   a. Tell students precisely why they are in the program.
   b. Establish the fact that the adults involved in the program are experienced professionals with the skills needed to help students.
   c. Emphasize the seriousness of the situation, and that serious work will need to be done.

4. Expect students to live up to high ethical and intellectual standards.
   a. Begin academic work at students' current levels of achievement, but don't water down the content.
   b. Make no false assumptions about students in terms of lacking ability.
   c. Do not give students insulting labels like "reluctant learners."
   d. Refrain from patronizing students (i.e., giving "warm fuzzies" or inappropriate external rewards).
5. Teach discipline and responsibility.
   a. Do not automatically expect students to possess and display these characteristics.
   b. Understand the difference between teaching discipline and imposing obedience, and do not confuse the two.
6. Avoid treating students anonymously or impersonally.
   a. Always acknowledge their presence or absence.
   b. Demonstrate genuine concern for their well-being.
7. Present an alternative strategy for learning.
   a. Have students do real schoolwork.
   b. Provide the kind of learning that students need to mature intellectually.
8. Locate the program in a place where students can feel a sense of belonging.
   a. Avoid putting it in classrooms that are used by other teachers whenever possible.
   b. Give students an opportunity to develop a sense of ownership.
9. Balance the program between fitting into the total school program and having enough autonomy to allow the kinds of decisions teachers must make in order to assist at-risk students.
10. Make strong efforts to help discouraged students see:
    a. The point of what they are being asked to do
    b. How it will improve their lives

Teacher Effectiveness. Address the question, "What makes teachers of dropout prevention programs effective?" by selecting teachers who have the following qualities:

1. *Toughness* (ethical, emotional, and intellectual)
   a. Can handle angry and confrontational students
   b. Keeps critical issues in focus
   c. Can work with difficult youth day after day
2. *Compassion*
   a. Understands the grimness of many students' lives
   b. Is willing to spend time with students getting serious work done
3. *Professionalism*
   a. Knows why graduation from high school is important
   b. Values, enjoys, and is willing to talk to youth about the pleasure and importance of learning
4. *Seriousness*
   a. Is clear about end results he or she wants for students, and flexible about how to get them
   b. Believes in serious work and that all students are capable of doing it
   c. Knows that the "I don't care" attitudes of students are for self-protection, and does not accept or put up with such attitudes
5. *Knowledge* (is knowledgeable about)
   a. Teaching and learning
   b. Learning styles
   c. Motivational theories and practice
   d. The reasons some youth become discouraged and defeated
6. *Creativity*
   a. Knows many ways to introduce and explain new topics and ideas
   b. Perseveres until all students "get it"
   c. Stimulates youth to think
7. *Authoritativeness*
   a. Leads through own expertise and sense of competence
   b. Does not constantly quote rules and regulations
8. *Sense of purpose*
   a. Has high ethical and intellectual expectations for self
   b. Acts accordingly
   c. Knows why he or she likes teaching and why he or she is working with difficult youth

9. *Cultural competence*
   a. Wears education and culture with pride
   b. Uses language effectively
   c. Enjoys knowledge and expertise
   d. Values own and students' cultural heritage

Student Needs. Answer the question, "What do probable dropouts need from adults and a dropout prevention program?"

1. Structure and predictability
   a. Provide a supportive structure.
   b. Make purposes and benefits of work clear.
2. Flexible means and consistent ends: Provide different approaches (traditional ones have not worked).
3. High ethical and intellectual expectations: Realize that these students are discouraged; they are not dumb.
4. "Do-able" academic work
   a. Select work that provides intellectual challenges without academic threats.
   b. Help students "catch up" in skills and self-image.
5. Contact with adults
   a. Do not have youth work in isolation, setting their own pace.
   b. Provide engagement with adults students can trust and respect.
6. Adult leadership
   a. Confront students with their behavior when they behave poorly.
   b. Handle student confrontations with skill and compassion, not as ego threats or battles to be won.
7. Serious, useful schoolwork
   a. Avoid busy work.
   b. Be sure students know the use of the work they are doing.
8. Trust
   a. Don't assume these students have chosen failure.
   b. Help them learn to break the pattern.
9. Increased self-esteem: Provide opportunities for achievement in worthwhile endeavors.

Modifications/ Considerations

This set of suggestions can be modified and expanded as needed for any setting or situation. The basic premise—that students who are at risk deserve a serious, dedicated approach to helping them succeed—must remain constant. Regular re-evaluations of existing programs should be required, and compliance should be specified in detail. Districts may wish to incorporate suggestions on what makes teachers effective in this sort of program into the qualifications required in hiring them for such programs.

Monitor

The most important data to keep from a program such as this would be the number of dropouts. In addition to knowing the numbers, concerned individuals should follow up and interview each dropout (see MONITOR 9 in Appendix A). Once located, several questions should be asked of dropouts. The two most obvious are: "Why did you drop out?" and "What would it take for you to return?"

Reference

Conrath, J. (1988). Dropout prevention: Find out if your program passes or fails. *The Executive Educator*, *10*(8), 15–16.

STAYING IN SCHOOL: PROGRAM FOR MOTHERS AND TODDLERS

Background

The idea behind this project is that if young mothers who have problems reading are taught to read, they will be better parents. They will be able to read to their youngsters and to interact generally with them, and will be better prepared to communicate with their children's teachers at school.

The background for programs of the type explained here, where mothers and their youngsters go to school, is the federally supported program referred to as Even Start.

Young mothers who have trouble reading and/or have not graduated from high school would be assisted by this program. Not only would they be given reading and basic skills instruction, they would be provided with skills that should help them become better parents. The youngsters of the mothers who participate in this program should also be assisted, because as their mothers learn to read and develop skills for parenting, the probability is increased that their mothers will read and interact more with them, and that will further their development.

Who Can Benefit

Following are six goals of a typical Even Start program:

Procedures

1. Raise the educational level of the parents of preschool children through instruction in basic skills.
2. Increase developmental skills of preschool children to better prepare them for academic success.
3. Enhance the relationship of the parent and child through planned, structured interaction.
4. Demonstrate to parents their power to affect their child's ability to learn.
5. Encourage early identification and treatment of physical or mental handicaps that may inhibit the children's learning ability.
6. Encourage identification and treatment of any handicapping condition in the adults that may inhibit their ability to care for their children.

Following is a plan for realizing some of those goals:

1. Recruit two groups of mothers who have reading problems and who have toddlers (about five pairs to a group).
2. Arrange for one group to come to the location (a school or some other community building) on Monday and Thursday, and the other to come on Tuesday and Friday for 3 hours a visit.

3. Determine initially the mothers' and toddlers' levels of functioning. Ask the mothers to read a number of community-relevant materials (e.g., newspapers, magazines, novels, recipes, bus schedules). For the toddlers, administer some of the items from standard screening inventories.

4. Engage a teacher to work with the mothers as a group and another teacher to work with the toddlers for a 2-hour period. Instruct the mothers on aspects of functional reading and other basic skills. The instruction for the toddlers should be on standard preschool activities.

5. Pair the mothers with their toddlers for the final hour of the session. During that time, assist mothers to read and interact generally with their youngsters.

6. Give the mothers homework assignments for themselves and their toddlers at the end of each session. Encourage them to read to themselves at home and to read and interact with their toddlers. Show the mothers how to monitor the extent they carried out these assignments.

7. Go over the mothers' homework assignments when they return to the classroom for another session prior to giving them the next assignment.

8. Help prepare the mothers to take the GED examinations as they become more proficient with reading and other basic skills.

9. Assist the mothers to take advantage of other services in the community.

Modifications/ Considerations

Transportation and attendance are matters that must be taken into account when starting projects such as the one explained here. Since some of the mothers may be a bit disorganized and not motivated to attend school, arrangements should be made to accommodate them. It may be necessary to pick some of them up. It may be advisable to place the centers in locations that are within walking distance of the mothers and their children.

Some projects of this type start off the sessions with a breakfast (or lunch). This is something to consider, because a good meal may be the key to their attendance.

Some programs of this type are scheduled during the day and others are offered in the early evening. There are advantages and disadvantages to either, but the time of the sessions should be considered when arranging Even Start programs.

The type of instruction and the curriculum for the mothers and their youngsters would obviously depend on their abilities. Whatever it is should be directed toward improving their quality of life as soon as possible.

Monitor

There are three sets of curriculum, objectives, and measures for this project. Gather data on the reading of the mothers (and perhaps other skills). Have them read from newspapers, TV guides, recipe books, training manuals, and other functional materials. Acquire data on correct and incorrect oral reading rates and their rates for retelling information from what they read, as a comprehension measure (see MONITORS 1 and 10 in Appendix A). Also, keep data on the extent they read at home and on the types of material they read.

As for the toddlers, keep data on such behaviors as identifying objects, naming colors, counting and matching similar and dissimilar objects, arranging objects in sequence and in categories, and following directions.

With respect to interactions between mothers and their youngsters, keep data on some of the following: questions asked by the mothers, the extent they give praise, give examples, show, tell, the extent their toddlers ask questions (see MONITOR 18).

Federally supported Even Start Programs.

Reference

LEARNING FROM BUSINESS: WHAT IT TAKES TO LIVE IN THE REAL WORLD

The reason for including this tactic is that many adolescents are totally unaware of the expectations and

Background

realities of the world. Recently, when a group of high school students was asked what they wanted to do when they grew up, many of them didn't have a thought, but they were uniformly adamant about not wanting to work in a local factory. When asked why, they replied that the work was demeaning (not their word) and repetitive. Although they may have been right (I don't necessarily believe that they were), they did not really know what those workers did. And sadly, they had absolutely no idea as to what those workers made and what their benefits were. And even more sadly, they had no idea what it would take to land a job at the factory. Many of the youth simply assumed that they could always get that type of job, when in reality it is doubtful that many of them could.

Who Will Benefit

The idea advanced in this tactic, to bring youth more in line with reality, would serve most adolescents, because the majority of them are not precisely in touch with the world outside school. This tactic would be particularly helpful for at-risk and remedial youth, those who are apt to quit school and go it on their own, because it may shake them up when they find out what it takes to get along "out there." Possibly, when they know what is required, they may be more motivated to stay in school and better prepare themselves for life after high school.

Procedures

1. Identify a few things that adolescents say they want—a car, for example.
2. Ask a series of questions about the costs of purchasing and maintaining some of those "things." A car: What will it cost? What about insurance? What about maintenance? What about gasoline? What about parking costs?
3. Set up a few exercises with the youth so that they seek out the answers to those questions.
4. Ask them about the cost of renting an apartment, since many of them can't wait to move away from their parents and be "on their own." What about the monthly rent? What about the first and last month's rent? The damage deposit? How about utilities? Is there a garage for their car? How will they furnish the place?

5. Set up similar exercises to come up with the costs of independence.
6. Ask them, once they know what it takes to buy things and to live in their own place, how much money they must earn to pull it off. Add a few more questions: How much will groceries cost? What about transportation costs, if they don't have a car? What about cleaning supplies and other incidentals to take care of their place?
7. Ask the big question. Now that they know a bit about what the expenses are in the real world and have some idea about how much they will have to earn to live the way they want to: Where will they get a job? If they want to be a fireman, do they know how much they will make? Do they know what the requirements are? The same and many other questions could be asked about every job: a busboy in a cafe, a policeman, a waitress, a gas station helper, a welder, a bricklayer, a plumber, a teacher, a preacher.

Modifications/ Considerations

All types of questions could be asked in an effort to assess the extent adolescents touched reality. Ask them about social security, about health care, about the income tax process, about insurance programs, about investments, about the stock market, about the courts, religions, about community organizations, about home repairs. We would probably be disappointed by many so-called bright youth if they were given such "folk" assessments. We would be even more alarmed by the responses of at-risk individuals.

Monitor

A series of pretests and posttests could be scheduled to determine the effects of reality instruction. (A teacher could develop a set of questions.) Take the automobile discussion, for example. Prior to the youth being instructed to look up and calculate the costs, simply ask them what it would take to buy and maintain a car. Readminister the assessment after they have brought together some facts and figures (see MONITOR 12 in Appendix A).

Reference

"Learning" (television program). (April, 1989). Sponsored by the Chrysler Corporation.

LEARNING FROM BUSINESS: NEEDS-GOALS, VROOM EXPECTANCY, AND PORTER-LAWLER MODELS

Background Motivating individuals is of great interest to both schools and businesses. With businesses this concern is often linked to productivity, whereas in schools it is associated with performance. Some of the programs that businesses have developed from various motivation models can also be implemented to motivate students. Of the existing models, three that might be adapted to school settings form the basis of this tactic: (a) the Needs-Goals model, (b) the Vroom Expectancy model, and (c) the Porter-Lawler model.

These models build on one another in such a way that a picture of how motivation occurs emerges when they are considered as a unit. The components of the most complete model, Porter-Lawler, incorporate the two basic features of the Needs-Goals model: (a) felt *needs* (which cause) (b) human *behavior*, and the suggested additions of the Vroom Expectancy model, which states that motivational strength (the intensity of desire to perform a behavior) is a function of the perceived value of the result of that action and the perception of how probable it is that the result will materialize.

The picture is more fully developed in the Porter-Lawler model, which stresses three additional characteristics: (a) Both intrinsic and extrinsic rewards determine the perceived rewards, (b) the requirements of the task and one's ability to perform the task determine how effectively it will be accomplished, and (c) the amount of satisfaction one experiences depends on one's perception of how fair the reward is.

This tactic attempts to translate the precepts of these motivational models into teaching strategies designed to motivate students to learn more and earn higher grades.

There are several advantages to using an approach originating in the business world when working with students who are not highly motivated by academic work. The very fact that these are "real-world" ideas that have actually shown results in settings other than schools should add credibility to whatever educational purpose a teacher sets out to achieve. By familiarizing students with models, and allowing them to apply the concepts to their own situations, teachers can increase the chances that students will begin to look at things they must do to succeed in a more realistic and positive way.

Who Can Benefit

1. Explain briefly the three motivation models identified earlier: Needs-Goals, Vroom Expectancy, and Porter-Lawler (see Figure 4.3).
2. Present Maslow's needs hierarchy (Figure 4.4). Ask students to think of needs that would fit the categories he has suggested.
3. Give examples of how the needs students have suggested may be translated into supporting behaviors directed at achieving their goals (e.g., hunger) that can then be transferred to behaviors (e.g., buying, cooking, and serving food) that support the goal, eating.
4. Ask students to state their needs in relation to school, home, work, or social situations. Then, guide them through the process of identifying behaviors that might support the attainment of the goals that would satisfy each need.
5. Write their suggestions on the board and discuss how effective the behaviors they have suggested could be in helping them reach their goals. Elicit alternatives if necessary.
6. Add to the two basic components of the Needs-Goals model the modifications suggested by the Vroom Expectancy model: motivation strength (perceived value of reward, and perceived likelihood that the reward will materialize). Give examples.
7. Redirect students' attention to the original lists of needs and goals to consider them in terms of motivation strength.
8. Point out the all-inclusive and expanded scope of the Porter-Lawler model. Show students how it incorporates all the elements of the first two models.

Procedures

FIGURE 4.3 Outline of Three Motivation Models

Needs-Goals Model

Felt *needs* cause *behavior* aimed at reducing those needs.

Vroom Expectancy Model

The degree of desire to perform a particular behavior is determined by:

1. an individual's perceived value of the result of performing the behavior and
2. the perceived probability that the behavior will actually cause the result to materialize.

Porter-Lawler Model

1. The perceived value of a reward for a particular behavior is determined by both:
   a. intrinsic and
   b. extrinsic rewards that result in need satisfaction when the behavior is accomplished.
2. Individuals can effectively accomplish a task only if they:
   a. understand what the task requires and
   b. have the ability to perform the task.
3. The perceived fairness of a reward influences the degree of satisfaction generated when the reward is received.

---

9. Ask students to examine the examples they have offered to identify intrinsic and extrinsic rewards that would come from attainment of their goals.
10. Help students evaluate the tasks that would be involved in achieving those goals in terms of skills they think would be required and whether they have the ability to perform them.
11. Ask their opinions about the fairness of the available rewards, and rate the rewards according to the responses.
12. Review the elements of all three motivation models, referring to students' examples on the board or offering additional ones.
13. Assign students to groups of two or three and give each group a need to analyze in terms of the three motivation models (see worksheet in Figure 4.5).

FIGURE 4.4   Maslow's Hierarchy of Needs

1. Physiological Needs	Relate to normal functioning of the body which, until met, consumes a significant portion of an individual's behavior.
2. Security (Safety) Needs	Involves keeping free from harm which, when obtained, allows future behavior to be aimed at social needs.
3. Social Needs	Made up of a desire for love, companionship, and friendship, reflecting a desire to be accepted by others which, when satisfied, shifts behavior to satisfying esteem needs.
4. Esteem Needs	Refers to an individual's desire for respect—generally divided into two categories (self-respect and respect for others)—which, when achieved, readies the individual to become self-actualized.
5. Self-Actualization	The desire to maximize whatever potential one possesses; the highest level of Maslow's hierarchy.

Note. Adapted from Certo, S.C. (1986). *Principles of modern management: Functions and systems.* (3rd ed., pp. 344 and 345). Boston: Allyn & Bacon. Reprinted by permission.

Modifications/ Considerations

As examples are offered to stimulate student participation, choose those that provide clear, positive cases. Monitor students' responses to see that they follow the steps and stay on target. You may wish to help interested students identify the needs inherent in some goals they wish to attain, and their plans for reaching those goals, by considering the goals in light of the motivation models in this tactic.

The discussion on human needs (step 2 in the Procedures section above) can be extended by introducing Argyris's (1957) Maturity-Immaturity Continuum and/or McClelland's (1976) Achievement Motivation theory.

Monitor

After students have had an opportunity to fill out their motivation worksheets, collect them and analyze the responses. Among several possible ways to analyze those data, it would be interesting to study the consistency and logic with which each student

FIGURE 4.5 Worksheet for Use in Learning from Business

MOTIVATION WORKSHEET

NEED: _____

GOAL: _____

N e e d s	felt need	
G o a l s	human behavior	
V r o o m	perceived value of reward	‾‾‾‾‾‾‾‾‾‾‾‾‾‾‾‾‾‾‾‾‾‾‾‾‾‾‾‾‾ –5 –4 –3 –2 –1 0 +1 +2 +3 +4
E x p e c t a n c y	probability that reward will materialize	‾‾‾‾‾‾‾‾‾‾‾‾‾‾‾‾‾‾‾‾‾‾‾‾‾‾‾‾‾ –5 –4 –3 –2 –1 0 +1 +2 +3 +4
P o r	intrinsic rewards	
t e r	extrinsic rewards	
L a w	requirement of the task	
l e r	the ability to perform the task	

Constance Ballew, 1989.

filled out his or her form. It would also be informative to look for similar patterns across students.

Since this is an open-ended and theoretical tactic, and teachers who arrange it would implement it in different ways, there are a variety of ways in which to evaluate it. One approach that would be suitable for most styles of delivery is to videotape a discussion that followed study of one or all of the models (see MONITOR 15 in Appendix A). Data of several types could be acquired from such a tape: simple questions, responses, interactions, topic switches, agreements/disagreements.

References

Argyris, C. (1957). *Personality and organization.* New York: Harper & Row.
Certo, S.C. (1986). *Principles of modern management: Functions and systems* (3rd ed., pp. 338–363). Boston: Allyn & Bacon.
McClelland, D.C. (1976). Power is the great motivator. *Harvard Business Review,* March/April, 100–110.

LEARNING FROM BUSINESS: LIKERT'S MANAGEMENT SYSTEM

Background

After studying several different sizes and types of organizations, Likert, the developer of the motivational strategy on which this tactic is based, reached the conclusion that management approaches basically fall into four categories or systems. These systems range from those that treat people poorly to those that treat them extremely well, with resulting productivity that correlates positively with the latter.

Likert's approach is focused on helping managers develop management systems based on the principle of supportive relationships, as defined by the elements of a System 4 style (see Figure 4.6 for fur-

FIGURE 4.6 Likert's Management Systems

Treating people poorly

System 1. This management style is in operation when employers have no confidence or trust in their subordinates. Subordinates do not feel free to discuss their jobs with superiors and are motivated by fear, threats, punishments, and occasional rewards. Information flow is primarily directed downward, with upward communication viewed with great suspicion. The bulk of all decision making is at the top of the organization.

Treating people less poorly

System 2. This style of management is noted when employers have condescending confidence and trust in subordinates (such as master to servant). Subordinates do not feel free to discuss their jobs with superiors and are motivated by rewards and some actual or potential punishments. Information flows mostly downward, whereas upward communication may be viewed with suspicion. While policies primarily are made at the top of the organization, decisions within a prescribed framework are occasionally made at lower levels.

Treating people fairly well

System 3. This style of management is apparent when employers have substantial, but not complete, confidence in their subordinates. Subordinates are somewhat free to discuss their jobs with their superiors and are motivated by rewards, occasional punishment, and some involvement. Information flows both up and down. Upward communication is often accepted but at times is viewed with suspicion. While broad policies and general decisions are made at the top of the organization, more specific decisions are formed at lower levels.

Treating people extremely well

System 4. For this style of management, employers have complete trust and confidence in their subordinates. Subordinates are completely free to discuss their jobs with superiors and are motivated by such factors as economic rewards based on a compensation system developed through participation and involvement in goal setting. Information in this system flows upward, downward, and horizontally. Upward communication is generally accepted, but if it is not, justifications are generally offered and the matter is discussed. Decision making is spread widely throughout the organization and is well coordinated.

Note. From Certo, S.C. (1986). *Principles of management: Functions and systems* (3rd ed., p. 356). Boston: Allyn & Bacon. Reprinted by permission.

ther information on the four systems). The advantage to developing such a style in the business setting is that as more human needs are satisfied (by moving from System 1 toward System 4), improved working relationships between workers and management will develop.

Although it may not be feasible in a school setting to apply all the elements of System 4, since it is based on economic rewards, there are elements that can be incorporated (e.g., participation and involvement in goal setting, and up, down, and lateral communication). Therefore, although a System 4 management style is most desirable, elements from both Systems 3 and 4 have been incorporated to develop this tactic.

Students who are trustworthy and freely express their ideas and concerns should profit the most from these procedures.

Who Can Benefit

1. Demonstrate confidence in students by allowing them to manage certain classroom procedures after they have been trained to do so (e.g., taking roll, checking papers, recording scores).
2. Provide time and opportunity for students to discuss their concerns about assignments and interactions with fellow students, teachers, administrators, and others with whom they are involved in the course of a school day, as these factors relate to their learning.
3. Identify clearly the benefits and rewards for productive academic and appropriate social behaviors, and establish fair and consistent consequences for unmet expectations and exceeded limits.
4. Define general school and specific classroom policies, but involve students in the decision-making process as to the applications of these policies to specific incidents and situations that affect individuals and certain groups.
5. Encourage students to set goals for themselves and for those groups they may be a part of in school.
6. Keep students informed about new or revised policies and procedures, and encourage them to comment and discuss the feasibility and fairness of those regulations through suggestion boxes, class meetings, letters to the editor of the school newspaper, and so forth.

Procedures

7. Provide ample feedback on students' performance in all of these areas, and increase their levels of responsibility in as many ways as possible.

Modifications/ Considerations   Unfortunately, many schools (and businesses for that matter) have traditionally adopted management approaches that mirror the more negative and authoritarian elements of Systems 1 and 2. It will, therefore, take some time to make the necessary changes, so be prepared for a drop in the amount and quality of work, and possible increases in nonproductive behaviors in the short run. This commonly turns into increases in desired behaviors once workers (students) adjust, because, when needs are satisfied, good working relationships between workers and management (students, teachers, and administrators) develop, which tends to increase productivity.

Monitor   To monitor this theoretical program, students could be asked to survey a number of businesses and other organizations with respect to the four management systems. To do so, they might read about them, interview individuals from management levels and others from middle management or entry levels, interview individuals who have dealt with these outfits, and so forth (see MONITOR 9 in Appendix A). Students might also be asked to list presumed advantages and disadvantages of the systems with respect to achieving short- and long-term objectives.

Reference   Certo, S.C. (1986). *Principles of modern management: Functions and systems* (3rd ed., pp. 338-363). Boston: Allyn & Bacon.

HEALTH

5

WELLNESS

As an introduction to this tactic and to others in this Health chapter, three notes are offered. One, it is my belief that these matters (wellness; nutrition; eating disorders; physical fitness; emotional health; smoking, drinking alcohol, and substance abuse; and sex education) should be dealt with by the entire teaching staff, at least indirectly. If, for example, a science teacher learns that a youngster in his class is experiencing some problems in one of those areas or has some greatly mistaken belief that could lead to a serious problem, that teacher should act. He should either intervene himself or refer the youth to someone else who has been designated to deal with the particular matter. He should not wait, thinking that the health or family living teacher will handle the matter when the youth takes that class.

Background

The second point in relation to these topics is that the suggestions in the eight topics are neither sequenced nor complete. Whereas the events laid out in the Procedures sections of most other tactics followed a step-by-step plan for carrying out the technique, that is not the case here. Instead, several facts and a number of ideas have been included that are intended to generate discussions.

The third point with reference to this set of Health tactics is that teachers should be more informed about these matters than they generally are. Theories and facts about health care change from time to time and teachers should keep up with them. Fortunately, current, readable, and free materials are readily available. Federal, state, county, and city agencies are extremely helpful in furnishing written materials and consultants to schools. And the education or public relations sections of local hospitals will gladly supply dozens of helpful pamphlets.

Wellness is a relatively new concept in health care. The idea is to inform and educate individuals so that they take care of their own health. The concept of wellness does not mean that individuals will never go to a doctor; it means that they will accept the responsibility for their health and occasionally, and when necessary, consult a physician. Not long ago all health care was in the hands of attending physicians. With the rising, nearly prohibitive, costs of health care and the fact that many individuals want to take on more responsibilities for their well-being, the idea of wellness has become popular. This notion certainly goes along with several tactics in this program that deal with self-management.

Procedures

The ideas in this section deal with three related topics: scheduling checkups by physicians, managing a self-care program, and preventing accidents.

Scheduling Checkups. Youth, in spite of the fact that they believe they are invincible, immortal, and will be eternally healthy, should learn that it is a good idea to have periodic checkups from competent physicians. According to a pamphlet put out by Doctors, a physician referral and appointment service in the Northwest, the following examinations should be scheduled by adolescents: at 13—dental checkup, 14—medical and dental checkup, 15—dental checkup, tetanus vaccine (to be given every 10 years after last vaccine), 16—dental checkup, 17—medical and dental checkup. They further recommend the following examinations for young adults: health screening visit with physician at 18; for women, annual health screening to include Pap smear, breast exam, instruction on self-assessment, and pelvic exam; for men, health screening visits every few years to include testicular exam and instruction on self-assessment; for both men and women, check cholesterol, blood pressure, and discuss lifestyle and its associated risks with physician at health screening visits; dental checkup every 6 to 12 months.

Another area of discussions should deal with health care providers (e.g., hospitalization insurance, social security, Medicare, and related services). This would be an eye-opening experience for teachers and students. Inform youth that a few health care plans pay for periodic checkups and reduce other costs for individuals who schedule them. Although this concept of prevention and wellness has not swept the health care industry, it is a good idea.

Youth should also learn that there are competent and incompetent physicians, just as there are skilled and unskilled mechanics, teachers, and lawyers.

They need to learn that they can communicate with physicians—ask them questions, question their responses, inform them about their symptoms—and confirm their advice by checking in with others once in a while. They should learn about specialists— which type of physician to go to for what—and that they will save time, money, and their own health if they go to the proper one at the right time.

Managing a Self-Care Program. According to a recent Gallup poll, individuals who are committed to taking charge of their health (about 16%) have an increased sense of well-being, feel confident in their appearance, and overall are more satisfied with their lives (Overlake Hospital Medical Center, 1987). One of the best resources of health care information comes from local libraries. In the Seattle area, for example, there is the King County Consumer Health Information Network. This system, with dozens of 1-800 numbers, is designed to provide up-to-date and reliable information to the public. In addition to the 1-800 numbers, the library system furnishes health books, journals, videocassettes, and audiocassettes for patrons to make informed decisions about their health.

The range of home health tests is astonishing. Working from a kit or test, individuals can now detect or monitor their own blood pressure, blood in the stool, impotence, muscular degeneration, urinary-tract infection, sugar levels related to diabetes, and many other conditions. Furguson, president of the Center for Self-Care Studies in Austin, Texas, and co-author of *The People's Book of Medical Tests*, claims that the expanding medical self-test field is a logical extension of such traditional home tests as taking one's temperature or weighing oneself.

Preventing Accidents. According to researchers at the Harborview Injury Prevention and Research Center in Seattle (no date), the primary cause of "accidents" is our fatalistic acceptance of them. That group has offered several facts about accidents:

1. Injury is the most costly of all major health problems facing our nation.
2. Trauma costs taxpayers $130 billion per year, more than cancer and heart disease combined.

3. Washington State taxpayers pay $5 million per year for motorcycle trauma.

4. Our federal government spends less than 2% of its total health budget on injury research and prevention.

5. Following are statistics regarding youth between 10 and 19 years of age per 100,000 of population per year: 14.2 deaths in motor vehicle accidents, 16.4 for suicides, 6.3 for drownings, 8.5 for homicides, 4.5 for pedestrians, 1.9 due to fires, 1.6 for bicycles, .6 for falls, and 32.4 for other types of injuries.

6. In comparing the homicide rates from 1980 to 1986 in Seattle and Vancouver, BC (which has stricter laws against handgun ownership), the Harborview group found that although the chances of being assaulted in general were the same in both cities, the chances of an assault with a firearm were seven times greater in Seattle.

7. In another of their studies, they found that 40% of the trauma victims admitted to Harborview or given autopsies by the King County Medical Examiner's Office tested positive for drug use.

8. About one-third of the injuries to pedestrians occurred in marked crosswalks.

Regarding the last point, a number of programs in schools and communities should be developed. Those might include better law enforcement aimed at violations against pedestrians, environmental modifications such as sidewalks and pathways, and training teachers and youth to deal with traffic. It is vitally important to exercise great caution, and toward that end here are a few tips: (a) Never cross a street simply because the light is green, the pedestrian light is on, or it is a crosswalk; (b) always run or walk facing the traffic, and be prepared to jump in the ditch at any moment; (c) be very careful of cars filled with young people coming from behind or approaching you; (d) never wear a radio with headphones as you run or walk—you need to listen to as well as see everything; (e) be extremely careful of individuals driving "hot" cars or 4x4 pickups; and (f) be especially careful of those who drive station wagons filled with children. In short, treat every vehicle (even bicycles) as a predator.

Another safety program that should be fostered is the use of bicycle helmets. Harborview researchers report that bicycle helmets reduced the risk of head injury by 77% and brain injury by 81%. In the Seattle area, there is a school program designed by the Harborview project to educate youngsters to use helmets. To introduce it, "Sprocketman" goes to the schools dressed in a stretchy orange-and-yellow racing suit, and orange mask and helmet. He offers facts, stimulates discussions, and makes recommendations.

Another campaign that should be constantly waged is for passengers and drivers to wear seat belts. Although more and more states have laws requiring people to wear them, there are still many drivers and passengers who do not, and many have been killed or seriously injured because they did not.

A number of aspects of home safety should be discussed at school; they have to do with fire, electricity, radon, asbestos, and other such materials, not to mention the keeping of firearms in the home.

Other safety programs that merit discussion deal with sports and recreation: swimming, boating, surfing, scuba diving, mountain climbing, hiking, and camping out.

Modifications/ Considerations

Wellness is an endless topic when it comes to generating important discussions, but yet another, not discussed here, regards health care and politics. Youth need to learn that some countries are more concerned with health care than others, and that some senators and representatives are more committed to health care issues than others. Youth should be informed that they can do something about this, just as they can have an impact on other social issues.

Monitor

A number of monitoring approaches could be arranged for ideas suggested in this tactic: Checklists could be designed to monitor aspects of home safety and wellness (see MONITOR 6 in Appendix A); interviews could be scheduled with physicians and others in the allied health field (see MONITOR 9); and logs could be written to detail the extent that individuals exercise, explain how they feel, and provide data on home testing (see MONITOR 10).

References Harborview Injury Prevention and Research Center. (no date). 633 Yesler Way #32, Seattle, WA 98105.

Overlake Hospital Medical Center. (1987). *Health confidence: How to take charge of your own health.* Bellevue, WA: Author.

PHYSICAL FITNESS: AN ASSESSMENT

Background Want to find a quick and easy way to help students determine whether they are out of shape? The activities in this writeup are designed to do just that.

First, there are some key terms that are essential to understanding the concepts involved in fitness. Good physical fitness is a familiar term meaning that the heart, lungs, and muscles are working to the best of their ability. A combination of flexibility, muscle strength and endurance, and cardiovascular endurance is involved. These terms may need to be clarified:

Flexibility refers to the ability to move muscles to their full extent. It is achieved through stretching, which can prevent injury and muscle soreness by loosening the muscles and getting the blood circulating.

Muscle strength is the ability to apply force, and *endurance,* the ability of the muscles to apply force for an extended period of time. Exercises that fatigue muscles can increase one's muscle strength.

Cardiovascular endurance refers to the extent the heart and lungs are able to supply oxygen to the working muscles. Adequate aerobic capacity enables one to perform activities over longer periods of time, and is believed to prolong life.

Simple tests to determine the condition of students with respect to those features are described on the following pages. They will serve as beginning fitness levels and as reference points against which improvements can be measured.

The assessment explained here would benefit all individuals, but it is particularly useful for at-risk and remedial adolescents; many of them are not in good condition physically. According to a number of fitness enthusiasts, there is a substantial relationship among physical fitness, emotional state, and cognitive development.

Who Can Benefit

Flexibility. The following test for flexibility will help students determine how loose and flexible their muscles are.

Procedures

1. Direct students to perform these steps:
   a. Find a box at least 12 inches high.
   b. Place a ruler on top of the box, with the end of the ruler touching the edge of the box.
   c. Take off your shoes and sit on the floor with your feet against the box.
   d. Reach forward with your arms in front of you and your hands on top of each other. (Do not bend your knees or bounce forward.)
   e. Repeat three times, and on the last one reach as far as you can.
   f. Hold that position for 1 second, and check the ruler to see how far you were able to reach.
2. Post the rating scale below and instruct students to evaluate their flexibility accordingly.

How Did You Do?

Men   Excellent shape = 5″ or more
Good shape = $2^3/_4$″ to $4^3/_4$″
Fair shape = $^3/_4$″ to $2^1/_2$″
Out of shape = less than $^3/_4$″

Women   Excellent shape = $6^1/_4$″ or more
Good shape = $4^1/_4$″ to 6″
Fair shape = $2^3/_4$″ to 4″
Out of shape = less than $2^3/_4$″

Muscle Strength and Endurance. One way to test for muscle strength and endurance is to count the number of bent-knee sit-ups a person is able to do in a timed test.

1. Instruct students to perform the following exercise:
   a. Lie on the floor with knees bent.
   b. Cross your arms and place hands on opposite shoulders.

    c. Have someone hold your feet or place them under a couch or chair to keep them on the floor.

    d. Sit up and touch elbows to your thighs.

    e. Return to starting position.

2. Count the number of sit-ups completed in one minute by each student. Refer to the chart below to evaluate individual muscle strength and endurance.

How Did You Do?

Men	Excellent shape = 51 or more
	Good shape = 45–50
	Fair shape = 38–44
	Out of shape = 37 or less
Women	Excellent shape = 42 or more
	Good shape = 33–41
	Fair shape = 29–32
	Out of shape = 28 or less

Cardiovascular Endurance. The distance one can cover in a timed run-walk test can indicate the capacity of the heart and lungs.

1. Establish a run-walk course outdoors, or mark a starting point on an indoor track (or gym floor) and measure the distance of the course or the circumference of the track.

2. Conduct 12-minute timings as students proceed along the course or around the track at a run-walk.

3. Measure the distance covered by each student at the end of the 12 minutes.
Note: If testing is done on an outdoor course, distance can be estimated by counting the number of telephone poles passed. They are generally about 200 yards apart. Also, the yard lines on a football field could serve as distance markers. Other alternatives would be to have someone follow in a car to measure mileage, or to have each student wear an odometer. If testing is done on an indoor track, count the number of laps and multiply by the circumference of the track.

4. Instruct students to rate their level of cardio-respiratory endurance according to this scale:

How Did You Do?

Men	Excellent shape = 1.6 miles or more
	Good shape = 1.5 to 1.6 miles
	Fair shape = 1.3 to 1.5 miles
	Out of shape = less than 1.3 miles
Women	Excellent shape = 1.2 miles
	Good shape = 1.1 to 1.2 miles
	Fair shape = .9 to 1.1 miles
	Out of shape = .9 miles

Estimating Fatness. In addition to those assessments, it is not a bad idea to face the facts about fat. Following are some simple tests to determine how fat you are. (These tests for males are summarized from a pamphlet put out by the National Dairy Council.)

Pot Belly Test. Compare chest with waist. Rate an "a" if waist is bigger, a "b" if chest is bigger.

Watch-It-Jiggle Test. Jog in place in front of a mirror. If anything jiggles mark "a," if not, mark "b."

Magic 36 Test. Subtract waist measurement from your height. If the difference is less than 36 inches mark "a," if more, mark "b."

A-Pinch-in-Time Test. Hold left arm out to side. Pinch skin on back of your arm and pull it away from the muscle. Have someone measure the distance. If more than 1 inch, mark "a"; if between $1/2$ and 1 inch, mark "b"; less than $1/2$ inch, mark "c."

The Spare Tire Pinch. Pinch 2 inches above your waist. If you pinch more than 1 inch, mark "a"; if between $1/2$ and 1 inch, mark "b"; and if less than $1/2$ inch, mark "c."

The "b" scores are the ideal. The "a" scores are larger and the "c" scores smaller than ideal.

Modifications/ Considerations

Certainly, physical education teachers could make use of these data and exercises, but other teachers could just as well. In fact, every teacher should point out and discuss with students the importance of staying in shape and engaging in consistent exercise programs.

Included here is a rather fundamental assessment; individuals could assay many other aspects of physical development. One assessment, for example, could assess ability to perform bent-leg sit-ups, knee-ups, side bends, standing twists, knee bends, leg curls, lying side leg raises, two-leg calf raises, standing cross-arm flies, push-ups off table, lying lower-back extensions, lat pulls, push-offs, standing front and lateral flies, standing curls, triceps push-offs, leg raises, side bends, seated twists, back bends, deep knee bends, step-ups, and many others.

Monitor

Instruct students to record their performance scores on the In-Shape Class Chart (Figure 5.1) to serve as a basis for comparison as they improve. Inform students that receiving "excellent" and "good" scores means that they are in good shape. Any rating below that means they need work. Compiled results of each method of testing will help you plan future goals and activities for the students in your classes (see MONITOR 5 in Appendix A).

Reference

You: A guide to food, exercise, and nutrition. (1987). Rosemont, IL: National Dairy Council.

PHYSICAL FITNESS: MAINTAINING A PROGRAM

Background

Once students have established their individual levels of fitness through the test exercises in the preceding activity, they should maintain a basic fitness program such as the one outlined in this activity.

Following are a few reasons for being involved regularly in an exercise program:

- It helps an individual handle stress. It bolsters enthusiasm and optimism.

FIGURE 5.1   Form for Recording Physical Fitness

IN-SHAPE CLASS CHART

Name _____

Activities	M	Tu	W	Th	F	Week's Ratings
Flexibility						
Strength/ Endurance						
Aerobic Capacity						
Flexibility						
Strength/ Endurance						
Aerobic Capacity						
Flexibility						
Strength/ Endurance						
Aerobic Capacity						
Flexibility						
Strength/ Endurance						
Aerobic Capacity						
Flexibility						
Strength/ Endurance						
Aerobic Capacity						

Kathleen Opie, 1988.

- It is a tension release and helps relaxation and sleep.
- It can help control weight. A trained muscle is better at burning fats and other calorie sources than an untrained muscle.
- It reduces body fat percentage and improves or at least maintains muscle mass. This is important during a weight loss program.
- It can improve the body's sensitivity to insulin, making it easier to burn glucose.
- It can increase bone density for younger people. For older women, exercise retards the progression of osteoporosis.
- It increases the "good" cholesterol (high-density lipoproteins) level in the blood.
- It assists the heart to be more efficient by pumping more blood per beat. This is true when the body is exercising or resting.

Who Can Benefit

It is important for all individuals to come up with an exercise program that they can maintain. As indicated in other tactics, it is particularly important for at-risk youth to set up an exercise program, because one of the prime characteristics of these individuals is that they are not physically fit.

Procedures

Some Key Points for the Beginner

1. It generally takes 3 to 6 weeks to go from a sedentary lifestyle to being minimally fit.
2. Exercise should be increased by about 10% per week.
3. Maintain exercise program. Use it or lose it!
4. The threshold heart rate for most teenagers is about 135 to 140 beats per minute.
5. Pain is your body's way of telling you that you are injured. Pay attention to it!
6. An exercise program consisting of one hour per day three to four times a week is sufficient.

Warm-Up and Stretching

1. Lead students in at least 1 minute of easy jumping jacks, jogging, or aerobic movement.
2. Follow with 5 to 10 minutes of nonbouncing stretching exercises (see Stretching Routine in Figure 5.2).

3. Choose an aerobic activity appropriate to your setting, or have students choose one they like to do at home: biking, jogging, swimming, or aerobic dancing (slowly, for about 5 to 10 minutes).

Aerobic Exercise

1. Teach students to calculate their threshold heart rate (number of heartbeats per minute during exercise). To figure this, subtract age from 220 and multiply by .65.
2. Conduct the aerobic activity so that students maintain their threshold heart rate for 20 minutes.
3. Stop, and direct students to take their pulse at rest by counting beats per minute from their wrist or neck.
4. Instruct them to walk about the room for 5 minutes, take their pulse, and compare that rate to their target heart rate.
5. Remind students that they should be able to carry on a conversation without panting, and to slow down if they cannot.
6. Encourage students to try to do a bit more every time.

Cool Down

1. Decrease activity level to 20% ($\frac{1}{5}$ of previous number of exercises) for the next 5 minutes.
2. End with 5 minutes of stretching exercises.

Modifications/ Considerations

Everyone should come up with an exercise program that fits him or her. Toward that end, individuals should sample a wide range of routines. They should try walking, running, swimming, aerobic dancing, rowing, or whatever, and should sample these activities before they buy expensive equipment for the first program they consider. Not only is it important for individuals to identify a type of exercise that they like, they should select at least one alternative. It can become boring to do the same thing day after day.

When discussing exercise and weight control it is not a bad idea to point out some relationships between various exercises and the time it takes to burn off calories. Start by informing students that

FIGURE 5.2 Stretching Routine

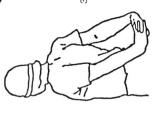

2. Interlace fingers behind your back. Slowly turn your elbows to inside as you keep your arms straight. Your chest should be forward and head straight. 15 seconds.

3. With arms extended over head, grab one hand with the other. Slowly bend at waist as you gently pull hand toward floor. Hold an easy stretch 10 seconds each side.

1. Pull elbow behind head—hold easy stretch 10 seconds each arm, 20 seconds total.

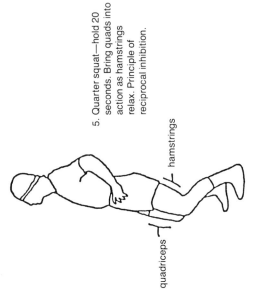

5. Quarter squat—hold 20 seconds. Bring quads into action as hamstrings relax. Principle of reciprocal inhibition.

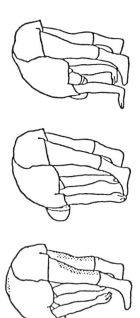

quadriceps — hamstrings

4. From a standing position, with legs straight, slowly bend at waist until you feel an easy stretch in the back of the legs. Do not overstretch. 30 seconds.

Return to a standing position by slightly bending your knees and then stand erect. This will take the pressure off the lower back and stretch out the hamstrings.

6. Repeat #4. Hold 25 seconds. Do not bounce when you stretch. Hold an easy stretch. Be relaxed.

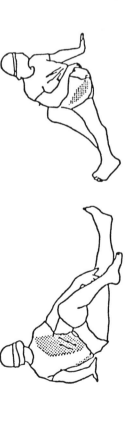

7. Sit down with heels 4 to 8 inches apart. With legs straight slowly bend forward at waist. Hold an easy stretch for 10 seconds. Slightly increase stretch into developmental phase of stretching. Hold for 10 seconds. 20 seconds. Use towel if necessary.

8. Spinal twist—10 seconds each side. 20 seconds.

9. Pull soles of feet together. With your hands clasped around your feet, slowly pull yourself forward until you feel a stretch in the groin area. Hold an easy stretch for 15 seconds. Slowly increase stretch as you feel yourself relax. Hold developmental stretch for 15 seconds. Keep elbows on outside of legs for great stability. 30 seconds.

Note. From *Stretching* (pp. 10 & 11). Copyright 1980 by Bob Anderson & Jean Anderson. Shelter Publications, Inc., P.O. Box 279, Bolinas, CA 94924. Distributed in bookstores by Random House. Reprinted by permission.

the recommended daily allowance for calories for a 150-pound man is 2,700 a day, and 2,000 for a 120-pound woman. Some informative discussions, leading to assignments, can be carried out regarding the amount of energy required to burn off calories from certain foods. A male, at the weight just noted, would have to play tennis for about 33 minutes to burn off the 233 calories in 20 french fries, walk 59 minutes to burn off the 307 calories in a cheeseburger, and run for 28 minutes to take care of the 354 calories in a slice of cheese pizza. A woman would have to bicycle for 6 minutes to burn off the 21 calories in a carrot, play tennis for 26 minutes to burn off the 150 calories in a half-pint of milk, and play basketball for 89 minutes to dispose of the 643 calories in a chicken dinner.

Monitor Assist students to develop a Workout Book in which they write down the number of times per week they exercised and the aerobic activity of their choice (see MONITOR 1 in Appendix A). Ask them to record their resting heart rate by finding their pulse (either on the neck or underside of the arm at the wrist) and counting the number of beats in 1 minute. Then, ask them to compute the threshold heart rate as described in the procedures section, and write both in the Workout Book.

Keep a chart posted in the classroom that shows each student's progress in the physical fitness program. At the end of each week discuss the progress they have made.

References Anderson, B. (1988). *Stretching*. Palmer Lake, CO: Stretching Inc.

Rice, S.G. (1988). 10 minute stretching routine. In *Athletic health care system* (6th ed.). Seattle: HMS Publishing.

Rice, S.G. (1988). *Computing your target rate zone*. Unpublished document.

NUTRITION

Background This tactic introduces students to sensible, well-balanced diet planning. The activities include an exercise that allows students to compare their current eating habits to a healthy diet, followed by tips and suggestions for improvement. A calorie chart is also provided to help monitor caloric intake (Figure 5.3).

Who Can Benefit

Since adolescents aren't generally concerned with nutrition, it is hoped that they will become more interested in a healthier diet as a result of these activities.

Procedures

Part A. Do You Eat Right?

1. Lead students in a discussion about what constitutes a well-balanced diet.
2. Survey and record their opinions on the board or on an overhead transparency.
3. Raise the question, "Are you deficient in any of the food groups?"
4. Present the "4-2-4-4 Rule" as a means of evaluating students' responses and leading into the activities:

4 servings from the *Milk Group:*
a. Provides body with calcium, riboflavin, and protein
b. One serving = 8 ounces of milk; $1^3/_4$ cup of ice cream; $1^1/_2$ ounces of cheese; 1 cup of yogurt

2 servings from the *Meat Group:*
a. Provides body with protein, niacin, iron, and thiamin
b. One serving = 2 ounces of beef, pork, lamb, veal, chicken, turkey, fish, seafood; 2 eggs; 4 tablespoons of peanut butter; 1 cup of dried beans, peas, or nuts

4 servings from the *Fruit-Vegetable Group:*
a. Provides vitamin A and vitamin C
b. One serving = a medium-sized apple, orange, or tomato; half a grapefruit; $1/_2$ cup cooked vegetables or fruit juice

4 servings from the *Grain Group:*
a. Provides carbohydrates, thiamin, iron, and niacin
b. One serving = 1 slice of bread; 1 roll; 1 ounce of dry cereal; $1/_2$ to $3/_4$ cup of cooked cereal

FIGURE 5.3 Form for Use in Monitoring Nutrition

STUDENTS' DAILY CALORIE CHART

Meals	Food Group	Calories
Breakfast	Milk	

1. _____ _____

2. _____ _____

3. _____ _____

4. _____ _____

5. _____

Lunch	Meat	

1. _____ _____

2. _____ _____

3. _____ _____

4. _____ _____

5. _____ _____

Dinner	Bread/Cereal	

1. _____ _____

2. _____ _____

3 _____ _____

4. _____ _____

5. _____ _____

Snack(s)	Fruit/Vegetable	

1. _____ _____

2. _____ _____

3. _____ _____

4. _____ _____

5. _____ _____

Daily
_____ Total

Daily
Student's Name: _____ _____ Goal

Difference + or − _____

Kathleen Opie and Constance Ballew, 1988.

5. Ask students what they think the average number of calories they eat in the course of a day should be.
6. Share the following recommendations for caloric intake with them:
    a. *Young women*—Require 2,000 calories a day to maintain their weight
    b. *Young men*—Require 2,700 calories a day to maintain their weight
    c. *For both sexes*—Add 500 calories to gain weight; subtract 500 calories to lose weight.

Part B. Finding Out.   After making students aware of the above information, lead them through the following steps to establish their current caloric intake.

Where You Are Now

1. Start by writing down everything you eat for 5 days.
2. Find out how many calories are in the foods you eat.
3. Check off the food groups of the foods that you eat.

Doing It Right

1. Compare your caloric intake and number of servings per food group to the recommended amounts (see numbers 4 and 6, Part A).
2. Are you deficient in any of the food groups? If you are, look for foods within that food group that you would consider adding to your diet.
    a. Add foods richer in calories.
    b. Enlarge or increase number of servings.
3. If you are over your caloric limit consider the following:
    a. Cut calories by eliminating butter, sauces, mayonnaise, coke, pastry, and potato chips.
    b. Watch those extra servings.
    c. Substitute low-calorie foods from the food groups in which you are deficient.
    d. Do not eliminate your favorite foods, just eat less of them.

Part C. Establishing a Healthy Daily Diet.   This activity will provide students with the basic knowledge they need to plan a well-balanced diet.

1. Present the sample diets for young men and women (see Part A).
2. Have students look up the nutrition and calorie information that corresponds to the foods listed for each meal.
3. Based on their findings, have students construct similar diet plans using other foods for variety.
4. Collect their plans and redistribute them to teams formed to verify their selections.
5. Appoint individual students within the team to serve as "expert advisors" on each facet of the plan: servings (quantity), calories, nutrition, vitamins, and overall appeal.
6. Establish a rating scale for students to apply to their evaluations of each diet plan. Example: 20 points possible for each facet.
7. Require group presentations of "findings."

Part D. Snacks.   Most people think of snacking as something they shouldn't do, but that's not necessarily true. *What* you choose to snack on may be more significant than *how much* or *how often* you "sneak a snack."

1. Hold a "Favorite Snack" election. Have students nominate their all-time favorite snacks, and then vote to elect the candidate for Favorite Snack.
2. Use information from previous lessons as campaign material to alternately support and discredit various candidates. Encourage additional research as well. (This would be a good opportunity to introduce students to various sources of information on health and nutrition.)
   EXAMPLE: "Do you realize that Candidate Dorito contains enough calories to add a pound a day to your waistline? Our candidate, Yogurt, on the other hand, not only contains fewer calories, she is an excellent source of protein!"
3. Offer some of the following healthy snacks as "Write-In" candidates:
   French Bread Pizza (200 calories)—Slice roll in half lengthwise. Top with spaghetti sauce, mozzarella cheese, and your choice of mushrooms, peppers, onions, some oregano, and garlic powder. Place under broiler or in oven until cheese melts.
   One Big Nacho (215 calories)—Place refried beans on a corn tortilla or tostada shell and top

with cheddar or Monterey Jack cheese. For extra spice add hot sauce or hot peppers. Bake in oven or under broiler until cheese melts.

Frozen Juice/Pudding/Yogurt on a Stick (85, 240, 170 calories, respectively)—Pour your favorite juice, pudding, or yogurt into a 6-ounce paper cup. Place wooden spoon or stick in center and freeze until solid. Peel off paper and go for it.

Portable Munchies (205 calories per ½ cup)—Mix shelled nuts, coconut, raisins, and other dried fruit. Bring them along to school, on a hike, or anywhere in case of the incurable munchies.

Part E. Sample Diets

For a young woman:

Breakfast—1 cup of raisin bran with 1 cup of skim milk, ½ cup of orange juice, and a piece of toast with 1 teaspoon of butter

Lunch—2 slices of whole wheat bread, 2 tablespoons of peanut butter, 1 tablespoon of jelly, an apple, 1 cup of milk, and some potato chips

Dinner—6 ounces of roast beef, 1 baked potato with 1 tablespoon of sour cream, ¾ cup of tossed salad with 1 tablespoon of French dressing, 1 cup of low-fat milk, and ½ cup of ice cream

TV Snack—1 cup of popcorn

For a young man:

Breakfast—1 cup of raisin bran, 1 cup of milk, 2 slices of toast with 2 tablespoons of butter and one tablespoon of jelly, and ½ cup of orange juice

Lunch—3 ounces of ham, 1 slice of Swiss cheese, 2 leaves of lettuce, 2 slices of rye bread, 1 teaspoon of mustard, 1 apple, potato chips, and 1 cup of milk

After School Snack—1 banana, 1 cup of milk, 1 slice of whole wheat bread and 1½ tablespoons peanut butter

Dinner—6 ounces of roast beef, 1 large baked potato with 1 tablespoon of sour cream, ¾ cup of tossed salad with 1 tablespoon of French dressing, 1 cup of milk, and ½ cup of ice cream

TV Snack—10 fluid ounces of apple juice

Modifications/ Considerations

Discuss with youngsters the implications of a poor diet over an extended period of time. For openers, ask them to observe others—in shopping malls, in the neighborhood, at concerts and athletic events—and determine the percentages of men and women who appear to be out of shape. Following those initial observations, discuss some of the conditions and diseases that may come about if a person eats too much of a certain food or group of foods or not enough of others. (Those discussions may relate to information in the next tactic, Eating Disorders.)

It is difficult to separate false claims from those that have some scientific basis when it comes to nutrition. With that in mind, 10 common myths are noted.

1. *High-fat foods cause cancer.* There is no evidence that *any* food *causes* cancer. Researchers have claimed, however, that if less fat is eaten the chances of getting cancer are lowered. Whereas high-fat foods do not cause cancer, they might promote it, particularly such cancers as breast and prostate. Scientists believe that many cancer cells are first produced by exposure to chemicals and other elements in the environment, and later nutrients take over to affect the growth and development of those cells. Many recommend that the fat contribution to our diet should not exceed 30% of the total calories. Furthermore, we should eat more fruits, vegetables, whole-grain breads, and high-fiber cereals.

2. *Fish oils lower cholesterol.* Many experts regard omega-3 (found in fish oils) as beneficial in making favorable changes in arteries, but to get enough of it in fish oil to make a difference, one runs the risk of an overdose. Rather than take fish oil, one should eat at least two servings of fresh fish a week. And that is effective in lowering cholesterol only in combination with a general diet program and exercise.

3. *Calcium pills prevent osteoporosis.* According to our medical friends, increased calcium at any age will slow bone loss, but the best way to prevent osteoporosis is to engage in a lifelong exercise program.

4. *Starchy foods are fattening.* Our experts say that starches, which consist of foods such as rice, potatoes, breads, and pastas, are not more fattening than protein. Starches are "complex

carbohydrates," which contain fiber and should account for 50% to 60% of our calories.

5. *Red meat is bad for you.* Not so, but one should exercise caution. Nutritionists tell us that regardless of the number of calories we consume, no more than 30% of them should be in the form of fat. Furthermore, the part that is saturated should be limited to less than 10% of the total. To provide an index of fat consumption, keep in mind that a 3-ounce piece of cooked, trimmed lean beef has 8.7 grams of total fat, of which 3.4 grams are saturated; 76 milligrams of dietary cholesterol; and 180 calories.

6. *Fiber helps you lose weight.* Don't count on it. Fiber acts like a sponge in the large intestine, absorbing many times its weight in water. When it passes through the body, it carries with it amounts of calcium and other nutrients. So it is back to the old advice, "Eat a wide variety of vegetables, fruits, and whole-grain cereal products," and you will likely get enough fiber and other necessary nutrients.

7. *Nondairy creamer is better for you than real cream.* Probably not, since most nondairy creamers are made from highly saturated plant oils. Although they contain no cholesterol, the high saturated fat content adversely affects the cholesterol count.

8. *Light (or lite) means light in terms of calories:* Actually, either term refers to light anything: calories, sugar, color, salt, or weight. The lightness of beer has to do with reduced alcohol and calories. Light corn chips are lighter than others only in weight; they are still fried in oil.

9. *A candy bar gives you a quick boost of energy.* Actually, it is more likely to deplete your energy. Within an hour, according to doctors, you'll feel more fatigued than you did before eating the candy bar, particularly if you are exercising. Furthermore, there is a lot of fat in a candy bar. Complex carbohydrates before exercise can help, however.

10. *Vegetable-flavored pasta is more nutritious than the regular kind.* Not much. Regulations require that vegetable pastas contain only 3% vegetable solids. Such small amounts add little to the nutritional content. (The preceding was

paraphrased from the *Journal-American* newspaper, Bellevue, WA, April 13, 1988.)

Monitor   Require students to keep a daily calorie chart showing the results of their eating habits for 5 days. Ask them to write down what they eat for each meal, then break the contents of their meals into food groups (see Students' Daily Calorie Chart in Figure 5.3). Set aside time in class to tally up the calories for each student (see MONITOR 1 in Appendix A). Have students write in their daily goals and calculate the difference between the daily total and daily goal. Students should be able to evaluate how well they stuck to their personal diet goals from the results.

Reference   *National Dairy Council. (1987). You: A guide to food, exercise, and nutrition.* Rosemont, IL: Author.

EATING DISORDERS

Background   Information is provided here on eating disorders of three types: obesity, anorexia, and bulimia. Hundreds of adolescents are too heavy, if not obese. Some of them are at risk and others are not, but unless something is done to assist these youth to lose weight, they are in for a lifetime of rejection, from themselves and others. Whether we like it or not, the slim body is prized. Indeed, it is oversold. But if others gauge us to some extent on the way we look, and if we see ourselves as others see us, then it behooves us to bring our bodies somewhat in line with the norm. As for the other two disorders—anorexia and bulimia—they are certainly not as prevalent as is obesity, but there are probably more young women who suffer from these disorders than we imagine.

Procedures   **Obesity.** Following are a few ways to leave your blubber (from a National Dairy Council pamphlet):

1. Don't waste time and money on fad diets, diet pills, or other methods that promise weight loss overnight.

2. Keep records of how much you eat, when and where you eat, what you're doing while you eat, and your mood. Go over your records and look for patterns or bad habits.

3. Try curing one bad eating habit at a time. Don't tackle another until you're sure you have the first problem licked.

4. Clean all the food out of your locker and your bedroom.

5. Measure or weigh all your food portions so that you know how much food you are eating.

6. Eat your meals at the same time each day. Condition your body to expect food only at certain times.

7. Eat breakfast. You will not save calories by skipping breakfast and snacking later.

8. Don't eat while watching TV or reading.

9. Drink a glass of water before you eat.

10. Eat slowly and put your fork down after every bite.

11. Don't shovel food into your mouth. Enjoy each mouthful.

12. Eat off a small plate; it makes little portions look bigger.

13. Try not to leave serving bowls and plates of food on the table while eating.

14. If you are tempted to eat more, wait 20 minutes.

15. Don't clean your plate just because of starving youngsters. Help them in other ways.

16. Remember, although no single food is fattening, too much of anything can be.

17. Keep in mind that two tablespoons of French dressing add 132 calories to your salad.

18. When you buy or bake a cake, slice it into small pieces and freeze them. There will be less temptation to grab a slice if you have to wait for it to thaw out.

19. If you are possessed with an uncontrollable desire to eat something, take a nap.

20. If you are lazy when it comes to snacking, keep snack food around that involves some work, like unpopped popcorn or an orange that has to be peeled.

21. As an incentive to maintaining a diet, put a photo of a thinner you or of someone else on the refrigerator or mirror.

22. Generally, the slower you take weight off, the longer you keep it off. Aim for a weight loss of one or two pounds a week.

Anorexia.   This is a complex illness in which individuals (mostly women) starve themselves. Research indicates that one in a hundred women aged 12 to 25 suffers anorexia, or 280,000 American women. Anorexia and other eating disorders are more likely to occur during periods in a person's life that require adjustment to or acknowledgment of significant changes: the beginning of menstruation, leaving home, divorce, the death of a loved one. Following are a few indicators of anorexia:

1. A weight loss of 25% or more is often a sign that something is wrong, particularly if the anorexic was of normal weight when she began her diet.

2. Dry, flaking skin. Because of a lack of necessary nutrients, the skin becomes rough and cracked, and scalp hair may fall out.

3. Cold extremities. Loss of weight means loss of the body's protective layer of fat. Many anorexics are cold in warm weather and wear unusual amounts of clothing.

4. Body hair. A fine growth of hair may cover much of the body.

5. Menstruation often stops before any loss of weight because the anorexic's highly charged emotional state causes a physical reaction.

6. Starvation seems to encourage obsessive thinking—a preoccupation with food that consumes most waking and sleeping hours.

7. Thinking is often disorganized and unrealistic as a result of the body's disorganization.

8. Anorexics may exercise to excess in an effort to lose weight or justify the food they do eat.

9. Anorexics become hyperactive. Their bodies are off balance, irritated, and keep them on the move.

10. Anorexics are often high achievers and want to be the best at what they do.

11. Anorexics often chew their food excessively, a mouthful could last 5 or 10 minutes before being swallowed.

12. Anorexia not only gives the victim the illusion of self-control, it allows her to control others.
13. Anorexics often see other people, who are in reality much heavier than they are, as being thinner than themselves.
14. They do not often eat with or in front of others.
15. They believe that the loss of just a few more pounds will solve many of their physical, social, and emotional problems.
16. Anorexics may see their illness as an expression of strength, believing that average people could not do what they are doing.
17. Parents of many anorexics are very demanding. They want and expect their children to be successful, and often their children do not feel that enough affection and support are provided.
18. Some anorexics do not like being female. They believe that society gives males more opportunities to feel worthwhile and valuable.

Bulimia. This refers to a cycle of behavior of consuming food and then eliminating it through vomiting or the use of laxatives and diuretics. Research indicates that as many as one million Americans have bulimia, mostly women. Bulimia usually develops around age 18, but can appear at any age. The intensity of the disorder ranges from those who have only an ice cream cone and vomit, to those who eat 55,000 calories in one day and purge themselves. Among the problems the bulimic may face as a result of the eating and purging cycle are onset of diabetes, malnutrition, erosion of tooth enamel and subsequent cavities, gum disease, digestive problems, intestinal problems, rectal bleeding, rupture of the esophagus, hernias, bleeding and infection of the throat, enlargement of lymph or salivary glands, and potassium depletion. Following are some general characteristics of bulimics:

1. They appear to be normal, healthy, happy, attractive, and successful.
2. They are achievers, good in school, sports, and in their jobs.
3. They learn that eating and then vomiting reduces stress, for a time. Over time and with repeated bulimic behavior, however, that period of stress-free feeling decreases. Therefore, to increase the

amount of time the bulimic feels free of anxiety, her only option is to increase the frequency of vomiting.

4. Bulimics believe that to be loved they must be perfect, and one aspect of perfection is to be thin.

5. Because they want to be liked so desperately, bulimics often overcommit themselves to people and projects.

6. They often overexercise, hoard food, are irritable or depressed, take numerous trips to the bathroom, eat all they want but never seem to gain weight.

7. They often shoplift, because they are too embarrassed to buy the numerous laxatives they need, and steal food from friends or stores.

8. Bulimics often complain about stomach cramps, severe constipation, loss of menstrual cycle, insomnia, muscle fatigue, feeling faint, weakness, dizziness, chills, headaches, bloodshot eyes, numbness of hands or feet, muscle spasms, and erratic heartbeat.

Modifications/ Considerations

It is too bad that we are so steeped in the idea that "thin is in." All of our magazines and advertisements on television feature people who are thin, young, and beautiful. (It would be an interesting assignment to determine the extent of that claim.) Dieting and exercising (to lose weight) are billion-dollar businesses. There are dozens of books, videos, and tapes on the subjects. To compound matters, many young people do not have perfect bodies, and they do not have strong self-concepts. During adolescence, boys and particularly girls are strongly influenced by what others think, and they believe that the only way to become popular (and that is what they want most) is to be thin and beautiful. Hence, millions of youth are prime candidates for an eating disorder. Although it is difficult, teachers and parents must try to counter these beliefs.

Monitor

There are several important features to take into account if a person is concerned about his or her weight. For openers, step on the scales at least once a week and record those data (see MONITOR 1 in Appendix A). Also, keep track of the calories eaten and the minutes involved in exercise.

Life Skills Education. (1983). *Anorexia: A lonely starvation.* Weymouth, MA: Author.

Life Skills Education. (1984). *Bulimia: Eating yourself sick.* Weymouth, MA: Author.

National Dairy Council. (1987). *You: A guide to food, exercise, and nutrition.* Rosemont, IL: Author.

References

EMOTIONAL HEALTH

It is just as important to attend to our mental health as to our physical health. Thankfully, a number of approaches and programs are available for dealing with this important matter. Although there is not a course as such in most secondary schools that deals specifically with emotional health, some teachers in home living, home economics classes, and a few others touch on this issue. Teachers of other subjects should also attend to these matters to the extent that opportunities arise. It is probably more important for many youth to increase emotional stability than to learn the periodic table of the elements or the major rivers of Austria.

Background

According to our surveys and interviews of teachers, many at-risk youth show signs of stress, suffer from periods of depression, and are likely to attempt suicide. Hopefully, the suggestions for observing youth and the exercises for alleviating certain debilitating symptoms will be of assistance to teachers and their students.

Who Can Benefit

In this section, comments are offered on three related topics: stress management, depression in adolescents, and adolescent suicide.

Procedures

Stress Management. Early on it is necessary to identify when one is under stress, to know about situations and conditions that promote stress, and to understand how to deal with stress. As for the effects of stress, it is important to point out and discuss a few facts.

1. About half of the uninjured survivors of natural and man-made disasters experience acute emotional, physical, or psychosomatic consequences.
2. Personality type can affect the risk for heart attack; that is, those characterized by high levels of achievement, striving, competitiveness, time consciousness, and impatience have been shown to have a high risk of developing coronary heart disease.
3. Social isolation has been observed to put people at special risk for unexpected mortality and morbidity.

Along with those facts, some theories about stress should also be discussed (from "Medicine for the Layman," 1985).

1. Stress can affect the cardiovascular system by increasing blood pressure and accelerating the atherosclerotic process.
2. Stressful situations can impair the mechanisms involved in immunity, particularly the body's ability to fight disease via cellular immunity.
3. Stress can cause peptic ulcers by stimulating hypersecretion of gastric acid.

So what can be done about it? Following are a few points to discuss with students, from a publication by Overlake Hospital, Bellevue, Washington:

1. Although you cannot control the external circumstances of your life, you can control your reactions to them.
2. Maintain good health: Exercise, eat properly, and get enough sleep.
3. Remember that things change. Don't try to keep everything the same.
4. Your beliefs are incredibly powerful.
5. Accept yourself as you are. Honor yourself as you are now.
6. Stay open to life's teachings.
7. Be patient.
8. Reducing stress is a daily commitment.

Following are some techniques and exercises designed to reduce stress:

1. Meditation is most successful when done in a comfortable, private place without distractions. Close your eyes and focus on one peaceful word or image.
2. Daydream by thinking about an entire relaxing environment in full detail.
3. Deep, slow breathing can interrupt stress responses and help one relax.
4. Deep muscle relaxation helps one to relax the entire body from head to toe by first tensing, then relaxing various muscle groups.
5. Autogenic suggestion can relieve stress. With this technique, individuals tell themselves how they want to feel.
6. Stretching and exercising can reduce stress. Some examples are the head and neck roll, back stretch, leg stretch, arm stretch, and most forms of aerobic exercise.

Depression in Adolescents. According to Sullivan and Engin (1986), over 30% of students in regular schools report moderate or severe levels of depression symptoms. And according to Shaffer and Fisher (1981), there is a frequent association between depressive symptoms and suicidal behavior in adolescents. It would appear, then, that it is important to recognize youth who are depressed and set up interventions.

Maag, Rutherford, and Parks (1988) queried guidance counselors and teachers as to the characteristics of depressed youth and came up with 10 categories. They are ranked in order according to the counselors: drug and alcohol abuse, low self-esteem, dysfunctional family, low academic performance, social incompetence, dysphoric mood (e.g., apathy), somatic disturbances (i.e., health problems), acting out, excess stress, and inappropriate locus of control (i.e., attributing positive events to external causes and negative events to internal causes).

Following are a few responses to forestall or mitigate depression from a column in the *Seattle Times* (Turner, 1987):

1. Don't push your worries behind you, out of sight, where they can heckle you. Bring them out front and look them over. Decide which ones you can do something about and which ones you have to live with.

2. Strive to turn a minus into a plus. If life hands you a lemon, make lemonade. A positive outlook sees some good even in unpromising situations.
3. Do something each day for someone else at some cost to yourself. In caring for the needs of others, we are less likely to concentrate on our own problems.
4. Live one day at a time. Will Rogers's motto on this score was, "Never let yesterday use up too much of today."
5. Nurture a sense of humor. To be able to laugh at ourselves is a sign of wholeness and wholesomeness.

Suicides in Adolescents. According to Neiger and Hopkins (1988), suicide rates have increased 200% for girls and 300% for boys aged 15 to 24 over the last 25 years. Half a million young people attempt suicide each year and 5,000 succeed. The numbers would be even higher if other forms of self-destruction such as fatal one-car accidents, drug overdoses, and self-administered poisonings were taken into account.

Although no one particular type of teenager commits suicide, there are certain characteristics that tend to increase the risk of suicide, and every teacher, counselor, administrator, and parent should be aware of them:

1. *Age.* Generally, risk increases with age, between the ages of 15 and 24.
2. *Sex.* Women attempt suicide three times more often than men, but twice as many men actually succeed in committing suicide.
3. *Race.* Blacks attempt suicide more often than members of other races, but whites complete the suicide more often.
4. *Geographic patterns.* There is a high rate of youthful suicide concentrated in the western U.S., especially in the intermountain region. Some research has related suicide to densely and sparsely populated areas.
5. *Depression.* As many as half of all teenagers suffer from regular bouts of depression.
6. *Acute suicidal behavior.* Indicators of suicidal ideation are actual suicide attempts, frequent discussions of death, making plans for death, purchasing or carrying deadly weapons, and taking deadly risks.

7. *Poor family relationships.* Feelings of helplessness and vulnerability make teenagers more prone to suicide, and factors such as family violence, intense marital discord, and loss of a parent through divorce or death can significantly increase this sense of helplessness.

8. *Alcohol/drug use.* There appears to be a direct relationship between the use of drugs and alcohol and suicide attempts by adolescents.

9. *Precipitating circumstances.* Often, a precipitating circumstance will push the teenager "over the edge": rejection by an important person, unwanted pregnancy, family crisis, poor performance in school, a fight with a peer, dispute with a close friend, fight with a parent, or mimicking another suicide.

10. *Other characteristics.* Suicidal adolescents are usually dependent, accident prone, restless or bored, obnoxious, easily fatigued, experiencing notable changes in sleeping habits, prone to frequent mood swings.

Modifications/ Considerations

As indicated, and dealt with in this tactic, there appear to be relationships among excessive stress, depression, and suicides. There are also relationships among self-concept, health, drug and alcohol abuse, noncompliance, social skills, and academic failure, themes of tactics in other sections of this book.

Six resources are generally available for treating youth who are depressed and are possible candidates for suicide; hot lines, psychiatrists and therapists, school psychologists, mental health agencies, school-based support groups, and psychiatric hospital units.

Monitor

Teachers, parents, and others should be sensitive to the moods and behaviors of teenagers and, if danger signs are noted, intensify their observations and actions and inform others of their concern. Checklists that indicate critical behaviors of youth could be developed for this purpose (see MONITOR 6 in Appendix A).

References

Benson, H. (1975). *The relaxation response.* New York: Avon.

Maag, J., Rutherford, R., & Parks, B. (1988). Secondary school professionals' ability to identify depression in adolescents. *Adolescence, 23,* 73–82.

Medicine for the layman: Behavior patterns and health. (1985). Washington, DC: U.S. Department of Health and Human Services, Public Health Service, National Institutes of Health.

Neiger, B.L., & Hopkins, R.W. (1988). Adolescent suicide: Character traits of high-risk teenagers. *Adolescence, 23,* 469–475.

Shaffer, D., & Fisher, P. (1981). The epidemiology of suicide in children and young adolescents. *Journal of the American Academy of Child Psychiatry, 20,* 544–565.

Sullivan, W.O., & Engin, A.W. (1986). Adolescent depression: Its prevalence in high school students. *Journal of School Psychology, 24,* 103–109.

Turner, D. (1987). Rx for depression: See the good that lies at hand, and "rejoice and be glad in it." *Seattle Times.*

SMOKING, ALCOHOL, AND SUBSTANCE ABUSE

Background   Offered here are some ideas for teachers to consider as they attempt to persuade youth not to smoke, drink alcohol, or use drugs.

Procedures   This section contains comments on each of the three habits. First, I spell out some risks involved, then offer a few ideas for breaking the habit. I'll deal with the easiest of the three first.

Smoking.   Following are some of the risks involved in smoking:

1.   *Shortened life expectancy.* The risk is proportional to the number of packs smoked and the length of time one smoked.

2. *Heart disease.* Smokers are twice as likely to have a heart attack as nonsmokers, and five times more likely to die suddenly from a heart attack.

3. *Peripheral vascular disease.* Because smoking accelerates "hardening of the arteries" and encourages platelet adhesion, it can negatively affect blood circulation in the legs, which can lead to gangrene and amputation.

4. *Lung cancer.* Smoking is responsible for over 80% of all lung cancers. This type of cancer is the leading cause of cancer deaths among men and will soon be for women.

5. *Larynx cancer.* Smoking increases the risk by about 3 to 18 times.

6. *Mouth cancer.* Smokers have 3 to 10 times as many oral cancers as nonsmokers.

7. *Smoking can cause cancer of esophagus, bladder, pancreas, and chronic bronchitis and emphysema.*

8. *Stillbirth, prematurity, low birth weight, and sudden infant death syndrome.* All these conditions are increased if a woman smoked during pregnancy.

9. *Affect on nonsmokers.* Breathing smoke-laden air can cause elevated heart rate and blood pressure in nonsmokers.

Now for the good news. Ten to 15 years after a person has quit, exsmokers' mortality rates approach those of persons who never smoked, and increased risk of heart disease decreases sharply after one year of nonsmoking.

Following are the six steps to quitting the habit:

Step 1: Fear of Quitting. Write down some of your past successes to indicate the power and sense of control and competence you had. Eliminate negative beliefs such as: "I'm afraid I'll gain weight if I stop smoking." "I've been smoking too long to stop." "Cigarettes relieve my tension."

Step 2: Create Commitment. There are many reasons to stop smoking; list yours. Following are a few to consider: It will reduce my chances of getting lung cancer. It will reduce my chances of developing heart trouble. I'll have more endurance when I exercise or participate in a sport. I'll be less likely to catch colds, flu, and other diseases.

Step 3: Begin Healthy Activities. Begin a regular program of exercise. Practice relaxation techniques and visualization.

Step 4: Plan Pleasure Activities. List a number of things that you like to do, and make sure you do them as much as possible. Plan rewards for quitting smoking.

Step 5: Plan Your Quit Day. Set a date for quitting 3 or 4 weeks from today. Plan special rewards for yourself in the short and long term. Sign a contract that you are quitting with your physician or other significant person. In preparing for "Quit Day," do not carry cigarettes, put away all ashtrays, go to places where you cannot smoke, go to bed earlier, keep your hands occupied, take frequent showers, drink non-alcoholic beverages.

Step 6: Quit Day. Get rid of all cigarettes, ashtrays, lighters, and matches. Tell your friends, your family, and your co-workers that you have quit. Remind yourself over and over again that the strange feelings you have when you quit will go away. It should take from 2 to 4 weeks.

Alcohol. Alcohol is a central nervous system depressant. Excessive or long-term use can be deadly. Following are a few more facts that should be pointed out and discussed.

1. Alcohol accounts for roughly 75,000 deaths annually in the U.S. About two-thirds of these are caused by accidents, suicide, and homicide, and one-third by acute and chronic alcohol-related illness.
2. Alcohol is a factor in half of all serious motor vehicle accidents. In December 1989, a man was convicted in Kentucky of killing 27 children and injuring dozens of others in the worst case of drunken driving in our history.
3. Frequent alcohol use has been shown to increase risk for a variety of chronic illnesses, particularly cancers and liver disease.
4. Alcohol appears to act with tobacco to multiply the risk of esophageal cancer.

5. There is clear evidence linking heavy alcohol consumption to fatty liver disease, alcoholic hepatitis, and cirrhosis.
6. Acute pancreatitis has also been associated with long-term alcohol abuse.
7. Nervous system disorders are a very common, yet less widely recognized problem associated with long-term alcoholism.
8. Alcohol has an effect on the endocrine system and is implicated in sexual dysfunction.
9. Alcohol has been shown to produce special risk to the developing fetus. Alcoholic mothers are twice as likely to suffer habitual spontaneous abortion and twice as likely to produce low birth weight babies as nonalcoholic mothers. Women who drink one ounce per day in early pregnancy show fetal alcohol syndrome rates between 1% and 10%.
10. Alcohol has been shown to have detrimental psychological effects on certain people. For example, suicide has been reported to occur 30 times more frequently among alcoholics than among the general population.

Substance Abuse. Certain characteristics of individuals and of their personal environments are associated with a greater risk of adolescent drug abuse:

1. Delinquents are more likely than nondelinquents to have depressed levels of autonomic and central nervous system arousal, and low arousal may contribute to sensation-seeking behaviors such as substance use among adolescents.
2. Youth characterized by withdrawal responses to new stimuli, biological irregularity, slow adaptability to change, frequent negative mood expressions, and high intensity of positive and negative expressions of affect more often become regular users of alcohol, tobacco, and marijuana in adulthood than children who evidenced greater adaptability and positive outlook early in life.
3. Researchers have found a higher prevalence of substance abuse disorders in late adolescence among youth diagnosed as hyperactive in childhood.

4. Poor parenting, high levels of family conflict, and a low degree of bonding between children and parents appear to increase the risk of adolescent problems generally, including the abuse of alcohol and other drugs.

5. Lack of maternal involvement in children's activities, lack of parental discipline, and low parental educational aspirations for children are associated with drug use.

6. Children from homes broken by marital discord are at higher risk of delinquency and drug use.

7. Parent-child interactions characterized by lack of closeness and lack of maternal involvement in activities with children appear to be related to initiation of drug use.

8. Poor school performance is a common antecedent of initiation into drugs and has been found to predict subsequent frequency and levels of use of illicit drugs.

9. A low degree of commitment to education appears to be related to adolescent drug use. Data show that the use of hallucinogens, cocaine, heroin, stimulants, sedatives, or nonmedically prescribed tranquilizers is lower among students who plan to enter college than among those who do not.

10. Peer use of substances has been found to be among the strongest predictors of substance use among youth.

11. Alienation from the dominant values of society, low respect for religion, and rebelliousness are positively related to drug use and delinquent behavior.

12. High tolerance of deviance, resistance to traditional authority, a strong need for independence, and normlessness have all been linked with drug use.

13. Earlier onset of drug use seems to signal the later extent to which drugs are used (Hawkins & Catalano, 1988).

According to Miksic (1987) the following are major actions required of successful substance abuse education programs:

1. Establish a clear, well-defined policy for teachers and students; detail how apparent or substantiated drug use or possession will be dealt with.

2. Encourage teachers to establish basic drug education curricula for their grade levels. Programs should be simple, brief, and nonjudgmental, and emphasize teachers' concerns for students' welfare.
3. Help teachers become aware of local drug problems and service agencies.
4. Provide an atmosphere in which teachers can develop the skills for resolving classroom and individual problems and for leading discussions about topics such as adolescent development and drug use.
5. Develop an intervention program that involves families as well as students by offering both one-on-one and group counseling and by making use of community resources.
6. Ask all teachers to review their role perceptions. If they feel their jobs are basically unfulfilling, and they are unable to empathize with students and deal with affective as well as cognitive training, they should perhaps seek other employment.
7. Develop peer-group approaches with positive role models for group or individual support.
8. Promote understanding of the emotional structure and perceptions that often accompany drug use. For example, drug-using students who feel they are incompetent and unreasonably rejected by adults and peers need a sympathetic approach rather than a disciplinary and judgmental attitude that confirms their belief that teachers and administrators are concerned only about keeping order, not about helping them.

Modifications/ Considerations

As mentioned in other tactics, only a few ideas are given here. Teachers who attempt to deal with these critical matters with students should gather considerable accurate and up-to-date materials on the subjects and study them carefully. They should then deal with these situations as they arise, regardless of the subject they are teaching.

Monitor

Data from this tactic pertain to the number of students who smoke, drink, or abuse substances. Hopefully, with increased understanding of these matters and efforts to cut down on their uses, the frequencies of these destructive habits will be decelerated (see MONITOR 1 in Appendix A).

References   Hawkins, J.D., & Catalano, R.F. (1988). *Risk and protective factors for alcohol and other drug problems in adolescence and early adulthood: Implications for substance abuse prevention.* Unpublished manuscript, Social Development Research Group, University of Washington, Seattle.

Medicine for the layman: Behavior patterns and health. (1985). U.S. Department of Health and Human Services, Public Health Service, National Institutes of Health.

Miksic, S. (1987). Drug abuse management in adolescent special education. In M.M. Kerr, C.M. Nelson, & D.L. Lambert (Eds.), *Helping adolescents with learning and behavior problems* (pp. 225–253). Columbus, OH: Merrill.

The Providence stop smoking handbook: A step-by-step guide to smoke-free living. (1989). Providence Respiratory Care Center, Providence Medical Center, 500 17th Avenue, P.O. Box C-34008, Seattle, WA 98124.

BEYOND SEX EDUCATION

Background   Let's assume that the adolescents with whom we are dealing, those who are at risk and others, know all about testicles, the scrotum, penis, vagina, fallopian tubes, and other vital parts. Let's assume also that they know a lot about masturbation and intercourse. We might even assume that they know about oral, anal, and other types of intercourse, are aware of the many positions for "doing it," and have some ideas about heterosexual and homosexual activity. That's not what this tactic is about. Our concern is that many adolescents are not aware of the consequences of having sex with someone of the same or opposite sex. Many of them do not appear to be aware of the fact, for example, that a baby can result from their sexual involvement, and not a few of them are naive about the diseases that are transmitted through sexual activity.

Offered here are some suggestions for teachers and counselors. There are many other facts and statistics that must be brought out to youth, but the ones noted here could be a start. It is my feeling, in developing this tactic and the others in this set, that all teachers should deal with these health matters. In my opinion, history, science, language, and other content teachers should assist with these important matters as they come up in their classes.

Procedures

I believe that teachers should engage youth in discussions on two important topics when it comes to sexual activity: the rearing of children and the awareness of sexually transmitted diseases.

Raising Children. A few discussions on this topic would not be out of line. For openers, talk about the responsibility of women while carrying the child, that they should not smoke, they should exercise, they should have prenatal care, and by all means, they should not drink alcohol, not a drop. (There was mention of this is the preceding tactic.) Discuss the man's and woman's responsibility insofar as preparing for the baby: going to classes, buying the necessary clothes and supplies, preparing the home, preparing others in the home for the arrival of a baby. Point out that a great deal of thought and preparation should take place prior to a baby's arrival. New parents shouldn't count on their own mom or dad to take on this responsibility. Talk about the many initial responsibilities when the baby arrives: feeding, changing, interacting. Emphasize the fact that what occurs early on in children's lives is of vital importance, and what happens in the first weeks, months, years, will set the stage for their personalities throughout their lives.

Invite young mothers and fathers to the class to talk about their baby. Have them bring the baby. They will tell the group, first of all, that the care and nurturing of a baby takes considerable time. It is not one of those things that you do for an hour or two then go on to another activity. It is a day after day responsibility. Indeed, it is a night after night chore. They will inform the class too, if they are at all honest, that they get tired of it, that they would like to meet with their old school chums and have a beer or a soda or do almost anything but tend the baby. They will tell the group that they get irritated, even mad, some nights when the baby wakes them up and they are tired. But that doesn't matter; the baby must still be loved and cared for.

Talk about the situations that have not worked out, where the woman or the man was too irresponsible, too immature, too selfish to properly care for the baby. Unfortunately, everyone knows about several instances like this in their neighborhoods. Talk about the girl who had an affair with someone of another race. They had a baby, the woman's folks disowned her; the man accepted no responsibility, and the baby was adopted by a family in another state. Talk about the couple who had a baby and the woman had another child from a former marriage. The man abused the older child and neglected the new one. The woman was equally irresponsible, and the boy's parents (in their late sixties) took the new baby, and the older child went with the woman's first husband. The first husband's wife didn't care for the boy, because he was a mess from all the commotion and distrust, and the boy's parents with the little girl have been tied up in custody battles. And talk about the boy who lived with a girl and had two children. The boy was a gambler and the girl a prostitute; neither cared about the children. The boy's parents (in their early sixties) now have the two children, but they would probably be sent to the woman if she went to court over it. (The same would apply to the second case: the set of parents who have the girl.) Not a pretty sight, but all that is happening within four blocks of where I live, and those are just the cases I know about!

Sexually Transmitted Diseases. We probably shouldn't, but let's assume that boys and girls know all about condoms. The boys know where to buy them and when to use them. Assume that they know enough to put them on after an erection, before penetration, and to take them off after they are through. Assume also that they know not to reuse them or to put oil-based lubricants on them (they may disintegrate the condom). But it probably isn't too good an idea to assume that they know much about sexually transmitted diseases.

You might start off the discussion with some information about *Acquired Immune Deficiency Syndrome* (AIDS).

What is it? It is a disease that is caused by the human immunodeficiency virus or HIV. Over time, HIV damages the body's immune system, resulting in infections and cancers that would not usually be a threat to healthy individuals. These illnesses are referred to as "opportunistic" infections and malignancies.

Who is at risk of getting AIDS? The great majority of those affected are men who have had sex with other men.

Why should I be concerned about AIDS? AIDS has a very high fatality rate; most persons die within 3 years from the time of diagnosis.

What are the symptoms of AIDS? A fever without a known cause for 2 weeks or more; night sweats when the room is not hot; a persistent dry cough not due to smoking; breathing difficulty, such as shortness of breath; loss of appetite; unexplained diarrhea; swollen lymph nodes; unexplained skin spots or lumps; and yeast infections that keep recurring.

How is AIDS diagnosed? The diagnosis is based on the person's medical history, the findings from a physical examination, and the presence of certain tumors or opportunistic infections when no other cause for an immune deficiency can be found.

How is AIDS contracted? It is transmitted and acquired only by direct intimate contact with infected blood or body secretions: by unprotected sexual contact with blood, semen, or vaginal secretions of a person who is infected; by sharing needles used to inject drugs; through transfusions of infected blood or blood products administered prior to 1985; by transmission from an infected mother to her infant in the uterus, during birth, or through breast feeding.

Can AIDS be prevented? The most certain way to avoid exposure to HIV is by abstaining from all sexual activity. Short of that, the person should stay with one partner and use condoms.

Gonorrhea is one of the most common sexually transmitted diseases. It is caused by the bacterium gonococcus.

What are the symptoms? A woman may have a discharge from the vaginal area or a slight burning sensation when urinating. As the disease progresses, she may develop pelvic inflammatory disease, a serious infection of the pelvic organs. If the woman is pregnant she can transmit the disease to the child during birth. The most common symptoms for a man are the discharge of pus from the penis and a burning sensation when urinating.

What is the treatment? Penicillin and tetracycline are the two most commonly used drugs. Although gonorrhea can be completely cured, it can be caught again. Untreated gonorrhea can lead to complications such as sterility, arthritis, meningitis, or heart problems.

Syphilis is a disease caused by a bacterium known as treponema pallidum that spreads throughout the body.

What are the symptoms? The first symptom is usually a small, painless sore on the penis or vagina. Later, a rash, swollen glands, fever, or tiredness may be noticed. It may then appear to be dormant for a time, perhaps several years. When syphilis re-emerges it may damage the brain, spinal cord, heart, or other organs. If a woman is pregnant and has syphilis she can transmit the disease to the unborn child through the bloodstream.

What is the treatment? The most common treatments are penicillin injections or tetracycline pills. Syphilis can be cured, but it can be caught again.

Genital herpes is a disease caused by the virus herpes simplex. There are two types: Type I causes fever blisters near the mouth, and type II causes genital herpes infections.

What are the symptoms? Blisters appear on the penis, vagina, or other infected areas from 2 to 12 days after sexual contact with an infected person. The sores break open and become painful. Later, there may be swollen lymph glands, fever, and aching muscles or joints. The time between the first infection and later eruptions may be months or even years. A woman with herpes can have a normal, healthy child if precautions are taken by her doctor.

What is the treatment? Although there is no cure for genital herpes, some relief is possible from the sores. Washing with mild soap and water helps. A woman who has had herpes should have a Pap smear every year, because she may have a greater likelihood of getting cervical cancer.

There are a number of other sexually transmitted diseases such as *nongonococcal urethritis, pubic lice, bacterial vaginosis, candidiasis, scabies, trichomonas, nonspecific vaginitis, pelvic inflammatory disease, molluscum contagiosum,* and *mucopurulent cervicitis.*

I realize that sex education, child care, and sexually transmitted diseases are sensitive topics. But they are serious topics and must be dealt with. As pointed out earlier, these matters should be handled as occasions arise. If, in a music class, a boy or girl expresses some mistaken idea about sexual encounters, it should be taken care of there, at least indirectly by making a referral to someone who is more competent to deal with it.

Teachers who discuss these matters with their students should obtain the most up-to-date and scientifically supported materials available. The ideas noted here are only outlines. Teachers' discussions should come from in-depth study on these topics; they should not shoot from the hip.

Modifications/ Considerations

The obvious and most important things to count with reference to this tactic are the number of youth who have children while still in school and the number who have contracted a sexually transmitted disease (see MONITOR 1 in Appendix A).

Monitor

Q and A about AIDS. (1989). The AIDS Prevention Project, 1116 Summit Ave., Suite 200, Seattle, WA 98101.
Sexually transmitted diseases. (1989). Division of Health, Sexually Transmitted Disease Section, LP-13, Olympia, WA 98504.

References

BASIC
SKILLS

6

READING: RECIPROCAL TEACHING

Background

The concept of reciprocal teaching was developed by Annemarie Palincsar and Ann Brown (1989). The technique was designed to help students better comprehend what they've read by following a four-step procedure: generating questions, summarizing, predicting, and clarifying. The ultimate goal of reciprocal teaching is for students to apply the technique to content area materials as a means to study and learn that material.

Who Can Benefit

This tactic would be beneficial for remedial as well as regular readers who are able to apply the four-step process. The technique would be of most benefit to intermediate and secondary students. It can be used with content area texts, as well as with basal readers.

Procedures

During the first few reciprocal teaching sessions, the teacher models all the steps to help students become familiar with them. Then the students take turns being the teacher, while the classroom teacher acts as a member of the group and assists the student teachers if they have difficulty with particular steps.

To begin the process, each member of the group silently reads a short passage or paragraph. When finished reading, each student silently generates answers to the four-step procedure in preparation for being the teacher. Once every member of the group has completed the reading, the classroom teacher selects one student to act as teacher. The student teacher works through the four steps orally and calls on other students when applicable.

Step 1: Question. The student teacher generates a question about the main idea of the paragraph. He or she might say, "The first step is a main idea question. A good main idea question about this paragraph is . . ." Once the question is posed, the student teacher may call on others for the answer.

Step 2: Summarize. The student teacher summarizes the passage in a brief sentence or two. The summary should include the main idea as well as any important details. He or she might say, "The next step is to summarize the paragraph. This paragraph is about . . ."

Step 3: Clarify. The student teacher asks if there are any words in the paragraph that are unfamiliar to anyone. He or she may generate the definition of a word to be clarified or may ask another student to give the definition. If no one is familiar with the word, the dictionary may be consulted.

Step 4: Predict. The student teacher predicts what the next paragraph will be about. The prediction should be based on the information in the current passage and on previously read paragraphs in the text. He or she might say, "Because the next to last paragraph described ducks, and this last paragraph noted what they ate, I predict that the next paragraph will be about where ducks live."

Students silently read the next paragraph or passage, and the classroom teacher selects the next student to act as teacher.

Modifications/ Considerations

Group size is an important consideration for this technique. The smallness of the group increases the turns each student will have and decreases the chance of any student becoming bored. The technique could be modified for a larger group by having different students act as teacher for each individual step.

The classroom teacher must be careful not to interfere unless absolutely necessary. He or she directs the lesson only when a student is unable to complete a step or completes the step incorrectly. Even then, the teacher should act only as a facilitator in helping students generate correct answers or questions.

The steps can be modified and presented in any order. Some teachers might put the clarifying step first. The ultimate goal is for students to internalize the steps so that they can use them when studying content area material.

Monitoring this technique might be done by giving students a paragraph to read silently, removing the paragraph when they had read it, then giving them a worksheet of questions pertaining to the text. This could be done on a weekly or biweekly schedule. The students could also be asked to tell or write freely about what they had read. They could be asked to do this once in a while prior to reciprocal teaching and once in a while as it was arranged. Teachers could count and chart the number of words said or written, the number of facts, or other features (see MONITOR 10 in Appendix A).

Monitor

Yet another way to evaluate this technique, particularly as it influenced comprehension, would be to involve the cloze procedure (see MONITOR 14). The teacher might describe one part of a story (perhaps the first) and ask a student to tell about the next. They could continue telling about alternate sections throughout the story. By so doing, the teacher and student would reciprocally involve a macro cloze technique.

Herrmann, B.A. (1988). Two approaches for helping poor readers become more strategic. *The Reading Teacher*, *42*, 24–28.
Palincsar, A.M., & Brown, A. (1984). Reciprocal teaching of comprehension-postering and comprehension-monitoring activities. *Cognition and Instruction*, *1*, 117–175.

References

READING: CREATING ACTIVE READERS

The purpose of this activity is to involve students in the reading process by requiring them to relate and apply their knowledge and experiences to written stories. It is based on various bodies of research that show that readers use their personal schemata to make sense of story events. A reader's comprehen-

Background

sion and interpretation of a story is based on the interaction between the reader's understanding of the current materials and the information and experiences on that topic prior to reading the material.

Who Can Benefit

Because this tactic stimulates interest and creativity, it is appropriate for unmotivated readers. It would also be effective for slow readers, for students are provided ample time to relate to characters and events and to write their responses. This tactic can be scheduled at the intermediate and middle school levels, focusing on basic story elements and language arts, as well as at the secondary level with questions or instructions focusing on more advanced critical thinking skills and elements of composition and interpretation. It can be arranged with fairy tales or other materials and with sophisticated short stories. The author of the cited research focused on sixth graders who were reading at the fourth-grade level.

Procedures

1. Select a story. Read it and mark with a red pen places in the story where feelings are aroused, where characters are introduced, when action occurs, when the story line takes a change of course, and so forth. These should be places where students can enter into the story and interact with the characters, the action, or the setting.

2. Type the story, skipping several spaces when you reach a red pen mark. Draw a solid line across the page to identify the point of interaction. Type specific directions to students in these spaces. For example: "Write four words to describe how you would feel if you were lost in a strange city." "Do you think Max should have kept the money he found?" Draw heavy lined boxes around these sections so they stand out. Photocopy.

3. Introduce this process to the class and model a story for them. Furthermore, introduce new vocabulary.

4. Provide students with ample time to complete the activity. The time allowed should take into account the length of the story. Begin with short passages or stories. Longer stories may take several days to complete.

5. Place completed stories in folders and allow students time to share them with classmates.

The teacher might request students to illustrate the story, write dialogue or write opinions, predict outcomes, create their own endings, record their feelings, evaluate character motivation or action. Once students are familiar with the activity, they can write interaction stories for their classmates. Secondary students could write interaction activities to be used by other students as study guides for particular works of fiction.

Modifications/ Considerations

This technique could be evaluated like the preceding one: Require students to freely write or tell about stories. Features of those write-ups or descriptions could then be counted and graphed. One could count the number of words written or spoken, number of phrases, number of judgments, number of descriptive words or action words. One could also evaluate the extent that all the ideas from a passage were covered, how well they were sequenced, or how well new material was blended with prior knowledge (see MONITOR 10 in Appendix A).

Teachers could evaluate the tactic described here by requiring students to describe materials a few times prior to scheduling the technique and on a few occasions as it was in place. Or, the teacher might alternate, over a period of several days, the involvement of the technique. In either design, data from one phase would be compared to those of the other phase to determine whether the procedure was effective.

Monitor

Gemake, J. (1984). Interactive reading: How to make children active readers. *The Reading Teacher, 37,* 462–466.

Reference

READING: A REASON TO READ

The RATE (Read and Then Evaluate) tactic is based on the notion that remedial students are often

Background

unmotivated because they have experienced a great deal of failure. Stimulating them to choose library books to read is difficult because most books at their reading level deal with content below their maturity level.

The RATE program is designed to provide remedial students with opportunities to select appropriate reading materials, form and express opinions about what they have read, and gain confidence in themselves as readers. RATE involves students in reading and rating library books by having them place color-coded stickers on the spines of books they have read. The rating stickers are visible to students who come to the library, and encourage them to read rated books and compare their evaluations with those of others. This program is intended to increase the reading ability and self-esteem of remedial students.

Who Can Benefit

This program may be most beneficial for middle school remedial students because of their special need to feel pride and experience success in reading. However, it could be arranged successfully with younger or older students.

Procedures

1. Explain the program; discuss and clarify the process of evaluating books.
2. Help students create a list of criteria for recommending or not recommending a book. For example, "exciting," "right for your age," "surprise ending," or "boring," "too long."
3. Read a book aloud to the students.
4. Practice rating the book and filling out a sample Rating Form (see Figure 6.1). Explain that green stickers are for highly recommended books, yellow for recommended, and red for not recommended.
5. Help students work together as a group to read two easy books, compare, and rate them according to their appeal and appropriateness for other students. (Reading easy books will help them become comfortable with the process before they do it independently.)
6. Assign student pairs and specific library shelves for which they are responsible. Students should rate at least one book per week from those shelves. They may work individually or in pairs.

FIGURE 6.1 Sample Rating Form for Reading Material

RATING FORM

Name: _____ *Dylan Smith* _____

Date: _____ *May 12* _____

Book Title: _____ *"Noah and the Rainbow"* _____

Author: _____ *Joe Jones* _____

Rating   green

Reason for rating: *It had good pictures.*

The words were not hard.

7. Give follow-up support in the form of art activities. Ask students to draw posters for books they have rated, and display them in the classroom or the library.
8. Keep rating records on file in the library.
9. Give each child who rates a book a "RATE Certificate of Merit Award."

Modifications/ Considerations

The students' involvement could be expanded:

1. Students could plan an advertising campaign for the program: design posters, make bulletin boards, visit classrooms, and make presentations about RATE.
2. Students who had rated books might go to elementary classrooms and share these books with the children through oral presentations, plays, or taped readings.

Monitor

To evaluate this program, students could keep charts to indicate the number of books they had read (see the charts with MONITOR 1 in Appendix A). Along the bottom of the chart, print successive days, and vertically on the left, print numbers from 0 to 100 or so. Each student could keep track of the number of books they read for a few weeks prior to involving RATE and continue charting the books read after the program was in effect. Students could, of course, maintain their own charts and set their own aims.

Reference   Jamison, P.J. (1985). RATE: A reason to read. *Teaching Exceptional Children*, Fall, 46-50.

WRITING: ACTIVITIES FOR THE WORLD OF WORK

Background   According to information in *The Bottom Line: Basic Skills in the Workplace* (1988), a large metropolitan bank discovered that a major reason for low productivity among the secretarial and clerical staff was that 70% of dictated correspondence had to be redone at least once because of spelling and grammatical errors. Anyone who has received correspondence from large firms or who has worked in such places can verify this sad state of affairs.

When potential employers were asked which writing skills they believed to be the most important for employees (Algozzine, O'Shea, Stoddard, & Crews, 1988), the following were noted in order of their importance: writing accurate messages, writing requests, noting assignments, completing forms, writing formal letters, completing checks and stubs, and completing money orders. In another survey of employers to identify the writing needs of employees, Emerson and Jenkins (1988) came up with four types of writing: filling out applications, writing incident reports, writing daily and weekly logs, and taking employment tests.

Who Can Benefit   Certainly, the primary beneficiaries of tactics that promote functional writing skills are those individuals who expect to survive in the world after school. The secondary recipients of rewards from such training are employers who despair over the lack of functional skills shown by those applying for jobs. To indicate the seriousness of this matter, the New York Telephone Company reported that only 3,619 of 22,880 (16%) applicants passed the examinations for jobs ranging from telephone operator to service representative (*The Bottom Line: Basic Skills in the Workplace*, 1988).

Procedures

A fundamental idea behind the suggestions in this tactic is that individuals must practice. Like learning to read, play the piano, or shoot free throws, there are right and wrong ways to do things, and individuals must be told which is which. After that comes the hard part: They have to do it right. And to do so, they have to practice every day. Included here are suggestions for becoming more proficient in four types of writing noted in the Algozzine et al. (1988) survey.

Writing Accurate Messages. One activity to promote this skill would be to practice giving messages over the phone, and taking messages for someone else. Another activity to promote message writing would be to give students one or more of the following assignments (all of which should deal with real activities and actual circumstances): Write to someone about what you did today; write to your teacher about your plans for the week, write to restaurants or other places that you attended and tell them whether or not you were satisfied with their services.

Writing Requests. As a possible assignment, one could write to (a) businesses or shops and request information on projects about which you are interested, (b) teachers and parents requesting information, (c) mail-order houses requesting additional information on certain items, (d) potential employers asking for information on hiring or other practices, (e) vocational or higher education institutions asking for materials, (f) branches of the military requesting information on benefits from service careers.

Noting Assignments. Being able to keep track of assignments is important in school and on the job. As with the other types of writing, students should practice noting their actual assignments, not contrived ones.

Completing Forms. According to a survey by Emerson and Jenkins (1988), the written employment application is the number two method used by employers to hire new employees (second only to the personal interview). The proportion of individuals who cannot properly fill out forms is extremely high. One of the problems in assisting youth to fill out applications is that there are so many types of forms. Nonetheless, students should be given experience in filling them out.

Teachers could select an application form that is most representative of others, run off several copies of it, and require pupils to fill it out. Teachers would learn quickly which items bothered certain pupils and could provide them extra help. Once pupils could fill in items accurately on that form, they could be given another. Although certain of their learnings would transfer to that second form, others might not. Teachers should take those opportunities to point out the differences in the forms. Students should stick with the second form until they can fill it in accurately in a reasonable time, and then be given a third, and so forth. They then should be able to generalize more and more information across types.

Modifications/ Considerations

Two other types of functional writing that should be promoted are writing checks and taking tests. For the former, teachers should regularly require students to write checks and keep records. The more in line with reality the better. As for taking employment tests, suggestions are available in two of the Study Skills tactics in Chapter 1.

Monitor

A simple chart could be developed to keep data on the number of messages kept and on other functional writing skills. Data could be acquired daily on the number of accurate and indecipherable messages that were written. Even more sophisticated data could be acquired on filling out forms. For this, the teacher could, first of all, have a few capable students fill out a form, and keep track of the time required to do so. Then, the teacher could plot the number of correct and incorrect statements per minute on a graph. Using those data as the standard, the teacher could require other students to practice filling out the forms (with help and encouragement, of course) until they had reached the aim (see MONITOR 1 in Appendix A).

References

Algozzine, B., O'Shea, D.J., Stoddard, K., & Crews, W.B. (1988). Reading and writing competencies of adolescents with learning disabilities. *Journal of Learning Disabilities, 21,* 154–160.

Emerson, J.C., & Jenkins, J.R. (1988). *Deriving job skills from the workplace: Employer survey results.* Unpublished manuscript, Experimental Education Unit, University of Washington.

The bottom line: Basic skills in the workplace. (1988). Washington, DC: A joint publication of the U.S. Department of Education and the U.S. Department of Labor.

WRITING: TEACHING PROOFREADING SKILLS

Background

Students are often asked to proofread, correct, and rewrite drafts of written assignments. The problem is that many times students don't know how to find errors in their writing, and are unable to correct the ones they do find.

Traditional writing methods teach each skill area separately (i.e., capitalization, punctuation, usage, etc.). It is assumed that students will make the transition from drill to general application in writing assignments. For students who are slow learners this transition may not occur.

This tactic is based on a program called *From Write to Right* (Melmann & Waters, 1985), the goal of which is to teach proofreading by leading students through a gradual progression of editing steps. The program does not aim to perfect the finer points of written language but to improve the readability of written assignments.

Who Can Benefit This tactic would be appropriate for intermediate or older students who need to improve their written language skills and their ability to proofread their writing for errors.

Procedures

1. Underline errors and give clues to students in order.
    <u>Her</u> was <u>there</u> money for the show <u>in</u> <u>friday</u>
    pronoun, homonym, wrong word, capital, period
2. Give error clues in random order.
    Six bird flue too a warm climet four winter.
    Look for: 3 homonym, 1 spelling, 1 plural
3. Underline errors but don't provide any clues.
    Paul<u>'</u>s was <u>stunged</u> <u>buy</u> a bee<u>.</u> but <u>T</u>he garden was in <u>ful</u> bloom.
4. Students find errors independently except for the clue, "Find five errors."
    Ate of hour boy eight the watermelons in less than an hour!
5. Students find errors independently.
    Yesterday, him play in the park.
6. Follow the same format but focus on paragraphs rather than on individual sentences.

Modifications/ Considerations When working with at-risk or remedial students, it is important to spend as much time as possible reviewing and practicing elementary level punctuation and grammar skills. This should be done prior to beginning the proofreading strategy.

Higher functioning students could practice editing each other's anonymous written language assignments. Students may find it motivating to be in the role of a teacher who does the correcting. For correcting spelling, students can go over their own work and circle the words they believe are misspelled, then look them up in the Random House *Bad Spellers Dictionary,* which lists commonly misspelled words.

Monitor Students' progress would need to be continually monitored to assure that they have mastered each step before progressing to a more difficult step. One way to do this would be to record the correct percentage each day of errors detected. When students reached 90% accuracy for 3 consecutive days, they could move on to the next step (see MONITOR 2 in Appendix A).

After the students have progressed through all five steps for both sentences and paragraphs, they are given a posttest that includes items from all five steps. To test for retention, the posttest could be readministered a few weeks after the completion of the program.

Melmann, M.A., & Waters, M.K. (1985). From write to right. *Academic Therapy, 20*(5), 583–586. **Reference**

WRITING: A MNEMONIC ORGANIZER

Writing, speaking, and reading are activities that have similar structures, introductions, main parts, and conclusions. Many students recognize these elements spontaneously, whereas others must be cued continuously to see them. This tactic was developed to give these students a strategy for organizing their writing, speaking, and reading. **Background**

Students who do not spontaneously organize their thinking or use study strategies will benefit the most from this technique. Students who already write with an acceptable structure may also profit from the reminders to examine their main points before writing and to search for errors when finished. **Who Can Benefit**

1. Introduce the rationale for a mnemonic organizer. First, language organizers ensure that students will follow recognized forms in papers and speeches. Second, by learning a mnemonic for organizing, students will be able to recall the form and use it in other writing and speaking situations. **Procedures**

2. Explain to students that the success of this strategy depends on their decision to use it carefully and apply it to other writing and speaking situations.

3. Present D-E-F-E-N-D-S (Figure 6.2) to students as a strategy for writing papers that defend their positions. (Each letter in the acronym stands for an action, and students should memorize what each letter stands for.) Work through a copy of the Organizer Form with a sample topic and position as each step is explained. Use an overhead projector to present the form.

D = DECIDE ON (my) POSITION ON THE TOPIC. (Tell students to think about what they're asked to do. Explain that they can't just decide on a topic; rather, they must know which side they are on and note their position on their planning form.)

E = EXAMINE THE TWO MAIN REASONS AND SUPPORTING DETAILS. (Require students to think of at least two reasons why they have taken their position. Make sure the reasons are different. Have students note these reasons on their planning form in the boxes provided, and note at least three details that explain each one.)

F = FIGURE THE BEST ORDER FOR THE REASONS AND DETAILS. (Ask students to decide which reason to write about first, second, and third, and note this on the form in the squares provided. Instruct them to order the details and note this on the form in the oblong spaces. Make certain that the students can defend the order logically, either verbally or in writing.)

E = EXPOSE (my) POSITION IN (my) FIRST SENTENCE. (Explain that the first sentence of the piece should state exactly the student's position.)

N = NOTE EACH REASON AND SUPPORTING POINTS. (Tell students to begin by stating the first reason they decided to write about, using a complete sentence. Make sure that students explain their reason using the details they selected in a logical order. Tell them to write what they think in their own words, using as many sentences as needed.

FIGURE 6.2 A Mnemonic Organizer

ORGANIZER FORM

Decide on exact position
  Examine the topic and think about what you're being asked to do.
  Decide what your position will be.
  Make sure your position takes a side.
  Note the position on your planning form.
Examine the reasons and details for the position
  Think of at least two reasons "why" you have taken your position.
  Make sure the reasons are different.
  Note these reasons on your planning form.
  Note at least 3 details that can be used to explain each reason.
Figure best order of reasons and details
  Decide which reason to write about first, second, etc., and note on form.
  For each reason, decide the order for the details and note on form.
  Make sure the order is logical.
Expose position in first sentence
  The first sentence of your essay should state your position exactly.
Note each reason and supporting points
  State the reason you decided to write about first using a complete sentence; explain your reason using the details you ordered earlier.
  Tell yourself to write more.
  Repeat for each new reason.
Drive home the position in last sentence
  Restate your position in the last sentence of the essay.
  Make sure you used different wording than the first sentence.
Search for errors and correct them
  Look for different kinds of errors in your essay and correct them using SEARCH: an editing strategy
    Set goals
    Examine your paper to see if it makes sense
    Ask if you said what you wanted to say
    Reveal picky spelling errors
    Copy over neatly
    Have a last look for errors

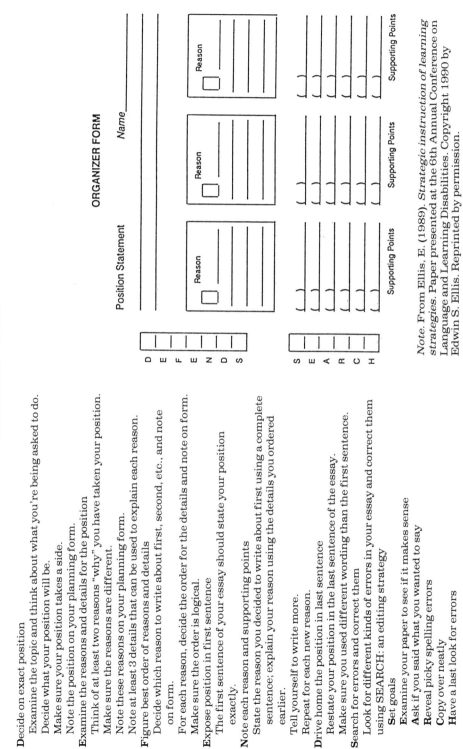

ORGANIZER FORM

Position Statement   Name_____

Reason   Reason   Reason

Supporting Points   Supporting Points   Supporting Points

D
E
F
E
N
D
S

S
E
A
R
C
H

Note. From Ellis, E. (1989). *Strategic instruction of learning strategies.* Paper presented at the 6th Annual Conference on Language and Learning Disabilities. Copyright 1990 by Edwin S. Ellis. Reprinted by permission.

Instruct students to repeat this process for each new reason.)

D = DRIVE HOME (my) POSITION IN THE LAST SENTENCE. (Make sure that students restate their position in the last sentence of the essay, using different wording from the first sentence. Encourage creativity in this step.)

S = SEARCH FOR ERRORS AND CORRECT THEM. (Require students to read the essay out loud to see if it makes sense, if it is convincing, and if they can make it more powerful by looking for redundancies and word usage errors. Set a limit for the number of errors allowed. Ask students to follow a checklist of errors such as incomplete sentences, noun/verb disagreement, misspelling, punctuation and capitalization mistakes. Have students copy it over neatly. Make sure that students recheck for errors.)

4. Following your introduction and example on the first day, ask students for questions or comments. They may say they recognize an introduction and a conclusion in the form. Inform them that the most important part of this writing exercise is for them to develop a form in "their head" and to use it. They should practice using DEFENDS so they get used to the steps for logically defending a position.

5. Review the points in DEFENDS for the next couple of days. Quiz students on the steps. See to it that they get practice by writing at least one paper using the steps.

6. Grade the paper using the criteria provided by DEFENDS.

7. Ask students to identify other classes or situations where they can use DEFENDS.

Modifications/ Considerations

1. Students can be assigned a position to take as well as a topic. This may be especially appropriate in beginning classes.

2. You may assign a position opposite to that desired by the students to stretch their ability to find supporting reasons. This works especially well in preparation for debates, because students should be equally prepared on the pros and cons of a topic.

3. Teachers can prepare materials for students to practice discriminating between a topic and a position. For example, "Write T before the entry if it's a topic, and P if it's a position on a topic."

____ I like pizza better than steak.

____ My paper is on the greenhouse effect.

____ I believe that voting needs to be changed.

4. The search step is an excellent place to individualize instruction, as the writing styles and errors of the students differ.

5. If you use student-to-student feedback in reading orally for errors, be sure to model how to give appropriate, gentle feedback.

6. Remind students to use DEFENDS in situations other than writing. Assign a speech or a debate. Point out that authors use DEFENDS to support their positions in newspaper articles.

Monitor

Require students to write several essays prior to learning the DEFENDS strategy, and write several after it had been scheduled. Essays should all be about the same length and written in about the same amount of time. Each student's sets of essays could then be given to judges. (They should neither be dated nor arranged in the sequences students wrote them.) It would be the judges' task to put the essays in either the "before" or "during" intervention pile and rate them on a number of features: clarity, organization, grammar and mechanics, neatness, and others (see MONITOR 13 in Appendix A).

Microcomputers could be used to evaluate aspects of writing, particularly certain quantitative elements. A number of word processing programs are available that allow writers to keep track of the number of words written, number of different or unique words, and many other features (see MONITOR 17).

Reference

Ellis, E. (1989). *Strategic instruction of learning strategies.* Paper presented at the 6th Annual Conference on Language and Learning Disabilities.

WRITING: READING TO ENHANCE WRITING

Background   This technique promotes the integration of reading and writing with content area instruction. It describes a long-term project designed to motivate students to create an original biographical story based on their knowledge acquired from other books. The student's enthusiasm for learning comes from pursuing a subject continuously for a period of time, building upon newly acquired knowledge by reading books on the same topic, seeking more information, and creating an original literary work related to the subject.

This technique is a carefully planned sequence of steps that builds on what knowledge the students have previously acquired. Its goals are for students to (a) learn about fictionalized biographies, (b) learn about a famous character, and (c) write an original fictionalized biography.

Who Can Benefit   The study (Zarnowski, 1988) was conducted in a fourth-grade classroom consisting of a mixture of students at various academic levels. This approach is recommended for instruction at the intermediate grades and for students at the secondary level who have difficulty reading (i.e., comprehending, making inferences, and learning from content area textbooks).

Procedures   The project that formed the basis for this technique took place over a 3-month period. It is a progression of steps to learn about fictionalized biographies, those in which authors add events that might have happened but for which there is no clear historical evidence that they did (Zarnowski, 1988). For this tactic students read biographies of several famous persons (e.g., Benjamin Franklin, Marion Anderson, or Kiri Te Kanawa) and recorded their reactions in a journal. When the students became knowledgeable about the character, they began writing their own fictionalized biography. Following are more details for carrying out the technique.

Step 1: Learning About Fictionalized Biographies

a. Read aloud several short biographies with narrations by a character who knows the famous person well (e.g., son, granddaughter, niece).
b. Construct a chart, and ask students to fill it in after listening to the story.

Learning About Fictionalized Biographies

Book title	Person telling the story	Famous person story is about	Things the person has done

---

c. Discuss as a class what was learned about the character.

Step 2: Learning About a Famous Character

a. Gather books from the school library, including a variety of material suitable for everyone (e.g., picture books, longer biographies, excerpts from writings).
b. Read to students 20 to 30 minutes a day about the historical figure.
c. Ask students to read silently from library books and write information they want to remember in personal journals.

Step 3: Writing an Original Fictionalized Biography

a. Prepare a fictionalized biography as an example and share it with the class.
b. Discuss the steps required for creating a biography by preparing a planning sheet that focuses on decisions to be made throughout the planning and writing process.

**Planning Sheet for Writing
a Fictionalized Biography**

1. Who could tell a story about Benjamin Frank-
    lin?

    Person:

2. What will the story be about? What happens?

3. What "facts" will you include?

---

   c. Work together on a draft of the story. As the stu-
    dents come up with ideas, the teacher writes them
    on the chalkboard.
   d. Repeat lesson several times using different infor-
    mation and a different narrative point of view.
   e. Ask students to begin writing their own fiction-
    alized biography. Encourage students to read one
    another's writing, and share ideas.
   f. Confer with students regularly.
   g. Ask students to illustrate books and proofread
    them for errors.
   h. Review planning sheet procedures as necessary.
   i. Set a time when books should be completed and
    submitted for evaluation.

**Modifications/
Considerations** This type of instruction offers a number of benefits
for students. Oral reading by the teacher familiarizes
them with many historical events, thus helping them
comprehend material they read independently. In the
cited study, students were allowed to choose their
own library books in order to collect interesting information. A teacher may invite students to bring their
own books on the subject or encourage them to check
out relevant material from the public library.

One concern may arise from this study: Will students lose interest in reading so many books on the
same topic? In the referenced study, the more the
children read, the more eager they were to continue
reading. Other studies have revealed that students of
this age are particularly interested in stories in
which a historical character provides examples of
worldly success.

By integrating reading, writing, and content area
instruction, less able readers are not deprived of information in content areas. They will receive needed
instruction in both reading and writing skills and

content areas without separating them from the regular classroom.

The procedure described here is one way to involve students in a purposeful reading and creative writing experience. The teacher must be supportive of all the pupils' efforts in order to attain successful results.

Monitor

A letter grade can be awarded to students who complete the assignment. Key areas of evaluation might be work habits, time management, pertinent content information, description of characters, originality, illustrative artwork, and neatness. To monitor students' involvement in this project, they could record the number of minutes spent reading each day on specified topics (see MONITOR 3 in Appendix A).

Reference

Zarnowski, M. (1988). Learning about fictionalized biographies: A reading and writing approach. *The Reading Teacher*, *42*(2), 136-141.

WRITING: SENTENCE-COMBINING

Background

Students' writing performance can be assessed on the elements of mechanics, grammar, semantics, syntax, organization, and content through the use of published checklists or by work sample analysis. The sophistication of a writing sample, as measured by sentence length and complexity, is the focus of this tactic.

Nutter and Safran (1984) proposed the T-unit analysis, which involves a main clause or a main clause and its accompanying subordinate clause. Typically, many handicapped students write simple sentences with a low number of words per T-unit. To increase the frequency of Ts, sentence-combining activities can be taught using the following guidelines.

Who Can Benefit   Given that written expression is a difficult task involving prerequisite skills such as reading, spelling, and handwriting, and that direct instruction for writing is not offered in most special education programs, this tactic may be especially useful for mildly or moderately handicapped students. It would also be appropriate for students who have limited scope of ideas, experiences, or vocabulary from which to draw for expressive writing activities.

Procedures

1. Evaluate several samples of students' written products and calculate a ratio of words per T-unit.
   EXAMPLE: Knight Rider is my favorite show. / It is about a man and a special car / he chases crooks / sometimes he fights. / He drives real fast. /
   > Total T-units: 5
   > Total Words: 25
   > Words/Unit: 5

   Record baseline on chart or graph.

2. Present lessons on sentence-combining.

   Step 1: Generate 4 or 5 simple sentences, utilizing words known to students. Write them on the board.
   > EXAMPLE: Tom went outside.
   > He looked at the flowers.
   > The flowers were dry.
   > Tom got some water.
   > He watered the flowers.

   Step 2: Write on the board and read aloud together a list of combining words: *because, when, but, and, or.*

   Step 3: Give instructions for combining simple sentences. Model the example verbally, and write the new sentence(s) on the board. Ask individual students to demonstrate various combinations.

   Step 4: Repeat with another set of simple sentences, followed by a structured worksheet on which simple sentences and combining words are supplied.

   Step 5: Next day: Review. Assign students independent writing for which they generate the simple sentences and combine them. Calculate and record the Word/Unit ratio.

Sentences that pertain to a topic of interest or that reinforce other vocabulary important to classwork should be chosen. When students have mastered the skills for combining sentences, more emphasis could be placed on generating creative writing ideas. Moreover, students could be challenged to combine various sentences in more than one way, and to discuss the changes in meaning.

Modifications/ Considerations

As suggested above, ongoing performances of students can be charted by using the T-unit analysis. Counting the number of words can be a tedious process, but low-ability or beginning writers will probably not write too much, unfortunately. Once the T-units have been marked students can count words, or the task might be assigned to parent volunteers or peer tutors. The teacher should establish what importance will be placed on other elements of writing, such as mechanics, before scoring (see MONITOR 1 in Appendix A).

Monitor

Nutter, N., & Safran, J. (1984). Improving writing with sentence combining exercises. *Academic Therapy, 19*, 449–455.

Reference

SPELLING: SEVEN METHODS FOR STUDYING WORDS

Memorizing weekly spelling words is a task that is easy for some, difficult for others, but nevertheless required of most elementary and many secondary students. Research studies have shown that several of the commonly scheduled techniques for studying spelling words (e.g., writing the words in the air, writing the words multiple times, studying the hard spots in words, allowing students to determine their own study methods) are not efficient and do not pro-

Background

mote success in spelling. To master spelling, students must be given research-based strategies for studying words. Below are seven such techniques.

Who Can Benefit

Pupils who have difficulty memorizing spelling words would benefit most from these techniques. However, they would be beneficial to any student or adult who has occasion to memorize the spelling of an unfamiliar word.

Procedures

Fitzgerald Method

1. Look at the word carefully.
2. Say the word.
3. Visualize the word with eyes closed.
4. Cover the word and then write it.
5. Check the spelling.
6. Repeat steps 1 through 5 if the word is misspelled.

Horn Method 1

1. Look at the word and say it to yourself.
2. Close your eyes and visualize the word.
3. Check to see if you were right.
4. Cover the word and write it.
5. Check to see if you were right. (If not, begin at step 1.)
6. Repeat steps 4 and 5 two more times.

Horn Method 2

1. Pronounce each word carefully.
2. Look carefully at each part of the word as you pronounce it.
3. Say the letters in sequence.
4. Attempt to recall how the word looks, then spell the word.
5. Check this attempt to recall.
6. Write the word.
7. Check this spelling attempt.
8. Repeat the above steps if necessary.

Visual-Vocal Method

1. Say word.
2. Spell word orally.

222222222

3. Say word again.
4. Spell word from memory four times correctly.

Gilstrap Method

1. Look at the word and say it softly. If it has more than one part, say it again, part by part, looking at each part as you say it.
2. Look at the letters and say each one. If the word has more than one part, say the letters part by part.
3. Write the word without looking at the book.

Fernald Method Modified

1. Make a model of the word with a crayon, grease pencil, or felt tip marker; say the word as you write it.
2. Check the accuracy of the model.
3. Trace over the model with your index finger, saying the word at the same time.
4. Repeat step 3 five times.
5. Copy the word three times correctly.
6. Copy the word three times from memory correctly.

Cover-and-Write Method

1. Look at the word. Say it.
2. Write word two times.
3. Cover and write one time.
4. Check work.
5. Write word two times.
6. Cover and write one time.
7. Check work.
8. Write word three times.
9. Cover and write one time.
10. Check work.

Modifications/ Considerations

To be successful with the techniques, students must be able to follow written, step-by-step directions. The teacher should most likely model the techniques several times, and closely monitor students as they learned the procedures step by step.

The teacher might make small copies of a particular technique to tape to the students' desks for quick reference. A wall chart would also be helpful.

Monitor   Because no one technique has been proven the most effective for all individuals, the authors of the cited research suggested that the teacher present each technique individually, schedule one for several weeks, and then teach the next one. The teacher should record all spelling test scores and note which technique was being used for which list of words. Once all techniques had been scheduled, the student and teacher could decide which technique was the most successful. Students can adopt that particular technique as their own study aid (see MONITOR 2 in Appendix A).

Reference   Graham, S., & Miller, L. (1979). Spelling research and practice: A unified approach. *Focus on Exceptional Children, 12,* 1–16.

SPELLING: IMITATION OF ERRORS

Background   Some students have a great deal more difficulty learning to spell than others. This tactic is designed for them. It is based on the notion that pairing incorrect and correct spellings will help pupils focus on the specific ways their incorrect responses differ from the correct ones.

   Many educators have been taught that they should not show students the incorrect way of doing something. The tactic described here departs from that idea, since according to research of Kauffman and others (Kauffman, Hallahan, Haas, Brame, & Boren, 1978), contingent teacher imitation of students' spelling errors may improve performance for certain types of students.

Who Can Benefit   This tactic would be an appropriate choice for students who have not responded to self-correction, positive practice, or other, more standard instructional techniques. In the research cited here, the authors studied mentally retarded and learning disabled students in primary and elementary grades. This tactic could be used effectively also for older pupils who had difficulty focusing on specific errors in particular words. This tactic might be particularly suitable with pupils for whom a sight word approach to reading had proven to be effective.

This tactic may be arranged as an adjunct to whatever type of spelling program was arranged for a targeted student. It may be scheduled as a variation of corrective feedback or it may be expanded to become the core of an individualized spelling program.

Procedures

1. Administer a pretest to students on an appropriate number of words on Monday. Pronounce each word individually, and have students write them on a worksheet. The words may be from a Dolch list, from a basal reader, or from a spelling program.
2. Using direct instruction or another instructional format, teach the words from the pretest, using the correctly spelled words as confidence-builders and clues to the spelling of other words whenever possible.
3. Administer a posttest in the following manner:
    a. Say the word.
    b. Have students say the word and write it.
    c. If the student writes the word correctly, praise him or her (words can be put on cards and given to a student when spelled correctly) and go on to the next word.
    d. If the student writes the word incorrectly, say "No, that's wrong" and cross out the word with a broad marker. Then say, "Here's what you wrote" (writing the word as an imitation of the student's error) "and here is the correct way to write it" (writing the word correctly). "Where is the error?"
    e. Have the student copy the correct model. (*Note:* Do not use colored pencils or other cueing devices to highlight the student's errors.)
    f. Go on to the next word, and continue until the posttest is complete. (Cards given for correct

spellings may be exchanged for appropriate reinforcers: books, magazines, school supplies.)

4. Begin next session at step 3 and repeat sessions daily until 90% mastery is reached.
5. Carry error words over to the next week.
6. Emphasize positive responses through meaningful reinforcement and underscore the "non-instances."

Modifications/ Considerations

This tactic may be especially effective for teaching phonetically irregular words. For some students, it may be better to revise step 3(e) by highlighting specific errors. For other students it might be effective if the corrected part of the word was written with larger letters. Attend carefully to the students' responses, and let your best judgment guide your selection of approaches.

Monitor

To assess accurately the effectiveness of this tactic, it is suggested that baseline data be gathered on spelling skill acquisition and maintenance prior to scheduling this procedure. If the same number of words was given for each spelling test, each pupil's score could be charted as percentage correct (see MONITOR 2 in Appendix A). Following the baseline and throughout a period when the imitation technique was scheduled, those data would continue to be gathered. By comparing a pupil's scores in one phase with those in the other, the teacher could determine the effects of the treatment.

References

Kauffman, J.M., Hallahan, D.P., Haas, K., Brame, T., & Boren, R. (1978). Imitating children's errors to improve their spelling performance. *Journal of Learning Disabilities, 11*, 217–222.

Nulman, J.A.H., & Gerber, M.M. (1984). Improving spelling performance by imitating a child's errors. *Journal of Learning Disabilities, 17*, 328–333.

MATH: A COGNITIVE STRATEGY FOR SOLVING WORD PROBLEMS

Studies with at-risk and mildly handicapped students indicate that many of them have a deficit in verbal math problem solving. This deficit is related not only to generalized reading abilities and computational skills, but to level of reasoning as well. Research that has focused on remediation of verbal math problem-solving deficits suggests that considerations must be given to developmental task analysis, cognitive strategies, and techniques to promote generalization.

    This example is designed to enable students to read, understand, solve, and check verbal math problems in general math at the secondary level. The strategy incorporates components of math problem solving and cognitive training such as corrective feedback, verbal rehearsals, self-questioning, and cueing with direct instruction.

Background

This procedure focuses on secondary students who have trouble with verbal word problems. The technique is particularly suited for those who must learn to apply newly acquired skills. The students in the referenced study (Montague & Bos, 1986) were LD students between the ages of 15 and 19.

Who Can Benefit

The verbal math problem-solving strategy includes eight steps:

Procedure

1. *Read* the problem aloud. The student asks the teacher to pronounce or define the unknown words.

2. *Paraphrase* the problem aloud. State important information giving close attention to the numbers in the problem. To provide focus on the outcome of the problem, self-questions should be posed (e.g., "What is asked?" or "What am I looking for?").

3. *Visualize.* Graphically display the information. Draw a representation or picture of the problem.

4. *State* the problem. This includes completing statements such as "I have . . ." "I want to find . . ." Underline important information in the problem.

5. *Hypothesize.* Complete statements such as "If I . . . then . . ." "How many steps will I need to use to find the answer?" Write the operation signs, such as addition signs or subtraction signs.

6. *Estimate.* "My answer should be around . . ." The skills of rounding and estimating are practiced in this step.

7. *Calculate.* Show the calculation and answer. Self-check features such as the current form of the answer, the correct place for decimal points, and the correct place for percent or dollar signs.

8. *Self-check.* Refer to the problem and check every step to determine accuracy of operation selected and correctness of response and solution. Check computations. Use a self-questioning technique.

Modifications/ Considerations

This tactic may be more successful for some students if they silently rehearse the steps rather than verbalize them. They might be given a cue sheet to follow as they go over the steps.

Once students are comfortable and successful with this technique, some of the steps could be eliminated. It is possible that shortened versions of the technique will sustain accurate performance for a number of students.

Monitor

The most obvious way to evaluate this technique is to require students to solve math problems for a few days without relying on the strategy, then teach it and encourage students to use it for a few days as they work similar math problems. If students successfully solve the problems with the technique, the teacher might request them not to use it, or to rely on only selected components to determine the extent the entire technique or portions of it are still required. Data from such an approach could be charted as correct and incorrect responses per minute (see MONITOR 1 in Appendix A).

Montague, M., & Bos, C.S. (1986). The effect of cognitive strategy training on verbal math problem solving performance of learning disabled adolescents. *Journal of Learning Disabilities, 19*(1), 26–33. **Reference**

MATH: A MNEMONIC STRATEGY FOR SOLVING WORD PROBLEMS

RIDGES is a simple mnemonic strategy that facilitates the understanding and organization of word problems. Like other learning strategies, an acronym is developed to help students remember the key steps of the technique. **Background**

This tactic could benefit intermediate and secondary students who experience difficulty with word problems that contain distractors and require organization of several steps. It should be of particular assistance to at-risk and remedial students, for they are characteristically lacking in abilities to deal with "story problems." **Who Can Benefit**

Step 1. Read the problem for understanding. The student should be aware that re-reading may be necessary to grasp the details of the problem. **Procedures (RIDGES)**

Step 2. I know statement. Student lists all the information in the problem.

Step 3. Draw a picture. The student should include all the information from Step 2 in a drawing, but it need not be elaborate. This step is particularly beneficial for students who have difficulty relating to abstract meaning.

Step 4. Goal statement declared in writing. The student writes, "I want to know _____." This statement may give the student a clue for the next step.

Step 5. Equation development. The student writes an equation that allows him or her to solve the problem.

Step 6. Solve the equation. The student "plugs in" the necessary information to reach the goal and solve the problem.

**Modifications/
Considerations**
During the early stage of the learning strategy, the teacher should carefully monitor the student to ensure that the steps are understood. Later, when students have become proficient with solving problems with this strategy, they should be encouraged to modify it to meet their individual needs.

Initially, the teacher should introduce rather simple word problems, to make certain that students correctly apply the strategy and accurately solve the problems. Later, as students become more comfortable with the technique and with calculating problems, more complex items should be assigned. To make them more difficult, require students to carry out two or more calculations, or add redundant figures, words, or phrases to the problems.

As a next step toward instructing students not only to solve but to understand the development and importance of word problems, ask them to construct their own. Naturally, those problems should be based on actual circumstances and situations the students encounter.

Monitor
As is the case with other learning strategies, the teacher may want to evaluate students' abilities to grasp the process (learn the strategy) and determine the effects of that learning on a product (in this

instance, becoming more proficient in solving word problems). For the former, students could be required to recite occasionally the steps of the strategy and explain what they mean (see MONITOR 6 in Appendix A). As for the latter, the teacher might set up a two-phase experiment. During phase one, word problems would be assigned prior to instructing the strategy, and during the next phase, the technique would be provided. Data from the two phases would then be compared.

Reference

Snyder, K. (1987). RIDGES: A problem-solving math strategy. *Academic Therapy*, *23*(2), 261–263.

MATH: A MATHEMATICS LABORATORY

Background

Limited planning time coupled with large class sizes make it impossible to meet the individual needs of students with traditional whole-class instruction. The Mathematics Laboratory, a method of individualizing instruction, utilizes principles of active learning to accomplish this.

Science and math can best be learned as laboratory exercises that involve three-dimensional objects, and when natural forces can be observed. A classroom can be organized by encouraging students to carry out experiments and activities.

Math Lab can be a remedial high school course, a course for average students, or a resource for gifted students. It is an area for hands-on discovery designed to give students successful math experiences. In the lab, students receive a combination of teacher-directed group instruction, paired discovery, and computer-assisted individual instruction.

Math Lab gives students and teachers a much needed break from textbook-style math. In the lab, students can learn interrelationships among concepts; moreover, Math Lab is a confidence-builder that enables students to be successful at making discoveries for themselves.

Who Can Benefit Junior and senior high students who failed or did poorly in basic math courses are the prime candidates for this tactic, although non-English-speaking students could also benefit. Math Lab is especially suited to those students who have "holes" in their overall math knowledge, since they may double up on Math Lab experiences while taking a concurrent math course. As Math Lab requires limited verbalizations, it is a suitable arrangement for students with reading and language disabilities. Math Lab can also be an appropriate arrangement for average students to explore cooperative problem solving, to learn about relying on others as learning resources, and to build spatial and logical skills. Carefully planned, the Math Lab can serve as a teaching site for gifted students.

Procedures A Math Lab can evolve over time. Some teachers set up a "Math-Lab Corner" within the classroom, and allow small groups of students to use it during the period. Students can visit the lab one day a week. Math Labs often carry over to other classes and teachers. Schools with labs can work out a loan service to share materials. Teachers in schools that build a central Math Lab can sign up for the room based on their units in the curriculum. Analyze the school's need for facilities by asking:

- Is limited or occasional use of the lab being planned?
- Are lab projects an integral part of the math program, or are they optional and not necessarily related to it?
- How large are the classes in which lab methods are being used?
- Is there team teaching in the school that can be utilized in a Math Lab?
- Can a new facility be planned, or must the existing classroom be adapted?
- How many teachers will be using the lab approach?
- How much money is available for the purchase of lab materials?

Consider the following points:

1. Support an active approach to learning.
2. Gain necessary approval from school administration, as the noise and activity level in the Lab may differ from traditional classes, and you may need new furniture arrangements.
3. Coordinate Math Lab materials with the rest of the curriculum. Construct activities that provide for multiple embodiment of each concept. Provide a wide range of activities. Relate learning to past experiences, yet provide new experiences when needed. Schedule interesting problems for student investigation. Accommodate individual differences by tagging each group of materials with the developmental level required. Provide necessary directions for beginning the activities. Guard against telling students precisely what to do, while providing them with enough direction to prevent confusion or discipline problems. Area centers can include:
   - Carpentry and automotive tools
   - Photographic equipment
   - Electrical equipment
   - Mechanical devices and machines
   - Textbooks and other reading materials
   - Weighing and measuring devices and equipment
4. Familiarize yourself with the materials that you have selected for the Math Lab. As you make this "trial run," consider the following questions:
   - What prerequisite skills are needed before these materials are introduced?
   - Are the directions clear and can they be followed easily?
   - Are there enough leading questions?
   - Do the activities match students' abilities, and do they embody desired mathematical concepts?
   - What are potential problem areas, and how might they be avoided?
5. Lay out the room carefully so that work can proceed efficiently. Locate a work table or two. Provide chalkboard or wall space for charting. Plan sufficient storage facilities. An option is to

create temporary shelves separated by bricks, which can be altered as necessary.

6. Begin implementing the activity-oriented lessons on a small scale. Give students time to adjust to a different learning atmosphere. Time is required for students to operate effectively in a learning environment that requires them to collect, organize, and analyze empirical data. Once you have made it clear that group leadership must come from within, students will adjust. Teach them the structure of the scientific method:
   a. Identify and state the problem.
   b. Find a method of attack.
   c. Carry through the plan of attack.
   d. Draw conclusions and compare results or methods.

   Demonstrate several applications of this.

7. Instruct students in ways to make transitions between work stations.
   - Assign students to small work groups and encourage group interaction. Avoid competitive situations between students; a non-threatening atmosphere is more conducive to learning.
   - Do not rush from the concrete to the abstract level. Allow students to build an understanding of the symbolic level.
   - Do not pack too much lab work into one session or hurry the students.
   - Try to alternate active periods with quiet ones.
   - Go outdoors when possible.

8. Collect as much information about the students as possible during the first week of instruction. Conduct informal oral testing or administer a teacher-made written test to determine where remediation is needed as well as boundaries for group instruction. Proper placement can ensure success for students. Continue to record observations every day as immediately as possible. Ask questions and listen to the answers, being careful not to assess the progress of the entire group by one student's response. Be alert for clues that suggest the need for new activities.

9. Appoint students to supervise cleaning up. Each student can be responsible for one area.

Put away material that is not in active use, as it may lose not only some of its appeal but some of its parts as well. Teach students to be responsible for the care of materials. Help them realize that in many cases the loss of one piece may make a whole device or game unusable.

10. Provide follow-up activities such as discussions of readings, reports, projects, and replications of activities. Ask questions that require students to analyze and synthesize their results, or require extrapolation and speculation on the outcome of related events. Ask willing students to demonstrate their learning to other classes or younger grades. Spend some time with students in evaluating lab experiences. After each activity is completed, ask students to share its strengths and weaknesses and make suggestions. Discuss ideas with colleagues.

Modifications/Considerations

Students in Math Labs have scored equal to and above students in regular classrooms in experimental situations, but the effects of such a program should be continually evaluated.

Keep Math Lab materials rich and open-ended. Do not set ceiling levels that restrict the use of materials in a particular grade. Nongraded sessions with a few students from several grades can prove fruitful. Given concrete situations, usual age and ability groupings can be misleading. Older children can help in the lab as assistants or buddies.

Sample Program Plan

In one school, Math Lab is offered once a week. Each quarter, students rotate through eight different labs. Individual lab packets are designed to be completed by a team of two students within a class period. Two teams can work at each lab with separate equipment. All materials needed to complete each lab are stored in numbered tubs. The tubs are set out prior to class, thereby reducing organizational time. Students find their lab station by checking a class chart. Math Lab is designed to serve up to 64 students, although 50 is ideal. By the end of one year, most students will complete 64 lab packets. Each teacher must assume responsibility for equipment maintenance, since no extra staff is allocated to operate the Math Lab.

TABLE 6.1 Computer Activities

Week	Group Instruction	Computer-Assisted Instruction
1	Testing	Introduction to Computers
2	Mental Math	Drill and Practice Software
3	Programming BASIC	Drill and Practice Software
4	Math Talk (integers)	Learning Games
5	Mental Math (integers)	Drill and Practice Software
6	Problem Solving and Logic	Drill and Practice Software
7	Application (integers)	Drill and Practice Software
8	Testing and Programming in BASIC or LOGO	Learning Games or Problem-Solving Software
9	Math Talk (fractions and/or decimals)	Drill and Practice Software
10	Mental Math (fractions)	Drill and Practice Software
11	Mental Math (decimals)	Drill and Practice Software
12	Problem Solving and Logic	Problem-Solving Software
13	Application Problems (fractions and decimals)	Drill and Practice Software
14	Geometry	Drill and Practice Software
15	Math Talk (percent)	Drill and Practice Software
16	Mental Math (percent)	Learning Games
17	Application (percent)	Drill and Practice Software (review)
18	Review and Testing	Drill and Practice Software (review)

Note. From Driscoll, M., & Confrey, J. (1986). *Teaching mathematics: Strategies that work* (p. 118). Portsmouth, NH: Heinemann Educational Books. Reprinted by permission of Mark Driscoll and Jeri Comfrey.

One unit of the Math Lab has to do with computer-assisted instruction (CAI). During the first week of CAI, students are introduced to the hardware. Vocabulary, operational procedures, and rules are stressed. Students run canned programs during the first week, such as entering class schedules and obtaining print-outs.

Students record their own progress on all computer-assisted work (see MONITOR 17 in Appendix A). A packet of worksheets is issued to each student containing a daily record form, self-correcting worksheets, and practice tests. Students pick up their envelopes on entering the room and have everything they need to begin work.

Drill and practice assignments are entered on the appropriate disk for each student. Some students prefer to work on only one disk at a time; others prefer two or three. When a student completes a disk, a short written test and brief informal oral test are administered. Any question that a student has difficulty with can be reassigned, reviewed, and retested. Certain topics that are difficult can also be reinforced with worksheets. Included in Table 6.1 is a list of suggested computer activities.

References

Driscoll, M., & Confrey, J. (1986). *Teaching mathematics: Strategies that work.* Portsmouth, NH: Heinemann.

Kidd, K.P., Myers, S.S., & Cilley, D.M. (1970). *The laboratory approach to mathematics.* Chicago: Science Research Associates.

COMPLIANCE

BEGINNING THE SCHOOL YEAR: OFF ON THE RIGHT FOOT

Background

Recent research and common knowledge have indicated that the way a teacher begins the school year is crucial to a classroom atmosphere conducive to learning. Although few would suggest that teachers let up during the year with respect to organization and preparation, it is absolutely necessary to establish firm and realistic expectations at the start of the term.

Who Can Benefit

Certainly, the teacher and the majority of the students will profit in the long run if the class gets off to a good start at the beginning of the year or semester. This is particularly true of many remedial and at-risk pupils for whom concise and firm expectations are requisites to their performance.

Procedures

Following are a few ideas for teachers to consider as they begin a new term:

Before Opening Day

1. Read your school's policy manual and re-acquaint yourself with the rules and procedures: opening and closing hours, attendance policies, fire drill routines, cafeteria rules.
2. Make the first day a real day. Prepare written lesson plans and have the necessary materials ready for students.
3. Plan the beginning and ending of class periods carefully. Many teachers lose control of students during these times.
4. Establish a few classroom rules. Select rules that establish an orderly environment and contribute to successful learning.
5. Set procedures for laboratory periods (i.e., cleanup of work areas or equipment, safety routines, distribution of supplies and materials).
6. Establish procedures for grading and for homework assignments.

Beginning Few Days

1. Identify your "standard operating procedures." Be sure that everyone knows the rules.
2. Monitor students' compliance with rules and standards closely the first few days. Uniformly and fairly apply sanctions for failure to comply.
3. Recognize the students' needs for a break now and then.
4. Convey the idea to students that they will be successful in your class. Tell them that you expect everyone to succeed and that you are there to help them.
5. Take it easy with respect to assignments the first few days. Set up situations whereby all the students succeed.
6. Become acquainted with each student's ability and motivational level, and determine, to the extent possible, each student's strengths.
7. Establish a system to assist new students to learn the rules. When a new student enters the class, ask a student who has learned the rules and procedures to spend time teaching them to the newcomer.
8. Take advantage of every opportunity to meet the students' parents. Explain your goals and expectations to them. Suggest ways they can help their youth at home with assignments.

Modifications/ Considerations

Use the checklist in Figure 7.1 to identify procedures you follow in your class.

Monitor

One way to monitor this project would be to keep data, from one year to the next, on the number of rules and procedures that are instructed at the beginning of the year and about how long it takes to do so. Related, the teacher might keep data on the number of infractions, tardies, and skips that are noted during the first few weeks of the semester (see MONITOR 1 in Appendix A).

Reference

Hutchins, C.L. (Senior Author). (1988). *A+chieving excellence: A site-based management system for efficiency, effectiveness, excellence.* Kansas City, MO: The Mid-Continent Regional Educational Laboratory.

FIGURE 7.1 Checklist for Beginning the School Year

BEGINNING THE YEAR CHECKLIST

Use this checklist to identify procedures you follow in your classroom. Put a check mark in the space to the left of each item for which you <u>do</u> have a set procedure. Place an asterisk next to those items you <u>do not</u> have procedures for but think you should. Circle items you think should be taught on the first day of school.

I. Beginning Class
_____A. Roll Call, Absenteeism, Tardiness
_____B. Academic Warm-ups
_____C. Distributing Materials
_____D. Class Opening

II. Room/School Areas
_____A. Shared Materials
_____B. Teacher's Desk
_____C. Drinks, Bathroom, Pencil Sharpener
_____D. Student Storage/Lockers
_____E. Student Desks
_____F. Learning Centers, Stations
_____G. Playground, Schoolgrounds
_____H. Lunchroom
_____I. Halls

III. Setting up Independent Work
_____A. Defining "Working Alone"
_____B. Identifying Problems
_____C. Identifying Resources
_____D. Identifying Solutions
_____E. Scheduling
_____F. Interim Checkpoints

IV. Instructional Activities
_____A. Teacher/Student Contacts
_____B. Student Movement in the Room
_____C. Signals for Students' Attention
_____D. Signals for Teacher's Attention
_____E. Student Talk During Seatwork
_____F. Activities to Do When Work Is Done
_____G. Student Participation
_____H. Laboratory Procedures
_____I. Movement In and Out of Small Groups
_____J. Bringing Materials to School
_____K. Expected Behavior in Group
_____L. Behavior of Students Not in Group

V. Ending Class
_____A. Putting Away Supplies, Equipment
_____B. Cleaning Up
_____C. Organizing Class Materials
_____D. Dismissing Class

VI. Interruptions
_____A. Rules
_____B. Talk Among Students
_____C. Conduct During Interruptions
_____D. Passing Out Books, Supplies
_____E. Turning In Work
_____F. Handing Back Assignments
_____G. Getting Back Assignments
_____H. Out-of-Seat Policies

VII. Other Procedures
_____A. Fire Drills
_____B. Lunch Procedures
_____C. Safety Procedures
_____D. Peer or Cross-age Tutoring

VIII. Work Requirements
_____A. Paper Headings
_____B. Use of Pen or Pencil
_____C. Writing on Back of Paper
_____D. Neatness, Legibility
_____E. Incomplete Work
_____F. Late Work
_____G. Missed Work
_____H. Due Dates
_____I. Makeup Work
_____J. Supplies
_____K. Coloring or Drawing on Paper
_____L. Use of Printed or Cursive Writing

IX. Communicating Assignments
_____A. Posting Assignments
_____B. Oral Assignments
_____C. Provisions for Absentees
_____D. Long-term Assignments
_____E. Returning Assignments
_____F. Homework Assignments

X. Student Work
_____A. In-class Participation
_____B. In-class Assignments
_____C. Homework
_____D. Stages for Long-term Assignments

XI. Checking Assignments in Class
_____A. Students Exchanging Papers
_____B. Marking and Grading Assignments
_____C. Turning in Assignments
_____D. Students Correcting Errors

XII. Grading Procedures
_____A. Determining Grades
_____B. Recording Grades
_____C. Grading Long Assignments
_____D. Extra Credit Work
_____E. Keeping Papers, Grades, Assignments
_____F. Grading Criteria
_____G. Contracting for Grades

XIII. Academic Feedback
_____A. Rewards and Incentives
_____B. Posting Student Work
_____C. Communicating with Parents
_____D. Students' Record of Grades
_____E. Written Comment on Assignments

Note. From Hutchins, C.L. (Senior Author). (1988).
A +chieving excellence: A site-based management system for efficiency, effectiveness, excellence (p. 58). Kansas City, MO: Mid-Continent Regional Educational Laboratory. Copyright 1990 by McREL Institute, Aurora, CO. Reprinted by permission.

MANAGING TIME: SCHOOL BEHAVIOR AFFECTS HOME PRIVILEGES

Background When traditional school disciplinary measures have failed to curtail maladaptive behaviors of adolescents, involving parents in setting up contingencies in the home has been effective. Daily written reports on student behavior provided by teachers, counselors, or school administrators are delivered to parents, who then institute the appropriate home reward or punishment, depending on the nature of the report.

Some benefits of this method are the following: (a) It does not demand much extra teacher time; (b) it involves parents positively in the educational process; and (c) it brings powerful home consequences (e.g., driving privileges, allowances, curfews) to bear on school behavior. In a study by Trice, Parker, Furrow, and Iwata (1986), treatment resulted in improved attendance, homework completion, compliance, class preparation, time on task, and weekly grades. Of the four types of communication that were used, Good Day Cards were the simplest and most effective; the procedures that follow focus on that method.

Who Can Benefit The cited study (Trice et al., 1986) was conducted in a senior high school. Participants were four 16-year-old males who were enrolled in a 10th-grade support program for disruptive and underachieving students. Chronic serious misconduct was the basis for their placement. All four boys had normal IQs, but were 2 to 4 years behind grade level in reading and math. They were all mainstreamed into regular classes for about half of the school day. Each lived with a single mother who was employed during school hours. This tactic could be arranged for at-risk or mildly handicapped students with conduct problems as well.

1. Ask each of the students' teachers to record students' behaviors on a daily form containing the following items (see Daily Report Form in Figure 7.2):
    a. Attendance
    b. Prepared for class (in place at late bell with all materials)
    c. Homework complete
    d. On task throughout period
    e. Classroom behavior
    f. Compliant (following are examples of noncompliance: refused to work, fell asleep, nonparticipation)
    g. Space at the bottom of the form for comments
    h. Space to put a letter grade for the week on the Friday forms

2. Give a satisfactory rating for the day if the student receives no more than two negative ratings from all the teachers. Make certain that students are aware of the rating criteria.

3. Contact parents by telephone to describe what they can do at home to help change their student's behavior at school. Following are some suggestions:
    a. Impose a Friday curfew of 8:00 p.m. if less than four satisfactory daily reports are received in a week.
    b. Give one-fourth of the weekly allowance to the student for a good daily report.
    c. Take away one-fourth of the weekly allowance for a bad daily report.

4. Send home Good Day Cards bearing a single message: "Your (son/daughter) had a (good/bad) day today." Be sure each card is dated.

5. Baseline measures taken prior to the implementation of this procedure could provide verification of its effectiveness. A percentage of improvement over baseline rates could also be reported as part of the students' grades, or noted in the deportment section of their grade cards at the end of each grading period.

6. To determine levels of parent compliance with the delivery of home-based contingencies, ask students each Monday how much allowance they received the previous week and whether they had been given a Friday curfew.

Procedures

FIGURE 7.2 Time–Managing Form

DAILY REPORT FORM

Date _____   Student _____

Behavior	Appropriate	Inappropriate
Attendance		
Prepared for Class		
Homework Complete		
On Task Throughout Period		
Classroom Behavior		
Compliant		

COMMENTS:

Weekly Average Grade _____ (Fridays only)

7. At the end of each 9-week period, assess whether students are delivering reports to their parents by asking parents to return all Good Day Reports delivered to them during that time.

Modifications/ Considerations In the cited study (Trice et al., 1986), three other interventions were tried with varying degrees of success. The second most effective was comprehensive reports, followed by personal letters and phone calls (to parents). In other situations one of those methods might prove to be as effective as the Good Day Cards were in the cited study, so they are briefly described.

Comprehensive Reports. A summary of the teachers' daily five-item checklists. Scores were tallied and either "satisfactory" or "unsatisfactory" was circled.

Personal Letters. Written to the parents, summarizing the student's day on the following points. (It is likely that a computer program is available that can generate these data.)

1. Statement of whether the day had been satisfactory
2. Summary of teacher ratings
3. Summary of teachers' unstructured comments
4. General statement of student progress, emphasizing the positive aspects of conduct and achievement

Phone Calls. Parents were called each day, following the same format as the personal letter.

Parents and teachers in the study liked the Good Day Cards best because they were the easiest to understand, and took the least amount of time to prepare and read. The telephone call condition was found to be the least effective, because it was often difficult to reach parents and there was a delay between the phone call and actual consequences. Another factor that may have some bearing on the relative unpopularity of these interventions was that they provided opportunities for lengthy conversations that could convey more negative information, therefore making them less rewarding for both students and parents.

An administrator, school psychologist, or counselor who could act as a consultant in this process might serve as a more impartial third party, and could save the teacher time.

Monitor

See the comments regarding evaluation on points 5, 6, and 7 of the Procedures section. Parents could be interviewed a few times while this program is in effect. They could be asked about the procedures they have involved, how successful they have been, and to comment on changes they might put into effect in the future (see MONITOR 9 in Appendix A).

Reference

Trice, A.D., Parker, F.C., Furrow, F., & Iwata, M.M. (1986). An analysis of home contingencies to improve school behavior in disruptive adolescents. *Education and Treatment of Children*, 6(4), 389–399.

BEHAVIOR MANAGEMENT: METACOGNITIVE TRAINING TO IMPROVE SOCIAL SKILLS

Background

Research has suggested a link between learning disability and delinquency. The cited study (Larson & Gerber, 1987) investigated the relationships among learning disability, metacognitive problem solving, social effectiveness, and the risk for delinquency. The authors hypothesized that deficits in social metacognition (the ability to discriminate situational requirements for effective problem solving) increase the risk for delinquency in youth with learning disabilities. The assumed reason social metacognitive skills are so instrumental in allaying delinquency is that those skills mediate improved social behaviors and enhance social competence. Many learning disabled and at-risk youth exhibit problems in social metacognitive skills, and ordinarily delinquents show more metacognitive problems than do nondelinquents.

Who Can Benefit

Learning disabled and non-learning-disabled offenders at a large state correctional institution served as the students in the referenced study. Their ages ranged from 16 to 19, and they had extensive histories of delinquency including offenses such as homicide, kidnapping, armed robbery, aggravated assault, burglary, and sale of narcotics. The following intervention is extensive and involved because of the severity of the population it served. This tactic, however, could be beneficial for many youth who lack basic social skills.

Procedures

1. Divide the training into three components: verbal self-instruction, metacognitive awareness, and metacognitive control.

2. Allow 90 minutes per day for the training sessions.
3. Focus the training around the following goals:
    a. Share experiences applying the skills learned.
    b. Read the goals of the lesson aloud.
    c. Discuss questions relating to the lesson.
    d. Drill steps and problem-solving procedures.
    e. Role-model specific skills.
    f. Assign homework task to practice the specified skill.
    g. Ask students to self-evaluate progress in applying skills.
    h. Share these evaluations with the group.

Verbal Self-Instruction.   Enables students to covertly cue themselves to stop and think before responding to social situations that are risky.

1. Set aside three lessons for verbal self-instruction.
2. Simulate a social situation that is potentially volatile or unpleasant.
3. Ask students to either act out (with restraint) or state how they would respond in this situation.
4. Instruct students to re-imagine the situation. Instead of responding impulsively, they must stop and think before acting.
5. Teach students to evaluate whether it is better to ignore the provoking situation or engage in logical systematic problem solving.

Metacognitive Awareness.   Teaches students what to think about when facing a problem.

1. Allow nine lessons for metacognitive awareness training.
2. Teach students to discriminate between "self" and "other" in problem situations.
3. Ask students to imagine a typical aversive interpersonal situation that they have encountered.
4. Ask them to identify the problems, and label them as "self"-owned or "other"-owned as they see them.
5. Help students to identify correctly the ownership of problems, and how that relates to their responsibilities in the situations.

Metacognitive Control. Provides students with a way to think when they encounter a difficult situation.

1. Schedule 10 lessons to teach metacognitive control to students.
2. Introduce the youth to the seven-step general problem-solving strategy for effective use of the social metacognitive awareness information.
   a. State the problem specifically.
   b. Generate solutions.
   c. Decide on the best solution.
   d. Be prepared with a back-up solution.
   e. Anticipate obstructions.
   f. Work out step-by-step procedures for carrying out chosen solutions.
   g. Execute as planned and check out feedback.

Modifications/ Considerations

Results for the delinquents with learning disabilities showed significant improvement between those receiving treatment and those who did not. The treatment also seemed to improve specific behaviors as well as generalize to situations outside of training. Behavior improvements were noted without specific reinforcement or cueing from others.

A point to emphasize about this technique is that the recommended training is complex and intense. A shortened version of the training may not result in the same positive effect. A scaled down approach, however, might be beneficial for less severe cases.

Monitor

Develop a group chart for recording the number of offenses that occur throughout the training procedures. Title the chart "The Overt Behavior Chart," and label the vertical axis "number of offenses" and the horizontal axis "number of days." Assign each student a symbol and chart those data each day (see MONITOR 1 in Appendix A).

Reference

Larson, K.A., & Gerber, M.M. (1987). The effects of social metacognitive training for enhancing overt behavior in learning disabled and low achieving delinquents. *Exceptional Children, 54,* 201–211.

BEHAVIOR MANAGEMENT: INCREASING TASK PERSISTENCE

Background

This is a long-term tactic designed to provide students with easily accomplished tasks and prompt positive feedback that in turn will raise self-confidence and result in increased task persistence. Consequently, a decrease in behavior problems in the classroom will result.

Many at-risk and remedial youngsters exhibit behavior problems in class (e.g., don't attend, cannot stay on task, talk out, and disrupt) that have been linked to a history of academic frustration and failure, social isolation, and poor self-concept. The idea of self-efficacy is that people's beliefs in their abilities determine how they go about solving a task, with what effort, and how long they persist in performing the task. A person's prior performances influence these beliefs.

Research indicates that success and failure experiences affect expectations, and demonstrate a positive relationship between self-efficacy and task persistence. The longer students can stay on task, the less opportunity they have to engage in annoying, disruptive behavior. Schunk's (1985) study showed that students' self-efficacy and skill development was enhanced when they participated in setting goals for daily work assignments. Students set the amount of work they intended to complete in a period. Their expectation of how much they could finish matched their self-efficacy scale rating. As students met and eventually surpassed their self-determined daily goals, their self-efficacy increased, which prompted them to set higher daily goals, which they attained. Additionally, their academic skills (in this case, math) improved greatly.

Who Can Benefit

The students in the cited study (Lyman, Prentice-Dunn, Wilson, & Bonfilio, 1984) were learning disabled sixth graders in a resource room. Intermediate or secondary level students who were anxious about or feared failure, and whose classroom conduct indicated an inability to stay on task, could benefit. Allowing students with conduct problems to participate in setting their goals will assist them to view outcomes (academic and behavioral) as being due to their own actions, thus instilling internal controls.

Procedures

1. Select the assignment for the particular class (e.g., math problems, vocabulary, history questions). Announce to students the amount of time that will be scheduled for the assignment. A short period is suggested at first (e.g., 20 minutes).

2. Give the following instructions to the students: "While working problems, it helps to have in mind what you are trying to do. Decide how many pages (problems) you intend to complete today. Choose a number between 4 and 10 pages (20 to 50 problems). If you do more, that's even better, but try to finish at least the number you choose. How many pages (problems) would you like to complete?"

3. Tell students to write the number of pages (problems) they have decided to attempt on the upper left corner of their paper.

Modifications/ Considerations

It is important to state a reasonable minimum amount of work that students should complete, otherwise they may sit back and do little or nothing (except talk and create disturbances). If students attain their self-set goals before the allotted period is over, either encourage them to attempt more or reward them with free time with the stipulation that it will cease if they disturb anyone else in the room (specify the types of behavior that are disturbing).

Monitor

There are a number of ways to monitor the effects of this approach. One could measure, for example, the amount of time a student spent on a task. Such data could be acquired by observing pupils at a predetermined interval (e.g., 10 seconds) over an extended period of time, noting whether they were working, calculating the number of intervals they attended to task, and plotting that percentage (see MONITOR 4 in Appendix A).

Lyman, D., Prentice-Dunn, S., Wilson, R., & Bonfilio, A. (1984). The effect of success or failure on self-efficacy and task persistence of conduct-disordered children. *Psychology in the Schools, 21*(4), 516-519.
Schunk, D. (1985). Participation in goal setting: Effects on self-efficacy and skills of learning disabled children. *Journal of Special Education, 19*(3), 307-316.

References

BEHAVIOR MANAGEMENT: HOME-BASED REINFORCEMENT

Background

The idea behind this tactic is that parents control a significant number of events that reinforce or control certain of their youngsters' behaviors. Not a few parents would debate this statement, because they have difficulty influencing, much less controlling, the behaviors of their youth. Nonetheless, considerable research is available to show that if parents define behaviors of concern, set up arrangements to give or take away something contingent on those behaviors, and stick to their guns, they will successfully alter the course of the behaviors. And related, teachers can take advantage of this power of parents and enlist them to help set up arrangements so that youngsters' behaviors improve at school.

Who Can Benefit

Tactics that depend on parents and their support are particularly beneficial to youngsters who have parents who will cooperate with the schools. Unfortunately, not all parents will. Some parents are so disinterested, unavailable, or disorganized that the approach explained here will not be effective. Schools should never write parents off, however. Every effort should be made to assist them to help their youngsters. Numbers of parents will show increased respect for schools, and make efforts to cooperate with them, if they know that schools are interested in them.

Procedures

1. *Specify the behavior of concern.* This should be done by the parent(s), the teacher, and the youth. All parties should know exactly what the target behavior is. A few behaviors that have been increased by this procedure are completing assignments, following instructions, participating in class, and helping others. Behaviors that have been decreased by this procedure are talking without permission, being disruptive, fighting, ignoring teacher directions, and violating classroom rules.

2. *Acquire baseline data.* Prior to setting up the intervention, someone should count the number of times that the target behavior occurs for a few days. These data could be gathered by the teacher, by a parent, or by the youth.

3. *Analyze the data.* Following this baseline, the teacher, with the pupil, should look at the data. If the behavior of concern is not occurring at a desired frequency (too few or too many), then something should be done. These data should also be shown to the parents.

4. *Ask for parent support.* Call in the parents (or one parent) and explain the situation to them. Show them the data and explain that, depending on the behavior, it should be happening more or less often, and ask for their assistance. Point out, if they do not know already, that they hold many reinforcers, and if they arrange them consistently, they can control certain important behaviors of their youngsters.

5. *Develop a school-home card.* Print on the card the behavior(s) that have been identified for change. On the example card (Figure 7.3) are seven behaviors: came to class on time, brought necessary materials, followed directions, stayed on task, asked for help when needed, didn't disturb others, and completed assignments satisfactorily. At the end of a period the teacher would circle either "Y" or "N" to indicate whether the student complied with the item, and send the card home with the student.

6. *Develop a reinforcement system.* In cooperation with the parents, set up a contingency system—that is, prepare to give the student something or take away something dependent on the occurrence or nonoccurrence of the specified behav-

FIGURE 7.3 Example Card for Home-Based Reinforcement

Name _____		
Date _____		
Teacher _____		
Came to class on time	N	Y
Brought necessary materials	N	Y
Followed directions	N	Y
Stayed on task	N	Y
Asked for help when needed	N	Y
Didn't disturb others	N	Y
Completed assignments satisfactorily	N	Y

ior(s). Following are some things that parents can give or withhold: money, TV time, tickets to movies or sports events, use of the car, favorite food, time to come home, time on the telephone, having friends over, going to friends' house, extra money for clothes or records. Explain to the parents that they should give certain of those things (or withhold them) contingent on a specified level of performance. For example, parents might allow their youngster to borrow the family car for 5 minutes for each event that is positively checked throughout the week. If all seven events were checked with a "Y" for 5 days, the student could use the car for 175 minutes.

7. *Gather data.* Keep track of the number of occurrences of the target behavior(s). As indicated, this could be managed by the teacher, a parent, or the student. The frequency of the occurrences should be plotted on a chart from day to day, and an aim should be printed on the chart so that everyone knows what is expected.

8. *Monitor the system.* Contact the parents periodically about the program: Is the student bringing home the card? Is the youth changing any of the markings? Is he or she improving? Is it possible to manage the contingencies? Should the level of expectancy be changed? Should the target behavior be changed? Should the reinforcer be changed? Should other changes be made in the system?

9. *Fade the school-home card.* When the student successfully meets all the expectations, it might be advisable to fade out the program. This could be done in a number of ways. For one, the entire program—the card, the reinforcers, the chart—could be terminated. For another, the teacher and the pupil could keep track of the behaviors at school, but not communicate this to the parents. Or, the parents could be informed periodically how their student was getting along. Yet another way to fade the procedure would be to schedule it intermittently and unannounced.

Modifications/ Considerations

As indicated earlier, this procedure is quite flexible; it can be arranged for a wide variety of behaviors. Furthermore, a number of reinforcers are available that parents can arrange.

As for considerations, teachers and parents must be consistent in carrying out this plan. Teachers must reliably check the behaviors of concern each day and make sure the card is sent home. Parents must see to it that they follow through with their part of the plan.

Monitor

As indicated, frequency data should be kept throughout this project (see MONITOR 1 in Appendix A), and those data should be charted on a graph like the one in MONITOR 1 (Figure A.1). There could be three phases to this project. The first would be the baseline, the period before the parent intervention. The next phase would be the home-based reinforcement period. The next phase would be a follow-up, during which time the teacher and student continue to gather information, but the parents are not involved.

References

Rhode, G. *Home based reinforcement systems: Effective communication between home and school.* (no date). Unpublished manuscript, Salt Lake City Public Schools.

Schumaker, J.B., Hovell, M.F., & Sherman, J.A. (1977). An analysis of daily report cards and parent-managed privileges in the improvement of adolescents' classroom performance. *Journal of Applied Behavior Analysis, 10,* 449–464.

BEHAVIOR MANAGEMENT: TECHNIQUES FOR HOSTILE-AGGRESSIVE YOUTH

Background

The techniques noted here by Jean Medick (Hutchins, 1988) were inspired in part by Glasser's Reality Therapy, Groves's Focus Program, and Gordon's Teacher Effectiveness Training Program. Glasser encourages teachers to do what they can to prevent children from developing failure-identities. Underlying Groves's program is the belief that an individual moves in emotional development from self-knowledge to knowledge of others. According to Gordon, four major concepts must be dealt with when developing appropriate social behaviors: the language of unacceptance, the language of acceptance, the concept of problem ownership, and the no-lose method of resolving conflicts.

Who Can Benefit

Medick (Hutchins, 1988) outlined techniques for deviant youth of three types: hostile-aggressive, passive-aggressive, and those with a withdrawn failure-image. The techniques noted in this tactic pertain to hostile-aggressive youth. According to Medick, they push, hit, intimidate or threaten others, call them names or ridicule them, and damage property. They antagonize others and are easily angered. They rarely smile, register little emotion, and appear indifferent. They "play it cool," swagger, frown, grumble, and are sassy.

Procedures The following points should be considered when working with hostile-aggressive (HA) youth:

Step 1. Develop a "success-oriented" attitude. HA youths will try to elicit responses that put themselves down and humiliate themselves. This reinforces their negative self-image. Remain friendly and firm in the belief that success will follow.

Step 2. Make friends. Take every opportunity to reinforce responsible behaviors with friendly comments and gestures.

Step 3. Establish classroom rules in a meeting. One rule should be that no one will put down themselves or anyone else.

Step 4. Enforce classroom rules. Whoever breaks a rule must identify the rule, evaluate his or her behavior, make a plan to follow the rule, and carry out the plan.

Step 5. Continue to develop a friendly relationship. Ask HA youth how they are doing, find out what kind of things they like to do, laugh and joke and share your interests.

Step 6. Teach HA youth better ways to behave. Instead of hitting or kicking, for example, decide on better alternatives—walking away and cooling off, verbalizing the way they feel about the situation.

Step 7. Have classroom meetings on topics HA youth think are worth talking about and for solving classroom problems. These meetings help them learn vital skills of listening, speaking, and thinking.

Step 8. Involve the youth in helping run the classroom. Give responsibility to HA youth and, while doing so, behave as though you are talking to responsible students.

Step 9. Talk about appropriate versus inappropriate behaviors. Discuss acceptable and unacceptable behaviors in a number of school situations: at football games, concerts, in the cafeteria, on the bus.

Step 10. Engage help of the school staff. Ask them to be friendly but tough with the HA youth. These youth, like others, must learn to get along with many adults.

Step 11. Have a special parent conference early in the year. Tell them the strengths you see in their youth, followed by a description of disruptive behaviors. Detail the step-by-step plan you have set up for their youth. Explain the goal of each step of the plan and why you think it will work.

Step 12. Identify the HA youths' strengths and interests through observations, interactions with the youth, and by listening to them. If an HA youth has difficulty with reading, help him or her find books on subjects of interest. When the youth is actively involved, ask him or her to read a book to younger children.

Step 13. Use the HA youth's independence to achieve academic progress. Set up contracts in each subject: for so much work he or she receives so much of something.

Step 14. Integrate Step 1 (teacher's attitude) and Step 13 (HA youth's independence). If the HA youth will not do something at school, require him or her to sign a "I refuse to . . ." statement. Give him or her the choice of doing the work at home or at school, but not the choice of causing a ruckus about completing the task.

Modifications/ Considerations

Many of the techniques listed here would be appropriate for youth of several types. They are not restricted to those who have acquired the label of HA.

Monitor

The most direct way to evaluate these techniques would be to tally the frequency of inappropriate behaviors displayed by the target youth prior to involving the practices and continue gathering the data after the treatment is in effect (see MONITOR 1 in Appendix A).

Reference   Hutchins, C.L. (Senior Author). (1988). Student management tactic 4: Medick's approach. In *A+chieving excellence: A site-based management system for efficiency, effectiveness, excellence*. Kansas City, MO: Mid-Continent Regional Educational Laboratory.

BEHAVIOR MANAGEMENT: TECHNIQUES FOR PASSIVE-AGGRESSIVE YOUTH

Background   The techniques outlined here for passive-aggressive youth were developed by Medick. They were stimulated by the writings of three authorities on social skills development: Glasser, Grove, and Gordon.

Who Can Benefit   Medick describes passive-aggressive (PA) youth as those who hear only what they want to hear, drag their feet at transitions in the schedule, misplace belongings, complain that they can't find them, volunteer to carry out chores but manage to mess them up, and demand constant attention in the process. They talk, laugh, and make noises throughout the day, are frequently out of their seats, and have a steady stream of excuses for misbehavior and failure to do schoolwork. The individual behaviors of PA youth are not all that bothersome; it is the fact that they occur one after another, all day long, day after day, steadily chipping away at a teacher's patience and desire to get on with the task of instruction.

Procedures   To deal with PA youth, Medick has outlined a 10-step plan:

Step 1. Get hold of your feelings—think before responding. A major goal of PA youth is to cause teachers to display anger. Do not respond with annoyance, irritation, or anger.

Step 2. Make a list of PA behaviors that irritate you and rank them from most to least annoying. Work to eliminate the top five. When accomplished, about 90% of the battle will be won.

Step 3. Deal with PA behaviors related to schoolwork. Make clear that teaching is your responsibility and learning is theirs. Concede that you cannot force anyone to learn. They should also be told that if they do not work, you have a responsibility to inform their parents.

Step 4. Have a conference with the youth and share your plan with him or her. Tell the youth which behaviors are unacceptable and will not be tolerated, and what consequences will follow if he or she persists.

Step 5. Have an early conference with parents. Let them know which inappropriate behaviors you wish to deal with, and how you plan to handle them.

Step 6. Make a point of giving the PA youth some friendly attention every day. Those youth need to know about better ways to interact with others.

Step 7. Give youths an opportunity to talk about their feelings. Have discussions on what a friend is, about the effects of teasing, fighting, and competition. Help youths label their feelings, particularly those that have to do with anger, rejection, and loneliness.

Step 8. Give PA youth responsibilities. Before they start to do a job, ask them to tell you specifically what they are going to do. Help them organize the plan.

Step 9. Reinforce briefly all appropriate and thoughtful behaviors.

Step 10. Meet the final battle—poor attitude toward authority figures and the institution of school—head on. Ask the following questions: "What happens to youth who fight teachers and principals and who break rules?" "Who loses in these private little wars?" "Who do youths like these hang around with if they drop out of school?" "What do you think the dropouts do all day and how do they feel?" Lay it out calmly, courteously, and in a caring manner.

Modifications/ Considerations

Many of these suggestions would be helpful for youth of other types; they are not the exclusive province of PA individuals.

Monitor

Keep data before and during implementation of these techniques on the effects of these or other interventions with PA youth. Certain of their behaviors could be charted as frequency of occurrence per day (see MONITOR 1 in Appendix A).

The teacher might also be interested in identifying the events that precede (perhaps trigger) some PA behaviors and which events follow certain of those behaviors. To gather those data, the teacher might develop a sheet on which there are three columns: one for antecedents, one for behaviors, and one for consequences. With that sheet, an observer could indicate those events during certain times of the day over a period of several days. These observations would probably need to be carried out by an aide or paraprofessional, since they would be rather time-consuming. The results from the observations might be worth the effort, however, if clues to before and after events that influenced PA behaviors were gained (see MONITOR 7).

Reference

Hutchins, C.L. (Senior Editor). (1988). Student management tactic 4: Medick's approach. In *A+chieving excellence: A site-based management system for efficiency, effectiveness, excellence.* Kansas City, MO: Mid-Continent Regional Educational Laboratory.

DISRUPTIVE BEHAVIOR: A PEER-MEDIATED PROGRAM

Self-management strategies can be arranged to alter individuals' behaviors: Make the behaviors less aversive to others and replace them with behaviors that are more socially acceptable. There are several benefits for students and teachers alike when students self-manage: (a) More teacher time is available for instructing rather than disciplining; (b) there is societal support for self-management skills, because they are essential to our democratic value system; and (c) the behaviors are acceptable and last beyond the watchful eyes of teachers.

Background

The study cited here (Young, Smith, West, & Morgan, 1987) sought to replace gradually the resource room teacher with the student's peers as facilitators of the training for the following reasons: (a) A peer-mediated program would free up more teacher time; (b) peer approval and attention would be more reinforcing to the student; and (c) the program would serve as a cooperative experience for the student's peer.

Discussed in this tactic are three phases of the self-management intervention: behavioral self-management, peer training, and peer-mediated self-management in the regular classroom.

The referenced study (Young et al., 1987) took place in a high school, where mildly handicapped youth were provided self-management training. Nonhandicapped high school students served as the peers who took over the tasks performed by the resource room teacher. The self-management intervention could be arranged for at-risk or remedial students with behavior problems in settings where a teacher would have access to a nonhandicapped population.

Who Can Benefit

Procedures   **Behavioral Self-Management**

1. Assess the environmental expectations (e.g., teacher, school, community, parental expectations) that should be set for the target student. Establish performance levels by finding the median of acceptable behaviors of three or more students who are successful in circumstances similar to those experienced by the target youth.

2. Define the target behaviors and the criteria for acceptable performance so that individuals understand what is expected of them.

3. Determine any discrepancies between the students' current behaviors and the expected behaviors by collecting baseline data. Behavioral deficits are defined as behaviors that fail to occur frequently enough, lack adequate intensity, do not occur with the proper form, or do not occur under the expected conditions.

4. Make sure that following the baseline period students understand the criteria as personal goals, as it will be their responsibility to observe and record their own behavior.

5. Establish a reward and punishment system for performance of the target behaviors that is acceptable to the student and teacher.

6. Implement the self-management program by illustrating both positive and negative examples of the target behaviors for the student. Define classroom rules ahead of time.

7. Schedule 35-minute sessions divided into three 10-minute intervals followed by a 5-minute period when students rate their behaviors and match them with the teacher's ratings.

8. Inform students that they are to rate their behaviors on a 0- to 5-point scale, and the ratings will be converted to points that can be redeemed later for rewards.

9. Give students the Behavior Point Card (Figure 7.4) on which they are to circle the number that best described their behavior.

10. Mark the student's card with a colored pen by putting a slash through the appropriate number to indicate your rating. Following are descriptions of the ratings:

    5 = excellent: Followed all classroom rules during the entire interval.

FIGURE 7.4   Card for Use in Behavioral Self-Management

BEHAVIOR POINT CARD

Name _____   Date _____

    0 = Student's rating   / = Teacher's rating

1st Rating:

                         Points _____
0 1 2 3 4 5   + Bonus _____
                         = Total _____

2nd Rating:

                         Points _____
0 1 2 3 4 5   + Bonus _____
                         = Total _____

3rd Rating:

                         Points _____
0 1 2 3 4 5   + Bonus _____
                         = Total _____

             Total points for 1st rating   _____
           + Total points for 2nd rating   _____
           + Total points for 3rd rating   _____
                        Total =   _____
           Average rating (total : 3) =   _____

Note. From Young, K.R., Smith, D.J., West, R.P., & Morgan, D.P. (1987). A peer-mediated program for teaching self-management strategies to adolescents. *Programming Adolescents with Behavioral Disorders, 3,* p. 41. Reprinted by permission.

    4 = very good: Minor infraction of the rules but followed the rules throughout the rest of the interval. There were no warnings from the teacher.

    3 = average: Did not follow all of the rules for the entire interval, but there were no serious offenses. Only one warning regarding behavior was given.

    2 = below average: Violated one or more rules to the extent that behavior was not acceptable

but followed the rules part of the time. Two teacher warnings regarding behavior were given.

1 = poor: Violated one or more rules almost the entire class period. Three teacher warnings were given.

0 = unacceptable: Violated one or more rules throughout the entire period. Four or more teacher warnings were given.

11. Give one bonus point if the student's rating was within one point of the teacher's rating, plus the number of points the student earned.

12. Give no points for the period if there is more than a one-point discrepancy between the student's and teacher's rating.

13. Fade gradually the teacher-matching feature over the next couple of weeks, but schedule spot checks to keep the student "honest."

14. Reduce the student ratings to one per session toward the end of the study if teacher/student ratings continue to agree and if the student's behavior is improving.

Peer Training

1. Recruit and train nonhandicapped peers in the same manner just described with the targeted student. Their training should occur in separate locations but at the same time as that provided the target student.

2. Ask the peers to practice the procedures by rating their own classroom behaviors.

3. Instruct the peers to match their ratings with the teacher's ratings. (The teacher comes into the peer's classroom to rate his or her behaviors during this phase.)

Peer-Mediated Self-Management in the Regular Classroom

1. Replace teacher rating with peer rating during this phase of the study, which should begin when targeted youth is down to one rating per session.

2. Instruct targeted youth to self-monitor in the regular classroom (where their peers are attending the class).

3. Exchange points earned by the targeted students for rewards at the end of the class period when the teacher returns to collect the point cards.

Implementing the self-management intervention is time-consuming and requires the cooperation of staff and students outside of the resource room environment. Teachers should consider that involvement before adopting the program in their classroom.

A significant aspect of this program is that it can be taught by a number of school professionals including psychologists, counselors, social workers, general education teachers, and administrators.

Specific classroom rules and reward systems will be different across teachers. In deciding on rules and rewards, teachers should consider student needs as well as their own. Because the program is built around the attainment of personal goals and increasing self-control, the students must believe that they have taken part in the decision process and that it is personally agreeable to them; otherwise the program will not be successful.

Modifications/ Considerations

Keep track of behavior ratings made on the point cards throughout the study. Chart the number of points earned per day and indicate the extent the pupil's records matched those of the teacher.

This project could also be monitored by interviewing individuals who are significant to the selected individual. They could be asked a few simple questions before the program begins and after it is under way. The following questions, among others, might be asked: Has the student's behavior improved? Is he or she more compliant? Is he or she easier to live with? Is he or she happier? (See MONITOR 9 in Appendix A.)

Monitor

Young, K.R., Smith, D.J., West, R.P., & Morgan, D.P. (1987). A peer-mediated program for teaching self-management strategies to adolescents. *Programming Adolescents with Behavioral Disorders, 3*, 34–47.

Reference

DISRUPTIVE BEHAVIOR: PEER CONFRONTATION

Background

Peer confrontation—which consists of peer aware-ness of discrepancies in behavior, calling attention to those discrepancies, and indicating appropriate change for that behavior—has been effective in reduc-ing maladaptive behaviors in problem students. The present study (Sandler, Arnold, Gable, & Strain, 1987) was designed to discover how beneficial the peer con-frontation procedure is with adolescent behaviorally disordered students. The authors sought to deter-mine whether peer confrontation would reduce two target behaviors in their students: (a) off-task ver-balizations (defined as a verbalization of a student not directly related to the task in which he or she is presently engaged) and (b) noncompliance (defined as the failure to follow a verbal command after 10 sec-onds, which has been repeated one time). The study also sought to discover how peer confrontation works across several classroom situations: group discus-sions, independent work, and group-individualized instruction.

Who Can Benefit

Two boys, ages 9 and 11, and an 11-year-old girl, all special education students, participated in the cited study (Sandler et al., 1987). They had records of severe behavior disorders including noncompliance, oppositional/disruptive behavior, and verbal/physical threats of aggression. The techniques, as described, could be effective if arranged for remedial or at-risk youth who display those behaviors.

Procedures

Interval One

1. Select a target behavior that is likely to have the most negative impact on students' performance (e.g., noncompliance).

2. Gather all students in one area of the classroom and seat them in a circle.

3. Ask one student to serve as leader during the group discussion. The leader may ask students questions about the weather, calendar, or current events, to which the others are to respond. Make sure the problem students are given the opportunity to be the group leader at least once.

4. Observe and note the occurrence of the target behaviors during a 30-minute group discussion period.

5. Respond as usual with positive or negative consequences for behaviors displayed.

6. Initiate peer confrontation on the second day. Each time the problem student engages in a target behavior, ask the other students the following questions:
   a. Can you tell student X why that is a problem?
   b. Who can tell student X what he or she needs to do to solve the problem?

7. Record the number of target behaviors displayed during the peer confrontation intervention.

8. Schedule a group discussion the next day without peer confrontation.

9. Note the number of target behaviors engaged in during the group talk.

10. Continue the steps in Interval One until every student has served as the group leader.

Interval Two

1. Engage the students in independent work. During this time, they are to remain seated, work independently, and raise their hands if they have questions.

2. Observe and record the number of target behaviors that occur during the first day, over the 30-minute interval.

3. Begin the peer-confrontation technique the next day during the independent work time. Follow procedures from step 6 of Interval One for the peer confrontation intervention.

4. Repeat observation of the target behaviors during the independent work time without peer confrontation on the next day.

5. Continue the same sequence over the next couple of days.

Interval Three

1. Conduct a group-individualized instruction activity. During this time, students are to remain at their desks while engaged in group games, worksheets, or films.
2. Record the occurrences of target behaviors observed for a 30-minute block of time within the group-individualized instruction.
3. Begin the peer-confrontation intervention during the group-individualized activity on the following day. Follow the procedures from step 6 of Interval One.
4. Note any target behaviors that occur the next day during the activity. Do not initiate peer confrontation.
5. Alternate peer confrontation with no peer confrontation during the activity over the next couple of days. Continue recording target behaviors.

Modifications/Considerations

Results of the cited study (Sandler et al., 1987) indicated that peer confrontation was an effective method for modifying disruptive behaviors of behaviorally disordered youth. The intervention seemed to work best when implemented during individualized instruction. It appears that peer confrontation served as an aversive stimulus to students, in that they reduced the target behavior to avoid more confrontation. The students in the study reported enjoying the intervention, and spontaneously confronted target youth without teacher assistance. Moreover, target students sometimes approached other youth who were displaying *their* target behaviors.

A possible reason for the success of this procedure is that it instills in students a knowledge of the natural consequences of their behaviors, that of peer disapproval.

Teachers may find initially that peer confrontation is somewhat threatening for the targeted student. It is important, therefore, to determine over the first few days of involvement if the intervention becomes less aversive for the student, or if there is a reduction in target behaviors. If neither happens, the teacher should temper the peer confrontation to a level that is more acceptable and effective for the problem youth.

In this project it is important to record the frequencies of the target behavior during each of the phases (intervals). Keep track of the occurrences during the group sessions, independent work, and individualized-group situations. It could be that the progression of events, as laid out here, is necessary to assist some youth, but data over the three phases could also reveal that certain students are more influenced by one particular setting (e.g., the individualized-group arrangement) (see MONITOR 1 in Appendix A).

Monitor

The interactions of the students in a group could be monitored by a tape recorder. Although that could be an intrusive and inhibiting factor, if it were scheduled on a number of occasions, pupils may become accustomed to it. The playbacks from those sessions could be informative to pupils and teachers. Statements and interactions of several types could be counted (see MONITOR 16).

Sandler, A.G., Arnold, L.B., Gable, R.A., & Strain, P.S. (1987). Effects of peer pressure on disruptive behavior of behaviorally disordered classmates. *Behavioral Disorders, 12,* 104–109.

Reference

DISRUPTIVE BEHAVIOR: PRACTICING WITH MENTAL TV

The idea for this tactic came from research on mental practice conducted by Alan Richardson in which three groups of students shot basketball free throws. The first group practiced and improved 24%, the second group imagined that they were shooting baskets and improved 23%, the third group did neither and did not improve. Thus, visualization was just as effective as actual practice.

Background

Many students have observed Olympic athletes using mental rehearsal. According to some authorities, students can learn the method of mental practice (visualization) to control emotions and/or practice new behaviors. The following procedure provides an example of mental rehearsal using the common image of a TV screen to help students visualize positive behaviors.

Who Can Benefit

Imagination can be fostered in young children, but as a technique to teach self-management, mental practice may be more effective for older students who have had more experiences to draw on, and have the ability to recall and describe situations. The skill of visualization is taught here by using the prompting of a TV screen to help students conjure up images of themselves.

Procedures

The exercise may be introduced by sharing the background information, defining any new terms to be used, and providing the rationale for learning this method for controlling new behavior. In preparation, the group could be encouraged to practice imagery (appropriate to ability level) for several days prior to getting involved in the technique.

1. Introduce an example to illustrate the type of situation a student might wish to improve: "Suppose you have a hard time getting your work done as quickly or as neatly as the others. You sense the teacher's disapproval and your classmates tell you to hurry, or perhaps make hurtful comments. You don't like this and you decide to take positive action." Ask the class members to come up with other examples. Allow a minute or two for each student to think about a particular problem on which they will work.
2. Encourage students to get into a comfortable position, take deep breaths, relax, and close their eyes. Ask them to think about a situation in which they would like to change the way they usually act.
3. Lead the students through 10-minute mental practice sessions: "We're going to practice Mental TV. Picture a TV set with two channels. You

control the channels and can change them when-ever you want. Picture your Mental TV. Turn it on and flip the channels. Watch the picture change. Now you are ready to put your Mental TV to work. On channel 1 you will see a picture of how you usually act when you experience your problem. Watch yourself on the screen. Look at the way you are acting. See your face, your expressions and those of other people around you. Listen to what you say and the way you say it.

"Now flip the channel and you'll see the way you would like to act. On channel 2 you watch yourself in the situation you want to change. See yourself on the screen. See your face . . . listen . . . etc.

"Continue to flip back and forth between chan-nels until you are aware of all the differences between how you usually act and how you would like to act. You can turn off channel 1 now. Plan to turn on your Mental TV for the next few days. Turn it on to channel 2 for the positive picture. This will help you act the way you would like to in the real situation."

4. Lead discussions on mental practice as a means to replace old actions with new ones. Encourage students to discuss all facets of the exercise. Ask questions such as: "Does anyone have difficulty forming images? Could you get both channels? How did they differ? Were you pleased with what you saw on channel 2?" Emphasize the fact that, with practice, Mental TV will become easier and more helpful. As students practice, stress the importance of creating a vivid and complete picture.

Modifications/ Considerations

As noted, Mental TV can be used for attaining goals, controlling emotions, changing behaviors, or improv-ing performances. The authors (Lee & Pulvino, 1978) suggest common experiences such as taking tests, interacting with peers, giving a speech, and reacting to criticism as topics for practice. Certainly, other examples could be provided, depending on the ages and characteristics of the students and other factors. Teachers who schedule this tactic should consider the possibility of being accused of using "brainwash-ing" tactics—asking students to close their eyes and conjure up images. They should be able to respond convincingly to this and other criticism.

Monitor   There are several ways to monitor this project, most of which require the gathering of data on a particular behavior or set of behaviors (e.g., not blowing up when confronted) before and after the treatment is scheduled. The pupil could self-record the frequency of the behavior(s); the pupil or another person could fill out a rating scale; another teacher, parent, or student could be interviewed; or sociometric inquiries could be made if the person was attempting to change a behavior that might affect his or her relationships with others (see MONITOR 8 in Appendix A).

Reference   Lee, J.L., & Pulvino, C.J. (1978). *Educating the forgotten half: Structured activities for learning.* Dubuque, IA: Kendall/Hunt.

DISRUPTIVE BEHAVIOR: SELF-OBSERVATION AND SELF-RECORDING

Background   The concept of modeling has been effective in encouraging the growth of social skills. One technique is to show videos that depict well-behaved students. In the research summarized here, students were shown videos of themselves as models of good behavior.

Who Can Benefit   The students who participated in the cited research (McCurdy & Shapiro, 1988) were between the ages of 9 and 11, and attended a school for socially and emotionally disturbed individuals. Watching themselves on TV is an amusing activity for youth of all ages, so the tactic is applicable for many students with behavior disorders from first grade through high school.

Procedures

This tactic requires the use of a video camera, as well as the help of an aide or volunteer.

1. Discuss with the targeted pupil which behaviors you consider inappropriate or disruptive so that you are both clear on the desired outcome of the tactic: to reduce the frequency of the selected behaviors.
2. Ask the aide to monitor the student's behavior for one class period, marking down the number of times he or she displays any of the target behaviors. Do this for about 10 days.
3. Videotape the student, occasionally, for an entire period during the second week of monitoring. (This will require the help of a second volunteer, perhaps an older student who is interested in video equipment.) Before the taping session begins, instruct the target student to be on his or her best behavior for the filming.
4. Edit the tape and delete any disruptive behaviors so that you have at least one 10-minute film of the student displaying acceptable behaviors.
5. Send the pupil to another room at the beginning of the period to view the 10-minute tape during the third and fourth weeks. (If more than one 10-minute tape was made, alternate the tapes.) Continue to monitor the student's behavior for the remainder of the period.

Throughout this whole process, the pupil's daily misbehavior rates should be graphed so that both the pupil and the teacher can monitor the pupil's progress. It is desired that by the end of the fourth week the misbehaviors will have fallen to an acceptable rate.

Modifications/ Considerations

Modifications can be made in the number of days the tactic is scheduled, as well as in the way students' behavior is monitored and recorded. Students in question could be taught to monitor their own behavior and graph the results themselves.

It might be helpful in this project if the pupils viewed a video of themselves when they were misbehaving. Then, by viewing a tape in which they behaved properly, they could make direct and vivid comparisons of their behaviors.

It should be noted that whereas all the students in the referenced research (McCurdy & Shapiro, 1988) showed improvement as a result of the tactic, not all of them maintained their improvements in a follow-up study after the tactic was no longer in effect. With those students, the same approach could be arranged from time to time, or perhaps they should be encouraged to self-record certain of their behaviors.

Monitor A way to monitor this procedure has been referred to: Record the behaviors and graph the frequencies daily. With respect to video recording, see MONITOR 15 in Appendix A.

Reference McCurdy, B.L., & Shapiro, E.S. (1988). Self-observation and the reduction of inappropriate classroom behavior. *Journal of School Psychology*, *26*, 371–378.

REDUCING DISTRACTIONS: SELF-MONITORING

Background Numerous educators have shown that some handicapped children (e.g., learning disabled, behaviorally disordered) are distracted by features of their environments. By adapting the method whereby handicapped students are required to complete assignments, the teacher might reduce or eliminate the distractibility. One way to reduce distractions is to require students to complete assignments in study carrels. The following procedures are adapted to include a self-monitoring arrangement whereby students place themselves in a quiet study area when they feel that distractions are interfering with their work.

This model was used for emotionally disturbed children who were having difficulty attending to academic activities. It was primarily used for children in middle school and high school settings where academic performance was of paramount importance. Self-monitoring the targeted behavior was a component added to the original study.

Who Can Benefit

1. Discuss a specific behavior (one that deals with a student's distractibility) with him or her.
2. Set up two areas in the classroom where students can go when they feel distracted. (One should be a study carrel with sides that block the view of other students. This can be made of a cardboard box that contains a large appliance, or one purchased through a school company. The other study area should be in a section of the room that is free of traffic and distractions, but not as isolated as the study carrel.)
3. Inform students that when they feel distracted and cannot do their work, to remove themselves from the situation and go either to the study carrel or to the special work area. They are to remain there until their current assignment is completed.
4. Set up a chart on the student's desk. When he or she removes himself, and successfully completes an assignment, the student should place a mark on the chart. If the teacher notices that the student is being distracted and is not working on an assignment, the teacher should ask the student to go to the study carrel and make a mark on the chart to indicate the move.
5. After a specified number of marks (set by the student and teacher), the student is granted a privilege (e.g., extra time before class or listening to a Walkman).

Procedures

It should be emphasized that the assignments given students should be ones that they can accomplish.

In a resource room, the handicapped student is with the special teacher for only a part of the day. A modification that would support this tactic would be for the special teacher to describe it to the student's other

Modifications

teachers. Arrangements could be made in the other classrooms to accomplish the same goals.

Also, modifications in assignments could be arranged with the student's other teachers. If the assignment required the student to write a full-page composition, the teacher might begin by having him or her write only one sentence, then a paragraph, and gradually increase the requirement to a full page.

Monitor This tactic could be monitored by placing a chart on students' desks on which they record their own activities. To make sure students keep score properly, they could be required to mark a chart on the teacher's desk before going to the study carrel. Or, the teacher could keep a separate record and make sure the two charts are in agreement at the end of each day.

If the assignments to be completed in the special room are for a different teacher, then it would be necessary to check with that teacher to see whether the assignment was completed as directed.

Since computers are located in many classrooms, a special disk could be given to pupils. On it they could type in, at the end of a class period, the number of times they went to a special place, how many assignments they completed, how many remained to be done, and information on other matters (see MONITOR 17 in Appendix A).

Reference Haubrich, P.A., & Shores, R. (1976). Attending behavior and academic performance of emotionally disturbed children. *Exceptional Children, 42*(6), 337-339.

INAPPROPRIATE LANGUAGE: PEER-MEDIATED EXTINCTION

Background When adults attempt to diminish bad behavior of youngsters, they are often unsuccessful when the behavior is reinforced by peers. A behavior that is commonly encouraged by peers is foul language. An approach to dealing with this problem is to engage peers in the behavior management process. The referenced study (Salend & Meddaugh, 1985) found that when students ignored the targeted youth whenever he or she swore, that type of language was eventually eliminated. The authors defined an obscenity as any verbal statement related to body parts designed for sexual activity or waste elimination, sexual behavior, or uncomplimentary references to someone's parentage.

The student in the cited study (Salend & Meddaugh, 1985) was a 14-year-old learning disabled male who attended a rural public school. The extinction procedures described here could be effective with students of other types and ages in other settings.

Who Can Benefit

1. Count the number of times the target student swears for 7 days prior to arranging the extinction procedure. These data will serve as the baseline.
2. Hold a meeting with the class members without the problem student present. Describe the problem to the students, and quiz them on the description of the behavior to make sure that they understand what it is.
3. Ask the peers to identify the behaviors they engage in that promote the obscene language of the target youth, for example, laughing, staring, or jeering.
4. Inform the students that if they ignore the student's profanity throughout a period, they will as a class receive 10 minutes of free time.
5. Implement the extinction intervention for 10 days, and continue recording the frequency of foul language from the target student.
6. Do not give the peers the reward of 10 minutes of free time for ignoring the student's obscenities on the 11th day and thereafter. Ask them to continue ignoring the foul language, however. Record the frequency at which the student swears for the next several days.

Procedures

Modifications/ Considerations Peer-mediated extinction was successful in decreasing the obscene language of the problem student in the referenced study (Salend & Meddaugh, 1985). Peers also learned an effective way to cope constructively with a peer-maintained disruptive behavior. Use of the intervention decreased teacher time spent disciplining the problem youth, and increased group cooperation as well.

Some teachers may want to be more "up front" with their plan, in which case they should set up a meeting with the entire group, including the problem pupil. At this time they would explain the situation— that they were displeased with the individual's behavior, but also unhappy with those who stimulated and maintained it. The teacher might then record (or have students record) not only the incidents of the inappropriate behavior but the events that preceded and followed it (see MONITOR 7 in Appendix A). The teacher could also inform the group that they would receive some reward (each day, week, whatever) if the target pupil didn't engage in the inappropriate behavior, and if the others didn't egg him or her on.

Monitor Suggestions for monitoring this project were included in the previous two sections.

Reference Salend, S.J., & Meddaugh, D. (1985). Using a peer-mediated extinction procedure to decrease obscene language. *The Pointer*, *30*(1), 8–11.

INAPPROPRIATE LANGUAGE: THE USE OF EXERCISE

Background The benefits of exercise have been documented for some time. Among the many benefits thought to be derived from exercise are improved health, self-esteem, and attention span as well as aiding in the reduction of stress and tension. Several studies have in fact demonstrated a relationship between jogging and improved behaviors. The authors of the referenced study (Evans, Evans, Schmid, & Pennypacker, 1985) sought to determine whether vigorous exercise (jogging and touch football) would positively affect talking out of turn and completing math problems.

Six emotionally disturbed middle school students were selected for the cited study (Evans et al., 1985), all of whom had histories of severe conduct problems in schools. The following program could benefit other types of students, including those identified as remedial or at risk.

Who Can Benefit

Decreasing Talk-Outs

Procedures

1. Locate a quarter-mile track or field on which the students can run and exercise.
2. Inform the students that they have been selected to participate in a jogging and exercise club. Remind them to bring the proper exercise attire to school.
3. Record the number of "talk-outs" (defined as any verbalization made without teacher permission) that occur during a 50-minute period. The teacher may wish to spread the 50 minutes over five 10-minute intervals throughout the day. These data will serve as the baseline.
4. Require the students to jog for 15 minutes on the second day. If possible, stagger the starts so that each student is running alone. This should eliminate the effects of social reinforcement.
5. Record the number of talk-outs that occur during a 50-minute period on the same day as jogging.
6. Record the number of talk-outs on the third day. Do not schedule any exercise for the students on that day.
7. Engage the students in a 15-minute touch football game on the fourth day. Make sure that everyone participates.
8. Encourage the students to attribute their wins or losses to effort and concentration.

9. Observe and record the number of talk-outs that occur during a 50-minute period on the day of the football game.

10. Record talk-outs on day 5, but don't schedule a physical activity.

11. Compare the number of talk-outs on the exercise days with the number on the nonexercise days.

12. Choose the physical activity that has the most effect on your students, and arrange it on future occasions.

Increasing Time on Task

1. Record the number of math problems or other assigned problems that the student completes on the first day.

2. Rate each student's classroom behavior with a *1* for poor, a *2* for satisfactory, or a *3* for excellent on the first day.

3. Require students to jog for 15 minutes on the second day.

4. Record the number of problems completed and rate student performance on the same day that they jog.

5. Repeat steps 1 and 2 on the third day, without any exercise interventions.

6. Start a 15-minute touch football game for the students on the fourth day. Make sure that everyone participates. Follow the same rules as in step 8 of the first part of this section.

7. Record the number of completed problems and rate student performance on the same day as the touch football game.

8. Rate student performance and record completed problems on the fifth day. Don't schedule an exercise on this day.

9. Compare teacher ratings and the extent the students stay on task.

10. Select the exercise program that promotes the most improvement, or continue to alternate the activities.

Modifications/ Considerations The cited study (Evans et al., 1985) reported a relationship between participation in vigorous physical activity and improvement in selected behaviors. The authors found that touch football yielded the greatest improvements overall. Another discovery was that student attendance showed a significant increase during the exercise intervention.

Teachers may have other forms of exercise (e.g., aerobics) they could select or alternate with the ones chosen for this study. This would allow teachers to adapt the program to their schedules and the students' needs. The teacher might also assess the effects of exercise on classroom behaviors other than those discussed in the referenced study.

Monitor

Ideas for monitoring were included in the procedures. Along with keeping data on talk-outs and math problems, students could be asked to record the amount of time they were engaged in exercise (see MONITOR 3 in Appendix A). If data on the three behaviors were available to students (they might record all of them), they might see relationships across the behaviors. Perhaps as they increased or maintained a certain level of exercise, they talked out less and computed more.

Reference

Evans, W.H., Evans, S.S., Schmid, R.E., & Pennypacker, H.S. (1985). The effects of exercise on selected classroom behaviors of behaviorally disordered adolescents. *Behavioral Disorders*, *11*(1), 42-50.

SELF-CONCEPT

8

SELF-MANAGEMENT: BUILDING SUCCESSES

Background

Our society does not provide many opportunities for individuals to express positive feelings about themselves. Yet most of us enjoy expressing pride in our accomplishments. Opportunities for positive self-expression can be incorporated into a classroom by providing a forum for disclosing positive and growth-promoting attributes about oneself. Shakespeare explained the philosophy behind these expressions in King Henry V when he wrote: "Self love, my liege, is not so vile a sin as self neglecting."

Who Can Benefit

Students who do not often identify successes in their lives will benefit from the techniques noted here. This is an especially important area on which to focus for at-risk and remedial students.

Procedures

1. Decide how much class time you will spend on exercises to become acquainted with your students and to build their self-esteem.
2. Divide the class into groups of four or five students. Explain that the goal of these exercises is for students to get to know one another better and to share pride in each other's accomplishments.
3. Select an appropriate activity from those listed in the next point. These exercises are listed in order of difficulty, with the easier ones listed first.
4. Ask each student to make a statement about a specific behavior, beginning with, "I'm proud that I . . ." Encourage students to react to other items, such as the following:
   - Things you've done for your parents
   - Things you've done for a friend
   - Work in school
   - How you spend your free time
   - Habits you have or something you do quite often

- About your religious beliefs
- How you've earned some money
- How you usually spend your money
- Something you own or what you've bought recently
- Something you have shared
- Something you tried hard to accomplish
- Thoughts about people who are different from you
- Something you've done in regard to racism
- Something you've done in regard to ecology

5. Encourage students to picture in their minds objects or circumstances that recall past successes or accomplishments. Many of us have symbols of success such as photographs, certificates, newspaper clippings, ticket stubs, and trophies that we have saved because they remind us of our ability and popularity. Instruct students to share their feelings and meanings connected with specific situations, as well as the successes they symbolize.

6. Ask students to share an accomplishment or achievement they experienced before they were 10 years old. Then ask them to describe a successful experience they had between the ages of 10 and 15; then between the ages of 15 and the present time. (These age ranges can be revised.)

7. Ask students periodically to share a recent success or accomplishment: the past week, last month, over the weekend, during a vacation, over the summer.

8. Inform the students that each person has 5 minutes to boast about anything he or she wants to talk about: accomplishments, awards, skills, personal characteristics, whatever. Require group members to monitor their own nonverbal signals as they listen, and to refrain from talking until they are asked to comment on the exercise.

9. Ask students to identify their greatest success for the day. This provides them an opportunity to review the day, and to become aware of day-to-day happenings. Some students will find this difficult at first, but as others begin to share their experiences, they may realize that they too have had a few successes. Encourage students to comment on the successes of their classmates.

10. Request students to write a paragraph or two to explain their successes, rather than reporting on them verbally. This type of exercise provides an ongoing record of accomplishments that students can review from time to time.

11. Encourage students to list five successful experiences they would like to have in the next year, 5 years, or longer period. This assessment could be scheduled in conjunction with goal-setting activities.

If some students report that they haven't had successes to share, encourage them to identify a few by reminding them of an instance you know about:

Modifications/ Considerations

- You've been taking care of your younger brothers and sisters for 2 years; that's certainly an accomplishment.
- You helped Paul with some of his assignments when he missed several days of school.
- You were polite to the guest speaker last week, and asked some very good questions.
- You reminded me to send home the letters to parents last week about the open house.

If several activities are planned to build on one another, groups can be rotated to ensure that students make new friends and have opportunities to capitalize on practicing their revitalized self-esteem. Before beginning new activities, however, ask the students if they would prefer staying with the old group or shifting to a new one.

For a few minutes every day, students could be asked to list all the nice things about themselves. Those data could be charted as frequency per minute or session. Such data acquired for a few days before a treatment, then for a period of time as the treatment was in effect, could help determine the effect of the intervention. Data across phases could be compared in terms of mean, range, or trend (see MONITOR 1 in Appendix A).

Monitor

Canfield, J., & Wells, H.C. (1976). *101 ways to enhance self-concept in the classroom.* Englewood Cliffs, NJ: Prentice-Hall.

Reference

SELF-MANAGEMENT: SETTING OBJECTIVES

Background   Often, adolescents see only the short-term picture rather than a long-term view. Teachers are trained to break down long-term goals or expectations to daily objectives. Students can also be taught to set goals and plan strategies for themselves to meet their goals. Effective goal setting and goal reaching can be a powerful tool for building students' self-concepts.

Who Can Benefit   Students whose lives and classwork appear to be scattered or without purpose are prime candidates for this intervention.

Procedures   Time required: 20 minutes

1. Ask students to begin thinking about changes they would like to make at home and at school. Offer some starting points: making new friends, improving school attendance, achieving higher grades.
2. Inform students that they should set two clear objectives for the school year. Write three questions on the board that students should be able to answer as they write each objective.
    - Does it state clearly what I'll be able to do when I reach my goal?
    - Does it include a time deadline?
    - Is there some way I can judge whether I've reached my goal?
3. Request students to print *C* beside each objective below that is clear and *U* beside each one that is unclear.
    _____ I want to make five new friends by January.
    _____ I want to have a better life than my parents.
    _____ I want to be happy.
    _____ I aim to make money.
4. Ask students to describe a successful student (see Student Worksheet in Figure 8.1). List on the board the behaviors of those students that make them successful (e.g., turns in assignments, participates in class activities).

5. Instruct students to choose three behaviors of successful students that would help them become more successful. Star the most important one.
6. Write an objective for the starred item. The objective must be "do-able" and measurable. It should specify *what* the student will do, *when* he or she will do it, and *how well* it will be done. For example, "I will pass five classes this quarter," or "I will raise my grade from a D to a C this quarter."
7. Test objectives by requiring students to indicate which ones are measurable. Say, "Show me how you can do it."
8. Demonstrate how to break down an objective into its prerequisite behaviors. For instance, "To get a C in social studies, I must pass next week's test, do my homework, and study for the exam."
9. Set a definite time when the objective will be checked.

Modifications/ Considerations

This technique will work with an individual, a small group, or an entire class. Keep in mind "where" the students are before they set objectives, and that small objectives are more meaningful and attainable than broad, distant goals.

This lesson would be most appropriate at the beginning of a year or quarter, or perhaps at the return from a school break.

Monitor

As suggested in the write-up, each objective should be measured to determine whether progress is being made toward the goal. If a student's objective was to turn in 100% of his or her assignments in U.S. history and biology throughout a semester, or to begin doing that 6 weeks into the term, the student should chart each day the number of assignments given and, of those, how many were turned in (see MONITOR 1 in Appendix A).

Reference

Phillips, M. (1991). *The peer counseling training course. Classroom guidance manual.* San Jose, CA: Resource Publications.

FIGURE 8.1 Worksheet for Setting Objectives

STUDENT WORKSHEET

Name _____ Teacher _____

OBJECTIVE SETTING

1. Describe the successful _____ student. List the exact behaviors of a successful student.

   a. _____   d. _____

   b. _____   e. _____

   c. _____   f. _____

2. Write down three behaviors that would personally help you be more successful. Choose the most important one for you. Mark with a (*).

   a. _____

   b. _____

   c. _____

3. Write an objective for the starred item. The objective must be a goal that you can reach and one you can measure.

   _____

   _____

   _____

   _____

4. Test your objective. "Let me show you how I can: _____

   _____

   _____

   _____."

   Can your counselor see you do it?   Yes _____   No _____

5. List the exact behaviors involved in reaching that objective.

_____

_____

_____

6. Set a check-back time when you will check your progress with your counselor. _Write this here:_

_____

Note. Adapted from Phillips, M. (1991). _The peer counseling training course_ (p. 95). San Jose, CA: Resource Publications. Reprinted by permission.

SELF-MANAGEMENT: ACCEPTING RESPONSIBILITY

Background

At-risk students sometimes fall into a mode of learned helplessness; they feel that outside forces control their lives, and they have lost control. Teachers can intercept negative, blaming statements and teach students to replace them with more productive, self-controlling statements. Students can then attribute success to something they can manage. The attribution of success to effort sets up a cycle of effort that breeds success, and an improved self-concept.

Who Can Benefit

Students of "low ability" tend to improve their school performance when they attribute success to effort. Students who believe that they have lost control of their lives will benefit from the structure built into this lesson.

Procedures

1. Write on the board, overhead, or butcher paper: "I AM THE ONLY PERSON RESPONSIBLE FOR WHAT I DO."

2. Instruct students to think of times when this sentence is *not* true—when other people control what happens to them. Examples include job hiring of employers and rule making of parents and teachers. Point out to students that, although they believe that others control them, *they* are actually in control, because they make choices as to how to act when faced with expectations or rules. How they perform during a job interview, for instance, makes a difference in whether they are hired.

3. Encourage students to identify instances at home and at school when they believe they are not in control, and to list them.

4. Instruct students to form small groups of four or five and appoint a "secretary" to write down all the tasks at home and school for which they are willing to accept responsibility.

5. Complete a master list of accepted responsibilities in the classroom, and display it as a reminder to you and the students.

6. Assist students to organize what they have learned from this exercise by filling in a responsibility chart (see Figure 8.2). Each pupil should complete one of these, and you should check off the activities.

Modifications/ Considerations

1. This activity is not only useful for individuals in resource rooms, it can be practical in regular classrooms as well.

2. Students could make a list of the consequences for not meeting each responsibility, and list them on a separate chart.

3. Guests from the community could be invited to speak to the class on responsibility and self-control. It would be particularly interesting to bring in an employer and an employee or a management person and an entry level individual from the same business (perhaps not on the same day).

Monitor Within the context of improving students' self-esteem and relating that to self-control, it would be informative if individuals took a few minutes once a week to write down the events or circumstances of their lives that were out of their control. Students

FIGURE 8.2 Form for Use in Accepting Responsibility

RESPONSIBILITY CHART

NAME: _____   DATE: _____

TEACHER: _____   PERIOD: _____

RESPONSIBILITIES FOR THIS CLASS:	*Behavior/ Attendance*	*Materials*	*Assignments*
	1.	1.	1.
	2.	2.	2.
	3.	3.	3.
	4.	4.	4.

Other classes:

1.

2.

3.

4.

5.

HOME:	*DAILY JOBS*	*WEEKLY*	*OCCASIONAL JOBS*
	1.		
	2.		
	3.		
	4.		

Note. From Stoker, J. (1980). *Grab H.O.L.D.: Help overcome learner dropouts. Classroom guidance manual.* San Jose, CA: Resource Publications. Reprinted by permission.

could then write out a plan to either gain control or exercise more control over certain of those. The objective would not be to obtain total control over everything (no one has this or would probably want it), but to reach a level of control that elevates self-confidence.

Another way to monitor this technique would be to use a rating scale (see MONITOR 5 in Appendix A). A number of features that indicate the acceptance of responsibility could be listed on the vertical axis, and alongside them a set of numbers could be printed that refer to the degree those indicators were true. Periodically, the teacher or student could fill this out.

Reference Stoker, J. (1980). *Grab H.O.L.D.: Help overcome learner dropouts. Classroom guidance manual.* San Jose, CA: Resource Publications.

SELF-MANAGEMENT: ATTRIBUTION RETRAINING I

Background Two lines of research support this tactic. One is that self-esteem is related to attributions—that is, how we perceive ourselves generally and how we attribute our successes and failures are closely linked. The other line of research suggests that attribution retraining leads to increased self-esteem.

Who Can Benefit One of the prime characteristics of at-risk, remedial, and many mildly handicapped youth is that they have relatively low and fragile self-esteem. They do not think very highly of themselves. Moreover, many of these adolescents have attributions that differ from those of more successful students. It is not uncommon for these students to attribute their failures to bad luck, poor teaching, or some other external factor, whereas their more talented peers are more inclined to attribute their shortcomings to lack of effort or motivation. Similarly, pupils with low self-esteem are apt to believe their successes as well are because of luck, teaching, or another agent outside their control; whereas the more talented pupils would likely believe successes occurred because of their own persistence and motivation.

Procedures

Teacher Training

1. Schedule a workshop for teachers to assist them to offer attribution retraining.
2. Give the teachers a difficult task. In the cited research (Tollefson et al., 1980), teachers were required to indicate which of three Javanese words had the same meaning as a set of English words. Each participant was given a booklet consisting of a set of directions and three tests. Directions for some teachers indicated that performance on the task was primarily due to effort. Other teachers received the instruction that some people have a natural linguistic ability for this type of task, and that ability would influence the outcome. Another set of teachers were told that due to the difficulty of the task, successes or failures would be primarily due to luck.
3. Schedule a second activity. In the referenced study, teachers were given the *Raven's Progressive Matrices* and, according to its procedures, asked to choose one of six diagrams that best completed the relationship involved in particular designs. Give the teachers the correct answer and ask them to complete one of the following sentences, depending on their outcome: "My failure was primarily due to . . ." or "My success was primarily due to . . ."
4. Encourage the teachers, following that exercise, to share their thoughts regarding attributions and their performance on the task.
5. Provide teachers with a short description of attribution theory. Stress the significance of effort for at-risk youth; it may serve as a necessary balancing force to counteract their lack of ability and knowledge.
6. Conclude the workshop with a role-playing demonstration by two group members concerning the attribution retraining procedure they will conduct with their students.

Attribution Retraining Program

1. Prepare a list of 40 moderately difficult spelling words for each student, commonly used words they are unable to spell but should be able to with a little effort.

2. Select 10 words a week from the list and give them to the student with directions to study the words for an oral test.

3. Administer the spelling test. If the student spells a word correctly, say, "You spelled that word correctly; you tried hard to learn to spell it." If the student spells the word incorrectly, say, "If you spend more time studying, you could learn to spell that word correctly."

Modifications/ Considerations

Any number of tasks could be scheduled for teachers to give them the idea of attribution retraining. Likewise, several exercises could be arranged for students, depending on their abilities and the subject of concern. Moreover, teachers could provide other types of feedback to students, depending on the quality of their responses. The point is, however, to encourage students to consider effort and motivation as prime ingredients of success and failure.

Just as some researchers have pointed out relationships between attribution and self-esteem, others have noted positive correlations between ratings of perceived choice and feelings of internal control. A number of tactics in this program have focused on self-management.

Monitor

In the referenced study (Tollefson et al., 1980), three tests were administered to pupils prior to and following their training. These instruments were the *Rosenberg Self-Esteem Scale*, the *Intellectual Achievement Responsibility Scale*, and the *Task Attribution Questionnaire*. Beyond calculating difference scores from those tests to evaluate effects of attribution retraining, teachers could keep informal anecdotal records on some students to learn whether their attributions were improving. Some indicators of positive change would be the increase in remarks such as: "I didn't try hard enough." "I didn't pay attention in class." "I studied for 6 hours over the weekend." "I kept good notes and reviewed them before the test."

Yet another way to monitor effects of this program would be to involve an interval recording approach (see MONITOR 4 in Appendix A). With this technique, the student (or teacher) could make a check at preselected intervals (e.g., 1 minute) to indicate whether he or she was on task.

Tollefson, N., Tracy, D.B., Johnsen, E.P., Borgers, S., Buenning, M., Farmer, A., & Barke, C. (1980). *An application of attribution theory to developing self-esteem in learning disabled adolescents* (Research Rep. No. 23). Lawrence: Institute for Research in Learning Disabilities, The University of Kansas. **Reference**

SELF-MANAGEMENT: PROMPTING PRAISE

Background

Thinking positively about oneself cannot be overemphasized. Considerable research indicates that if individuals have proper estimates of themselves, they are better able to relate to others and are more able to learn skills in and out of school than are those with inadequate self-esteem. A prime contributor to self-esteem is praise and acknowledgment from others. We all need recognition from our peers, superiors, and elders; some of us more than others. The technique explained by Baer and Wolf (1970) is designed to help pupils contact a sometimes dormant but readily available natural community of praise. That is, pupils can learn to seek reinforcement from their teachers.

Who Can Benefit

A characteristic of at-risk youngsters and many others who have been in remedial or compensatory programs is that they have negative self-concepts. Many of them have had so many experiences with failure that their self-concepts are fragile. This technique would be a suitable approach for them, particularly those who are reinforced by teacher praise and who rarely receive any.

Procedures

1. Inform students that you want them to evaluate their performance accurately in some area. That could be in physical science, U.S. history, math, or another class.

2. Provide them with the necessary standards to do so; they must know what a "good performance" is. Give them the necessary teachers' manuals, tape cassettes, or whatever else is needed for them to compare their performance to a standard.

3. Work with the students on the selected skills until they can discriminate good from poor performance, and until most of their efforts are first rate.

4. Obtain data regarding the extent students can accurately evaluate their performances. Depending on the skill, the evaluation of their performance could be more or less sophisticated. For some subjects, students could be required to provide a precise measure of frequency, percentage, or the like. For other performances they might simply make a statement regarding its quality: "That was great." "That wasn't too good." "That needs help, but it's better than it was."

5. Inform pupils to go to their teachers and prompt them for praise, if their work is of high quality.

6. Provide students with statements to use when they seek reinforcement from their teachers: "Look how much I've done." "What do you think of this?" "How about this?"

7. Assist students to determine the proper time to approach their teachers and the times they should not go to them to prompt reinforcement. Pupils should not, for example, go to teachers when it is obvious that they are busy.

8. Keep data on the extent the pupils can go to teachers without becoming a pest. Baer, Holman, Stokes, and Fowler (1981) suggested that youngsters in a large class should not approach their teacher for praise any more than four times a day.

Modifications/ Considerations

The last point in the procedure must be kept in mind; an individual could obviously ask for too much praise. We have all known adults who constantly seek reinforcement and can be very annoying. Perhaps another factor that should be blended into this technique is the rate at which the seeker of praise dispenses reinforcement. It may be that individuals can ask for as many praise statements as they give or, more likely, can ask for one bit of praise for each four or five compliments they give.

If a teacher believes that students' self-concepts are improving as a result of this technique and that they know when and how to seek praise from teachers, the teacher might encourage students to do the same at home. There, instead of referring to their noteworthy schoolwork, students could make reference to their activities around the house: how they carried out assigned chores, how they voluntarily assisted in some way, how they remembered to pick up something. They should be reminded, as they seek reinforcement at home, to dispense praise to themselves and to keep their requests natural and under control.

Monitor

Pupils should keep track of the number of times they "ask" for praise. Furthermore, they should keep data on whether they were, in fact, praised when they asked for it, and on the circumstances of the interaction (e.g., time of day, what the teacher was doing when prompted). In other words, they should keep track of the antecedents and consequences that accompany their requests (see MONITOR 7 in Appendix A).

References

Baer, D.M., & Wolf, M.M. (1970). The entry into natural communities of reinforcement. In R. Ulrich, T. Stachnik, & J. Mabry (Eds.), *Control of human behavior* (Vol. 2, pp. 319–324). Glenview, IL: Scott, Foresman.

Baer, D.M., Holman, J., Stokes, T.F., & Fowler, S.A. (1981). Uses of self-control techniques in programming generalization. In S.W. Bijou & R. Ruiz (Eds.), *Behavior modification: Contributions to education* (pp. 39–61). Hillsdale, NJ: Erlbaum.

TEACHER MANAGEMENT: GROUP INTERACTIONS

Background

Most adolescents believe that no one has ever thought about some of the events and circumstances that they are experiencing. When they do learn that others share some of their concerns, they may realize the significance of those matters. Accordingly, they might take the thoughts of others more seriously.

Who Can Benefit

Students who feel alienated or isolated from other students should profit from this technique. Youth of that type may be of low or high ability. The entire class could gain from confirming one another's concerns.

Procedures

1. Set up chairs or desks in a circle.
2. Divide poster paper or a chalkboard into as many sections as there are students. Indicate the "up" side of the paper on each piece. Put a big background for a puzzle on the floor with the shapes drawn on it in the middle of the circle.
3. Give each participant a piece of the paper or assign him or her a section of the chalkboard. Ask students to take out their pencils or provide them with felt pens.
4. Ask the students to draw a symbol of what is happening in the world right now. Tell them to make it their own symbol, one that represents their feelings about our world. The picture must be of something that is meaningful to them: a concern, like, dislike, hate, or love. An alternative is to provide students with magazines and ask them to cut out images that are meaningful to them.
5. Tell them, when they are finished, to put their piece on the puzzle background. You may need to establish a time limit for this activity.
6. Introduce the exercise as an experience in reflective listening, one in which each person has the opportunity to express his or her feelings and to listen as others describe theirs.
7. Provide an example for the students. Ask, "Is there any symbol you would particularly like to hear about?" A participant then tells about his or her symbol. Reflect the participant's feelings:
   Teacher: "You feel hopeless."
   Student: "No, not exactly."
   Teacher: "Powerless to do anything?"
   Student: "Yeah, powerless and lonely, too."
8. Ask each student, one by one, to explain his or her drawing and to tell the class why it has meaning.

Before moving to the next person, get an affirmative answer from the students to one of these questions: "Do you think your feelings on this have been heard?" "Would you like to stop now even though your feelings may not have been completely heard?"

9. Plan follow-up activities that expand on the concerns of students. Allow them to suggest what they would like to do about their concerns. Use the information to practice group decision making. For example, word lists of feelings can be written as having directions—pleasure or love in one direction, and pain or hate in the other. Students can hang word lists for these feelings on the wall and add to them when they desire. Replace the paper when it gets too full and encourage more drawings.

Modifications/ Considerations

For some students, it is easier to express ideas in small groups than if they are with a number of other students. The technique explained here could begin with small groups and eventually be scheduled with more and more students.

Students should be assigned to groups so as to avoid cliques and unnecessary disturbances. Counselors could be asked to recommend students for various groups. They could, in fact, run some of the groups.

The sharing of concerns can be arranged in liberal arts classes such as history, English, and speech. Such sessions can also be scheduled in social studies classes, particularly those that deal with contemporary problems.

Monitor

For this project, it is important to acquire data on students' reactions. Not only is it informative to learn about the expressed concerns of the students, but equally so to know about the reactions of others to those issues. To gather data on the latter, students might be asked to write a few sentences occasionally that explain their feelings about certain points (see MONITOR 10 in Appendix A). Those data could be reviewed from time to time by each student to see if there is a pattern or trend to their thoughts. In some situations, where a teacher or counselor has established a feeling of trust among the students, some of those reactions might be shared with the group.

Reference Achterman, E. (no date). *Self-enhancing education project.* Santa Clara, CA: Author. (For further information, write: SEE, 1957 Pruneridge Avenue, Santa Clara, CA 95050.)

TEACHER MANAGEMENT: THE POSITIVE SANDWICH APPROACH

Background A positive approach to teaching is more effective than an aversive one. Though aversive comments may stimulate immediate results, their side effects often include decreased enjoyment and increased fear of failure.

Aversive comments in a classroom can result in a power struggle between students and teacher. When that occurs, the negative behaviors from students increase. The approach recommended here relies on social reinforcement or praise to strengthen acceptable behaviors.

Who Can Benefit Positive reinforcement creates a proper situation for learning skills and a positive environment for social interactions. The Positive Sandwich strategy was developed to de-emphasize or temper the criticisms or grades regarding classroom behaviors and reinforce students' efforts and performances. It is most effective with students with low self-esteem and those with newly formed skills.

Procedures 1. Identify students who have low self-esteem and a low tolerance for criticism; they may be high or low achievers. Look for signs of sensitivity to criticism such as tears, face-hiding, or brash statements.

2. Implement a three-step strategy of sandwiching a constructive comment between two positive comments.
    a. *First*, tell the student what he or she did well. Reinforce effort, which student can control. Your goal is to prepare the student emotionally for a constructive comment.
    b. *Second*, provide the student with specific directions about new behaviors to develop or about corrections to make. Gear the instruction to the needs of each student. Keep your expectations high.
    c. *Third*, complete the interaction with a second positive comment to leave the student with a reinforcement. Consider when Joel is late to class for the fifth time. You make a constructive comment to him about his behavior. Your statement might be, "I'm glad you made it today, Joel. However, do you know how many tardies you have already? (Wait for response.) You need to be in your seat before the bell rings. I know that you can do better."
3. Over time, systematically shape the target behavior positive responses to criticism by gradually increasing your expectations for the student, while keeping them realistic and attainable.
4. To maintain a student's behavior, the timing and schedule of comments is crucial. Initially, offer a comment as close to the occurrence of the behavior as possible. Frequent reinforcement will strengthen the behavior and provide feedback. Once behaviors have developed, they will persist longer with intermittent comments.

Modifications/ Considerations

1. Positive comments cannot be given or received as phony, or your credibility will suffer.
2. Students with the greatest need for this strategy can only accept mild criticism.
3. If a targeted student has a low image of himself or herself, make other teachers or counselors aware of your efforts, and involve them in the use of the Positive Sandwich treatment.
4. Discuss explicitly with the student the strategy of sandwiching constructive comments with positive statements. Encourage the student to make positive statements to others, particularly if he or she intends to criticize them for something.

5. Discuss the Positive Sandwich strategy with class members as a means to build better interactions with others by delivering sincere and constructive comments.

Monitor Keep a notebook of interactions to write in immediately after each class period or at the end of the day. Record both your actions and the student's reactions to your comments (see MONITOR 7 in Appendix A).

Reference Smith, R.E., Smoll, F.L., & Curtis, B. (1979). Coach effectiveness training: A cognitive-behavioral approach to enhancing relationship skills in youth sport coaches. *Journal of Sport Psychology*, *1*, 59–75.

TEACHER MANAGEMENT: TEN EXERCISES

Background Today's teachers deal with adolescents who display a variety of emotional states. Some adolescents are more aware of their feelings and those of their mates than are others. One indication of sensitivity is that they begin to recognize that they and others express a number of negative statements. Once they become aware of their negative statements and those of others, they can begin responding to them with positive restatements. To aid adolescents to develop this skill, teachers should take advantage of situations that arise in the classroom to counter negative statements.

Who Can Benefit Adolescents, generally, and students with low self-esteem can benefit from these exercises. Indeed, most individuals, adolescents or otherwise, could do with a dose of this type of training.

Five Self-Esteem Exercises

Procedures

1. Instruct students to make a list of all the resources in their lives—including people, agencies, tools, and their skills—that they can rely on in difficult situations. Ask them to list a few of the times that they solved problems. Suggest that they talk to someone who loves them about a problem, and picture beforehand how that person might react.

2. Explain to students that they should give themselves credit for all the roles they play in life: student, son or daughter, friend, grandson or granddaughter, worker. Have them recall improvements they have made on problems in their lives with respect to their various roles.

3. Ask students to write down, in private, on a 3×5 card the worst thing they ever did, then tear the card up and throw it away. This action should help teenagers understand that they can get rid of bad memories and live for the present.

4. Tell students to ask themselves, in spite of everything they know about themselves, whether they want to be like themselves. Suggest that they say to themselves, "I don't want to be a star with all those hassles, I really like to be me. I wouldn't trade my life with anyone." This will give them motivation to keep going in their present circumstances.

5. Explain that the past can only limit what they do in the future if they let it.

Five Exercises for Teachers and Students

1. Ask students how they begin their day. Suggest:
    *   That they begin with a calendar on which special activities are noted for that day
    *   That if they have a worry on their minds, they should write it down, and then think of other, more positive thoughts
    *   That they might listen to their favorite radio station in the morning while they get ready for school
    *   That they should bring a book that has positive thoughts for the day, and read it

2. Share suggestions on how to deal with "snipers" in their life, those who take potshots at them (e.g., teachers, peers, siblings, bosses, or parents). Pre-

pare a defense statement to say to yourself: "I did my best." "I learned from my mistake, and I'll do better the next time." "It's not that big a deal."

3. Offer suggestions for dealing with yourself when you are your own most vicious sniper. When you tell yourself you did _____, say, "That's not like me." Define yourself positively, by saying, "I'm better than that."

4. Create a corner for selected pictures or clippings that are meaningful to students. Tell them that they should surround themselves at home and at school with positive messages. Suggest that they carry messages or photographs in their wallets and cars that are uplifting.

5. Suggest to students that they end their day by thinking of three good things. Explain to them that when they end the day on a positive note, they will sleep better and be better prepared to deal with life in the morning.

Post inspirational thoughts around the room, or ask students to create posters of their favorite quotes:

"In the game of life, success isn't playing a good hand, it's playing well the hand you're dealt."
"How you spend your time is how you live your life."
"Opportunity is always knocking. It's here in the circumstances of your life. It's not something that always comes from others. It's something you have to discover."
"Remember you'll always do your best when you can shape the circumstances, so shape them carefully. When you can't shape the circumstances, remember that you can shape yourself."
"Being obsessed with a wasted past wastes the present and surrenders the future. Don't dwell on the past and give it power. Celebrate the fact that you survived it. Dwell on selecting your best options now."

Modifications/ Considerations

1. Be familiar with the student's circumstances, and be prepared for emotional outbursts.
2. Ask students to develop or share their own strategies for self-affirmations.

3. You might consider playing some of the commercial tapes that are available on getting "pumped up" to achieve. Some of them are okay. They will at least stimulate discussions.

Monitor

Instruct students to count, throughout the day or for a specified period of time, the number of positive thoughts they can generate about themselves and the number they can think of about others. It might be a particularly good idea to have them say or write as many positive things as they can about a person they are not too fond of (see MONITOR 1 in Appendix A).

Reference

Ellis, A., & Harper, R. (1972). *A guide to rational living.* North Hollywood, CA: Wilshire Book Co.

ATTITUDE

9

SELF-MANAGEMENT: MAKING RESPONSIBLE CHOICES

More often than not, problems in classrooms arise from the actions of a few individuals who demand attention or have difficulties channeling their energies. Sometimes, however, a teacher is assigned a class in which most of the pupils cannot get along; they seek attention through deviant outbursts, or don't care about school. The tactic explained here should be considered in instances when an entire class needs to develop self-responsibility.

Background

The program in the cited research (Hellison, 1983) was implemented in a middle school physical education class. It was a co-ed, multiracial group of students who could not work with one another. The procedure explained here was successful and could be applied to other situations and to older students.

Who Can Benefit

1. Explain to the students that for 2 days of the week they have the choice of working on personal physical fitness concepts ("student time") or doing teacher-directed activities ("teacher time"). If they choose the former, set up contracts for working on physical fitness activities.
2. Tell the students that to be successful on their contracts they must be self-motivators and self-controllers.
3. Include in the contract a test on the skill being taught in the gym class that week (e.g., dribbling a ball or rope climbing).
4. Schedule the fifth day of each week as "group activity day." On that day, self-control and cooperation are stressed. Teach students to implement the self-awareness levels outlined in the next point.

Procedures

5. Instruct pupils to rate themselves on their "awareness" levels on group activity day with the following scale:

   0 = Little self-control, verbal and physical abuse of others, not involved, puts down those who are involved, irresponsible, blames others, feels powerless

   1 = Under control, not involved but doesn't interfere with others' right to learn or teacher's right to teach

   2 = Under control, involved in subject matter, but only as directed by teacher

   3 = Self-responsible, self-motivated, able to work independently, able to take responsibility for actions and attitudes (accountability accepted and acted on)

   4 = All of the above, plus caring about others, involved with others in a helping way; sensitive to the needs of the group or willing to put ego aside to assist someone else

6. Require students who get into arguments to go to the "talking bench," which is situated along one wall away from the activities. There, they work out their disagreement, report back to the teacher, and later, make up the time they lost.

7. Make a chart containing vertical columns for each student (see Figure 9.1 for Self-Responsibility Chart). Write their names across the top of the chart. List the number of group activity days from top to bottom as Day 1, Day 2, and so forth. After each group activity day, ask students to write their self-evaluation score in the respective column next to the group activity day. Beside each score, students should write in the free time or privilege earned for that score. The chart informs both the students and the teacher about the students' progress over time.

Modifications/ Considerations The reason that the program in the referenced research succeeded was that it demanded responsibility, independence, and self-evaluation from the students. Students were allowed to make responsible choices and to see the effects of their decisions. One precaution should be taken, however, when setting up a program of this type: There should be close agreement between the students' self-evaluation

FIGURE 9.1 Chart for Making Responsible Choices

SELF-RESPONSIBILITY CHART

Group Activity Days	Self-evaluation score	Privileges earned	Self-evaluation score	Privileges earned	Self-evaluation score	Privileges earned
day 1						
day 2						
day 3						
day 4						
day 5						
day 6						
day 7						
day 8						
day 9						
day 10						

Kathleen Opie, 1988.

scores and those of the teacher. Without agreement, students could gain access to privileges they hadn't earned. If there is a significant level of disagreement on a student's ratings, it may be advisable either to arrange some type of reward for students whose agreements between self- and teacher-ratings are high, or to involve some penalty for those whose scores are not in accord.

This was an excellent experience for middle school youngsters, but it could also be scheduled effectively in high schools. Furthermore, the tactic could be arranged in classrooms, as well as gyms, where students spend a majority of their time working alone. In those former situations, the reinforcer could be group work rather than personal time.

Monitor
See suggestions in number 7 of the Procedures above and MONITOR 5 in Appendix A for more information on Rating Scales.

Reference
Hellison, D. (1983). Teaching self-responsibility. *Journal of Physical Education, 54,* 23–28.

SELF-MANAGEMENT: ATTRIBUTION RETRAINING II

Background
Students with a history of failure frequently attribute their shortcomings to the lack of ability and their achievements to teacher bias, luck, and task ease. Successful students, on the other hand, tend to attribute both their successes and failures to effort (or lack of effort) rather than to factors outside their control. As a result, successful students have a tendency to work harder and longer at tasks. The following tactic seeks to train failure-oriented students, many of whom are remedial or at risk, to reattribute their successes and failures to effort, in an attempt to improve academic performance. The training involves three phases: self-observation, substitution, and cognitive restructuring.

Who Can Benefit
Ninety seventh- and eighth-grade students from a Los Angeles school participated in the referenced study (Reiher & Dembo, 1984). They were selected

because of their low effort attribution scores on the Intellectual Achievement Responsibility Scale.

The potential for generalization to a variety of academic tasks, the group training approach, and the simplicity with which the steps can be organized and presented to teachers are all valuable aspects of this tactic. The emphasis on self-instruction and placing the responsibility for change in attitude on the students makes this a skill that can benefit students long after they have left a particular teacher, classroom, or school.

Prepare students for the program by introducing the concept that one's internal dialogue can influence his or her behavior.

Procedures

Self-Observation

1. Encourage students to list some of the inappropriate self-statements they have made in various academic situations (e.g., "I'm not smart enough to do it," "I don't really care," "I couldn't do it even if I tried").
2. Instruct them to compare self-statements with one another, noting similarities and differences.

Substitution

1. Explain to the students that through self-suggestion they can utilize the power to imagine. For example, ask them to reflect on positive statements or images that evoke good feelings or prompt relaxation (e.g., "I remember how I felt when I got an A," "When I try real hard I can do about anything," "I don't have to do it all at once; I can do some of it each day for a week or so").
2. Ask students to volunteer examples of positive self-statements, compiling a list for future reference.

Cognitive Restructuring

1. Train students to self-monitor their levels of effort by having them rate their intention to participate in an assigned academic task on a scale of 1 to 10 (1 = least; 10 = most).

2. Direct their attention to the specific nature of the task and have them clarify it as follows:
   a. Decide what the task is about.
   b. Determine *exactly* what you are supposed to do.
   c. Reward yourself verbally for completing this step. (Say something like "Way to go," or "That's good.")
3. Instruct students to identify the necessary sequence of steps in a task, and reward themselves on successful completion.
4. Instruct students to rate their efforts, using a 1 to 10 scale once again. *Note:* See Self-Instructional Training Guide in Table 9.1 for examples of how to execute steps 3 through 5 of the cognitive restructuring phase.
5. Practice self-instruction and self-suggestion on an actual academic task for 40 minutes—for example, reading a table of contents in an atlas, solving basic math problems, using library reference skills, or comprehending reading passages.

Modifications/ Considerations

The cited study (Reiher & Dembo, 1984) was successful in improving academic performance by training students to attribute their achievements to effort; that is, to change their attitudes about themselves and their abilities. One could provide additional examples of how to increase positive thinking and self-esteem. For example, it is sometimes inspirational to tell students about successful people who overcame poor beginnings to achieve what they have. Likewise, it can be motivating to tell stories of individuals who had poor attitudes at one time or who had fallen into states of moral or psychological decay and who, because of a change of attitude, pulled themselves out of it.

Monitor

Instruct the students to keep two types of data. First, they should keep track of the intensity with which they worked on assignments; second, they should keep data on whether or not assignments were completed. A more precise measure of the latter would be to acquire data on how well the assignments were carried out, perhaps by using grades.

TABLE 9.1 Self-Instructional Training Guide

Procedure	Blackboard Guide	Example
WHO is performing the task?		
The student used a simple self-rating measure to identify his or her intention (effort) to participate in the assigned academic task. This was accomplished by using a scale of 1 to 10. The student was asked to hold up in the air the appropriate number of fingers (0 = no intention [effort], 10 = maximum intention [effort]) to demonstrate self-monitoring of effort. This procedure was repeated again at the end of the task to reaffirm the level of intention. This WHO question represented the most critical aspect of the training with regard to the effort attribution shift.	1. Decide how much effort you wish to apply to the task. 2. Hold up the number of fingers that tell how much effort you are going to make (0 = no intention [effort], 10 = maximum intention [effort]). 3. Reward yourself verbally (with a "that's good" statement) for your effort.	"Let's see (student holds up 9 fingers), I really want to apply my best effort here. Okay, that's good, I'm really going to try hard on this."
WHAT is the nature of the task?		
The second question directed the students' attention to the specific nature of the task involved. The student was asked to clarify the academic task at hand. This was accomplished through the use of three guiding statements on the blackboard (see Blackboard Guide).	1. Decide *what* the task is about. 2. Decide *exactly* what you are supposed to do. 3. Reward yourself verbally (with a "that's good" statement) for completing this section.	"All right now, what exactly is the task? I'm supposed to look at the table of contents of this atlas and then answer the question at the bottom of the page. That's good, I've got that straight."
HOW is the task to be performed?		
The third question attempted to enhance the self-instruction in the effort and positive reinforcement statements, and identified the necessary sequence of steps in the academic task.	1. Decide *how* you will take your first step in completing the task. 2. Decide how you will take the next step in the task. 3. Reward yourself verbally (with a "that's good" statement) and continue the process until you have completed the task. 4. Give yourself an effort rating (hold up fingers 1 through 10).	"Now, how should I proceed? First, I'll skim over all the information to see what it contains. Good, I have a pretty good idea of what's in here. Now, they want to know on what page the map of West North Central United States can be found. Okay, let me look for West North Central United States. Ah, okay, here it is on page 6."

Note. From Reiher, R.H., & Dembo, M.H. (1984). Changing academic task persistence through a self-instructional attribution training program. *Contemporary Educational Psychology, 9,* p. 88. Reprinted by permission of Academic Press.

It might be of interest also to have students write down two "effort" rankings—one before they began an assignment, and one after they finished it. Pupils would learn a lot about the difference between their intentions and their performances. Those ratings could be charted as frequencies (see MONITOR 1 in Appendix A).

Reference   Reiher, R.H., & Dembo, M.H. (1984). Changing academic task persistency through a self-instructional attribution training program. *Contemporary Educational Psychology, 9,* 84-94.

TEACHER MANAGEMENT: DEALING WITH ALIENATION

Background   To break the cycle of alienation experienced by students and teachers in urban schools, we must accompany calls for order and high expectations with relevance for students and professionalism for teachers. That is the challenge laid out by Firestone (1989). According to him, and many would agree, teacher alienation and student alienation feed on each other. Therefore, in order to establish better attitudes on the part of teachers and students, both parties must be considered. Firestone cautioned that in attempts to deal with poor attitudes, the Joe Clark, get-tough orientation may be oversold; safety and order are too often purchased at the price of personal freedom and self-respect.

Who Can Benefit   Students and teachers alike should benefit from this program. As their attitudes improve, so would those of their parents and the community at large.

In this study (Firestone, 1989), researchers gathered information about how the cycle of alienation worked in some schools and how it had been broken in others. To obtain this information, they constructed measures of both forms of alienation, then rated each school's overall levels. Their data showed that the correlation between teacher and student alienation was .92, indicating a high degree of association.

Procedures

Some opinions from students on what promotes a good situation:

1. A good teacher is fun, caring, devoted, patient, intelligent, a role model, expressive, personal.
2. The assignments should be interesting and relevant.
3. Teachers should explain things again and again when students do not understand something the first time.
4. Students don't like it when teachers talk down to them.
5. They don't like it when teachers embarrass them in front of others.
6. Students need personal reasons to meet standards.

And from teachers:

1. They like it when students listen to them and hang around to ask questions about the work.
2. They want to be listened to and respected by administrators.
3. Teachers don't like the punitive attitudes of some administrators.
4. They like supportive working conditions. These included quality of the buildings and the adequacy of materials.
5. They work best when there is an atmosphere of collegiality among teachers.
6. Teachers want to have influence over the things that affect them.

Table 9.2 summarizes the specific practices observed that tended to reduce student and teacher alienation. According to Firestone (1989), an emphasis on relevance and respect provides students with reasons to stay in school, minimizes the forces that encourage

Modifications/ Considerations

TABLE 9.2 Factors That Reduce Student and Teacher Alienation

	Daily Actions of Principals and Teachers	Formal Decisions by Principals	Formal Decisions by District Office
Order	Consistency on the part of the principals		
	Respect from all adults in school		
Expectations		School incentive programs (like academic letter jackets)	Districtwide coordinated student testing and curriculum articulation programs
			Districtwide inservice and staff development programs
Relevance	Quality counseling	Career programs	Career programs
			Adequately staffed counseling programs
Professionalism	Personalized administrative support for teachers	Administrative actions, from parties to retreats, to promote collegiality	Districtwide inservice programs
	Sharing among teachers about professional issues	Sharing influence and decision making with teachers	Opportunities for teacher influence over relevant district decisions (like testing and curriculum alignment programs)

Note. From Firestone, W.A. (1989). Beyond order and expectations in high schools serving at-risk youth. *Educational Leadership,* February, p. 45. Reprinted with permission of the Association for Supervision and Curriculum Development. Copyright 1989 by ASCD. All rights reserved.

students to leave, and fosters an environment where their needs for belonging and recognition are met. Professionalism (e.g., involving teachers in decision making and providing desirable working conditions) creates a climate that helps teachers treat students with respect.

Data could be kept on student and teacher absences. **Monitor**
Furthermore, qualitative surveys could be administered to students and teachers prior to altering the
attitudes, and while the program is in progress. For
this, selected teachers and students could be asked to
respond to a number of queries: "How do you like
working at (going to) school?" "Has the climate
improved in the past 6 months? If so, how is it different?" "What changes could be made so that this was a
better school?" "Do you know of other schools that
have better educational climates or atmospheres?"
"What concerns or distresses you the most about this
school?" (See MONITOR 9 in Appendix A.)

Firestone, W.A. (1989). Beyond order and expectations in **Reference**
    high schools serving at-risk youth. *Educational Lead-*
    ership, February, 41–45.

TEACHER MANAGEMENT: MATH ANXIETY

Math anxiety is a phenomenon that increases in mid- **Background**
dle school when math becomes more abstract. Basic
courses often have a high concentration of students
who neither like nor understand math. It is essential
to assist these students. This tactic presents a few
suggestions for teachers to use with math-anxious
students.

Pupils who perceive themselves as slow or of low abil- **Who Can**
ity in math will benefit. This includes those who **Benefit**
arrive at class without completed homework, cram
work into folders so that no one will see what they did,
and erase entire problems when their answers are
wrong rather than look for the errors. Math anxiety
applies to males and females, and affects high- as
well as low-ability students.

Procedures
1. Estimate the degree of math anxiety of your students by asking them to complete this sentence on the first day of class:
"To me, math is _____."
2. Preview the attitudes presented and select or create tactics that respond appropriately to students' concerns and problems.
3. Discuss in class the students' attitudes about mistakes, anxiety, or failure in math.
4. Identify resources in your school and community that may assist in dealing with math anxiety.

Problem 1. Lack of confidence in math can lead students to ask continuously for reassurance. Some pupils refuse to go on to another problem until they have been told that their answer is correct. Poor math students often "talk" to themselves in ways that are negative and nonproductive.

Tactics to apply

1. At the beginning of a course, answer all questions so that students realize you are helpful. Encourage creativity in solving problems. Avoid saying, "This is how you solve the problem." Lead students with questions such as the following: "What would be your first step?" "How did you know that?" "What were you saying to yourself?" "What would you do next?" "Is there another way of doing it?" As the semester progresses and students gain more confidence, answer questions in less detail, and put more questions back to the students. Remain available, however, even if students don't have questions, as this keeps communication open.

2. Make it clear that being confused about a problem can be the first step in learning. Consider these comments: "Is it okay to make a mistake? You bet it is; I make them all the time." "We learn a lot from our mistakes." "When you don't have the right answer the first time, don't erase it; analyze your method, try another, and you might get it right." If students are truly stuck with a problem, suggest that they put their work away, do something else, and go back to it later.

3. Another approach is to assign students to small groups that include pupils who were formerly anxious about math. There, peer tutors can discuss

topics that were initially confusing for them, and outline strategies they relied on to solve the problems.

4. Teach math by using methods that are standard in other subjects, such as assigning nontextbook material, term papers, or alternative exercises such as looking for patterns and differences on different pages. Encourage students to use study skills that were taught in other classes, such as reading the text, working examples, underlining keywords, taking and studying notes, writing definitions in their own words, and discussing ideas with other students.

5. Encourage students to brainstorm ways to feel less anxious about numbers. For example, students can cut out big numbers from construction paper and hang them from the ceiling where they look less forbidding.

Problem 2. Methods employed by students who don't like math are not particularly effective, and are almost certainly not those used by instructors. Often these students rely on memorization, and treat math as a huge list of rules and steps that have to be learned, much like a recipe. Unfortunately, these students don't always memorize the context in which the rules are applied, and end up applying them in the wrong places. Learning by memorization is no fun, and it contributes greatly to a student's fear of the subject. When a question is asked that is a little different, students who try to memorize everything know they won't be able to answer it.

Tactics to apply. Be aware that students who don't like math often have reasons for the ways they attempt to solve problems. Note their strategies and make use of them as clues as to how they think. Make students aware of the methods they are using and how they might be improved. Only after an old method has been thoroughly laid to rest can a student's mind be free to listen to a new one.

Problem 3. A common source of math anxiety is word problems.

Tactics to apply

1. Teach without ambiguous language. Point out that mathematics is a language of numbers, and that

FIGURE 9.2 Practice in Translating Words to Mathematical Symbols

the sum of	greater than
one number over another	less than
added to	twice
a fractional part of	two thirds of
increased by	he has 4 left
quotient of	as many as
together they have	longer than
divided by	shorter than
more than	7 inches more
square of	6 pounds extra
smaller than	decreased by
difference between	4 less
times	one half the product
subtracted from	the cube of
multiplied by	8 exceeds x by
product of	the excess of 10 over x

Note. From Dahmus, M. (1970). How to teach verbal problems. *School Science and Mathematics, 70,* p. 132. Reprinted by permission of the School Science and Mathematics Association.

mathematical expressions are just shorthand for longer word phrases. Write out words next to the symbols. Give students practice in translating mathematics terms before actually working story problems (see Figure 9.2).

2. Request students to read the problems out loud to help them make sense, and to help you discover their misconceptions.

3. Use word problems that were written by students.

4. Use word problems created by professionals (e.g., merchants, doctors).

5. Think of practical applications that use hands-on activities, such as rolling dice, manipulating survey data, or meeting job requirements. As employees in "pretend" companies, students can fill out formal job applications with references and W-2 forms, keep time cards, review their paychecks, and file for tax refunds. Involve the senses, especially in areas like geometry.

Problem 4. A common misconception of students is that if you're good, math problems should be accomplished instantly or at least very fast. They may have only seen problems completed in class by teachers who already knew the answers.

Tactics to apply. Show students your false starts and piles of scratch paper, and explain the time it takes to work problems. Explain the process you follow, using pencil instead of pen, and estimating answers or checking them with a calculator. Give students time to explore problem situations. Ask them to generate questions from their observations. Assign fewer problems and require students to redo their answers until they are correct.

Problem 5. Certain types of instruction favor competitive and aggressive students to the detriment of students who are not. Research shows that lower level math skills are often taught with timed tests and instructional games. Students who tend to lose also drop in achievement.

Tactics to apply. Don't assume that all students enjoy competitive games. Choose equitable teaching methods and be sensitive to the needs of various students. When teachers use cooperative-learning strategies, girls often achieve more than boys on higher level math activities.

Gather adequate information about your students before attempting to remediate problems. Be aware of the fact that many students experience a "sudden death" situation with mathematics: One day in a math class they were embarrassed or made to feel stupid and they "quit." Do not push students into feeling this sense of inadequacy, and encourage them to try changing their perceptions.

Modifications/ Considerations

It is not an easy task to evaluate the effects of approaches designed to decrease students' anxiety toward mathematics. It is even more difficult to ascertain whether students' attitudes toward academics generally improve as they become less anxious about mathematics.

The best indicators of the former would be reflected in some of the following: increased atten-

Monitor

dance in mathematics classes, more assignments turned in on time that were satisfactorily completed, better grades, more enthusiasm shown for the subject and fewer negative remarks, more advanced mathematics courses taken, more applications made of mathematics concepts and principles to real-life situations. A checklist that includes those and other items could be completed from time to time (see MONITOR 6 in Appendix A).

References

Akst, G. (Ed.). (1981). *Improving mathematics skills*. San Francisco: Jossey-Bass.

Mahlios, J. (1988). Word problems: Do I add or subtract? *Arithmetic Teacher, 36*, 48–52.

SCHOOLWIDE CHANGES: STUDENTS HELP AT SCHOOL

Background

Considerable numbers of secondary students have bad attitudes toward their teachers, classes, and most everything associated with school. It is hard to say when and how those attitudes were developed. It seems that many poor attitudes begin in the intermediate grades and continue into middle school or junior high, and on through high school (unless students drop out, and more and more do just that). It is also difficult to pinpoint the reasons for these poor attitudes. But many students become disenchanted and alienated with schools because they have not been given any responsibility for upkeep, much less the governance of the school; furthermore, many believe they are not acquiring information that relates directly and immediately to their lives.

Who Can Benefit

Ideas in this tactic should be considered to influence the poor attitudes of many remedial and at-risk students, as well as others who appear to be disfranchised by education, schools, and teachers.

Listed here are three suggestions for bringing students around so that their attitudes are more positive toward school:

Procedures

1. *Upkeep and maintenance.* Many pupils have little feeling of ownership or responsibility for their schools. This is noted not only in their verbal disrespect for the school but by the acts of vandalism that are more serious. Those students believe that schools were built as prisons; schools are places that contain them and keep them from doing what they want to do. One way to change the attitudes of these students is to involve them in the day-by-day routines of the school. For example, a school secretary at a high school was asked one afternoon to watch a boy who had been sent to the office for disciplinary reasons (the vice principal was not there). Since the secretary was busy and could not simply sit with the youth, she enlisted his help with a number of chores. The young man liked the work and asked, a few days after his "sentence" had been served, if he could help some more. Because help was needed, he and others were put into service on a variety of tasks. Consequently, those students were praised for their work, realized they were contributing to the school, and to some extent, behaved more respectfully toward their school.

2. *Pupil governance.* Many schools do not elicit the opinions of students on school matters. This is unfortunate, because there are a number of activities and policies about which students' ideas should be requested. Students, like their elders, appreciate being considered when decisions are made on issues that affect them. Although there are a number of issues about which students should probably not be consulted—the wisdom of the teachers, parents, and school boards should prevail—those matters are probably fewer than most of us would like to believe. Pupils could be given some say in the scheduling of classes, the assignment of teachers, the scheduling of assemblies, parties, and other special occasions, the menus in cafeterias, bus routes, and even teacher evaluations. That isn't to say that they should have total responsibility in deciding about those

highly important matters, but their opinions should certainly be solicited.

3. *Learning relevant skills.* It is difficult for most youngsters to listen to lectures and read books about events and circumstances that are not immediately relevant to their lives. Although not every important topic in all their classes can be immediately relevant to pupils, many topics are. For example, a seventh-grade earth science class was studying conservation. Their teacher had planned a library assignment to cover this topic, but when a number of his students asked if they could do more than just talk and write about it, he redesigned the unit to involve them with their community. The students learned about where and how paper could be collected, what happens to that paper, how paper was made originally, and the effect of recycling paper on workers' jobs in their town. Some other activities: Students learned on what days the papers would be collected, how they should be tied together, and how many pounds of paper equal one tree. They asked neighbors to save papers for their paper drive, wrote letters on conservation to the local paper, and loaded paper on the trucks.

Modifications/ Considerations
There are a number of other ways to help students acquire better attitudes and become less alienated with schools—they depend on the teaching staff, the community, and the types of students—but more should be done. Another way to look at this matter would be for adults to spend some time in schools to learn firsthand about the experiences of children. (One thing that adults would probably want to change about schools, if they spent an entire day sitting in classes, would be the chairs. They are very uncomfortable, and an uncomfortable seat does nothing for a positive attitude.)

Monitor
It is difficult to measure attitudes, either good ones or bad ones, but somewhat easier to monitor the manifestations of those attitudes. Some factors related to good and bad school attitudes are the following: vandalism, absences, fights, referrals to the principal or other disciplinary figure. A checklist could be devel-

oped that includes those items and others. It could be completed by teachers, parents, and students (see MONITOR 6 in Appendix A).

Krumboltz, J.D., & Krumboltz, H.B. (1972). *Generating enthusiasm for school: Changing children's behavior.* Englewood Cliffs, NJ: Prentice-Hall.   **Reference**

SCHOOLWIDE CHANGES: CHANGING ATTITUDES REGARDING EDUCATION (CARE)

The CARE program was designed to help educators become aware of students who are developing attitudes toward education that are not conducive to learning. It provides them with a way to intervene with these students to change their negative attitudes, and offers a range of preventive activities as well.

Background

A team made up of an administrator, teachers, a counselor, and parents has the responsibility of taking referrals, proposing a plan of action for students who have been referred, and reviewing their progress. Anyone may refer a student to this team for intervention.

Intermediate or middle school students displaying characteristics that have been observed in studies (Hess, Wells, Prindle, Liffman, & Kaplan, 1987) conducted with high school dropouts (i.e., low reading ability, above or below average age for class, among other characteristics) are targeted through referrals for intervention by the CARE team. It is hoped that attempts to intervene with these at-risk youth at an early age will prevent them from dropping out later on. (See Figure 9.3 for a listing of characteristics of these youth.)

Who Can Benefit

FIGURE 9.3 Changing Attitudes Regarding Education

REFERRAL FORM
(To be completed by referring person)

Student's Name _____

Teacher _____

School _____

Referral Date _____ Student Number _____

Chronological Age _____

Parent's Name(s) _____

Address _____ Zip _____

Home Phone _____ Office Phone _____

The above named student is being referred based on the responses to the following:

Characteristics	Never				Always

I. *Academic*

1. The student displays a low reading ability.   1 2 3 4 5

2. The student fails to achieve in regular schoolwork.   1 2 3 4 5

3. The student possesses either a low scholastic aptitude *or* average to high scholastic aptitude but with performance consistently below potential.   1 2 3 4 5

4. The student's grade level placement is below average age for grade.   1 2 3 4 5

II. *School Patterns*

5. The student displays irregular attendance/frequent tardiness.   1 2 3 4 5

6. The student displays antagonism to faculty.   1 2 3 4 5

7. He or she causes discipline problems.   1 2 3 4 5

8. The student had a frequent change of schools.   1 2 3 4 5

III. *Social*

9. There is little acceptance of student by school staff.   1 2 3 4 5

10. The student's friends are much younger or older.   1 2 3 4 5

11. He or she has few friends.   1 2 3 4 5

12. There is a marked difference in student from schoolmates in:
    a. size   ☐
    b. interests   ☐
    c. physique   ☐
    d. social class   ☐
    e. nationality   ☐
    f. dress   ☐
    g. personality development   ☐

13. The student participates in extra-curricular activities.   1 2 3 4 5

14. The student has a record of delinquency.   1 2 3 4 5

IV. *Family*

15. The student is not able to compete with, or is ashamed of, brothers and sisters.   1 2 3 4 5

16. The student has an unhappy/unstable family situation.   1 2 3 4 5

17. The parents of the student did *not* graduate from high school.   1 2 3 4 5

18. The student has a low socioeconomic status.   1 2 3 4 5

19. The family has an inability to afford the normal expenditures of schoolmates.   1 2 3 4 5

V. *Health*

20. The student has a serious emotional or physical handicap.   1 2 3 4 5

21. The student has or has had chronic illness.   1 2 3 4 5

Note. From Duval County Schools. (1986). *CARE, Changing Attitudes Regarding Education* (pp. 3, 4). Jacksonville, FL: Author. ERIC Document Reproduction Service No. ED 285 923. Reprinted by permission.

Procedures **Guidelines for the CARE Team.** Here are suggestions for developing and running a CARE team:

1. (Principal) Appoint members of the CARE team: principal, a classroom teacher, guidance counselor, referring teacher, and parents.
2. Select a chairperson for the team.
3. Meet a minimum of once every 9 weeks to:
   a. Act on new referrals
   b. Review current and previous cases
4. (Recorder) Complete individual reporting forms and log each case.
5. (Counselor) Flag cumulative record to make tracking possible, and place a copy of the Individual Report Form in cumulative folder.
6. Initiate intervention.
7. Monitor and modify interventions as necessary.

Intervention for Project CARE. The purpose of Project CARE is to help students care about education and know that educators care about them. Students who have been identified as candidates for the program become members of Project CARE according to guidelines established by the team in their school. Following are suggestions for establishing the structure and function of this group:

1. Conduct monthly meetings with students of similar age to decide on and put together a project to show that they care about their school, education, and teachers.
2. Ask interested teachers to volunteer to meet with Project CARE students to coordinate the projects.
3. Support students' attempts to write and give a CARE skit for individual classes or the whole school.
4. Encourage students to write CARE thoughts and read them over the intercom.
5. Encourage students to welcome new students and take them on a tour of the school.
6. Give each student involved in the project a CARE button to identify them and instill a sense of pride.

Taking Individual Action. For students with academic difficulties, the following may be useful:

1. Provide assistance through appropriate referrals:
    a. A homework assistance program
    b. Volunteer tutor
    c. Peer tutoring
    d. Primary resource teacher
    e. Special programs such as Chapter I
2. Set up counseling groups for work and study skills.
3. Write behavioral contracts with the referring teacher and student to improve daily work and study skills.
4. Conduct parent workshops to teach students ways to assist their children.
5. Use selective class scheduling.

Family Concerns

Divorce/death/new family

1. Provide individual and group counseling.
2. Give parents referral information such as family counseling services and homemaker services.
3. Establish parent education groups for parents with similar concerns.

Chronic/serious illness

1. Arrange for individual counseling.
2. Make referrals to:
    a. School social worker
    b. Parents regarding information on available services
    c. Home reinforcement services if appropriate

Abuse or neglect.   Refer to home reinforcement services.

Unidentified family concerns. Request assistance from school social worker who can:

1. Assess needs
2. Offer help with possible resources

Frequent school changes

1. Assign a Big Brother or Big Sister to the referred student.
2. Formulate a plan including:
    a. Early contact with counselor, principal, and other appropriate staff
    b. Frequent follow-up in first weeks to alleviate the stress of change

3. Contact next school when student leaves about:
   a. Academic difficulties
   b. Need for referral to outside agencies

Frequent tardiness/absence

1. Have a parent conference to explain need for attendance.
2. Engage the assistance of the school social worker, attendance officer, or others when appropriate.

Health Concerns

Uncertain health concern. Contact school nurse or school social worker to:

1. Determine existence and nature of health problem
2. Assist parents in securing needed assistance

Cleanliness/hygiene

1. Counsel with student.
2. Have parent conference.
3. Refer to nurse or social worker.
4. Refer to home reinforcement services if appropriate.

Chronic illness

1. Conference with parents to learn about:
   a. Nature of the illness
   b. Related limitations
   c. Special needs
2. Counsel with student to help him or her deal with the illness and its effects.
3. Involve student in support or counseling groups with others who have chronic health concerns (e.g., diabetes or epilepsy).
4. Assist parents to get help through hospital or homebound programs.
5. Inform all school staff who have contact with the student about the nature and limitations of the illness.

Physical or emotional handicap

1. Make appropriate referrals:
   a. Services available through the school
   b. Hospital
   c. Counseling services

2. Provide individual or group counseling.
3. Arrange for school presentations by mental or physical health organizations.

Interpersonal Relationship Concerns

Problems with peer group

1. Make staff members who work with the student aware of his or her situation, and work with them when dealing with behaviors such as tattling, teasing, and name calling.
2. Conduct classroom sessions on building interpersonal skills, acceptance of individual differences, and a cooperative classroom spirit.
3. Provide individual or group counseling on interpersonal relationships (i.e., how to develop friendships, finding a way to belong to the group).
4. Involve the student with problems as a "buddy" for a younger student who needs a friend.
5. Help student find:
   a. A hobby
   b. A sport to get involved in
   c. A club to join
   d. Music or art activities
6. Develop behavioral contracts with the students to help them change negative behaviors (e.g., fighting, bullying, teasing).
7. Refer to outside agencies if needed.
8. Ask parents to help plan cooperative efforts to provide youth with more positive interactions.

Problems with school staff

1. Plan strategies with adults who work with the student to change the cycle of negative interactions.
2. Conduct workshops to help staff improve relationships with such students including:
   a. Communication skills
   b. Improving self-concept and positive discipline approaches

Modifications/ Considerations

These strategies have been recommended to give staff immediate ways to deal with students who are displaying negative attitudes toward school. Whenever possible, it would be more desirable to act early in each student's school experience to prevent these attitudes from developing at all.

Monitor A program such as this should be evaluated by keeping track of who is involved (students and faculty), the time spent on the program, and by detailing the program's components that are involved. Beyond gathering those descriptive data, all (or at least representative) individuals involved in the program should be interviewed periodically to determine whether they are pleased with the progress or would recommend changes (see MONITOR 9 in Appendix A).

References Duval County Schools. (1986). *CARE, Changing attitudes regarding education.* Jacksonville, FL: Author. (ERIC Documentation Service No. ED 285 923)

Hess, A.G., Jr., Wells, E., Prindle, C., Liffman, P., & Kaplan, B. (1987). "Where's Room 185?" How schools can reduce their dropout problem. *Education and Urban Society, 19*(3), 330–335.

GOALS

10

PLANNING: ARRANGING CONTRACTS

Background

Remedial, at-risk, and learning disabled students often lack the academic skills and study habits valued by teachers, and those required for success in schools. As a result, those students receive poor grades and scant praise, and consequently become unmotivated and demoralized. In a response to this problem, the cited research (Tollefson, Tracy, Johnsen, & Chatman, 1986) implemented a training program to teach self-management behaviors that included skills in goal setting and planning.

The method used to monitor these self-regulated behaviors was a weekly contract made up of several interrelated features: (a) setting realistic (attainable) academic goals; (b) developing a plan to reach these goals (the contract); (c) implementing, monitoring, and evaluating progress; and (d) accepting responsibility for success and failure in attaining goals. The latter relates to effort attribution, the perception individuals have of the role that effort plays in achievement. To succeed in this task, all four components are essential.

Who Can Benefit

The technique described in the cited research (Tollefson et al., 1986) was conducted with junior high learning disabled students in a resource room. These practices could be set up for other types and ages of students in a variety of settings. To ensure success, the student and teacher must be committed, and must carry out their part of the contract. The student must attempt to accomplish that which is set out; the teacher must give the student consistent feedback on his or her efforts.

Procedures

1. Record the number of assignments (the precontract) the student is asked to complete. These data will serve as a baseline.

2. Encourage the student to select a subject or behavior in which he or she wants to improve. Combine information from the student, as well as your own ideas about problem areas in establishing a weekly contract (see Weekly Contract in Figure 10.1).

3. Explain a contract to the student noting that it is a promise to fulfill a certain requirement or task. Emphasize the fact that students are obligated to fulfill the task they selected, and when they do, they will receive a reward.

4. Develop a study plan to meet the goal. Specify activities, time and place the work should be done, and who students can ask for help when needed.

5. Direct students to monitor their daily work by placing a (+) or (–) to indicate whether the plan was followed that day. If the plan was not carried out, students should write in a reason why it was not.

6. Instruct students to record their "level of satisfaction" on the form at the end of a week.

7. Explain to students that their level of satisfaction is attributed to their success in establishing a realistic goal and completing the contract. If students have failed, inform them that their failure is due to the quality and amount of effort put forth, and not to luck or ability.

8. Review the completed contract once a week and introduce the one for the next week, which is to be filled out prior to each new week.

Modifications/ Considerations

The cited research (Tollefson et al., 1986) was successful, probably because the weekly reviews between teacher and students provided the feedback necessary to help students attribute their successes and failures to their personal efforts rather than to external factors such as luck. A second reason to account for the success of the project was that the goals set by the students were attainable.

Related to attribution and the attainment of goals, it was interesting to note that in the cited research (Tollefson et al., 1986), the students' self-esteem remained high, perhaps because they were in control of their performances.

FIGURE 10.1   Form for Usc in Planning

WEEKLY CONTRACT

Subject: _____   Student Name: _____

Period: _____   Teacher Name: _____

from _____   to _____

Goal Statement: _____

_____

COMPLETION DATES: TASK 1 _____

TASK 2 _____
(fill in as needed)

Study Plan: Activities   Work Time   Place   Helper

Monday
Tuesday
Wednesday
Thursday
Friday

_____

_____

Goal _____

Accomplished   Not Accomplished   Reasons

_____

_____

Level of Satisfaction: Very Satisfied _____

Satisfied _____

Not Satisfied _____

Reward

Teacher Signature _____

Student Signature _____

When it comes to writing performance contracts, a number of modifications are possible. The complexity of the contract could be changed—some could be simpler, others, more sophisticated. Contracts could be drawn up in several of a student's classes. The number and type of individuals involved in setting up and carrying out the contract could be varied from the student and teacher situations described here. For example, contracts could be written that involve friends, administrators, or parents. The component of time could be varied as well, moving from weekly to longer term contracts.

Monitor   The type of data to be kept for this project are rather obvious: number of goals set and attained per week (or other period of time) (see MONITOR 1 in Appendix A). Beyond those measures, data could be acquired on the quality of students' performance, their attitude toward the subject, and their grades.

Reference   Tollefson, N., Tracy, D.B., Johnsen, E.P., & Chatman, J. (1986). Teaching learning disabled students goal-implementation skills. *Psychology in the Schools, 23,* 194–204.

PLANNING: COMPLETING LONG-TERM ASSIGNMENTS

Background   When students do not make productive use of class time, due to disruptive or off-task behaviors or failure to meet teacher expectations, learning is adversely affected. Systematically teaching students to assume responsibility for managing their own behaviors is one way to address these problems.

The establishment of a teacher-managed reinforcement system, wherein responsibility for maintenance is gradually shifted to students, is an effective approach for dealing with those concerns. Outlined here is a method for teaching the self-management skill of completing assignments as a starting point from which other behaviors can be managed by students.

Students who accept responsibility for improving a particular behavior as a personal goal are likely to benefit from this program. When students successfully modify a behavior by self-evaluation in one setting, that technique can likely be successfully arranged for other behaviors in different settings. Greater success in school and work are the ultimate benefits to these students. **Who Can Benefit**

Introduce the WATCH approach for completing long-term assignments (e.g., book reports, term papers, and special projects). **Procedures**

Introduction

1. Prepare the following materials:
   a. Display of the WATCH acronym (poster, transparency, or written on board):
      W = <u>Write</u> down the assignment, the due date, and any special requirements for the assignment.
      A = <u>Ask</u> yourself if you understand the assignment, and ask for clarification or help if necessary.
      T = <u>Task-analyze</u> the assignment, and schedule the tasks over the days available to complete the assignment.
      CH = <u>Check</u> each task as you finish it for completeness, accuracy, and neatness.
   b. Copies of blank Assignment Planner and Point Card (see Figure 10.2) for each student
   c. One example copy of a completed Assignment Planner and Point Card
   d. Three example assignments for your class, with corresponding Assignment Planner and Point Card sheets filled out for each
2. Tell the students that they will learn to use a Planner (much like adults use on the job) to schedule and monitor their work.

FIGURE 10.2 Assignment Planner

Week of: ____to____

| WATCH |
| Assignment Planner and Point Card |

Name:_____

Assignment_____

        a. Due Date_____

Special   b._____

Require- c._____

ments   d._____

        e._____

| Do I Understand the Assignment? (   ) |
| Do I Need to Ask for Help? (   ) |

		(Optional) Citizenship/Points		Watch/Points		Total
Monday:_____	I C/A/N	☐	_____	☐	_____	☐
Tuesday:_____	I C/A/N	☐	_____	☐	_____	☐
Wednesday:_____	I C/A/N	☐	_____	☐	_____	☐
Thursday:_____	I C/A/N	☐	_____	☐	_____	☐
Friday:_____	I C/A/N	☐	_____	☐	_____	☐

Assignment_____

        a. Due Date_____

Special   b._____

Require- c._____

ments   d._____

        e._____

| Do I Understand the Assignment? (   ) |
| Do I Need to Ask for Help? (   ) |

		(Optional) Citizenship/Points		Watch/Points		Total
Monday:_____	I C/A/N	☐	_____	☐	_____	☐
Tuesday:_____	I C/A/N	☐	_____	☐	_____	☐
Wednesday:_____	I C/A/N	☐	_____	☐	_____	☐
Thursday:_____	I C/A/N	☐	_____	☐	_____	☐
Friday:_____	I C/A/N	☐	_____	☐	_____	☐

Note. From Young, K.R., West, R.P., & Morgan, D.P. (1987). *Teaching self-management strategies to adolescents: Instructional manual* (p. 112). Logan: Department of Special Education, Utah State University. Reprinted by permission.

3. Emphasize the fact that this will help them organize and keep records of what they have done so they won't forget things such as:
   a. Directions for completing an assignment
   b. What materials to use (e.g., pencil or pen, lined or unlined paper)
   c. Due dates
4. Formulate a list of possible reinforcers (see Table 10.1, Reinforcement Preferences).

Instructions

1. Give a blank copy of the Planner to each student; explain that it is to be used as part of the WATCH program.
2. Point to the display of the acronym WATCH and inform students that they will learn what each letter means and how to carry out each step.
3. Explain what they can gain by learning and using the WATCH procedure:
   a. Better organization skills
   b. Record of information pertaining to assignments (due dates and materials)
   c. More self-control (rather than control being maintained by teacher or adult)
4. Use the posted acronym and examples of Planners with sections completed for each step to explain the corresponding meaning and application.
5. Read assignments given by you or another teacher during class. Present examples of correct and incorrect entries on the Planner. Discuss why each entry was either correctly or incorrectly written, reviewing the W, A, and T steps as necessary.
6. Hand out three or four blank Planners to each student. Read your prepared assignments (see 1(d) in Introduction, above) and ask students to complete the W-A-T steps. Provide corrective feedback.
7. Evaluate students' understanding of the WATCH procedure by reading one more assignment and having students organize their plan to complete it. Review and give corrective feedback, but review as necessary for students who are experiencing difficulty.

TABLE 10.1 Reinforcement Preferences

Ten Most-Preferred Reinforcers/Privileges
(suggested from a sample of high school students)

Male Students	Female Students
1. Free period (no work)	Free period
2. In-class movie/video	Listen to music on tape
3. Listen to music/tape	Extra grade points
4. Extra grade points	Listen to radio
5. Extra lunch period	Pizza party
6. Pizza party at school	Field trips
7. Listen to radio	Soft drinks
8. Soft drinks in class	In-class movie
9. Credit for gas/auto supplies	Tickets for local movie
10. Play games on computer	Time to visit with friends

Ten Least-Preferred Reinforcers/Privileges
(in descending order; 1 is the least preferred)

Male Students	Female Students
10. Tutor in junior high/elementary school	Commendation from principal
9. Rent a piece of equipment	Earn school supplies from teacher
8. Free reading time	Use of hand-held video games
7. Meal at teacher's home	Pass to gym
6. Pat on back from teacher	End-of-year awards ceremony
5. Commendation from principal	Meal at teacher's home
4. Weekly lunch with teacher	Rent a piece of equipment
3. Posting student names on board	Weekly lunch with teacher
2. Stickers on papers	Pat on back from teacher
1. Trial-size health and beauty	Stickers on papers

Note. From Young, K.R., West, R.P., Smith, D., & Morgan, D.P. (1987). *Teaching self-management strategies to adolescents: Instructional manual*, p. 100. Logan: Department of Special Education, Utah State University. Reprinted by permission.

Modifications/ Considerations   It is essential to the success of any self-management program that students accept the fact that they need to acquire self-management skills. Careful preparation and indication of student commitment to this goal are necessary before introducing the program.

The Planner suggested in this tactic is one example of a form that may be used. Teachers could design others that are more pertinent to the needs of their students, make use of student-developed approaches, or adapt commercially designed assignment books or planning calendars.

Each time corrective feedback is offered (see step 6 in Instructions, above, for an example), students can be reinforced for accepting criticism. In the A segment of the WATCH strategy another opportunity to reinforce a desirable behavior presents itself. The Planner is structured in such a way that students must acquire pertinent information before starting their assignments. Those behaviors represent attributes that teachers and employers frequently identify as important at school and on the job.

The results of step 7 in Instructions, above, should indicate whether additional instruction is necessary on any of the WATCH steps. Depending on which, if any, areas show weakness, students may receive this additional assistance either on an individual basis or in groups according to their deficit areas.

Monitor

A suggestion for monitoring this program is provided in step 7 of the Instructions (above). That concerns students' ability to involve the WATCH process (see MONITOR 6 in Appendix A). Beyond that, teachers or students could acquire data on the number of assignments completed, how long it took to finish them, and how well they were carried out.

Reference

Young, K.R., West, R.P., & Morgan, D.P. (1987). *Teaching self-management strategies to adolescents: Instructional manual.* Logan: Department of Special Education, Utah State University.

PLANNING: SETTING PRIORITIES

Background

This activity is based on the Q-sort technique, which involves sorting a set of cards into piles to form a normal distribution. The sorting process serves to actively involve students as they evaluate the relative importance of each item.

Who Can Benefit At-risk, remedial, and students of other types should profit from this technique. Explained here is a process for evaluating and prioritizing goals in three general areas: interpersonal, intrapersonal, and material.

Procedures Listed here are preparations to take care of prior to involving students in this technique and the steps required for carrying it out.

Preparations

1. Create one set of goal cards, on which the goals on the Goal Classifications List (Table 10.2) are printed (one per card) for each student.
2. Construct a folder that opens flat for each student.
   a. Attach an envelope containing the goal cards to the bottom left inside of the folder.
   b. Above the envelope, print the following instructions: "In the envelope below you will find 75 cards. A goal is written on each one. On the other page there are seven pockets. The top pocket is for goals you care the most about. The bottom pocket is for those you care the least about. The other pockets are for in-between goals.

      "Read each goal and decide how important it is to you. Put the three goals you care most about in pocket number 1 at the top. Put the three goals you care least about in pocket number 7 at the bottom. In pockets 2 through 6 place the other goal cards from the most to the least important to you. Place only the number of goal cards that are supposed to be in each pocket."
3. Tape seven pockets, vertically arranged, on the right side of the folder.
   a. Label the top end "Goals I Most Care About."
   b. Label the bottom end "Goals I Least Care About."
   c. Include instructions specifying the number of cards to be sorted in each pocket as shown on page 446.

TABLE 10.2   Goal Classifications List

Interpersonal (Relationships with Others)	*Intrapersonal* (Personal Concerns)	*Material* (Concrete Possessions)
Be a good friend	Be close to God	Have enough money to help others
Have close friend(s)	Go to heaven	Work to make money
Spend time with friends	Help people learn about God	Have enough money to buy what I want
Be close to my family	Do exciting things	Have a job I enjoy
Help my family	Have a lot of change in my life	Advance in my job
Do things with my family	Try everything I want to	Be good at my job
Marry someone I love	Be an attractive person	Travel to foreign places
Be happily married for a long time	Be well liked by others for what I am	Travel in the U.S.
Marry someone I know well	Respect myself	Meet people in other countries
Have children	Feel free to be different from others	Have a recent model vehicle
Spend time with children	Be able to think on my own	Have good equipment on my vehicle (car, pickup, van, etc.)
Be a good example for my children	Make a living on my own	Own my own home
Have leadership qualities	Learn as much as I can	Have a nice place to live
Be thought of as a leader	Get the best education I can	Keep my home in good condition
Be a leader in many areas of my life	Do well in school	Collect possessions (things) of interest
Do volunteer work	Work to improve my weaknesses	Have many possessions (things)
Work with community organizations	Develop my strengths and talents	Take care of my possessions (things)
Do things for others in the community	Know myself better	Have a lot of clothes
Understand others better	Eat the right foods for health	Wear fashionable clothes
Talk easily with others	Exercise for good health	Have comfortable clothes
Be a good listener	Be healthy all my life	Attend shows and other events
Be active in sports	Be more patient with myself and others	Eat at expensive restaurants
Understand sports	Accept things I cannot change	Have a large library
Promote sports	Be willing to wait for good things	
Live with someone	Look natural	
Remain single		
Be free without ties to anyone		

Note. Adapted from Cummings, M.N., Chamberlain, V.M., & Kelly, J.M. (1979). The Q-sort approach to helping adolescents with goal setting. *Illinois Teacher of Home Economics, 23,* p. 48. Adapted by permission.

Pocket	Number of Cards
1	3
2	8
3	16
4	21
5	16
6	8
7	3

Steps

1. Discuss goal setting as a way to enhance the quality of one's life and to plan for the future.
2. Tell students that this activity will help them choose their goals.
3. Provide each student with a folder.
4. Instruct students to read the instructions and begin the sort.
5. Ask students to make a record of their goal distribution on a separate sheet of paper.
6. Initiate class discussion about different ways to work toward achieving high-priority goals.
7. Help students develop individual plans for achieving their goals.

Modifications/ Considerations

Whereas the 75 goals printed here were selected by others, students or teachers could choose different ones. Furthermore, the goals in this research were from three categories and fit into seven sections (from least to most preferred). Fewer or more categories could be used, and fewer or more dimensions (pockets) could be selected.

Monitor

Once students have identified a few important goals to be achieved in a short or long period of time, they should be encouraged to monitor the extent to which they are attaining them. If, for example, one of Sarah's goals was to have a library of 500 classics, she could first list the books she intended to purchase, then check them off as they were added to the collection (see MONITOR 6 in Appendix A).

Reference

Cummings, M.N., Chamberlain, V.M., & Kelly, J.M. (1979). The Q-sort approach to helping adolescents with goal setting. *Illinois Teacher, 23*, 46–49.

ATTAINING GOALS: COMPLETING HOMEWORK

This technique assists students to set goals, a skill that must be learned and practiced. After pupils have had practice setting goals in the classroom, they can be encouraged to apply this skill to homework assignments and to personal goals. When students learn to monitor their own progress with this tactic, teachers can expect to save time.

Background

The referenced article (Nielson, 1983) was based on studies with adolescents. However, good self-management skills are important for everyone, since they are the means whereby long-term goals are attained. Specifically, this tactic is designed for students who need to turn in homework assignments on time. Those who have had experience satisfying instructional contracts should acquire self-management skills fairly quickly.

Who Can Benefit

1. Assist students to set performance goals that are slightly beyond their present levels; tell them what their present levels are; explain to them what constitutes a reasonable goal; and provide examples of goals with upper and lower limits. Explain to students that their goals must be easy to keep track of so that credit for progress can be easily documented.

Procedures

2. Assist pupils to develop their own reward systems. They could reward themselves for reaching their goals, for approximating them, or for reaching them a number of days in a row. Penalties rather than rewards could also be arranged, but generally the denial of a reward alone is sufficient.
   Note: Make sure the reinforcement system is generous at the beginning of the program by arranging for daily rewards. Later, the rewards should be faded.

3. Design contracts with students that detail assignments to be completed, schedules to be met, and rewards to be given (see Figure 10.3, Student Contract for Homework).

4. Assist pupils, initially, to set attainable goals, yet ones that require effort. Once they understand how to set reachable goals and have attained a few, allow them to set their own, continuing to make sure they are attainable, easy to measure, and specified for a short period of time.

5. Require students to submit progress reports that explain the extent to which they achieved their goals. Show them how to keep track of their progress by charting it daily.

6. Help students rewrite their contracts periodically. The first few should be written to cover only a day or two.

Modifications/ Considerations

This tactic has potential benefits beyond its initial purpose, that of increasing the extent to which students turn in their homework. Pupils could also develop important self-management skills that would serve them well in many areas for years to come: saving money, breaking unwanted habits, using time wisely, improving relationships with others. Moreover, students could learn generally about goal setting. They could learn to set goals that are attainable and experience the satisfactions derived from reaching them. It could be that some students, prior to experiences such as these, had never set goals for themselves, much less attained them. Those successes could go a long way in bolstering the negative self-concepts of some students, those who had never been asked to participate in their own instruction and had rarely accomplished anything related to school.

It is important to write contracts for a short period of time at first. After pupils have complied with the features of a few short-term contracts, the times for those agreements could be extended.

Once students have successfully written and carried out a few contracts dealing with homework, they could be instructed to set up other contracts at school, at home, and on the job.

Monitor

There was some mention on monitoring these suggestions in the Procedures section. Specifically,

FIGURE 10.3   Student Contract for Homework

Name _____

Date _____

STUDENT CONTRACT FOR HOMEWORK

Assignments to Be Turned In:

_____

_____

_____

_____

_____

_____

_____

By:

_____

_____

_____

Rewards:

_____

_____

_____

_____

_____

students should begin monitoring their short-term homework assignments. This could be done with a simple chart on which they plot the number of assignments given each period (e.g., week) and the number submitted on time. Later, students should be encouraged to identify long-term goals (e.g., completing term papers) and to keep data throughout an extended period on how they worked toward the goal (see MONITOR 3 in Appendix A).

Reference   Nielson, L. (1983). Teaching adolescents self-management. *The Clearing House, 57,* 76–80.

ATTAINING GOALS: TIPS FROM THE WORLD OF WORK

Background   The following suggestions for time management, tied with the realization of goals, were written by Pauline George, a management training specialist. According to her, it is not a case of managing time, because time is a constant; rather, it is a case of managing ourselves. Therefore, tough choices have to be made. We need to keep in mind that "if we do this, then we can't do that."

Who Can Benefit   Most of us, teachers and students alike, can benefit from techniques on how to get the most out of our time; at-risk and remedial students stand to profit the most, because they are often disorganized and, as a result, nonproductive.

Procedures   Following are the eight Ps for success according to George:

1. *Purpose*—Make priorities and objectives specific, measurable, realistic, and scheduled. Write

them down and review them. If an objective from one week is no longer important, push it down the list or remove it completely.

2. *Patterns*—Your habits are your key to management. Analyze your days to discover your habits. Ask others to tell you how you waste your time. They can see things you can't.

3. *Plans*—Many people stop after they plan; they don't schedule an activity. Make a to-do list every day. Those things that are scheduled have a better chance of being carried out.

4. *Parasites*—These are such pernicious time-wasters as watching TV, answering and talking on the phone, waiting for buses and appointments, being interrupted, and engaging in idle chitchat. Try to eliminate them or devise ways to profit from them.

5. *Paperwork*—Analyze it and try to handle each piece of paper only once. Don't set it aside without taking appropriate action. If that means throwing it away, throw it away.

6. *Partners*—We're in this together. Be a good listener; it saves lots of time and prevents many problems. Show people you respect their time. Know who to go to for what type of assistance.

7. *Procrastination*—Admit it when you're procrastinating. Stop rationalizing and you'll be more likely to act. Identify your stalling techniques and eliminate them. Learn to do it now, and do unpleasant things before pleasurable ones.

8. *Personal*—Be good to yourself. Get enough rest, eat properly, and exercise regularly. Doing that will increase your energy, decrease tension and stress, and allow you to focus better on the identified tasks.

Modifications/ Considerations

Although the eight points noted here were designed for individuals in business, most of them apply to students in schools. It may be informative to students to learn that it is important for individuals of all ages and of all types to get a handle on their use of time. It needs to be pointed out that all of us are given the same amount of time, and that some people do "have their acts together."

Monitor   Most of the eight points identified by George could be evaluated separately. Take point four, for example—Parasites. Students could be encouraged to keep track of the minutes spent each day watching TV, loafing, hanging around, or whatever else that keeps them from attaining their goals. Those data could then be charted (see MONITOR 3 in Appendix A). It would also be revealing if students plotted the number of minutes they devoted to obtaining their number one goal on the same chart. They might see a relationship.

Reference   *Plan ahead: Mind your Ps.* (May 7, 1989). Scripps Howard News Service, printed in the *Seattle Times*.

PARTICIPATION

PARTICIPATING IN DISCUSSIONS: SELF-MONITORING

It is generally believed that students benefit more from classroom experience if they participate through asking questions, giving opinions, and sharing ideas. Yet, the number of techniques for stimulating classroom participation is limited. This tactic seeks to introduce the concept of self-monitoring as a way to increase classroom participation among students.

Background

A study involving college students (Delprato, 1977) was the basis for this tactic. Because the instruction of high school students often follows a lecture-discussion format like that of college students, the benefits of the techniques described here should apply to high school students as well. Students of any age, however, would benefit by increasing their level of class participation.

Who Can Benefit

Too often, remedial, at-risk, or mildly handicapped students who are mainstreamed into regular class settings are hesitant to ask questions or express opinions. This tactic could serve as a method for helping them become more involved in classroom interactions.

1. Select one student to serve as an observer. Inform the student of the participatory behaviors he or she should watch for (i.e., asking questions and offering opinions or answers).
2. Instruct the observer to make a check for every participatory behavior observed for each pupil. Continue this for a few days, and consider those as baseline data.
3. Discuss with the class the behaviors that indicate classroom participation, in this case asking questions and offering opinions or answers.
4. Explain to students the importance of their participation in class discussions: When they ask or

Procedures

answer questions it indicates they are staying in touch, and those interactions inform the instructor about the level of their understanding.

5. Inform students that they may be able to improve the extent of their participation by monitoring their own interventions.

6. Instruct them to make a check on a slip of paper each time they ask or respond to a question.

7. Advise the student observer to continue recording the participatory behaviors as unobtrusively as possible.

8. Ask the observer to total the number of responses for the entire class each day and enter that score on a chart.

9. Ask students to keep charts showing their frequencies of participation. Those charts could reflect the composite contributions of each pupil, or two symbols could be charted daily to differentiate questions from answers.

Modifications/ Considerations

It is possible that improvements in behavior from self-monitoring alone may be insignificant for some individuals. For them, the teacher may add another incentive to the procedure.

Some students could be encouraged to set aims. They could indicate on their personal chart the number of interactions they would like to offer per day or week. Teachers could help them arrive at these goals. For that matter, the class as a whole could set a goal. Based on achieving those goals, individual or group rewards could be arranged.

As some students reach aims, they could be encouraged to record other types of interactions during the lecture and discussion sessions. Some interactions might be follow-up comments, remarks that integrate pieces of information, alternative solutions or options, information from sources other than the lecture or text.

It should go without saying, but if teachers desire that youth contribute to discussions, they should allow them plenty of opportunities to do so and should reinforce them when they do.

Monitor

Suggestions for monitoring the effects of this procedure were offered in steps 7, 8, and 9 of the Procedures section. See MONITOR 1 in Appendix A for more information on gathering and charting frequency data.

Delprato, D.J. (1977). Increasing classroom participation with self-monitoring. *The Journal of Educational Research*, *70*(4), 225–227. **Reference**

PARTICIPATING IN DISCUSSIONS: LOOKING ALIVE

Successful students learn to attend to the teacher, and behave appropriately. Furthermore, their body language generally indicates that they are tuned in and motivated. Less successful students do not attend, misbehave, and are not tuned in. The latter is indicated by their verbal behaviors and body language. Many of these students, however, can be taught to recognize various social and body gestures, to know the meanings or implications of those expressions and movements, and to incorporate them into their interactions with teachers and others. By looking like they are participating, these students may prompt more interactions with teachers, hence become regular participants.

Background

Students at any age can learn metacognitive strategies, given explicit explanations. This strategy is particularly suitable for remedial students who are insensitive to body language.

Who Can Benefit

1. Introduce the SLANT strategy to students as a way they can appear to be paying attention.
2. Explain to them that this strategy works because individuals' body language sends out strong messages.

Procedures

3. Ask students to consider: "What body language are you using and what is it saying to the teacher?"

4. Write the letters of the SLANT strategy on the board, and ask students to go over them with you.

   S = SIT UP. (Sit up straight in the chair, with your feet in front of you.)

   L = LEAN FORWARD.

   A = ACT LIKE YOU'RE INTERESTED. (Have materials ready and write notes.)

   N = NOD YOUR HEAD. (When you agree with something, show it.)

   T = TRACK THE TEACHER WITH YOUR EYES. (Teachers will see that you are following along.)

5. Get students involved in the process by asking them to explain why the steps might be effective.

6. Instruct students to memorize the steps for the strategy and practice it in your class until it comes naturally. Then, ask students to use SLANT in other classes and report back to you on how it worked.

7. Encourage students to look for examples of this type of body language from other students, their teachers, and in situations outside of the school.

Modifications/ Considerations

Students could watch another group in a class modeling the SLANT strategy for a few minutes. They could also interview successful students, asking them what they do to maintain their interest and to appear interested.

If pupils use this strategy they might be called on by the teacher. To prepare for that, students should learn another strategy for interacting with the teacher, such as the following three-step plan:

1. Paraphrase what the teacher said.
2. Ask questions.
3. Say what you think is important.

Apart from the strategy advanced here to encourage involvement and participation, students could be asked to offer other ideas and techniques. They could, for example, embellish on the following ideas for attending and not daydreaming:

1. Jot down distracting thoughts and put them aside.
2. Write down at least one word that pertains to the topic every 30 seconds.
3. Write the numbers 1 to 10 on a blank sheet and write in an item from the lecture for each number.
4. Write questions about the lecture.
5. Draw pictures or symbols to reflect the ideas of the lecturer.

Monitor

A videotape might be used to help students identify the subtleties of body language. The tape could be of a class in which some listeners used body language to indicate they were interested and motivated. Other participants could, with their body language, show that they were terribly bored with the lecture (lots of students would audition for those roles). Viewers of the tape would point out the various forms of body language and note, when possible, the effects of that language on the speaker (see MONITOR 11 in Appendix A).

Reference

Ellis, E. (in press). A metacognitive intervention for increasing class participation. *Learning Disabilities Focus.*

PARTICIPATING IN DISCUSSIONS: POINTS FOR INTERACTING

Background

It is important for students to participate in class discussions. Teachers want students to respond to questions voluntarily and when called on, and want them to contribute relevant information to class discussions. Furthermore, teachers would like for all the pupils to contribute, not just a few. When students participate, teachers are informed as to who, first of all, is listening, and in addition, how well they understand the information and are able to assimilate it.

Who Can Benefit

The procedures explained here should be considered for many at-risk, remedial, and other students who are reluctant to participate voluntarily in class discussions.

Procedures

1. Explain to the students why it is important to participate in class discussions.
2. Review the rules before each discussion: Raise hand to speak, speak only when called on, offer relevant comments, put your hand down when others are speaking, listen to others while they are speaking.
3. Pass out a list of questions to each student at the beginning of each discussion period that relate to the material being discussed.
4. Give examples of relevant and irrelevant contributions.
5. Designate a student to record the relevant and irrelevant contributions and disruptions (as determined by the teacher and students) of the pupils during the discussions.
6. Give a point for each relevant remark and take away one for each disruption.
7. Give compliments to youngsters for particularly good contributions.
8. Paraphrase some contributions to help clarify them.
9. Explain to the students that their point total will make up a portion of their daily grades.
10. Inform them that they will receive, for example, a C if they end up with 0 points, C+ for one point, B– for two, and so forth.
11. Post the weekly grade averages on the bulletin board.
12. Inform students that their weekly grades make up 25% of their quarterly grade.

Modifications/ Considerations

It is important to maintain a rapid pace for offering contributions. The teacher should set the stage for the discussions, keep the students' comments in line with the topic, guide them back on topic if they stray, and encourage pupils to make their comments as succinct as possible.

Inform students of various types of contributions: providing examples from the text, offering samples from other reading or personal experience, comparing two points of view, relating two or more contributions of others, questioning the logic or reasoning of some comments. The teacher should give several examples of these types. The students might watch videos of talk shows or other audience participation shows and note relevant, irrelevant, and stupid comments and questions.

A group chart could be developed on which "Number Contributed" is printed on the vertical axis and "Successive Days" on the horizontal axis. Individual charts could be made that reflect the number of points per day for the students (see MONITOR 1 in Appendix A).

Monitor

Smith, B.M.S., Schumaker, J.B., Schaffer, J., & Sherman, J.A. (1982). Increasing participation and improving the quality of discussions in seventh-grade social studies classes. *Journal of Applied Behavior Analysis*, *15*, 97–110.

Reference

ANSWERING QUESTIONS: REPHRASING QUESTIONS

On numerous occasions when students are asked questions they ask for the question to be repeated, mutter something to themselves, or drop their notebook onto the floor as a diversionary tactic. At other times pupils don't respond at all. A contributing factor to these weak or blank responses is the failure to

Background

understand what was asked. The following technique helps students answer questions by requiring them to repeat the question before answering it.

Who Can Benefit

The approach described here would be suitable for many at-risk and remedial students. Many of them do not attend to teachers' instructional programs, and rarely contribute to class discussions.

Procedures

1. State the question simply. Do not elaborate or rephrase the question at this point; that might further confuse students. It will help to have clearly thought out the questions prior to asking them to ensure that you say exactly what you want to say the first time.

2. Instruct students to ask themselves the question in their own words, whether or not they are called on. This nonverbal exercise will help them understand the question.

3. Call on a student to respond. Require the student to precede his or her answer with a rephrased form of the question.

4. Ask the pupil to restate the question even if he or she cannot answer it. This is an excellent form of feedback to help determine if the question was effectively communicated. If not, rephrase the question yourself.

5. Repeat step 3. If a particularly good response is given, you may wish to have another student rephrase it. If students expect this type of routine, they will be more attentive to the answer.

Modifications/ Considerations

The instructor should always ask a question, *then* call on a student. If the student is called on before a question is asked, other students may not listen to the question because they know that someone else has to answer it.

This tactic should benefit "askers" as well as "answerers," in that teachers and pupils should learn the importance of asking clear and unambiguous questions that increase the chances of answering questions correctly. The importance of asking good questions could be pointed out in reverse by asking long, drawn-out questions or ones that are confusing in other ways. Students would learn quickly how difficult it is to paraphrase them, much less answer them. (For questions of this type, the class could listen to the questions asked by reporters at a presidential press conference.)

Continuing with the last suggestion in the preceding section, the teacher could prepare two sets of questions, both on topics that are interesting or have been studied by the students. One set of questions would be clear and concise, those on the other set would be vague and rambling. The teacher could then mix up the questions and ask them of the students. The students would have three tasks: Note whether the question is "good" or "bad," rephrase it, and answer it. A checklist could be developed to acquire those data (see MONITOR 6 in Appendix A).

Monitor

Webb, C.D., & Baird, H.J. (1980). Three strategies for motivating pupils. *The Clearing House, 54*, 27–29.

Reference

ASKING QUESTIONS: FIVE SUGGESTIONS

According to some research, about 80% of classroom exchanges are initiated by teachers. The common pattern for these exchanges is for the teacher to ask a question, a student replies, and the teacher evaluates it. In the procedure explained here, the teacher is a question-creator: one who sets up discussions in which pupils are given more autonomy; hence respond more freely.

Background

Many at-risk and remedial students, as well as a number of others, should profit from this tactic.

Who Can Benefit

Procedures Following are five techniques teachers might consider to assist students to ask questions:

1. Ask questions prior to reading the story. Give a brief sketch of the story, then stimulate students to ask questions about what the author might tell them.
2. Encourage students to ask questions after they read the story that were not answered; that information would contribute to their interest in the story.
3. Direct students to ask themselves and others about what information or experiences they had prior to reading the story that might have been related to the story.
4. Request students to ask questions and stimulate discussions about what the author might write about next if he or she wrote a sequel to the present story.
5. Ask *who*, *when*, and *why* questions following certain passages. Ask pupils, following a portion of the story, if the story pertained more to one of those types than another.

Modifications/ Considerations Using one of these five techniques, the teacher could encourage pupils to question each other's questions. The teacher, using this approach, can continue to guide discussions and evaluate the content and relevance of the various contributions.

Following are a few other ideas for stimulating question asking, beyond those offered in this tactic and in others in this section of the book. Write out a few questions from a passage on slips of paper, and give them to certain pupils (perhaps the ones who have problems coming up with questions), or have a drawing to determine which students receive the slips. Or certain students, those who have difficulty forming questions, could be required to earn the question slips. When they asked questions they would be rewarded. Yet another approach would be to set up a cooperative situation whereby groups of youngsters are formed following the reading of a passage. As a group, they would write out sets of questions that were later asked of group members in turn. Also, a group contingency plan could be arranged. For this, groups of the students would be required to ask questions, one at a time. When they had all posed their query, they would all receive some reward.

For openers, it would be informative to keep data on pupils' contributions when the ordinary type of classroom interaction is in effect, then keep data on pupils' contributions when any of the procedures explained here are arranged (see MONITOR 1 in Appendix A).

Monitor

Kitagawa, M.M. (1982). Improving discussions or how to get the students to ask the questions. *The Reading Teacher, 36*(1), 42–45.

Reference

APPENDIX A: MONITOR

Monitoring means to measure and evaluate, to gather data. Although the reason to monitor the tactics in this program (or on any other educational procedure, program, or technique) should be obvious, a few words of justification are offered nonetheless. Teachers should monitor their tactics to learn whether the tactics are effective; teachers need to know if the student is improving.

It is important to gather data regarding the effects of tactics, because we can often be fooled about their effects. We can, without proper data, believe that a technique is assisting youngsters to achieve some goal, when in fact they are languishing. It is also possible that pupils are actually progressing toward some objective, but without the help of data, we believe otherwise.

How to Gather and Use Data

By encouraging teachers to keep data to monitor the worth of scheduled tactics, I am not implying that they do not now keep data. Most teachers administer achievement tests of several forms. They often give unit tests supplied by publishers, sometimes gather data on student learning objectives set by their district, and give dozens of other informal measures and quizzes. The problem with many of those tests is that they are not linked with a program; what is taught is one thing and what is measured is another. Data should be associated with what is instructed and should reflect pupils' efforts regarding those programs.

Types of Data

Data should have the following features.

Directness. The primary characteristic of data that are sensitive to students' efforts is that they are *direct*. As mentioned earlier, data should be acquired that truly reflect the nature of the activity. If, for example, a teacher arranged a tactic to assist a youngster to read want ads or similar types of materials, he or she should set up a situation to gather data as the pupil reads want ads and similar materials. Although the teacher could measure that activity in a number of "unnatural" or indirect ways, those data would not necessarily pertain to the objective.

Importance. The most *important* aspect of the behavior being taught—not necessarily the easiest—should be measured. If the teacher wishes to advance a student's ability to comprehend material from a newspaper, he or she should monitor the extent to which the student understands that material. The teacher should not, in that case, measure how well the youth could read orally from the newspaper, unless, of course, that was another objective. This feature, importance, is closely related to the first feature, directness.

Frequency. A third characteristic that should be taken into account when selecting a measurement approach is *frequency*. The teacher should obtain data regarding the pupil's performance rather often, certainly more than once a semester or year, as is so often the case.

Using the Data Data regarding students' performances are not an end of themselves. Once they are acquired they must be studied; they must assist teachers to make decisions. Accordingly, the more important the decision, the more data should be kept and analyzed.

Following are a few educational decisions that are made, some of them often: (a) to place a pupil in a special or a regular situation; (b) to shift a student to more or less difficult material, assign more or less material; (c) to practice on a behavior more or less often; (d) to shift from one instructional technique or set of materials to another. Data are also used to report progress accurately to pupils themselves, to teachers, parents, administrators, and to state and federal agencies.

Of course, it takes time to monitor accurately the progress of pupils. Many teachers complain that when they measure students' activities they lose valuable time that could be spent teaching. But those teachers might ask themselves: "Unless you are measuring, how do you actually know that you are teaching?" For example, the Boeing aircraft company could certainly turn out more 747s, 737s, and other planes if they cut back on their testing. But you and I pray they don't do that, because we are concerned about our safety as we fly from one place to another and feel reassured knowing that Boeing must schedule a test now and then to increase the probability that their planes take off, stay in the air, and land when they are supposed to.

So teachers must find a way to measure the important behaviors of their pupils. For some behaviors, data can be obtained from a number of students all at once. That saves time. For other activities, information can be obtained from small groups, whereas peers can collect certain types of information. In a number of instances, data can be acquired by the pupils themselves, and other behaviors can be measured by paraprofessionals or volunteers. Regardless of how data are gathered and whoever acquires them, they must be obtained, because it is vital to know whether the tactics arranged for students have helped them.

But It Takes Time!

Included here are brief explanations of 19 ways to acquire data. Some are simpler than others, some more widely useful than others, some more suitable for academic skills, and others more appropriate for social behaviors. Most of the evaluation approaches were arranged by researchers of tactics that were paraphrased for this program.

Each of the various tactics that form the bulk of this book contains a "Monitor" section. Within this section, the teacher is referred to one of the numbers that follow in the MONITOR section. This section contains a general explanation of each measurement approach. More specific suggestions for evaluating the technique are included in the "Monitor" sections.

Readers should keep in mind that these measurement ideas are only suggestions. They should feel free to select from other measurement approaches

How to Use This Section with the Tactics

described in this section or from others that have not been included. It is vital, however, that some measurement approach be selected and it be chosen, to the extent possible, with the three features of proper measurement in mind: directness, importance, and frequency.

THE MONITOR APPROACHES

This section contains a listing and description of the various approaches.

MONITOR 1. Frequency Count

To obtain data of this type, the teacher first defines the behavior (e.g., asking for assistance or helping others) and counts the number of times that behavior occurs. Those counts could be taken over an entire day, during one period (e.g., biology), or for a selected time (e.g., one minute). The measurement period would depend on the behavior and other factors.

Those data could then be charted in a number of ways. They could be plotted as frequency per period or session (e.g., 50 minutes) or per minute. Furthermore, two rates can sometimes be charted: correct and incorrect rate per period. See Figure A.1 (equal interval chart) and Figure A.2 (semilog chart).

MONITOR 2. Percent

To obtain these data, the teacher would determine how many times a pupil responded to a set number of items. If, for example, there were 20 opportunities to respond and the youth accurately responded to 15 of them, the percentage would be 75 (divide the number correct by the total number). This has been a common way to measure academic behaviors and could be chosen to monitor certain social and language behaviors as well. This may be a good choice if the number of items presented is the same or at least is known from one session to the next. (When this form of

FIGURE A.1   Frequency Chart—Equal Intervals

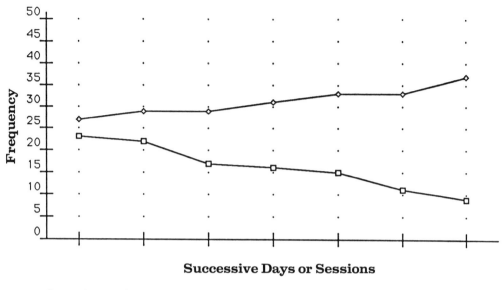

Successive Days or Sessions

◇ Corrects   ▫ Incorrects

FIGURE A.2   Frequency Chart—Semilogarithmic

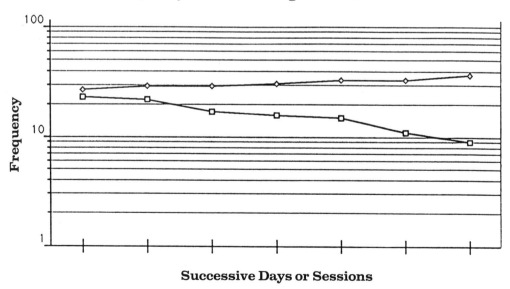

Successive Days or Sessions

◇ Corrects   ▫ Incorrects

FIGURE A.3 Percentage Chart

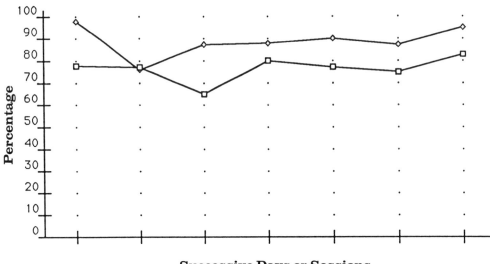

◇ Student 1   □ Student 2

assessment is chosen, however, the teacher is not informed about the amount of time required to make the responses.) These data can easily be charted on a graph that ranges from 0 to 100 on the vertical axis (see Figure A.3).

MONITOR 3. Duration or Latency

To obtain a measure of *duration* the teacher would determine how much time the student devoted to the activity. The teacher would indicate with a watch when the activity began, note when it ended, and calculate the elapsed time. This may be an appropriate measure if the teacher wants to know only how long a pupil worked on a task.

Latency indicates the amount of time between the stimulus and the response. A teacher might want to know, for example, how long it took a student to get to work after he or she had been asked to do so. To acquire the data, like those for duration, a watch would be required. Duration and latency data could be charted on a graph such as that in Figure A.4.

FIGURE A.4 Duration/Latency Chart

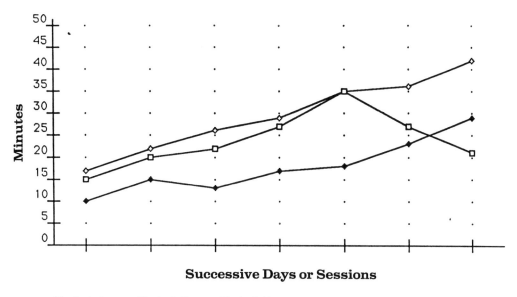

◇ Student 1   □ Student 2   ◆ Student 3

For this approach, the teacher identifies a pupil's behavior (e.g., working on an assignment) and periodically observes that student to determine whether the behavior is occurring. That interval could be for a few seconds, a few minutes, or whatever length of time the teacher chooses (see Figure A.5). Data from that type of assessment are usually reported in terms of percentage of occurrences. For this, the teacher would decide to take the same number of samples of the behavior each session (e.g., 20). At the end of the session the teacher would determine the percentage of times the behavior was noted and graph that number on a percentage chart.

This type of measurement has been widely used for social and academic behaviors. When this approach is selected, the samples could be obtained by individuals other than the teacher, because this is a relatively expensive form of gathering data. Data could be acquired by a peer, a volunteer, or in some instances, by the target individual himself or herself.

To obtain this type of data, the teacher would develop a rating scale on which a number of items to be evalu-

MONITOR 4.
Interval
Recording

MONITOR 5.
Rating Scale

FIGURE A.5 Time Sample Form

Minutes

10	10	10	10	10	10	10	10	10	10	10	10	10	10

Minutes

10	10	10	10	10	10	10	10	10	10	10	10	10	10

ated were printed on a form (see Figure A.6). Also, a series of numbers would be printed to indicate the extent to which the pupil carried out or engaged in the item. In the example, the numbers 1, 2, and 3 are printed: 1 = rarely, 2 = occasionally, and 3 = most of the time. This would be a suitable approach if the teacher knew the characteristics on which he or she desired information.

Rating scales have been used for a wide variety of social, language, and interaction situations. They could be administered before and after a tactic had been scheduled. In so doing, a student's pretest scores on each item could be compared to those scores on a posttest.

MONITOR 6. Checklist

To acquire this type of data, the teacher would prepare a list of events or statements such as that in Figure A.7. The teacher would then make a mark of some type to indicate whether the statement described the student or whether the student had carried out the activity. Various marks have been used to indicate whether the activity was totally or partially completed, whether it was completed independently or with some assistance, and whether cues or prompts were given. This approach has been widely used for a variety of social and academic behaviors.

Checklists could be administered before and after the tactic was scheduled as well as during the

FIGURE A.6 Rating Scale

ORGANIZING AND PARTICIPATING IN CLASS

3 = most of the time
2 = occasionally
1 = rarely

	3	2	1
Attends Class			
Brings Materials			
Comes Prepared			
Asks Appropriate Questions			
Listens to Others			
Begins Assignments on Time			
Works Steadily			
Contributes to Class Discussion			
Accepts Criticism			
Does Well on Tests			

period it was in effect. With those data, the teacher can compare the pupil's scores in general, or on specific items, from one period of time to another.

Observation forms such as the one in Figure A.8 are helpful if the teacher wants to know not only what the pupil did, and perhaps how often he or she did it, but what events occurred before (antecedents) the behavior and what happened after (consequences) the behavior. This type of measurement could be scheduled throughout the period when a tactic was in effect.

**MONITOR 7.
Before-
During-After
Observations**

FIGURE A.7 Checklist

CHECK ITEMS THAT PERTAIN TO PUPIL

☐ Makes friends easily

☐ Is easily distracted

☐ Complains a great deal

☐ Generally has a positive attitude

☐ Is critical of others

☐ Compliments classmates

☐ Is dependable

☐ Offers excuses for mistakes or shortcomings

☐ Is generally agreeable

☐ Seems to enjoy school

Although data of this type are more expensive to gather than some others, they would provide information on the narration of events before, during, and after. This would be a reasonable choice for monitoring a number of social behaviors.

MONITOR 8. Sociometric Ratings To acquire these data, the teacher asks pupils a question or two. He or she might ask them to indicate their best friend, the person with whom they would like to work, the one with whom they would not want to work, or a number of other questions (see Figure A.9). The teacher would then tally those responses on a sheet that indicated the names of all the individuals in the group from which the selections were made.

This technique has been widely used to determine the likes, dislikes, and preferences of students. It could be appropriate to schedule a sociometric device before and after some treatments that set out to alter the selections of youngsters or the extent to which some were chosen.

MONITOR 9. Interviews This type of monitoring could be set up for a number of circumstances with a number of individuals. One example would be to interview youth before and after

FIGURE A.8 Observation Form

Before/During/After Observations

Name_____

Date_____

Target Behavior_____

Antecedent (Before)	Behavior (During)	Consequence (After)

Summary_____

_____

_____

_____

FIGURE A.9 Sociometric Ratings

Indicate the degree you would like to work with each student in the class on a science project.

	Not At All	Perhaps	Very Much
Arnold	X		
Betty		X	
Carl	X		
Dorothy			X
Everett		X	
Faith	X		
Gayle		X	
Harold			X

they had experienced a tactic. The interview could be open-ended, or some prompting questions could be asked. For other situations, the youth's parents, siblings, or teachers could be interviewed prior to and following some treatment to determine whether they noted any effects and to comment on the situation generally. Data from interviews could simply be reported or they could be analyzed and coded in some way.

This type of approach could be suitable for a number of academic, social, vocational, or other situations.

MONITOR 10. Free Expression For this approach, students could be asked to talk or write about the circumstances in which they were involved. This practice has been widely used in reading where students are asked to either describe or write about what they have just read. They could be asked to recall, as much as possible, to sequence the ideas, to paraphrase the story, to evaluate the material, or to blend the material with previous knowledge. From that information, the teacher could count the number of facts said, the number of words written, the number of judgments, or whatever. These data could then be charted on a graph as frequency per period of time or as rate (correct and incorrect) per minute. Data of this type could be kept throughout the time a tactic was scheduled or simply before and after the technique was in effect.

MONITOR 11. Written Items: From Pool

To use this form of monitoring the teacher writes a number of questions from a text passage or set of lectures. Those items could be multiple choice, fill the blanks, short answer, true or false, or other forms. The teacher would then draw a number of items randomly from this pool for each session. Those items would then be presented to students and data from their efforts would be acquired. Any number of items could be developed for the pool and any number could be randomly drawn. In one project, teachers wrote 50 short answer questions for the pool and pulled out 25 for each session.

One advantage of a program of this type is that microcomputer programs are available (for example, Study Guide, from MECC, 3400 Lexington Avenue North, St. Paul, MN 55126). Using one of these programs, the teacher types in the questions only once then draws out as many as desired from one session to the next. With some programs the questions are not only randomly selected, they are printed out in various sequences.

A program of this type is suitable for most subjects at the secondary level (i.e., social studies, science, language arts, mathematics). The students' scores from these tests can be acquired in terms of number correct, percentage correct, or as rate (correct and incorrect) per minute.

MONITOR 12. Written Items: Different

For this approach, the teacher could use the quizzes provided by textbooks at the ends of units or chapters. Many textbooks offer questions of several types (i.e., multiple choice, matching, true or false, and essay). This would be a reasonable way to evaluate progress in some content areas, particularly if there were a number of these tests of about the same degree of difficulty that contained about the same number and type of items.

Some teachers have used this monitoring approach to evaluate the effects of particular interventions, by gathering data throughout several phases and alternating, by phases, the scheduling of the interventions. The publisher's (or teacher-made) tests could be administered after each phase. Students' scores from those tests could then be gathered and charted as frequency per session, as percentage correct, or as rate per minute.

MONITOR 13. Construct

For some behaviors, this approach is the most straightforward way to evaluate the effects of a tactic. The student, following some type of instruction, is asked to write a story, to play a game, to perform on an instrument, to build a bird cage, to bake a potato, to go to town, to locate an address, to solve a problem, to paint a picture, to draw a diagram, or to set a table. Teachers could use this method with about any academic, social, or vocational activity.

Data from this approach could come in a variety of forms: The product could be evaluated by the teacher or an expert in the field, a checklist could be followed to determine how well the product was developed, or time taken to produce the item could be calculated.

MONITOR 14. Cloze Procedures

For this approach, the pupil is asked to complete something: a sentence, a paragraph, a mathematics problem, a graphic, or whatever. This technique would be a suitable choice if the purpose was to instruct a sequence or arrangement of symbols.

The cloze procedure is a common one in reading, when every nth word is occluded and youngsters are asked to supply it. This technique could be arranged in a variety of other situations, however. Some teachers have used this form of monitoring with graphics by supplying a few shapes and some accompanying words and requesting youth to fill in the missing shapes and symbols.

With the availability of portable "camcorders," it is possible to capture performances of students visually and orally. This could be an excellent way to assess certain social, communication, or vocational behaviors. It is quite likely that the effects of this form of measurement on performance (and we need to be aware that most, if not all, assessments have an effect on the performance) would be lessened to the extent that the recording equipment was unobtrusive and usual.

**MONITOR 15.
Video
Recording**

Data from this approach could be evaluated in a number of ways. For one, film taken before and after a treatment could be shown to independent judges. They could be asked to determine, first of all, which film was the "before" and which was the "after." Judges could then be required to point out profound and subtle changes in the student's behavior. Another way to evaluate the film would be to develop a checklist of events or circumstances that were to be noted and allow a teacher, the student, a peer, a parent, or someone else to check off the items.

An audiotape could be made while youths read, discuss, or interact. Using tape recorders to record the performances of students as they read has been a common procedure, but it could be a useful technique for acquiring information in a number of other situations. These recordings could be evaluated in several ways. For one, the teacher could, while listening to the tape, count the number of words read, the mistakes made (and the type), and the number of pauses. For another, an independent judge could evaluate tapes from before and after treatment and determine which was which, and pass judgment on the comparative qualities of each.

**MONITOR 16.
Audio
Recording**

A number of microcomputer programs are available that perform multiple functions. With them, a program is offered the pupils (e.g., math), they are given feedback of various types as they respond, and their responses are captured and later displayed. Some of those programs show the pupil's data following a session as percentage correct, others as correct and incorrect frequency, and still others provide data on the duration and latency of responses. Some of these

**MONITOR 17.
Computer-
Assisted
Evaluation**

programs even display a pupil's scores over a period of time, and a few of them plot the student's scores on a graph and even signal when one tactic should be withdrawn and another scheduled. Some of these programs are AC·CEL (West, Young, West, Freston, & Johnson, 1985; distributed by PTMA, Precision Teaching Materials and Associates, Sarasota, FL) and *Mathematics Instruction Decision-Making* (computer software for summary and analysis of educational performance data; West, Young, & West, 1983).

MONITOR 18. Interaction Analysis

Data of this type would be gathered if the teacher desired to know the extent a youth interacted with others. If the teacher wanted data from the youth and one other individual, he or she could mark a tally each time the youth initiated an interaction with the other and make a different kind of mark when the other person replied. These data for keeping track of these interchanges could be relatively simple. The data could be more sophisticated by making one kind of mark for initiations, another for responses, and yet others for the types of initiations and responses. A number of interaction codes are available for teachers who desire this type of data (e.g., Glucksberg, Krauss, & Weisberg, 1966). Indeed, there is a computerized recording system available for achieving data of this type (West, Young, & West, 1988). Data of this type could be charted as frequency per session or as rate per minute. If several types of data are gathered, they could all be entered on the same chart by using different symbols.

MONITOR 19. Contrived Situations

Although one of the features of a good measurement approach is for it to be natural, there are occasions when the teacher desires to assess a behavior and, to do so, must set up a simulated environment. Situations of this type are often arranged when it is necessary to practice on a skill, and it would be difficult to have enough opportunities to try this approach out in the "real world." A teacher might, for example, want to assist students to improve their abilities to engage in an interview. For this, he or she could arrange a situation in which someone played the part of the employer, another the employer's secretary, and others acted out different roles. With those characters, the teacher could ask youths in his or her class to go in for job interviews.

Role-playing arrangements could be established in several other situations, many of which have to do with social, vocational, and communication behaviors. As for the data, the teacher might have a prepared checklist of items to indicate the extent to which the target youth reacted to the various items.

References

Glucksberg, S., Krauss, R., & Weisberg, R. (1966). Referential communication in nursery school children: Method and some preliminary findings. *Journal of Experimental Child Psychology, 3,* 333–342.

West, R.P., Young, K.R., & West, W.J. (1983). *Mathematics instruction decision-making* [Computer program]. Logan: Utah State University.

West, R.P., Young, K.R., & West, W.J. (1988). *Easy Code: A device for collecting, summarizing, and analyzing behavioral data* [Computer program]. Bountiful, UT: Pelikan Technology.

West, R.P., Young, K.R., West, W.J., Freston, C.W., & Johnson, J.I. (1985). *AC·CEL* [Computer program]. Logan, UT: AC·CEL Enterprises.

APPENDIX B:
HOW TO PRESENT THE TACTICS

I have attempted here to provide workshop presenters with ideas for helping teachers, or others to whom these tactics are shown, achieve a frame of reference for accepting and understanding them. These remarks have come from my experiences at the University of Washington in teaching a tactics class. I am sure that I did not provide some of those students (many of whom were teachers) with a proper framework with respect to tactics, and they left those sessions with the wrong idea about what tactics were and what could be done with them, or with a restricted notion about accepting new ideas. Those individuals, although they were in the minority, were not impressed for perhaps one of the following reasons: They believed that many of the tactics were too simple; they did not focus on the "main" ideas of education; they didn't believe that certain tactics would help with their current crop of students; they did not believe that certain tactics would fit in with their school's policies; they thought that some tactics would require too much time; they rejected certain tactics because they had tried ones like them, and they were not effective, or they were told by other teachers that such tactics would not work; they rejected an entire set of tactics because they wanted others. Dozens of other reasons have been given for not learning about different instructional approaches.

But it has been my experience that if the 10 points outlined here are discussed prior to explaining the tactics (and along the way as they are presented), most teachers will accept the new ideas.

1. What is a tactic?

Tactics are tools. Just as carpenters have a collection of tools—saws of various sizes and types, hammers of all sorts, many kinds of levels, a variety of planes and T-squares—and just as mechanics have their snap-on kits filled with dozens of tools, so should teachers have a large set of tactics. Carpenters and mechanics use their tools to create, maintain, and repair. Teachers use their tactics for the same reasons. They *create* by teaching new behaviors; they *maintain* by helping students review previously taught skills; and they *repair* by offering remedial assistance.

In describing tactics to teachers it is important to point out that tactics do not necessarily replace programs. In fact, they support them. At the secondary level, for example, if a teacher arranges a study skill in biology or U.S. history, that tactic should support the content of the biology and U.S. history class. It is also important to point out that tactics do not replace teachers, because a "good" tactic (tool) will not of itself do the job; it takes an expert teacher (mechanic).

2. Are some tactics better than others?

In a sense, no one tactic is any better than any other. True, some tactics are scheduled more often than others, and certain ones are arranged on rare occasions (the latter are often scheduled when all else has failed), but they can all be good.

Our friends the mechanics have several tools that are frequently used. They have others that are rarely selected. I have been told that there is a little wrench that is used only on one small part of the fuel injection system of certain BMWs. It won't work on all BMWs or for other parts of BMWs, and it won't work on fuel injection systems of Fords, Toyotas, Porsches, or any other car. But when the mechanic needs that particular wrench for that BMW, he needs it. It is a valuable tool. The same holds true of educational tactics. Although some of them are not called for very often, when they are needed they are valuable.

3. Are there some bad tactics?

Not really. As explained, certain tactics are more frequently used than others, but when one is needed and successfully used, it is a good tactic. An important consideration for all tactics is to make the proper selection; that is, to match up the tactic with the behavior. Again, back to our mechanic. If he used a box wrench of one size for a job when he should have selected an end wrench of another size, and the box wrench didn't work, that doesn't mean that it was a bad tool. The box wrench was selected when it should not have been. So rather than say the tool was bad, it would be more appropriate to say that the mechanic was bad; he needed help in selecting tools. The same holds true of teachers and tactics. The teacher should not only have a vast storehouse of tactics, but should know how and when to use them.

A bad tactic might be one that was poorly explained. If a teacher read about it and tried to put it into operation but could not really figure it out, then that was perhaps a bad tactic. (Actually, that would be an instance of a bad write-up of what might have been a good tactic.) Certainly, tactics need to be adequately explained. A teacher should not be expected to simply pick up a kit or package without an explanation and immediately put it into operation any more than our mechanic friend would be expected to pick up a new tool from his snap-on friends and begin using it without first reading up on what to do with it.

4. Where do tactics come from?

First of all, to qualify as a tactic one would recommend to teachers, there should be some data to indicate that in some situation the tactic was successful; it helped alter a selected behavior in the desired direction. Even with that restriction there are dozens of educational and psychological journals that supply tactics. Following is a list of the 10 journals that contributed the most tactics for this book: *Journal of Learning Disabilities, Academic Therapy, Teaching Exceptional Children, Learning Disability Quarterly, Exceptional Children, Journal of Applied Behavior Analysis, The Reading Teacher, Journal of School Psychology, Behavior Disorders*, and the *Clearing House.*

5. Are they written as tactics in the journals?

No, unfortunately. What appear as tactics in this book did not begin their lives in that format. In fact, most of the articles were not written for teachers, they were written as research reports for university professors. Many of those articles comprise several sections, the first of which is a brief review of literature and a statement of the research problem. Next is a procedures section in which the researcher explains the setting, the subjects, and other conditions of the study. Following are the results and discussion sections. Many journal articles are lengthy and difficult to read, and depending on the journal, they are to a greater or lesser degree laced with educational jargon.

So the research translators must read these articles and rewrite them for teachers. That does not mean to be patronizing; it means to paraphrase or translate researchers' projects so that they can be arranged in classrooms. Tactics must be written in such a way that teachers who read them "get a feel" for carrying out the procedure. They must also be written so that the integrity of the original piece is maintained. That is a trick, but considerable data are available to support the format in which these tactics are written. Most of the tactics in this book are from 500 to 750 words in length, and all are made up of five sections: Background, Who Will Benefit, Procedures, Modifications/Considerations, and Monitor. The references that formed the basis for the tactic are also provided.

6. How can I tell if a tactic is effective?

Well, you need some data. And here I don't mean the scores from achievement tests that are probably unrelated to what teachers teach, but some measure that is directly related to what they teach.

Included in this program are explanations of 19 ways to obtain data on tactics (see Appendix A); many variations are possible with each of them. Even with those many possibilities, there are certainly numerous other ways to measure performances.

Regardless of which measurement approach is selected to monitor behaviors, however, it should be chosen as carefully as are the tactics themselves. No measurement approach is inherently good or bad, just as no tactic is always good or bad. Remember the mechanic.

As noted in the MONITOR section (Appendix A), teachers should select the simplest and most natural way to measure important behaviors. Moreover, they should measure them rather often; once is not enough. One should evaluate important behaviors at least twice: once before treatment and once after.

Some teachers complain that when they measure performances, that takes away time from their teaching. Nonsense. If teachers don't measure, how do they know they are teaching? They may simply be taking up time.

Not only are some teachers hesitant to measure, there is a general reluctance to carry out educational research. Interesting (read that *deplorable*) that so little money is devoted to educational research when compared to the money spent on "education." I read the other day that about 10% of the total education budget is spent on research, whereas about 30% is spent on research in business. But arguing and lamenting on this topic could go on and on.

7. Can some tactics be adapted to fit other situations?

Yes, but therein lies one of the biggest problems when presenting tactics to teachers, because teachers are not known for their generalization skills. It is not uncommon that, when presented with tactics used originally with third-grade youngsters, second- and fourth-grade teachers will tell you that this tactic will not work with their children because they are either younger or older. The same statements come up when one shows data to middle school and high school teachers. If the presenter explains a tactic that came from a 10th-grade biology class, some 11th-grade biology teachers and many of the English teachers and social studies teachers will not attend the presentation. They will say or imply that they could not make use of the information in their situations because the students or subjects are different.

Teachers who can extrapolate from a tactic being presented to their situations, whatever they may be, are refreshing. They apparently ask themselves—as tactics are presented from grades or ages other than theirs and topics or subjects different from theirs—how they could modify the tactic so it would work in their situations. Following are some possible modifications they are considering: change the manager, from teacher to pupil or pupil to teacher; use easier or more difficult material; schedule the technique for more or less time; provide different types of feedback or reinforcement.

8. Why do I need to know about these tactics?

There have always been students in secondary schools who have not been motivated to learn and who have had great difficulty getting along in schools, but recently those numbers have increased. Following are a few reasons for this: (a) More youth are alienated from school for one reason or another, (b) fewer parents are able to reinforce their youngsters properly and instill the idea that education and schools are important, (c) more bilingual and non-English-speaking students are enrolled in schools, and (d) more special education students are being mainstreamed into regular classes.

Many of those students must be dealt with differently. For some, the materials must be presented differently; for others, the motivational system must be adjusted. For several, the time they work on tasks must be adjusted, and for still others, more reminders, cues, and prompts must be provided.

Good teachers—that is, professionals—must have hundreds of tactics on hand if they are to meet the instructional and motivational needs of their pupils. Perhaps one of the differences between an amateur and a professional is the number of tactics (tools) at their disposal and, of course, their ability to know when, where, and how to use them.

9. How can I remember the tactics and the way to use them?

Teachers will certainly remember the tactics they just recently used and probably the ones they scheduled last year with a few students, but they probably will not recall all of the techniques they arranged a few years ago. If a teacher knows of dozens, perhaps hundreds, of tactics and wishes to use them from time to time, he or she must write them down and file them in a handy place. They could be outlined on 3×5 cards and kept in a box, written on sheets of notebook paper and placed in a three-ring binder, assembled in a book such as *Tactics for Teaching*, or written in a computer program such as RIDE (Responding to Individual Differences in Education). But they must be written and filed someplace.

If a teacher has access to dozens of tactics, that teacher is a terrific resource to other teachers, and this is significant, because when teachers need help they generally go to other teachers. We collected data on this topic a few years ago, and this was true at both the elementary and the secondary level. Of course, certain teachers go to school psychologists and others who are available in their particular schools for assistance. But ordinarily, teachers don't have a 1–800 number to call for advice.

10. Who should know about tactics other than teachers?

Resource personnel such as teacher consultants, school psychologists, and special education resource teachers should know a lot of tactics, for as just noted, teachers occasionally go to them for advice, suggestions, and support. It would not be a bad idea if building principals or other administrators knew a few tactics. If they were able to suggest a couple of helpful techniques to teachers from time to time, they would certainly score a lot of points with their staff.

APPENDIX C: SUPPLEMENTAL LIST OF PROGRAM CONTENTS

Eleven categories of tactics, corresponding to the chapters, make up the contents of this program. They were determined by analyzing the data from a survey of teachers. Five categories form this supplementary table. Tactics from the original categories have been reassigned to these new groups. The additional categories should increase the use of this program for inservice providers and teachers.

STUDY SKILLS: Completing Homework: Self-Monitoring

Self-Management (25)

STUDY SKILLS: Taking Tests: Debriefing
STUDY SKILLS: Managing Time: Staying on Task
STUDY SKILLS: Managing Time: Being Prepared
SOCIAL BEHAVIORS: Getting Along with Others: Structured Learning with Self-Monitoring
ATTENDANCE: Attending: Self-Recording and Public Posting
MOTIVATION: Increasing Interest in Schools: Allowing Students to Participate in Grading
MOTIVATION: Self-Management: Increasing Performance
MOTIVATION: Self-Management: Identifying Antecedents and Consequences of Behavior
MOTIVATION: Self-Management: Saving a Life
BASIC SKILLS: Reading: A Reason to Read
COMPLIANCE: Behavior Management: Increasing Task Persistence

COMPLIANCE: Disruptive Behavior: A Peer-Mediated Program

COMPLIANCE: Disruptive Behavior: Self-Observation and Self-Recording

COMPLIANCE: Reducing Distractions: Self-Monitoring

SELF-CONCEPT: Self-Management: Building Successes

SELF-CONCEPT: Self-Management: Setting Objectives

SELF-CONCEPT: Self-Management: Accepting Responsibility

SELF-CONCEPT: Self-Management: Attribution Retraining I

SELF-CONCEPT: Self-Management: Prompting Praise

ATTITUDE: Self-Management: Making Responsible Choices

ATTITUDE: Self-Management: Attribution Retraining II

GOALS: Planning: Arranging Contracts

GOALS: Planning: Setting Priorities

PARTICIPATION: Participating in Discussions: Self-Monitoring

Peers (25) STUDY SKILLS: Learning from Textbooks: Visual-Spatial Approach

SOCIAL BEHAVIORS: Getting Along with Others: Arranging Psychosocial Activities

SOCIAL BEHAVIORS: Getting Along with Others: Solving Interpersonal Problems

SOCIAL BEHAVIORS: Getting Along with Others: A Four-Step Process

SOCIAL BEHAVIORS: Peer Tutoring: Guidelines for Setting Up Programs

SOCIAL BEHAVIORS: Peer Tutoring: Developing Better Writing Skills

SOCIAL BEHAVIORS: Peer Tutoring: Moving Toward Better Relationships

SOCIAL BEHAVIORS: Peer Tutoring: A Classwide Program in Social Studies

SOCIAL BEHAVIORS: Cooperative Learning: Circles of Learning

SOCIAL BEHAVIORS: Cooperative Learning: Student Teams–Achievement Divisions (STAD)

SOCIAL BEHAVIORS: Cooperative Learning:
Teams–Games–Tournament
SOCIAL BEHAVIORS: Cooperative Learning:
Cooperative Integrated Reading and Composi-
tion (CIRC)
SOCIAL BEHAVIORS: Cooperative Learning:
Jigsaw II
SOCIAL BEHAVIORS: Cooperative Learning:
Group Investigation
SOCIAL BEHAVIORS: Cooperative Learning:
Co-op Co-op
ATTENDANCE: Attending: Peer Group Support
Plus Rewards
ATTENDANCE: Attending: Social Rewards
MOTIVATION: Modifying the Classroom: Arrang-
ing Peer Forums
BASIC SKILLS: Reading: Reciprocal Teaching
BASIC SKILLS: Reading: A Reason to Read
BASIC SKILLS: Math: A Mathematics Laboratory
COMPLIANCE: Disruptive Behavior: A Peer-Medi-
ated Program
COMPLIANCE: Disruptive Behavior: Peer Confron-
tation
COMPLIANCE: Inappropriate Language: Peer-Medi-
ated Extinction
SELF-CONCEPT: Teacher Management: Group
Interactions

STUDY SKILLS: Reading: Multipass to Increase
Comprehension
STUDY SKILLS: Reading: Visual Imagery and Self-
Questioning to Improve Comprehension
STUDY SKILLS: Writing: An Error Monitoring
Strategy (COPS)
STUDY SKILLS: Memorizing Information:
Mnemonics
BASIC SKILLS: Writing: A Mnemonic Organizer
BASIC SKILLS: Math: A Mnemonic Strategy for
Solving Word Problems
COMPLIANCE: Behavior Management: Metacog-
nitive Training to Improve Social Skills
GOALS: Planning: Completing Long-Term Assign-
ments
PARTICIPATION: Participating in Discussions:
Looking Alive

Metacognition (9)

Parents (9)   SOCIAL BEHAVIORS: Learning to Compromise: The Art of Negotiation
ATTENDANCE: Punctuality: Three Techniques
ATTENDANCE: Attending: Praise and Rewards
ATTENDANCE: Attending: The Quarter Credit Plan
ATTENDANCE: Attending: Involving Parents and the Community
ATTENDANCE: Attending: Parental Involvement and Improved Instruction
ATTENDANCE: Dropout Prevention: A Three-Week Plan
COMPLIANCE: Managing Time: School Behavior Affects Home Privileges
COMPLIANCE: Behavior Management: Home-Based Reinforcement

Instructional Modification (6)   STUDY SKILLS: Learning from Textbooks: Study Guides
STUDY SKILLS: Learning from Textbooks: Graphic Organizers
STUDY SKILLS: Learning from Textbooks: Visual-Spatial Approach
STUDY SKILLS: Learning Vocabulary: Precision Teaching Vocabulary Sheets
STUDY SKILLS: Organizing Lectures: Advance Organizers
COMPLIANCE: Reducing Distractions: Self-Monitoring

AUTHOR INDEX

SUBJECT INDEX